This volume, with over fifty authors and consulting editors from around the world, reflects the maturing member care movement. The diversity of its content and contributors is a clear sign that two aspects of global mission are more fully appreciated than in the past. First, the shift of Christianity to the Global South (now two-thirds of all Christians), is reflected in both who needs member care and who is providing it. Second, integral mission, emphasizing both proclamation and demonstration, is highlighted throughout. This volume is forward-looking and paves the way for the wellbeing of future generations of Christian workers around the world. Well done Drs. O'Donnell and colleagues!

Todd M. Johnson, PhD
Co-director, Center for the Study of Global Christianity,
Gordon-Conwell Theological Seminary

Over the years, Kelly and Michèle O'Donnell have made valuable contributions to COMIBAM and to the mission movement in Ibero-America. Their member care articles, research, and books are strategic tools in our hands, supporting the growth and maturity in caring for our mission workers around the world. I am sure that *Global Member Care Volume 3* will likewise have a strong impact on our mission movement in our commitment to responsibly support our staff. I am very encouraged to see the seriousness and scope of the topics covered by the book's many authors. I highly recommend this book to pastors, mission leaders, and everyone who is involved in sending and caring for mission workers. Thank you, Kelly, and Michèle! It will be great to see this material in Spanish and Portuguese too!

Cristian Castro
Executive Director, Cooperación Misionera Iberoamericana (COMIBAM)

A chorus of over forty authors, including many from the Global South, offers practical insights and tools for staff care that can be studied and adapted throughout the growing global mission movement and overlapping sectors. It is a timely, strategic compilation to further establish member care more globally and to take it further into mission frontiers.

Howard Dueck
Founding Director of Member Care, TeachBeyond

Yet again Kelly and Michèle O'Donnell have brought together an impressive array of thought leaders in member care and mission to give valuable updates and to point to the future. Academically solid and highly practical, this is core reading for member care managers and strategic mission thinkers, member care practitioners and trainers.

Graham Fawcett
Consultant Clinical Psychologist, Thrive Worldwide

Indigenous mission leaders and workers in the region have benefited from the member care tools and experiences shared by many colleagues from around the world including Kelly and Michèle O'Donnell. Their third book in the *Global Member Care* series promises to be another valuable resource to promote quality member care and faithful service for everyone called to missions. I am especially appreciative of the emphasis on supporting mission workers in difficult territories among the least reached peoples and places.

FAYEZ ISHAK
Founder, Bridges of Hope, Egypt

Global Member Care Volume 3 is a timely addition to the valuable member care resources from the O'Donnells over the years. Its broad scope and breadth of contributors can greatly benefit those member care workers from the Global South whose need for such resources is great. As one whose focus for the past three decades has been in caring for children (especially Asian MKs/TCKs) and families serving cross-culturally, I believe there is an undeniable nexus between cross-cultural workers "staying the course" if the family and their children are cared for intentionally and holistically. I am pleased to know that many of the authors include and even mainstream these areas in their chapters. I am very grateful for this collaborative effort, and I highly recommend it!

JOHN BARCLAY, DMin
Asian MK/TCK advocate, Melbourne, Australia

The O'Donnells excel in producing books that rally together the mission and member care community across the globe. This exceptional volume is an example of how member care practice will be enriched and ministry among unreached peoples and places will be strengthened as we learn from each other and embrace our diversity in global mission.

GLADYS K. MWITI, PhD
Consulting Clinical Psychologist, Founder and CEO of Oasis Africa

Once again Kelly and Michèle have given us a gemstone for understanding and developing a more *global and holistic* member care. Various authors emphasize cultural diversity, the Global South, and worldwide challenges and opportunities. The stories, strategies, and extensive resources are other core features. This book is a must for everyone in mission and member care!

PRAMILA RAJENDRAN, PhD
Miila Consulting, India

The O'Donnells' newest volume strategically brings together the written contributions from dozens of member care colleagues from both the Global South and Global North. I am eager to start reading it and reflecting on how to engage in member care practice further from the individual through the global levels. While several pioneers such as Dr. Marjory Foyle got the member care movement rolling in the 1980s and 1990s, it was Drs. Kelly O'Donnell and Michèle Lewis O'Donnell that especially helped to systematize our thinking and collaborative practice for member care. Over the past four decades, they have continuously looked at member care through the microscope to sharpen our focus on specific topics and issues and through a telescope to place it into the wider context of global issues and mission frontiers.

Dr. Gisela Roth
DMG, Tumaini Counseling Centre, Member Care Psychiatrist, Kenya & Germany

This ground-breaking book models how we can learn from one another and transcend cultural or other divides by putting "Master Care" at the core of our relationships. I encourage the diversity of people in mission and member care—including Christians working across sectors—to read, discuss, and apply its rich and relevant contents to support healthy and effective mission workers among all peoples.

Ruth E. Van Reken
Co-author, *Third Culture Kids: Growing Up Among Worlds*
Co-founder, Families in Global Transition

GLOBAL MEMBER CARE

VOLUME THREE

Stories and Strategies for Staying the Course

EDITORS
Kelly O'Donnell & Michèle Lewis O'Donnell

CONSULTING EDITORS
Bruce Barron, Samuel Girguis, Tim Hibma, Michael Pollock,
Nik Ripken, Ruth Ripken, Tim Sanford, Grace Shim, David Tan

visit us at missionbooks.org

Global Member Care (Vol. 3): Stories and Strategies for Staying the Course

© 2024 by Kelly O'Donnell and Michèle Lewis O'Donnell. All Rights Reserved.

For updates on the Global Member Care series, including new links and resources, visit: https://sites.google.com/site/globalmca.

No part of this book may be reproduced, stored in a retrieval system, or transmitted in any form or by any means—electronic, mechanical, photocopy, recording, or otherwise—without prior written permission from the publisher, except brief quotations used in connection with reviews. This manuscript may not be entered into AI, even for AI training. For permission, email permissions@wclbooks.com. For corrections, email editor@wclbooks.com.

William Carey Publishing (WCP) publishes resources to shape and advance the missiological conversation in the world. We publish a broad range of thought-provoking books, and the publishers and editors do not necessarily endorse all opinions set forth here or in works referenced within this book. The responsibility for the interpretation and use of the material lies with the reader and neither the publishers nor editors shall be held liable for damages arising from its use.

The URLs included in this workbook are provided for personal use only and are current as of the date of publication, but the publisher disclaims any obligation to update them after publication.

All Scripture quotations, unless otherwise indicated, are taken from the Holy Bible, New International Version®, NIV®. Copyright ©1973, 1978, 1984, 2011 by Biblica, Inc.™ Used by permission of Zondervan. All rights reserved worldwide. www.zondervan.com. The "NIV" and "New International Version" are trademarks registered in the United States Patent and Trademark Office by Biblica, Inc.™

Scripture quotations marked NASB are taken from the NASB® New American Bible®, Copyright © 1960, 1971, 1977, 1995, 2020 by The Lockman Foundation. Used by permission. All rights reserved. lockman.org.

Scripture quotations marked Amplified are taken from the Amplified Bible, Copyright © 1954, 1958, 1962, 1964, 1965, 1987 by The Lockman Foundation. Used by permission.

Scripture quotations marked NLT are taken from the Holy Bible, New Living Translation, copyright ©1996, 2004, 2015 by Tyndale House Foundation. Used by permission of Tyndale House Publishers, Carol Stream, Illinois 60188. All rights reserved.

Published by William Carey Publishing
10 W. Dry Creek Cir
Littleton, CO 80120 | www.missionbooks.org

William Carey Publishing is a ministry of Frontier Ventures
Pasadena, CA | www.frontierventures.org

Cover and Interior Designer: Mike Riester

ISBNs: 978-1-64508-591-1 (paperback)
       978-1-64508-593-5 (epub)

Printed Worldwide

28 27 26 25 24   1 2 3 4 5   IN

Library of Congress Control Number: 2024939943

For Jesus Christ
Preeminent One
Pierced One
Precious One

Contents

Foreword   xiii
    Beth Gill, Becky Lewis, Linda Dorr, and Tricia Johnson
Preface   xvii
Introduction: xxiii
    Going and Growing Together Among All Peoples

PART ONE
Staying the Course in Mission Frontiers

Introduction to Part One   3
    Consulting Editors: Nik Ripken and Ruth Ripken

Chapter 1   9
    Prioritizing the Frontier Peoples:
    Strategic Implications for Mission and Member Care
    Rebecca Lewis and Tim Lewis

Chapter 2   25
    Following and Serving Jesus Globally:
    A Framework for Engaging with Our World
    Kelly O'Donnell and Michèle Lewis O'Donnell

Chapter 3   41
    Into the *Missio Dei*: Promoting Wellbeing for All People and the Planet
    David Johnston and Charlotte Johnston

Chapter 4   57
    International Psychology for Mission and Member Care
    Joyce Yip Green and Karen Brown

Chapter 5   73
    For All People and All Peoples:
    The Universal Declaration of Human Rights
    Kelly O'Donnell

PART TWO
Staying the Course in the Regions

Introduction to Part Two   85
    Consulting Editors: Samuel Girguis and David Tan

Chapter 6   91
    Supporting the Wellbeing and Effectiveness of Chinese Mission Workers
    Rainbow Cai and Raymond Yang

Chapter 7   107
    Contextualizing Member Care:
    Lessons from Counseling Korean Mission Workers
    Steve Sang-Cheol Moon and Mary Hee-Joo Moon

Chapter 8   121
    Ministry in the Diaspora:
    Supporting Philippine Christians in the Middle East and Hong Kong
    Grace Margaret Alag and Jorge de Ramos

Chapter 9   137
Developing Member Care in Indonesia:
Collaborations with Goers and Senders
Traugott Boeker and *Hanni Boeker* with *Hendry Pangaribuan*

Chapter 10   155
Doing Member Care Well in India
Isac Sounderaraja and Lancelot Paul

PART THREE
Staying the Course in the Sectors

Introduction to Part Three   171
Consulting Editors: Michael Pollock and Tim Sanford

Chapter 11   177
Mental Health as Mission: Our Journey into Trauma Training and Care
Emily Hervey and Dean Mellerstig

Chapter 12   193
Being a Prophetic Voice in Mission:
Living in Integrity and Confronting Corruption
Kelly O'Donnell and Michèle Lewis O'Donnell

Chapter 13   209
Room at the Table:
Welcoming People with Disabilities in the Church and Missions
Jenny Smith

Chapter 14   225
Climate and Environmental Issues:
Code Red for Member Care and Mission?
Debbie Hawker, David Hawker, Jamie Hawker, and Biniam Guush

Chapter 15   243
Staff Care in the Fight Against Human Trafficking
Timothy Friesen

PART FOUR
Staying the Course in Good Practice

Introduction to Part Four   261
Consulting Editors: Grace Shim and Tim Hibma

Chapter 16   265
Tough People for Tough Places:
Member Care Reflections from Team Expansion
*Doug Lucas, Jacquie Kubr, Mary Kranick, Jonathan Trotter,
and Renee Witkowski*

Chapter 17   279
Member Caring and Linking Ministries:
The Strategic Role of the Local Church
Jeremy Thomas and Anastasia Thomas

Chapter 18   295
    Caring for Mission Workers Through Coaching:
    Good Practices in the Global South
    Mulugetta Demissie Dagne, Rich Hansen, and Keith Webb

Chapter 19   309
    Physical Health for Mission and Humanitarian Workers
    Ted Lankester and Brian Wainaina

Chapter 20   323
    Pastoral Coaching: A Team Model for Member Care
    Edward Bruce, Kendall Johns, Chloe Raphael, and Denise Lee

Afterword   337

Index   339

Foreword

Beth Gill, Becky Lewis, Linda Dorr, and Tricia Johnson

In the early 1980s, our parents, Ralph and Roberta Winter, were undergoing some of the physical and psychological challenges that face long-term workers. Our mother, while working in the healthcare field among one of the twenty-three ethno-linguistically distinct Mayan Indian tribes in Guatemala, suffered for over two decades with the debilitating effects of undiagnosed hypothyroidism. Had an adequately trained member care team come alongside her at her lowest points, they might have recognized physical symptoms that differentiated her symptoms of fatigue from depression. This might have resulted in a much earlier diagnosis of hypothyroidism—a classic disease associated with the iodine-depleted soils of the highlands of Guatemala.

We are so grateful for the incredible legacy that our parents and grandparents left to the four of us. We have many happy childhood memories of growing up on the mission field in the rural highlands of Guatemala. Our parents led by example, with our mother helping as a nurse to develop health materials for the Mayan Indians in our area. Meanwhile, our father taught new skills to young Mayan men, to help them become financially stable through one of the over twenty micro-enterprises he set up. But it didn't stop there.

The Winter family in 1966.
In the front row (left to right) are Ralph, Becky, Beth, and Roberta.
In the back row (left to right) are Tricia and Linda.

We moved to Southern California in fall 1966 for our dad to join the newly formed faculty of the School of World Mission at Fuller Seminary. Our parents started a publishing company to publish in book format the doctoral and master's theses that his students were writing, so that others could benefit from lessons learned. It was all hands-on deck, as our mother and all four Winter girls began working at William Carey Library Publishers after school. As we pitched in on many projects over the years, the cause of the least reached peoples irretrievably captured our minds and hearts.

In 1975, our parents made the decision to leave Fuller and start the US Center for World Mission, focused on the "hidden peoples" with the fewest or no mission workers, no Bible translations, and no indigenous churches speaking their heart languages. This vision helped propel into existence new mission agencies focused entirely on these pioneer fields, which were often very remote or in restricted-access countries.

As our parents took up the challenge of redirecting mission efforts to unreached people groups (UPGs), they increasingly recognized how hard it was for mission workers to survive and thrive in these settings. UPGs had no indigenous fellowship of believers capable of reaching their own and hence were devoid of national brothers and sisters with whom to partner for ministry and mutual support. As the nascent member care field was emerging, our parents came to deeply value the research and work of two of its earliest pioneers, Kelly and Michèle O'Donnell. *Helping Missionaries Grow* (1988) and subsequent works caught their attention and resonated with their shared vision for least-reached peoples. Furthermore, being a health professional and because of her own health challenges, our mother cared deeply about people's wellbeing, both physical and emotional.

In 1992, the O'Donnells called for the prioritization of resources to the least-reached, with one example being Kelly's article "Agenda for Member Care in Frontier Missions." He stated, "Without adequate member care strategies, there is little hope for the ongoing maintenance of the frontier mission movement … these missionaries require special attention, so that in the context of sacrifice and isolation, they can still reach the peoples they are called to." This statement is still true today, as we continue to see how pioneering efforts call for pioneering, quality member care! This concern was further elaborated in the 1992 book the O'Donnells edited, *Missionary Care: Counting the Cost for World Evangelization*. Our parents wrote the foreword to this book because of their firm agreement with these perspectives.

Over the past three decades, all of us have each come to know Michèle and Kelly and their valuable and urgently needed contributions to mission workers' wellbeing and effectiveness. When one of us had a child who was severely traumatized on the mission field, Michèle and Kelly patiently and compassionately worked with our family, our children, and our mission over two years to untangle and treat the PTSD. Our extended Winter family is profoundly grateful.

This book builds on the previous two volumes (*The Pearls and Perils of Good Practice* and *Crossing Sectors for Serving Humanity*), adding significant insights into the global context in which we are living. As senior editors joining with over sixty colleagues from around the world (authors, consulting editors, publishing staff), the O'Donnells have collaboratively and competently further explored many of the complex and crucial issues related to member care. We are excited by this third book on global member care and commend it highly to you for its relevance now and into the future.

The Winter daughters and their families have all been involved with missions. Despite the geographic distance between them, they stay close to each other through their weekly group video prayer times.

Beth, the eldest, and her husband, Brad Gill, served in North Africa for thirteen years in small business development and anthropological research. Since 1998, they have lived near Detroit, Michigan, USA. Brad and Beth are both on the Frontier Ventures board (Brad is the chair) and they work together editing the *International Journal of Frontier Missiology*, Beth as copyeditor and Brad as senior editor.

Becky, the second daughter, and her husband, Tim Lewis, spent eight years in North Africa and helped to found Frontiers—serving in senior leadership for fifteen years. They continue in ministry, along with two of their four children, and are currently based north of Seattle, WA. They founded Telos Fellowship in 2018 to continue to clarify and advocate for "Frontier People Groups"—those UPGs still needing their own Christward movements.

Linda, the third daughter, is married to Darrell Dorr, with three adult children and ten grandchildren. The Dorrs and their young children lived in the United Kingdom for eight years on loan to Frontiers. They subsequently resided in the USA (Pasadena and Chicago). They now live in the greater Seattle area while continuing to serve with Frontier Ventures (formerly the US Center for World Mission).

Tricia, the youngest, is married to Todd Johnson and they worked for four years at the US Center for World Mission. With their three daughters, they have lived in Richmond, Virginia (USA), Singapore, and Thailand. They now live in the Boston area, where Todd is on the faculty of Gordon Conwell Theological Seminary and co-director of the Center for the Study of Global Christianity. Tricia has thoroughly enjoyed teaching English to adult immigrants for the past 16 years.

Preface

Behold, the tabernacle of God is among the people, and He will dwell among them, and they shall be His peoples, and God Himself will be among them, and He will wipe away every tear from their eyes; and there will no longer be any death; there will no longer be any mourning, or crying, or pain; the first things have passed away.
—Revelation 21:3–4 NASB

If you are interested in growing as a person, developing your member care skills, bringing help to tough places, being stretched to see the world differently, staying current with good practice, and expanding your global reach, then you have come to the right place. This third book and its two predecessors in the *Global Member Care* series are for you. Join us in staying the course as we follow Jesus Christ to share the good news and good works among all peoples and places. Welcome!

Global Member Care

Member care is an interdisciplinary, international, and trans-cultural field that focuses on supporting the diversity of mission personnel and sending groups. It is also a *cross-sectoral* field that is connecting and contributing to the many efforts to protect and promote the wellbeing of all people and the planet. Our vision for providing and developing quality member care in mission is more than forty years old and still growing!

The member care field has clear roots that can be traced back to the 1960s and 1970s, although its phenomenal growth has occurred during the last three decades. Just about everyone in Christian mission is aware of the notion of member care, albeit perhaps by different names such as personnel development, human resource management, staff wellbeing, or worker health. The wealth of concepts, resources, practices, and practitioners has contributed greatly to the people and purposes of the mission community—and beyond. These contributions will continue to increase in the coming years as the member care field expands further and develops globally. As a field, we are engaging in new opportunities for member care within the *missio Dei*—the vast realm of God's redemptive work in the world—marked by a diversity of good practitioners committed to both the Great Commission and the Great Commandment.

Book Series Overview

The *Global Member Care* series is dedicated to our colleagues around the world in mission who have member care responsibility. This includes field and team leaders, mission workers themselves, personnel department staff, professionally trained caregivers, educators, researchers, health advocates, and many others in formal or informal member care roles. The three books in the series build especially upon the fifty chapters in the 2002 edited book, *Doing Member Care Well: Perspectives and Practices from Around the World*. Together they represent the ongoing efforts to shape and support member care from the local to global scales, so as to equip all of us with the character, competence, and compassion necessary for good practice on behalf of the wellbeing and effectiveness of mission workers and mission senders.

The first volume of the series, *The Pearls and Perils of Good Practice*, is replete with practical resources and interactive applications, reviews of member care history, Global South perspectives, and future directions. It covers crucial issues of health and dysfunction in mission, as well as foundational ethics and human rights principles to guide member care practice. The second volume, *Crossing Sectors for Serving Humanity*, continued the emphasis on good practice by exploring different sectors, especially the humanitarian, human resources, and health sectors. We encouraged member care to expand in new ways and to take advantage of the many opportunities for serving humanity.

This third volume, *Stories and Strategies for Staying the Course*, emphasizes least reached peoples and places and features twenty chapters full of stories, strategies, reflections, and resources from member care and mission colleagues around the world. It provides a distinctive, directional platform to listen to and learn from global voices as we reflect on good member care practice in the context of challenging global issues, inspired by the vision to see member care develop globally—for all peoples and from all peoples.

For updates on the *Global Member Care* series, including new links and resources, visit the Global MCA website: http://sites.google.com/site/mcaglobal. We hope to see additional collaborative volumes in the *Global Member Care* series!

Thank You!

We want to express our deep gratitude to our many colleagues and friends over the years—including Calvary Community Church in California and Calvary Chapel in Connecticut—who have encouraged us in our member care work in global mission. We would not have been able to stay the course without you! We also sincerely appreciate the various colleagues around the world who have shared their passions, life experiences, and expertise so well in the book's twenty chapters. Thank you, faithful authors! And our sincere thanks to the dozens of chapter reviewers behind the scenes for your helpful feedback to the authors. Working with a great group of nine consulting editors was an additional highlight. We are so grateful for your contributions to strengthen and direct this book towards a more "global" member care marked with cultural humility, love for the persecuted Church, and the increasing role and importance of the Global South. Our deep thanks go out as well to the amazing Winter daughters (Beth, Becky, Linda, and Tricia) who launched the book in an "all peoples" direction with their insightful Foreword. Special thanks also to our lifelong friend, Ron Williams, for updating the graphics for the *missio Dei* Model of Global Member Care that appears throughout this book. Bruce Barron (Senior Editor of the World Evangelical Alliance) meticulously copyedited the book, and as a consulting editor offered timely and relevant suggestions for strengthening its contents. The book would not be the same without you—we cannot thank you enough! In addition, the superb team at William Carey Publishing skillfully guided the book through its many phases from start to finish. Thank you! Finally, our work would not be possible without the consistent and wise input from our Member Care Associates' board (Jane, Jim, Ralph, Steve, James, Nancy, and Daniel) and finance manager (Stan), the generosity of donors, and the supportive love of our friends and family. Our heart-felt thanks to all of you for traveling together with us on this global journey with Jesus Christ!

Member Care and Love

Member care is founded on the biblical and trans-cultural command to love one another (John 13:34–35) as well as on the ethical sense of duty to help vulnerable people (Prov 24:11–12). It is both sacrificial and celebratory. It is a duty and desire—and hopefully a delight! Such *agape* love, as affirmed in the multi-lingual epigraph on page xxi, never ceases. We grow together in the mission community, celebrate life together, and, as human vessels full of strengths and weaknesses, do our utmost to stay the course together in sharing the gospel among all peoples and all places, to the end of the age, for God's glory. Resilient love is the ultimate measure of the effectiveness of member care.

> This gospel of the kingdom shall be preached in the whole world as a testimony to all the nations, and then the end will come.
> —Matthew 24:14 NASB

Maranatha!

Kelly and Michèle O'Donnell
Geneva, Switzerland
June 2024

사랑은 언제까지든지 떨어지지
Axebber n wayen i d-yeṭṭasen
Kasih tidak berkesudahan
Anbu orukallum ozliyathu
Хайр хэзээ ч дуусдаггүй
Ljubav nikad ne prestaje
اَلْمَحَبَّةُ فَتَدُومُ وَلَا تَنْتَهِي
Armastus ei hävi ilmaski
ความรักไม่มีวันสูญสิ้น

לעולם תבל לא האהבה
Ime eque carpis
爱 是 永 不 止 息
Սերը բնավ չիյնար
Mbëggeel amul àpp
Uthando aluze lutshitshe
ፍቅር ለዘወትር አይወድቅም
Dashuria nuk ligshtohet kurrë
Kærleikurinn fellur aldrei úr gildi
Die liefde vergaan nimmermeer
Quintlasohtla nochipa in oc sequin
愛はいつまでも絶えることがない
Любовь никогда не перестает
Upendo hauna kikomo kamwe
A szeretet soha el nem fogy
E kore rawa te aroha e taka
Die Liebe höret nimmer auf
La charité ne périt jamais
Caritas numquam excidit
Miłość nigdy nie ustaje
O amor jamais acaba
Renmen pa janm fini
Kärleken förgår aldrig
Sevgi asla son bulmaz
Láska nikdy nevypadá
Meilė niekada nesibaigia
Kasih tidak berkesudahan
El amor nunca deja de ser
Charitatea nehoiz-ere ezta erorten
Tình yêu thương chẳng hề hư mất bao giờ
Ang pagibig ay hindi nagkukulang kailan man

ἡ ἀγάπη οὐδέποτε πίπτει

Love never fails.

1 Corinthians 13:8

Introduction

Going and Growing Together Among All Peoples

This book features stories and strategies from colleagues around the world:
People who are dedicated to helping mission workers and senders.
People who minister among least-reached peoples and places.
People who work together with integrity, skill, and resilience.
People who are committed to helping fellow humans in need.
People who are growing and going broadly in mission.
People who are staying the course in mission!

This third volume in the *Global Member Care* series, *Global Member Care: Stories and Strategies for Staying the Course*, is part of ongoing efforts over the past thirty years to shape and support the field of member care in mission. It is designed to reflect on member care practice in many settings and to forge new terrain for the future. We want to further equip the wide range of people around the world who have member care responsibility, including leaders, colleagues, friends, professional caregivers, trainers, and sending groups. In so doing we want to emphasize the richness of cultural diversity and the increasing influence of the Global South as we move towards a more *global* member care.

We have emphasized three points to make this collaborative volume—with its forty-three authors and nine consulting editors—as readable and relevant as possible. First, the chapters include personal stories, ministry descriptions, and strategies about member care for workers among and from the least reached peoples and places. Second, we provide examples of efforts by member care and mission workers who are ministering across sectors and cultures to help vulnerable people in many settings. Third, the chapters contain references and links to a variety of core materials and resources for readers who want more information.

We have solicited chapter contributions from colleagues around the world, including many senior-level colleagues and husband-wife teams with decades of experience. The book thus provides a directional, legacy platform for member care as we learn from the authors' seasoned, global voices. We hope it will serve as a strategic bridge to shape and support member care among all peoples, now and into the future.

Overview of the Book

We have organized the book into four parts, although many of the chapters overlap with two or more of the topics. Each chapter concludes with an application section consisting of three core strategies, three core resources, and three items for reflection and discussion.

Part One: Staying the Course in Mission Frontiers
The five cutting-edge chapters in this section launch us into the global context of this book. There are emphases on prioritizing unreached and frontier peoples, exploring a framework for global engagement, ministering in the *missio Dei*, applying international psychology principles, and understanding the importance of human rights. Collectively, these chapters help us to keep worldwide challenges and opportunities at the forefront of mission and member care.

Part Two: Staying the Course in the Regions
This section features five illuminating chapters with perspectives and practices for member care for five Asian countries: China, Korea, The Philippines, Indonesia, and India. The authors describe struggles and successes in developing effective mindsets and ministry for member care, noting that in many places member care is still very much in development. Caring for Filipino Christians working in diaspora settings and collaborating for culturally relevant, holistic care are some of this Part's many contributions.

Part Three: Staying the Course in the Sectors
This section's five, far-reaching chapters help us to better understand why connecting and contributing across sectors is strategic for mission and member care. The authors offer a personal and international lens for viewing areas of ministry that are crucial to mission and caring for mission workers in those areas. Topics include mental health and trauma, integrity and corruption, ministry to and by people with disabilities, climate and environment, and human trafficking and abuse.

Part Four: Staying the Course in Good Practice
A variety of important member care services and resources are addressed in this section's five thought-provoking chapters. Book-ending the material are chapters on how two different mission organizations have developed member care over the years. In between are three chapters that probe and affirm the importance of member care by the local church, coaching in the Global South, and health care for mission and aid workers.

We would have certainly included many other topics in this book if there had been space beyond the twenty chapters. Just a few examples include risk management, digital member care, spiritual vitality, addictions, member care leadership, member care in more regions and sectors, perspectives and practices by additional colleagues from the Global South, future directions, and dissertation summaries (e.g., Estelle 2023; Johnson 2024; Rajendran 2019; Shi 2020; and Wilcox 2024). For additional areas currently being discussed in member care, see the special member care issues by AFRIGO (2023) and *Evangelical Missions Quarterly* (2022), the edited book by Whiteman and Pujols (2023), TCK and family resources (Families in Global Transition), COMIBAM (2023), and the presentations from these recent member care conferences: Global Member Care Network Conference, Mental Health and Missions Conference, Pastoral Training in Member Care Conference, and Asia Member Care Network Consultation.

Making the Most of the Material

As you go through the material in this book, we suggest that you keep in mind the book's six goals, adapted from volume 2 in the *Global Member Care* series, *Crossing Sectors for Serving Humanity* (O'Donnell and Lewis O'Donnell 2013). Underlying these goals is the process of mutual learning, exchanging of resources, and building relationships as we seek to provide and develop member care in mission among all peoples and within our challenging global context. The six goals are as follows:

1. To support mission workers in their wellbeing and effectiveness.
2. To equip colleagues in mission who have member care responsibility.
3. To equip mission workers with tools and opportunities for their work with others.
4. To equip member caregivers who directly work with vulnerable populations and others.
5. To support colleagues in other sectors via materials in the member care field.
6. To stay informed as global citizens about current and crucial issues facing humanity.

This book, like the first two volumes in the series, can be used as a practical tool for member care workers, sending groups, and those with member care responsibility, and as a complementary text for training purposes in universities, seminaries, and mission settings. The intended audience is primarily the international Christian mission and member care community, as well as Christians working in other international sectors. We intend to supplement this text by hosting podcasts with many of the book's authors.

Some Notes on Member Care History

Over the last thirty-five years, member care as a field and movement has increasingly taken root around the world. At the core of member care is a commitment to providing and developing resources to support mission personnel, sending organizations, and sending churches. Colleagues and friends, specialty providers, and locals who are befriended can serve as key sources of such care. Some of the many tangible signs of member care's amazing growth are the many organizations, trainings, and practitioners that have emerged along with the national, regional, and international networks of member care, the first of which formed in the Middle East and North Africa in the mid-1990s (O'Donnell 2015b). The largest and most influential is the Global Member Care Network (GMCN). Created in 1998 as part of the World Evangelical Alliance's Mission Commission, it currently has about 6,500 people in its online community and launched its *Member Care Journal* in 2024.

Here is how we described the field of member care thirteen years ago:

> The development of member care really has its origins in the Biblical admonitions to "love one another" (John 13:34), "bear one another's burdens" (Galatians 6:2), "be kind to one another" (Ephesians 4:32), "teach and admonish one another" (Colossians 3:16), "encourage one another day after day" (Hebrews 3:13) and scores of similar "one another" verses that fill the New Testament. Member care, in this sense, is nothing new.
>
> Christians and Christian workers, for better or for worse, have been trying to practice these relationship principles down through the centuries. Yet what is new are the more organized attempts all over the world to develop comprehensive, sustainable member care approaches to support cross-cultural Christian workers. These attempts have drawn on the contributions of practitioners from such diverse health care fields as travel and tropical medicine, psychology and psychiatry, intercultural and transition studies, pastoral care and coaching, personnel and human resource development, and recovery and trauma care. (O'Donnell 2011b, 9)

Currently, there are an estimated 445,000 foreign mission workers and 13.5 million national Christian workers (citizens) from all denominations (Zurlo, Johnson, and Crossing 2024). In addition, millions of Christians are involved in the overlapping areas of "sector care" and "humanity care." They are engaged in such fields as humanitarian relief, healthcare, development, peacemaking, and human rights. Moreover, many other Christians are working in countries all over the world as "tentmakers," seeking to share their faith and good works. Added to these numbers are Christians among the diaspora of peoples who have relocated for economic, educational, sociopolitical, and/or security reasons: international workers, students, refugees, and internally displaced peoples. They may not be "mission workers" per se—that is, they were not formally sent out by any organization—but they are part of God's overall plan to see the good news shared among all peoples and places.

More Materials on Member Care History and Developments

- "Highlighting Member Care History," chapter 1 in *Global Member Care, vol. 1* (O'Donnell 2011b)
- "The Missional Heart of Member Care" (O'Donnell 2015b)
- Magazine and Journal Issues on Member Care (1983–2017) (Member Care Associates 2017)
- "Member Care History" (Member Care Associates)
- "Tributes to Member Care Pioneers and Developers" (Member Care Associates)
- "100+ Member Care Books" (Member Care Associates)

Three Frameworks to Support Member Care

We work with Member Care Associates, Inc. (MCA), a Christian organization committed to supporting workers and sending groups within the mission community, especially those serving among least reached peoples and places. We also connect and contribute to the overlapping health, humanitarian, development, human rights, and peace sectors and especially to the areas of global mental health (e.g., Global Mental Health-Map) and global integrity (e.g., Global Integrity Day).

We have developed three succinct frameworks to guide, and indeed often goad, our member care work and how we collaboratively help to shape and support member care around the world.

Framework 1—Member Care Profile: Good Practice Parameters

Member care is the ongoing investment of resources by sending groups, service organizations, and workers themselves, for the nurture and development of personnel (O'Donnell and Lewis O'Donnell 1992). It is both people-oriented and task-oriented, as it actively engages in good practice for the wellbeing and effectiveness (referred to as *WE*) of mission workers and sending groups. Member care seeks to be inclusive, proactive, holistic, comprehensive, culturally relevant, and strengths focused.

It focuses on every member of the organization, including children and home office staff, plus locals, nationals, and volunteers who are part of or working with the sending group and organization.

It includes preventative, developmental, supportive, and restorative care in culturally relevant ways. A core part of member care is the mutual care that workers provide to each other. Connecting with resources and people in the local host community is also crucial.

It seeks to implement an adequate flow of care from recruitment through retirement.

It develops resilience, skills, and virtue, which are central to helping personnel stay healthy and effective in their work. Member care thus involves both developing inner resources (e.g., perseverance, stress tolerance) and providing external resources (e.g., team building, logistical support, skill training).

Framework 2—Global Member Care Model: *Missio Dei Domain*

This member care model (Member Care Associates 2017; O'Donnell and Lewis O'Donnell 2016b) builds on the original model developed in 1999–2000 by Kelly O'Donnell and Dave Pollock with some initial input from Marjory Foyle (O'Donnell 2001). It now features two additional spheres (making a total of seven), which are also described in terms of "flows of care," and it places global member care solidly within the realm of the *missio Dei* domain.

Missio Dei is an inclusive term that represents God's vast redemptive work in the world—the overall mission of God on behalf of humanity. Theologically, at the core of all we do is the message and work of Jesus Christ, whom we understand to be the world's only true and blessed hope, and whose gracious salvation is proclaimed and whose virtuous character is to be embodied by the Church. This expanded model of global member care continues to emphasize Jesus Christ at the core of member care, including our relationship with him, member care/mission workers serving him, and his love for all people.

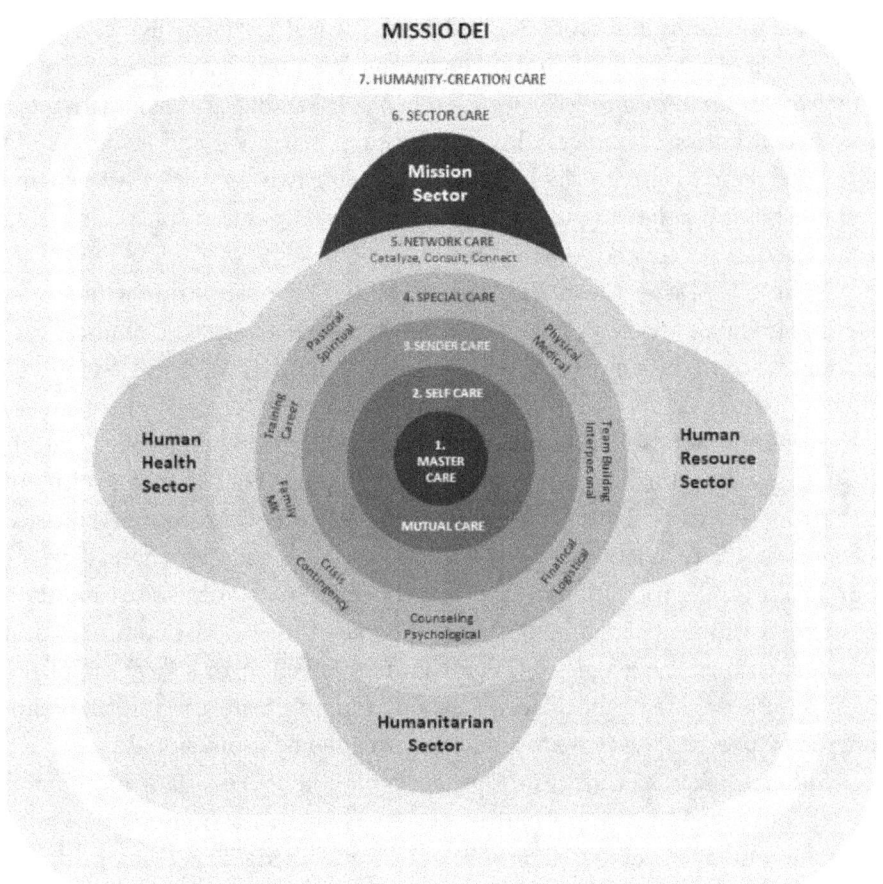

Global Member Care Model: Missio Dei Domain (seven spheres)
©2024 Kelly O'Donnell and Michèle Lewis O'Donnell

The first five spheres from the original model were used in *Doing Member Care Well* (O'Donnell 2002) as the grid for organizing that book's 50 chapters. It has also been discussed and used widely in mission, member care, and academic settings (e.g., Eriksson 2012). The sixth sphere, sector care, was added in *Global Member Care, vol. 2* (O'Donnell and Lewis O'Donnell 2013) and emphasizes the sectors of mission (primary), humanitarian, health, and human resources. The seventh sphere, humanity—creation care, reflects the growing interest and involvement in linking the gospel and good works in new ways on behalf of the wellbeing for all people and the planet (Burdick 2022). It surrounds the other six spheres and is itself contained within the *missio*

Dei, that is, the overall work of God in the world through divine, secular, ecclesiastical, missiological, and other means. We note that all seven spheres can involve providing and receiving member care. Sending groups and member care networks, for example, not only offer supportive care and resources but also need them to remain viable. Member care is a two-way street with shared responsibilities! Following is a brief description of the seven spheres, starting from the core sphere and moving outward.

Sphere 1. Master Care: *The Flow of Christ.* Our relationship with Christ is fundamental to our wellbeing and work effectiveness. Member care resources strengthen our relationship with the Lord and help us encourage others in the Lord.

Sphere 2. Self and Mutual Care: *The Flow of Community.* Self-care is basic to good health. Self-awareness, monitoring one's needs, a commitment to personal development, and seeking help when needed are signs of maturity. Likewise, quality relationships with family and friends are necessary for our health and productivity. Staff are encouraged to form and maintain close friendships of accountability with people in their home culture and in the host culture. Colleagues who love and are loved form a key part of the "continuum of care" needed for longevity, ranging from the informal care offered by peers to the more formal care provided by professionals.

Sphere 3. Sender Care: *The Flow of Commitment.* An organization's staff members are its most important resource. As such, sending groups—both churches and agencies—are committed to working together to support and develop their personnel throughout the work-life cycle. They demonstrate this commitment by how they invest themselves and their resources, including finances, in staff care. Sending groups aspire to have a comprehensive, culturally relevant, and sustainable approach to member care, including a commitment to organizational development, connecting with outside resources, and effective administration and management. Note also that not all mission workers are sent out by a formal group such as a church or agency; those with looser organizational connections need member care too, including support teams and local resources to back them up.

Sphere 4. Special Care: *The Flow of Caregivers.* Various skills and services are needed by both member care specialists and others with member care responsibilities, such as field leaders, team leaders, and fellow workers. Special care includes four *dimensions* of care (prevention, development, support, and restoration) and several *types* of care (such as psychological, physical, family, and team—the seven types of care listed in the diagram are not comprehensive). The goal is to help personnel develop the resiliency and capacities needed to minister well (healthily and effectively) to others. "Specialists" delivering care should be properly qualified and should normally work in conjunction with sending groups. They must often go beyond familiar or convenient comfort zones to provide services in challenging contexts within professional ethical limits.

Sphere 5. Network Care: *The Flow of Connections.* Member care providers are committed to relating to each other, working together, staying up to date on events and developments, and sharing consolidated learning from their member care practice. They are involved not just in providing their services, but in actively "knitting a net" to link resources with areas of need. Partnerships and close working relationships are required among member care workers, service organizations, sending agencies, and regional member care affiliations. Especially important is the ongoing interaction between member care workers from different regions and different emphases (spiritual life, trauma care, coaching, etc.).

Sphere 6. Sector Care: *The Flow of Common Ground.* People with member care responsibility must stay in touch with sectors that are relevant for their work. They should cross into new areas to find common ground—emphases, projects, disciplines, and fields within related sectors—for mutual learning, exchanging resources, and developing skills. Crossing sectors doesn't necessarily require becoming an expert in any given sector. Rather it entails a continuum of involvement which is carefully considered in view of one's primary focus in member care: being informed by, integrating with, and/or immersing in a given sector or part of a sector.

Sphere 7. Humanity—Creation Care: *The Flow of Common Good.* Major problems are affecting the wellbeing of people and the planet. Both member care and mission provide opportunities for mature Christians who possess character, competence, and compassion to become strategically involved at all levels, from local to global settings. Those with member care responsibility are encouraged to connect and contribute to our globalizing world and the intertwining people–planet nexus in new ways for the common good while maintaining their focus on supporting the health, resiliency, and effectiveness of mission personnel and their sending groups (e.g., note some of the chapters in Thompson 2023). A healthy planet is conducive for healthy people—and thus creation care is crucial for the health and wellbeing of mission workers and the people and places where they serve.

Framework 3—Global Integration Collaborative: Common Ground and Common Good

Global Integration (GI) is a framework that we have been developing over the past fifteen years as we consider, like so many others, how to help make our troubled world a better place. GI involves a commitment to actively and responsibly engaging in our world, from local to global levels, for God's glory. It emphasizes prioritizing our relational connections and making relevant contributions to wellbeing on the issues facing humanity and the planet, in light of our integrity, commitments, and core values (e.g., ethical, humanitarian, human rights, faith-based) (O'Donnell and Lewis O'Donnell 2016a).

We began to conceptualize GI in 2010 and developed it further via many entries on the *CORE Member Care* weblog (O'Donnell 2011a; O'Donnell 2015a). The theological concept of common grace is key, as it acknowledges God's sovereign goodness and kindness to all people without distinction. Furthermore, crossing sectors for mutual learning and support—as mentioned in Sphere 6 of the Global Member Care model above—is a key process of GI (O'Donnell 2013; O'Donnell and Lewis O'Donnell 2013). We also use the term "global integrators" to refer to colleagues of integrity who link their skills, values, and relationships to address major issues in our world (O'Donnell and Lewis O'Donnell 2016a).

GI encourages a variety of people to be at the "global tables and in the global trenches and everything in-between" in order to help research, shape, and monitor agendas, policies, and action for all people and the planet. It intentionally links *being* the people we need with *building* the world we need. *As people of "faith, hope and love," practicing Christian spirituality, a foundational motive for GI is to seek God's glory in all we do.* We believe the GI framework and principles are crucial for (a) member care/mission practice and direction; (b) colleagues working in different sectors and settings; and (c) all those who endeavor to live as global citizens (i.e. our common sense of belonging, identity, and mutual responsibility as humans)—people of good will committed to find common ground for the common good (O'Donnell and Lewis O'Donnell 2023).

Final Thoughts

Global Member Care Volume 3 is part of an ongoing effort to help us keep abreast with both our globalizing world and the global field of member care. It summons all of us to serve faithfully in mission through quality member care and to develop member care skills considering the major challenges affecting the world. We earnestly encourage all participants in the field to take advantage of the wealth of opportunities for connecting and contributing globally toward the wellbeing of the diverse and remarkable people who serve in mission as well as on behalf of the wellbeing of all people and the planet.

We anticipate that there will be future volumes in the *Global Member Care* series compiled and edited by different colleagues around the world. We are especially eager to see more colleagues from the Global South involved in shaping and supporting the development of "global" member care. This ongoing series can be one of the many strategic streams that bring member care colleagues together to share relevant reflections, resources, and research for good practice. We hope that others will develop works with more specific thematic or regional emphases.

Global Member Care Volume 3, like the two preceding volumes in this series, points us to the *raison d'être* for our mission efforts: imparting the gospel of Jesus Christ and our lives (1 Thess 2:8) in culturally relevant ways, prioritizing least-reached peoples and places, and improving the lives of fellow human beings—many of whom are denied basic human rights and living in places beset by multidimensional poverty, protracted calamities, and intractable conflicts. We sincerely hope that this third volume will both inspire and instruct our colleagues around the world in their member care and mission work as they endeavor faithfully to serve among all peoples. *Ad majorem Jesu Christi gloriam*!

References

AFRIGO. 2023. "Trauma and Member Care: Help for Our Hurting Missionaries." 8 (3). https://afrigo.org/issues/volume-8-3/.

Asia Member Care Network Consultation: https://www.barnabas.org/member-care/events/asia-member-care-network.

Burdick, Brent. 2022. *Gospel Issues for the Global Church*. Independently published.

COMIBAM (2023). Report 2022. https://comibam.org/wp-content/uploads/2023/04/Annual-Report-COMIBAM-2022-compressed.pdf.

Eriksson, Cynthia. 2012. "Practical Integration in Cross-Cultural Member Care." *Journal of Psychology and Theology* 40 (2): 112–115. https://doi.org/10.1177/0091647112040002.

Estelle, Julie. 2023. "The Effectiveness of Preparation and Support for Missionaries' Mental Health: A Qualitative Primary Data Collection Analysis." MSc diss., London School of Hygiene and Tropical Medicine. https://drive.google.com/file/d/1-ZWvNsyfbXI7t11EMF1e_QkJKUt5A2sR/view?usp=sharing.

Evangelical Missions Quarterly. 2002. "Special Issue on Member Care." 58 (2). https://missionexus.org/emq/emq-archives/emq-volume-58-issue-2/.

Families in Global Transition. https://www.figt.org/.

Global Integrity Day: https://sites.google.com/view/global-integrity-day/.

Global Member Care Book Series: https://sites.google.com/site/globalmca/.

Global Member Care Network Conference: https://globalmembercare.com/conference-2024/.

Global Member Care Network. Member Care Journal. https://globalmembercare.com/journal/.

Global Mental Health-Map: https://sites.google.com/site/gmhmap/.

Johnson, Danielle. 2024. "The Impact of COVID-19 Traumatic Stress on Global Workers." PhD diss., Regent University. https://go.openathens.net/redirector/regent.edu?url=https://www.proquest.com/dissertations-theses/impact-covid-19-traumatic-stress-on-global/docview/3032998781/se-2.

Member Care Associates. "100+ Member Care Books." https://membercareassociates.org/featured-materials/100-mc-books/.

Member Care Associates. "Member Care History." https://membercareassociates.org/mc-foundations/notes-quotes/.

Member Care Associates. "Tributes to Member Care Pioneers and Developers." https://membercareassociates.org/mc-foundations/tributes-2/.

Member Care Associates. 2017a. "Global Member Care Model: Member Care in the Missio Dei." Member Care Update 94 (February). https://us4.campaign-archive.com/?u=f34fc856e7776d7b69dafd3b3&id=7155c94ed6.

Member Care Associates. 2017b. "Special Issues on Member Care: Journals and Magazines (1983–2017)." Member Care Update 93 (January). https://us4.campaign-archive.com/?u=f34fc856e7776d7b69dafd3b3&id=cd2c8801e9.

Mental Health and Missions Conference: https://www.mti.org/mhm.

O'Donnell, Kelly. 2001. "Going Global: A Member Care Model for Best Practice." *Evangelical Missions Quarterly* 37 (2): 212–222.

O'Donnell, Kelly, ed. 2002. *Doing Member Care Well: Perspectives and Practices from Around the World*. Pasadena, CA: William Carey Library. https://passionexchange.files.wordpress.com/2008/10/doingmembercarewell.pdf.

O'Donnell, Kelly. 2011a. "Member Care—Mental Health: Global Integration." *CORE Member Care* (10 weblog entries: July 13 to December 15, 2011). https://us4.campaign-archive.com/?u=f34fc856e7776d7b69dafd3b3&id=7155c94ed6.

O'Donnell, Kelly. 2011b. *Global Member Care, vol. 1: The Pearls and Perils of Good Practice*. Pasadena, CA: William Carey Library.

O'Donnell, Kelly. 2013. "Charting Your Course Through the Sectors." In *Global Member Care, vol. 2: Crossing Sectors for Serving Humanity*, edited by Kelly O'Donnell and Michèle Lewis O'Donnell, 5–20. Pasadena, CA: William Carey Library. https://membercareassociates.org/wp-content/uploads/2018/01/Charting-Your-Course-through-the-Sectors-final-ODonnell-2013.pdf.

O'Donnell, Kelly. 2015a. "Global Integrators." *CORE Member Care* (25 weblog entries: January 15 to December 31, 2015). http://coremembercare.blogspot.com/search/label/global percent20integrators.

O'Donnell, Kelly. 2015b. "The Missional Heart of Member Care." *International Bulletin of Mission Research* 39 (2): 91–96. https://membercareassociates.org/wp-content/uploads/2021/03/Missional-Heart-of-MC-article-pub-version-from-IBMR-website-2015.pdf.

O'Donnell, Kelly, and Michèle Lewis O'Donnell. 1992. "Perspectives on Member Care in Missions." In *Missionary Care: Counting the Cost for World Evangelization*, edited by Kelly O'Donnell, 1–23. Pasadena, CA: William Carey Library. https://drive.google.com/file/d/1zIU2CnfBfA9d52Vk6L2fgd9GQUoe4t5W/view.

O'Donnell, Kelly, and Michèle Lewis O'Donnell, eds. 2013. *Global Member Care, vol. 2: Crossing Sectors for Serving Humanity*. Pasadena, CA: William Carey Library.

O'Donnell, Kelly, and Michèle Lewis O'Donnell. 2016a. "Global Integration: Addressing the Pressing Issues Facing Our World—Overview and Opportunities for Mental Health Professionals." *Christian Psychology Around the World* 8 (1): 191–194. https://emcapp.ignis.de/8/#p=1.

O'Donnell, Kelly, and Michèle Lewis O'Donnell. 2016b. "Multi-Sectoral Member Care: Engaging Our World as Global Integrators." *Journal of Psychology and Theology* 44 (1): 303–314. https://membercareassociates.org/wp-content/uploads/2016/12/ODonnells-2016-JPT-article-published-pdf.pdf.

O'Donnell, Kelly, and Michèle Lewis O'Donnell. 2023. "Global Integration Overview Member Care." Associates. https://membercareassociates.org/global-integration/gi/.

Pastoral Training in Member Care Conference: https://www.barnabas.org/member-care/events/ptm.

Rajendran, Pramila. 2019. "Contextual Realities in Caring for Global Missional Leaders." PhD diss., Indian Institute of Inter-Cultural Studies. https://drive.google.com/file/d/1MgXhoTJa1TJLbxlZNMP6cvlbdfbTCyml/view?usp=sharing.

Shi, Qi. 2020. "Don't Leave Stay Strong: Enabling Chinese Mission Workers to Thrive in the Context Where They Serve." PhD diss., School of Intercultural Studies, Fuller Theological Seminary. (See the condensed version from January 2024 including contact and website information here: https://drive.google.com/file/d/1omOXjpF-O8hYpFiSmVGTgQVXOkAo0No7/view?usp=sharing).

Thompson, Kate, ed. 2023. *Psychological Support for Workers on the Move: Improving Global Staff Care*. New York: Routledge.

Whiteman, Geoff, and Heater Pubols, eds. 2023. *Essentials of People Care and Development: A Collection of Best Practices, Research, Reflections, and Strategies*. Wheaton, IL: Missio Nexus. https://missionexus.org/essentials-for-people-care-and-development/.Wilcox, Teressa. 2024. "Retreat+ Program Development for Missionaries Living in Host Countries." DMFT diss., Hope International University.

Zurlo, Gina, Todd Johnson, and Peter Crossing. 2024. "Fragmentation and Unity." *International Bulletin of Mission Research* 48 (1): 43–54. https://www.gordonconwell.edu/wp-content/uploads/sites/13/2024/01/Status-of-Global-Christianity-2024.pdf.

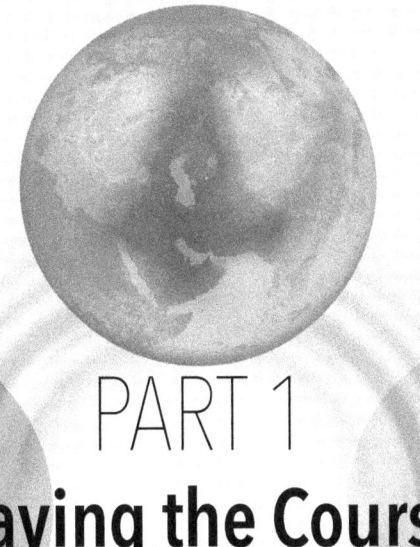

PART 1
Staying the Course in Mission Frontiers

Nik & Ruth Ripken, Consulting Editors

Introduction to Part 1

We (Nik and Ruth) are overseas mission veterans with over thirty-seven years serving in places where the good news had no access among thousands of people in Malawi and South Africa. We also lived in Kenya while ministering into Somalia as part of an $11 million relief effort. Entering the world—and mission frontiers—of famine, civil war, and persecution was life-altering for us. The twin biblical truths of crucifixion and resurrection were regular experiences that shaped and strengthened our faith.

In Matthew 10, Jesus tells his disciples that he is sending them out as "sheep among wolves." Our training in educational settings, however, had mostly prepared us to be sheep among sheep. We were not ready, for example, to witness the systematic martyring of most Somali believers. In addition, our son died suddenly while we were in Somalia, and Ruth's mother died far away in the USA. Yet sojourning among believers in persecution helped us see how we could be prudent and victorious even among wolves. We also learned firsthand how member care, with an emphasis on team members supporting one another, is vital in the "sheep among wolves" realities of mission frontiers—the focus of Part One.

Overview and Perspectives

Chapter 1 by Rebecca and Tim Lewis, is a clarion call to the church and mission community to send well-trained and well-supported workers to the frontier peoples. It calls for forming strategic collaborations, learning local languages and cultures, and incarnating Christ within families and communities. The Lewises remind and at times reprimand the church and mission-sending world, pointing out that more than one billion people have little or no access to the good news of Jesus Christ.

There are different and overlapping ways to state the statistics about the unreached. The Joshua Project, for example, suggests that among peoples that make up 40 percent of the world's population, less than 2 percent are followers of Jesus. Another metric from the Joshua Project is that the 100 largest unreached people groups total over 1.8 billion people, or nearly one-fourth of all humanity. The important point for the authors is to "see the world through people group eyes" and to reprioritize mission efforts to focus on the remaining frontier peoples.

Many frontier peoples dwell in locations marked by insecurity, poverty, health hazards, and environmental extremes. The longevity and effectiveness of those serving among these peoples depend upon teams caring for one another and regularly worshiping together. In addition, people who are highly trained, skilled, and experienced in member care and trauma care are vital to the holistic health of those serving in such difficult environments. The Lewises call upon the church and mission community to prioritize the special training and member care needed to support staff long-term among frontier peoples. This challenging chapter sets the frontier mission tone for the book and launches it into the loving heart of Christ for all peoples.

Chapter 2 by Kelly and Michèle Lewis O'Donnell, features a global framework for linking skills, relationships, and integrity on behalf of the major issues facing our world. The O'Donnells encourage us to use it as a "grid to guide and a guide to goad" as we actively and responsibly engage with our world, locally through globally, for God's glory.

Broadly speaking, two types of law codes have formed the basis of governments, both historical and modern: Roman law and common law. Though there are variations within these governing traditions, these two law codes define how governments engage the world and the peoples living under their control. Roman law's premise is that its citizens are born with the "right to nothing." It is the purview of the state and its proxies to determine what, if any, are the rights of its peoples. Common law, in contrast, evolves from the desires and ambitions of its people. Its premise is that all citizens are born with the "right to everything." Roman law's power is based within the governing entity; common-law governments are elected by and serve its people.

The O'Donnells have emphasized the best that common law has to offer while understanding the realities of Roman law. They appeal to the aspirations that exist in the hearts of all people. They make the case that followers of Christ and like-minded partners are stewards of the human condition and of creation itself. Kelly and Michèle share a variety of United Nations documents and international efforts, summoning colleagues from various backgrounds to collaborate for the best of all people and the planet. They also share various truths from the Bible to encourage seeking common ground for the common good.

Chapter 3 by David and Charlotte Johnston, combines their remarkable personal stories in the MENA region with numerous micro-narratives of others. They skillfully relate these accounts to the ambitious seventeen Sustainable Development Goals (SDGs) of the United Nations. Their concept of caring for people and the world like a shepherd is consistent with both Old and New Testament motifs.

The Johnstons guide us to reflect on the seventeen SDGs and to seriously consider meaningful and strategic participation in them as Christ-followers. Involvement with healing the sick, feeding the hungry, good governance, and capacity building is not solely the task of secular organizations such as the United Nations and international organizations. God's people must permeate and partner at all levels of the human experience as part of an "all of society" approach to promoting the wellbeing of all people and the planet.

The United Nations has the purview and resources for creating significant opportunities to support long-term national and global change. But the impetus to identify and meet local needs and effect long-term change needs to be done in collaboration with local communities and their governing entities. The international community can help to supply the opportunity and resources needed for long-term change (sustainable development), but no outside entity can provide the will to implement that change. Our *shared* task in development is the same as in frontier mission: help people to access information and skills so that they can make informed choices, and don't try to choose for them. We concur with the Johnstons' message that Christians should serve on the ground and within the United Nations in such a way as to meet human needs and encourage participatory governance at all levels. It is our God-given responsibility to mobilize the wealthy and powerful while providing a voice for the poor and powerless. Opportunities abound for Christians to make our world a better place for Christ's glory!

Chapter 4 by Joyce Yip Green and Karen Brown, stirs up some hurtful recollections for us. How we desperately needed what these authors provide before we left the United States for Africa four decades ago! Under the framework of international psychology (IP), they offer wise counsel for anyone who desires to walk alongside those whose cultural norms are a treasure to mine. The authors provide principles and narratives that serve as a roadmap to access the hearts and minds of others whose languages and cultures differ from our own. With their help, we could have recognized earlier the need to become lifelong learners. We would have recognized earlier that God had sent us into the world for his investment in us as much as our investment in our host culture. And we could have recognized earlier how God was already present in the cultures and countries where we were sent.

We say a resounding "amen" to this chapter and how it models a thoughtful integration of IP with mission and member care.

We sat under a South African professor in one of our doctoral classes. He observed that Western workers often analyze another culture from a "bird's-eye view." He insisted that we adopt the perspective of a "worm's-eye view" that learns at the feet of local cultures. I (Nik) still remember my shock when approaching a gathering of starving, nomadic camel herders in rural Somalia. Their extended family was in a dire situation. Immediately I suggested a feeding initiative through which we could save the majority of the men, women, and children within these families. But the men refused. They insisted that I first address the needs of their camels. Observing the shock on my face, one of the elders forcefully stated, "If you feed our wives and children and allow our camels to die, then all of us will soon be dead. If you will treat and feed our camels, then we will be able to meet the physical needs of our families. Save our camels so that we can feed our families." Clearly, we needed an on-the-ground view—then and always!

These experienced authors offer concrete perspectives as they unpack concepts such as "cultural sensitivity" and becoming "contextually informed." As Christians and psychologists, they offer their IP wisdom and hard-earned lessons for seeking "cultural relevance." Their chapter abounds with advice and a narrative that inspires and informs. Also highly instructive is the inclusion of five short IP applications from a seasoned mission consultant in Asia. Prepackaged programs seldom provide long-term solutions. Loving enough to listen and learn is a major step toward participating in a shared humanity and part of lifelong mutual learning.

Chapter 5 by Kelly O'Donnell, presents the right to pursue a better life as individuals in our global family. No culture or institution has the right to demand or implement certain actions from those of other cultures and belief systems. Furthermore, governing institutions, just like peoples of faith, must always retain the moral imperative to see that "human beings shall enjoy freedom of speech and belief and freedom from fear" and "social progress and better standards of life in larger freedom" as proclaimed in the preamble of the UDHR.

Such is the dream of the UDHR. It is our dream and prayer too that the 30 articles enshrined in this document will become accepted and implemented globally, because they represent the heart of God. As this chapter asserts, exploring and understanding the relevance of the UDHR for mission and member care cannot be overemphasized.

The vision and the rights articulated in the UDHR are so compelling and so biblical that we are adamant that the only response to the UDHR should be a resounding yes. Sadly, the UDHR's aspirations will never be completely fulfilled. But people and governments of good will should nonetheless endeavor to live and act by them. The UDHR reflects the heart and command of the Creator to respect the worth and dignity of all people, since all people are made in the image of God.

Final Thoughts

These five chapters reflect the best that God's servants desire to offer the peoples of the earth. John 1:14 proclaims concerning Jesus that "The Word became flesh and made his dwelling among us." Jesus's incarnation is for us the model of the crucible wherein transformation germinates and burgeons into new realities. Member care workers are called to embrace lifestyles of *micro-incarnation* by entering into the worlds of mission workers. May you embrace grace from God and strength from one another as you lay down your lives to care for those serving among all peoples, the mission frontiers, and the major issues and suffering facing our world. This type of care is compassionately wrapped in a human touch, a hug, a cup of cold water, and tears shed because of shared brokenness.

We join with the authors to encourage you and the international mission community to prudently connect with and contribute to the resources and efforts of international entities—including United Nations agencies—that are also working in the *missio Dei* frontiers as part of the overlapping humanitarian, human rights, health, peace, and development sectors. Furthermore, the contextualized member care for which these authors advocate intertwines with the ongoing reality for mission workers of crucifixion nested within the opportunity of resurrection. May we all prayerfully support one another in faithfully incarnating the gospel and resolutely staying the course in mission!

Ruth Ripken and Nik Ripken have been married for forty-seven years. They are the parents of three sons and have two "daughters-in-love" along with two grandsons. The Ripkens have supervised workers throughout North Africa and the Middle East, hold workshops around the world, and present podcasts about what they have learned from believers in persecution. They are the authors of several books and articles including Nik's *The Insanity of God* (2013), *The Insanity of Obedience* (2014), and *The Insanity of Sacrifice* (2019).

Prioritizing the Frontier Peoples

Strategic Implications for Mission and Member Care

Rebecca Lewis and Tim Lewis

Specialized training and member care are crucial to enable people to be effective with the most difficult people groups and places—and to stay long enough to make a difference. Without strategic awareness, mission workers can be inadvertently diverted from pioneering among Unreached People Groups (UPGs) to "easier" locations that already have higher concentrations of workers and stronger local support structures for children, families, and teams. Frontier workers must specifically be supported for the special challenges of pioneering work, or else they will tend to gravitate to "reached" people groups—i.e., those that already have indigenous Christian movements.

In this chapter, we highlight the incredible progress made in bringing Jesus into previously overlooked communities through an emphasis on people groups and through the development of new forms of member care designed to support pushes into pioneering areas. We then clarify why 25 percent of humanity remains in "Frontier People Groups" (FPGs), which are the least reached subset of UPGs. We propose the strategic priority of sending many more workers to start family-blessing movements to Christ in the largest FPGs. Lastly, we suggest ways to prepare and support today's workers to overcome the barriers that keep these groups outside the Kingdom.

We need to undertake significant rethinking of strategic training, innovations in outreach, and relevant member care for those involved in pioneering or frontier work. As this chapter explains, the remaining FPGs share specific challenges that help to explain why movements to Christ have not taken hold among these groups. Historically, the greatest progress has happened when support for mission workers is geared toward the unique difficulties of a particular mission context, such as happened with tribal people groups beginning nearly one hundred years ago. Lessons from that era still apply today.

Breakthroughs from Seeing with "People Group Eyes"

In the twentieth century, the rise of air transportation and radio/phone communication opened up access to isolated tribal peoples, nearly all of whom had never heard of Jesus. Great progress resulted from Cameron Townsend's insight that unless we see the world with "people group eyes," the spread of churches could give the false impression that the gospel was available to an increasing number of people groups, when actually it was not. In the 1930s, Townsend established the Summer Institute of Linguistics, Wycliffe, and "jungle camps" to train workers to survive amid even the most isolated tribal peoples, to learn their language, and to teach them literacy and the Scriptures. It quickly became clear that these difficult situations required specific types of training and specialized staff support (later called member care), which Wycliffe and others designed and provided. More recently, similar "desert camps" have been proposed to train people to work with the nomadic tribes of the desert (Philips 2002). A new training program for various types of nomadic peoples was launched in 2018, now called Nomadic Connect (Offereigns 2024).

The ethno-linguistic tribal focus was amazingly successful. The number of Protestant mission agencies more than doubled between 1945 and 1969 (Winter 1970, 54–55). The 1,500 tribal groups in New Guinea, for example, are no longer "unreached"—almost all of them have at least 2 percent evangelical Christians.

However, by the 1970s most of the denominational missions were saying the job of mission outreach was finished. "Missionaries, go home" was a mantra of some. Most mission workers worked among overseas Christians; they saw churches everywhere and assumed that the rest of the world was the same. Meanwhile, the people groups with no Christians were hidden from view. Today, after fifty years of expansion into Africa and Asia, over 80 percent of Christians still live in countries where more than 50 percent of the population identifies as Christian (Zurlo, Johnson, and Crossing 2023).

It again took "people group eyes" to reveal that, even after the emphasis on remote tribal groups, the pioneering or frontier mission task was far from finished. Moreover, many people groups untouched by the gospel were still "hidden" in highly populated areas too, not just in remote areas. In 1974, Ralph Winter conducted a famous global analysis, presented at Lausanne's first International Congress on World Evangelization. He was shocked to discover that *about 60 percent of the world's population still lived in people groups with no indigenous churches of their own* (Lewis 2018a).

The successful push to reach tribal peoples had somehow bypassed the major religious blocs of Islam and Hinduism, and the incredible work of China Inland Mission had been seemingly eclipsed by the Communist revolution. The stark reality was most easily seen on a pie chart Winter produced, called "Penetrating the Final Frontiers," which revealed huge areas full of "unreached" people groups without witness or churches in China, India, and the Muslim world (Lewis 2018a).

The pie chart also showed, surprisingly, that mission workers from the United States had settled almost entirely among the people groups and in geographic areas with high percentages of national Christians, helping with discipleship, pastoral training, and evangelistic outreach (Lewis 2018a). Therefore, member care resources were focused on the needs of this type of workers at that time. As the field of member care began to coalesce in the 1970s into a recognized movement, Christian mental health practitioners and people with firsthand experience in mission talked "openly and at times passionately about the challenges of mission life. Many writings from the 1970s addressed the areas of missionary preparation, selection/evaluation, field adjustment, longevity, children's issues, women's roles, and reentry: in short, how to better support and equip mission personnel" (O'Donnell 2015, 92). However, with the new data emerging on UPGs, member care personnel increasingly needed to address problems of workers facing the complexities of pioneering within huge people groups with no believers.

Astounding Progress Among Unreached People Groups

A new strategic challenge to "see" and reach out to UPGs was launched in 1975 and had taken hold by the mid-1980s. Some 17,000 UPGs were originally identified, and roughly 10,000 of them are now "reached"—which the Joshua Project defines as having more than 2 percent strongly committed or evangelical Christians and 5 percent other Christians. All believers who hold to a high view of Scripture and the need for heart conversion to Christ are considered "Great Commission Christians" or evangelicals, including Pentecostals and charismatics. Zurlo et al. (2023) estimated that there are over 2.6 billion Christians and over 400 million evangelicals globally.

Surprisingly, even though over 90 percent of global mission workers were still serving "reached" people groups, those who focused on working among UPGs made huge progress in establishing movements to Christ. As previously with the tribal peoples, whole new agencies arose to take on the challenge of the UPG mega-bloc, such as Muslims, while a growing number of Indian mission agencies and churches sent workers cross-culturally to that country's many UPGs. Despite facing difficult situations, with few member care resources focused on their needs, workers banded together in new structures, organizations, and teams to tackle the challenge of UPGs.

As a result of seeing with "people group eyes" once again, astounding progress in spreading the gospel has been made during the last forty years. Not only are half of the original UPGs now "reached," but another 40 percent of the remaining UPGs had growing indigenous movements to Christ. That left only 60 percent of the remaining UPGs with no sign of progress of the gospel (representing 25 percent of the world's population).

In 2018, Chris Maynard of Transforming Information created an updated version of Winter's pie chart (unpublished), using data from the *Atlas of Global Christianity*, Operation World, and Joshua Project. The new version of this chart (shown here) (Butler, Lewis, and Maynard 2024) graphically clarifies the remaining "frontier" mission task. It reveals the location of "Frontier People Groups," defined as those UPGs that still have no known indigenous movements to Jesus and have no more than one Christian of any kind for every 1,000 people (Lewis 2018a). We have produced an animated video of this new pie chart, which is now available in multiple languages (Joshua Project; Maynard and Lewis 2018).

The data show global progress of the gospel beyond all expectations. For example, today the gospel has finally been established in China among the Han Chinese, where millions of believers no longer view God as a foreign God but as their Creator and Father too. The Communist push to kill faith in God did not ultimately succeed! Many movements to Christ have emerged among Buddhist people groups; fewer than 2 percent of the remaining FPGs are Buddhist or associated with tribal or ethnic religions (32 million people out of 2 billion).

Even more importantly, though the world's population has nearly doubled, in just 40 years (between 1980 and 2020) the percentage of the world's population in FPGs dropped from 60 percent to only 25 percent. And the global ratio of committed followers of Jesus to people in FPGs improved from 1:10 to 1:2, as the population of committed followers of Jesus in the world quadrupled while the population in the remaining FPGs decreased by 20 percent (see bar graph accompanying the pie chart).

Prioritizing the Frontier Peoples

The Remaining Frontier Mission Task

This chart shows the global distribution of followers of Jesus and non-believers, including among Unreached People Groups (UPGs), and Frontier People Groups (FPGs), which are those UPGs with **no progress of the gospel, still needing movements to Jesus**. The 25% of humanity in FPGs—shown in black—still need pioneer workers and are mostly in India and Muslim-majority countries.

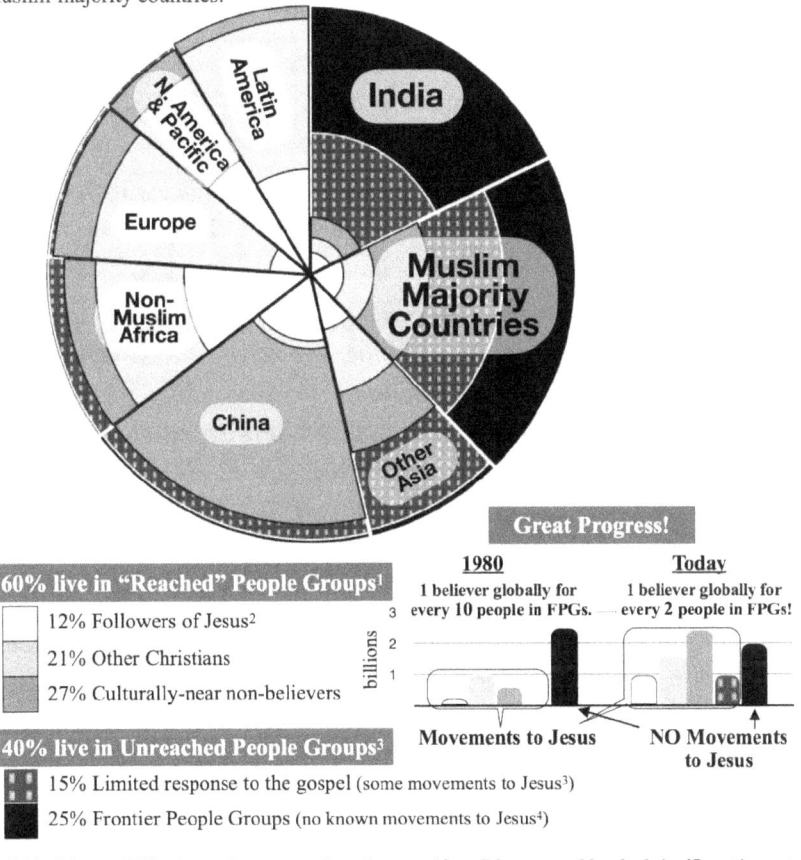

60% live in "Reached" People Groups[1]

- 12% Followers of Jesus[2]
- 21% Other Christians
- 27% Culturally-near non-believers

40% live in Unreached People Groups[3]

- 15% Limited response to the gospel (some movements to Jesus[3])
- 25% Frontier People Groups (no known movements to Jesus[4])

Great Progress!

1980: 1 believer globally for every 10 people in FPGs.

Today: 1 believer globally for every 2 people in FPGs!

Movements to Jesus — NO Movements to Jesus

[1] 60% of the world live in people groups where the gospel is well known and has had significant impact. (greater than 2% Evangelical or greater than 5% Christian Adherent)
[2] Estimate based on published figures for Evangelicals, Charismatics & Pentecostals.
[3] Up to 2% Evangelical or 5% Christian Adherent. [4] No more than 0.1% Christian Adherent.
Percentages based on a global population of 8 billion people, using data from JoshuaProject.net/frontier
Adapted with permission from the Go31.org *Prayer Guide—for the 31 largest Frontier People Groups*

Used with permission of Rebecca Lewis.

Understanding the Remaining Frontier Mission Task

But what does this new data reveal about the task still ahead of us? Data analysis using "people group eyes," though not perfect, has clarified some unexpected things. Here is what we can learn through the interactive map of FPGs at the Joshua Project, which is sortable by many detailed criteria such as size, country, religion, language, and diaspora:

1. *Two billion people live in nearly 5,000* FPGs—25 percent of the world's population.
2. *Around half of all the people in FPGs live in India*, with 70 percent of them in South Asia, including Pakistan and Bangladesh. Another 18 percent are in Central Asia, the Middle East, and North Africa combined.
3. *97 percent of the people in Frontier People Groups (FPGs) are either Muslims (50 percent) or Hindus (47 percent)*, with a mere 3 percent belonging to Buddhist, Sikh, animist, or other religious or non-religious groups.
4. *Nearly one billion people live in the 35 largest FPGs*, each of which have more than 10 million people (see Bless Frontier Peoples and Go31 for a prayer guide covering these largest groups).
5. *The most strategic approach to reaching FPGs is to start indigenous, self-propagating movements in the nearly 300 mega-FPGs* (those larger than one million people in size, totaling 1.6 billion people, 20 percent of humanity and 80 percent of the population of FPGs), which will impact the smaller FPGs that are frequently related. For example, there are over seventy distinct Kapu people groups in India.

The fact that more than 95 percent of the remaining FPGs, both by count and by population, are Muslims or Hindus (along with a few Sikh, Buddhist, Jain, or animist groups) has enormous implications for member care. Most of these people are in huge people groups that have been significantly neglected in mission outreach and/or who see Christianity as a threat. Most are in countries closed to mission work; many are hidden in South Asian megacities. It can be hard to gain positive access and relational acceptance in these people groups, just as in the isolated jungle tribes of fifty years ago. Member care will need to help workers from around the globe thrive in these FPG settings.

The Growth of Member Care Focusing on Unreached People Groups

Ralph and Roberta Winter helped to sponsor two conferences called "Psychological Resources for Frontier Missions," in 1980 at the Center for World Mission and in 1981 at Biola University, both in California. They understood that it is often difficult to survive and thrive in areas where there are no national brothers and sisters with whom to partner. These conferences were followed by two landmark books, *Overcoming Missionary Stress* (Foyle 1987) and *Helping Missionaries Grow* (O'Donnell and Lewis O'Donnell 1988). The O'Donnells subsequently began their decades-long advocacy for the intentional prioritizing of member care efforts and resources to the least reached (Member Care Associates). "Without adequate member care strategies, there is little hope for the on-going maintenance of the frontier mission movement … these missionaries require special attention, so that in the context of sacrifice and isolation, they can still reach the peoples they are called to" (O'Donnell 1992, 107). The need for concerted advocacy is still present today.

There have been great advances in what could be called "reactive member care," which helps with those who have faced trauma, burnout, and other serious problems and crises in their life and families. Significant progress has also been made in "proactive member care" in such areas as mutual support and interpersonal skills workshops, pastoral field visits, team building sessions, retreats, leadership and management training, homeschooling of children in areas far from schools (such as the Sonlight Curriculum that Rebecca helped develop in the 1990s), and child protection training for agencies.

Nevertheless, there are still many glaring gaps in member care mindsets and resources across the globe. In particular, we believe that much more specific training for member care personnel supporting workers in FPGs is needed, as attrition rates can be very high. Many workers struggle to connect with "families of peace" in today's chaotic urbanizing world, so they lack the deep relationships that would keep them encouraged and engaged. Due to the internet, workers can often remain dependent on their friends at home and their home culture, which undermines their ability to bond and adapt locally in FPG settings.

Thankfully, proactive coaching and counseling via the internet is now possible, increasing field longevity and helping to avoid burnout, deteriorating marriages, and family breakdowns. Greater preparation and timely help are especially needed for those experiencing what we call "theology shock"—when God doesn't act as expected and people's worldview and understanding of God's goodness are shaken to the core. Also, timely help is needed for those traumatized by the spiritual warfare that can accompany even successful movements, such as the persecution, jailing, or martyrdom of disciples or teammates. More spiritual, emotional, and missiological resources must be developed that are geared specifically to support frontier mission workers' adjustment, character, and competencies. This need is not merely for relatively well-resourced Western mission workers, but especially for the growing numbers of frontier mission workers from the Global South—including some coming from people groups that are still "unreached" but now have movements to Christ, such as in Indonesia.

The member care community itself must sustain a high level of commitment to helping people and families stay in and be effective among the FPGs, even though this work can be much more difficult than mission service elsewhere. Additional collaborative efforts, structures, and support networks are needed to deliver care for those fulfilling the varied roles required in FPG setttings (O'Donnell 2002). For example, our grandchildren have been blessed by joining other TCK teens from around the world in online language learning, home school co-op groups, and international Christian homeschooling networks such as Ambleside Online. These resources were not possible when we were raising our children in North Africa. Such opportunities should be in the toolbox of sending organizations and member care workers who can help families find innovative solutions and continue to thrive while being effectively engaged with a FPG. See the work of Missionary Upholders Trust in India for some good examples of the types of collaborative efforts and resources, many of which are described in their *Care and Serve* newsletter and in chapter 10.

Strategic Considerations for Effectiveness among Muslim and Hindu FPGs

1. Blessing the Families and Communities of FPGs

The great historian of Christian missions, Kenneth Scott Latourette, wrote, "Too often we have torn men and women one by one out of the family, or village, or clan with the result that they have been permanently de-racinated or maladjusted. … It is much better if an entire natural group … can come rapidly over into the faith" (Winter 1970, 90). Everywhere the gospel has been successfully established, we have *not* pulled believers out of their cultures and communities. Even in the religious mega-structure of the Roman Empire, Paul encouraged the Roman believers to remain in their families and communities, blessing them with their newfound faith and character. We need to understand and use Paul's principles to reach the FPGs (Lewis 2018b).

In today's major cities, it can appear that the family-based "ethnē" people-group thinking is no longer relevant, but that is not true. With the rise of the global internet and urbanization, and with the growth of migrant and diaspora communities, the identities of some people groups, especially among the younger generations, are being blurred into a superficial quasi-Western global youth culture. However, those bereft of the strong bonds of family-based ethnic people-group identities are increasingly seeking newer but weaker (and often unhealthy) bonds with identity groups based on ideology or grievances. People yearn for *belonging* amid their loneliness in the no-man's land of growing hybridity.

Early mission workers established most of the world's schools and hospitals, which have now been largely taken over by secular entities, either government or private. But there are many gaps where a government may have little desire to help or provides limited or no solutions. Families and communities in FPGs are often hurting. We can assist with adult literacy, job creation, and local entrepreneurship (Goldmann 2024). As ministers of compassion, we can also address problems such as addictions, disabilities, conflict, corruption, and trauma. "Making a Killing" (2019) urges workers to reclaim the historical mission response and oppose the various "global death industries" that are wreaking havoc on communities everywhere—especially among FPGs. Very few representative *communities* of FPGs (less than 1 percent of the total) are in the diaspora in open countries, so we must go to the homelands in ways that governments will allow, such as establishing profitable businesses and training, reclaiming agricultural lands, and improving infrastructure and supply chains.

The goal of bringing long-term blessing to FPGs requires understanding the big picture and valuing their God-given heritage and God's purpose for their people group. Mission workers must be prepared to become "belongers" in these resistant communities, listening with humility as locals share their hopes and problems. The diverse member care field with its multi-disciplinary and multi-cultural inputs and practitioners is positioned to help mission workers develop skills and explore ways to support holisic care and development with members of FPG communities.

2. Building on a Shared Humanity by Bringing Them Jesus, Not Christendom
As noted above, the highest priority is the remaining large Muslim and Hindu groups, where it is far too easy to get sidetracked in religious arguments. Not knowing how to overcome religious prejudice, we have historically ignored Muslim and Hindu groups. In fact, the centuries of outreach in India has almost entirely ignored the Hindu middle castes, now approaching a billion people, focusing instead on the highest castes or the outcastes and tribal groups (Anon 2024). We can build a bridge by emphasizing our common humanity with these groups, refected in many areas such as our common desires for healthy families and relationships, healing, hope, and deliverance from evil. They are not rejecting Christ but Christendom (Richard 2024).

We need to learn to speak with the grace and compassion that Jesus showed the Samaritan woman, *bypassing her religious arguments* by pointing out that God is Spirit and is seeking all those who will worship him in spirit and truth. We too can offer Jesus as "living water" to spiritually thirsty people. Jews refused to associate with Samaritans due to religious prejudice, but Jesus went to them. The whole Samaritan village, at the end of Jesus's visit, exclaimed, "Now we have heard for ourselves, and we know this man really is the savior of the world" (John 4:42). Jesus was no longer just the Savior of the Jews, but their Savior as well. *This exclamation is what we long to hear from the Muslims, Hindus, and other frontier peoples of the world*!

3. Planting Movements, Not Institutional Churches
Movements are needed to establish the gospel initially in a new people group; after that, appropriate indigenous churches can follow, designed by the believers themselves. Attempts to plant institutional churches, complete with a program, leadership structure, and religious culture, have traditionally failed to multiply in high-identity FPGs, attracting persecution instead. Historically, movements to Christ have usually preceded the formalization of believers into church structures, and movements have slowed once the focus of believers shifted to running programs, constructing church buildings, and founding hospitals, orphanages, and schools, as helpful as all these activities were.

Lasting movements can happen even in resistant high-identity groups when the gospel takes root in strong, pre-existing community structures, such as families and clans (Lewis and Lewis 2018). When Bible studies are done openly, with the whole family present to wrestle among themselves about what they are learning, then the family members can decide together whether or not to follow Jesus. Integral Disciple Making Movements

(IDMM) training combines the best of community blessing and Bible study movements (Charlotte 2024).

There have been more movements to Christ in the last 40 years within Muslim or Hindu groups than in the previous 200 years of Protestant outreach. As early as 1969, over 50,000 Muslims had become followers of Jesus in Southeast Asia (Winter 1970, 61). Now the vast majority of new movements are being started by movement leaders from other people groups nearby, and most of the remaining FPGs share a language with another UPG that already has movements to Christ, such as Arabic, Urdu or Hindi. Only 2000 of the 5000 Frontier People Groups speak languages in which there is no known movement (Parks 2024). For more on movements in India see specific articles in the special issue of *Mission Frontiers* magazine "Seeking Movements Among Frontier Peoples" (Anon 2024; Richard 2024; Smith 2024). *Nevertheless, the Muslim and Hindu worlds have not yet made the discovery that proved crucial to the Han Chinese coming to Christ, namely that the God of the Bible is not a foreign god and that Jesus is their Savior too.*

Additionally, extending indigenous movements into new cultures with no Christian witness has depended in each generation on new mission structures with that specific goal in mind. For 275 years (1517–1792), Protestant churches ignored or rejected the need for special mission structures and sent no workers to unreached peoples (Blincoe 2020). Even experienced movement leaders crossing into new cultures and languages will need structures, training, and member care to support their efforts.

Conclusion

What God has done in the last century, especially the last 50 years, is astounding. But 25 percent of the world's population still lives in people groups with no known movements to Christ and virtually no known believers. This task is considerable, but by God's grace we believe it is achievable. Eighty percent of this population is in just under 300 people groups larger than one million people in size, virtually all of them Muslims or Hindus, and 70 percent live in South Asia. *We believe that beginning a movement to Christ among these 300 Muslim or Hindu FPGs is the highest priority.*

However, since mission workers in FPGs are still barely 1 percent of the total global mission force, their needs are easy to overlook. Specialized member care training is needed so that member care personnel can support frontier workers who are seeking out new roles and new support structures for pioneering in our rapidly changing world. God is calling mission workers from many nations now, and each sending culture has its own special struggles, which call for contextually and culturally relevant solutions. To adopt Western solutions can be like David trying to use Saul's armor to fight Goliath (Goldmann 2007). We encourage sending groups and member care personnel to strategically prioritize and support frontier mission workers and their families in their cross-cultural callings, strategies, and sacrifices, in ways that will enable them to thrive and be effective among FPGs.

Applications: Prioritizing the Frontier Peoples

Core Strategies

1. Focus on the nearly 300 largest FPGs, so as to impact 1.6 billion people, representing 80 percent of the two billion people in FPGs.

2. Overcome barriers among FPGs by learning to bless their families and communities, building on our shared humanity, bringing them Jesus rather than Christendom, and promoting movements rather than institutional churches.

3. Innovate new roles, new training, and additional member care resources and structures specifically designed for the unique challenges that face workers among FPGs (internationals, nationals, and locals), including culturally relevant support and virtual technologies.

Core Resources

1. Data resources for FPGs. Joshua Project (including the sortable FPG map) and Telos Fellowship websites. Clarifying the Remaining Frontier Mission Task (Lewis 2018a) and What's Gone Wrong with the Demographics? (Lewis 2018c). See the animated video, Understanding the Remaining Mission Task (Joshua Project; Maynard and Lewis 2018).

2. Prayer resources for FPGs. For groups larger than 10 million people: Bless Frontier Peoples and Go31.

3. Member care resources. Global Member Care Network and Member Care Updates (Member Care Associates).

Reflection and Discussion

1. Discuss some reasons why it has been difficult for movements to Jesus to develop among Muslims and Hindus, who represent 97 percent of the remaining FPGs. Are there things that we have done or not done to make it more difficult for them to understand and embrace the gospel?

2. What attitudes and skills would help mission workers to thrive and form deep connections with families and communities in FPGs?
3. What member care structures and training are needed to support mission workers going to FPGs? How can they be collaboratively developed?

References

Anon, D. 2024. "Understanding Christward Movements in India." *Mission Frontiers*, March–April. https://www.missionfrontiers.org/issue/seeking-movements-among-frontier-peoples.

Bless Frontier Peoples. https://blessfrontierpeoples.org/.

Blincoe, Bob. 2020. (blog). https://robertblincoe.blog/the-catastrophic-protestant-mission-ice-age-illustrated-1st-of-8-timelines/.

Butler, Robby, Rebecca Lewis, and Chris Maynard. 2024. "The Remaining Frontier Mission Task" (chart). Adapted from Go31.org, *Prayer Guide for the 31 Largest Frontier Peoples*, 2023. https://joshuaproject.net/assets/media/handouts/the31-en.pdf.

Charlotte, D. 2024. "Wholistic Disciple Making: An Integral Approach for Multiplying Churches and Transforming Communities." *Mission Frontiers*, March–April. https://www.missionfrontiers.org/issue/article/wholistic-disciple-making.

Global Member Care Network. https://globalmembercare.com/.

Go31.org. "Prayer Guide for the 31 Largest Frontier People Groups." https://go31.org/resources/dig-en/.

Goldmann, Bob. 2007. "Saul's Armor and David's Sling: Innovative Sending in the Global South." *Mission Frontiers*, May–June. https://www.missionfrontiers.org/issue/article/sauls-armor-and-davids-sling.

Goldmann, Bob. 2024. "Entrepreneurial Strategies for Reaching Frontier Peoples." *Mission Frontiers*, March–April. https://www.missionfrontiers.org/issue/seeking-movements-among-frontier-peoples.

Joshua Project. https://joshuaproject.net/.

Lewis, Rebecca. 2018a. "Clarifying the Remaining Frontier Mission Task." *International Journal of Frontier Missiology* 35 (4). https://ijfm.org/PDFs_IJFM/35_4_PDFs/IJFM_35_4-Lewis.pdf.

Lewis, Rebecca. 2018b. "How to Reach a Frontier People Group: Following Paul's Principles." *Mission Frontiers*, November–December. https://www.missionfrontiers.org/pdfs/MF40-6_Nov-Dec_eBook-24-27_How_to_Reach_Frontier_Peoples.pdf.

Lewis, Rebecca. 2018c. "Losing Sight of the Frontier Mission Task: What's Gone Wrong with the Demographics." *International Journal of Frontier Missiology* 35 (1). https://ijfm.org/PDFs_IJFM/35_1-LewisFMTask.pdf.

Lewis, Tim, and Rebecca Lewis. 2018. "Planting Churches: Learning the Hard Way." *Mission Frontiers*, March–April. https://www.missionfrontiers.org/issue/article/planting-churches-learning-the-hard-way.

"Making a Killing: The Global Death Industries and Missionary Response." 2019. *Mission Frontiers*, September–October. https://www.missionfrontiers.org/issue/archive/making-a-killing.

Maynard, Chris, and Rebecca Lewis. 2018. "Understanding the Remaining Frontier Mission Task" (video). https://www.youtube.com/watch?v=SVmTU13rgo8.

Member Care Associates. "MC History. Member Care and Unreached Peoples." https://membercareassociates.org/mc-foundations/notes-quotes/.

Member Care Associates. "MC Updates—Special News." https://membercareassociates.org/resource-updates/mca-resource-updates/.

Missionary Upholders Trust. *Care and Serve*. http://mutindia.org/publication.html.

O'Donnell, Kelly. 1992. "An Agenda for Member Care in Frontier Missions." *International Journal of Frontier Missions* 9 (3): 107–112. http://www.ijfm.org/PDFs_IJFM/09_3_PDFs/9_3O%27Donnell.pdf.

O'Donnell, Kelly. 2002. "Developing Member Care Affiliations." In *Doing Member Care Well: Perspectives and Practices from Around the World*, edited by Kelly O'Donnell, 515–528. Pasadena, CA: William Carey Library. https://passionexchange.files.wordpress.com/2008/10/doingmembercarewell.pdf.

O'Donnell, Kelly. 2015. "The Missional Heart of Member Care." *International Bulletin of Mission Research* 39 (2): 91–96. https://membercareassociates.org/wp-content/uploads/2021/03/Missional-Heart-of-MC-article-pub-version-from-IBMR-website-2015.pdf.

Offereigns, Samira. 2024. "Nomad Connect: A Learning Journey." *Mission Frontiers*, January–February. https://www.missionfrontiers.org/pdfs/31-33_MF_46-1_JAN-FEB-24_OFFEREIGNS.pdf.

Parks, Stan. 2024. "The Best Hope for Reaching Frontier Peoples." *Mission Frontiers*, March–April. https://www.missionfrontiers.org/issue/seeking-movements-among-frontier-peoples.

Philips, David J. 2002. "Striking Camp with the Nomads." *Mission Frontiers*, March–April. https://www.missionfrontiers.org/issue/article/striking-camp-with-the-nomads.

Richard, H. L. 2024. "Devout Hindus: Anti-church but Not Necessarily Antichrist."*Mission Frontiers*, March–April. https://www.missionfrontiers.org/issue/seeking-movements-among-frontier-peoples.

"Seeking Movements Among Frontier Peoples." 2024. *Mission Frontiers*, March–April. https://www.missionfrontiers.org/issue/archive/seeking-movements-among-frontier-peoples.

Smith, Rekedal. 2024. "Testimony of a Viable, Indigenous Church Planting Movement."*Mission Frontiers*, March–April. https://www.missionfrontiers.org/issue/seeking-movements-among-frontier-peoples.

Telos Fellowship. https://www.telosfellowship.org/.

Winter, Ralph. 1970. *The 25 Unbelievable Years (1945–1969)*. Pasadena, CA: William Carey Library.

Winter, Ralph. 1973. "Two Structures of God's Redemptive Mission." https://frontiermissionfellowship.org/uploads/documents/two-structures.pdf.

Zurlo, Gina, Todd Johnson, and Peter Crossing. 2023. "World Christianity 2023: A Gendered Approach." *International Bulletin of Mission Research* 47 (1): 11–22. https://doi.org/10.1177/23969393221128253. (A link to the annual table of statistics can be found at https://www.gordonconwell.edu/wp-content/uploads/sites/13/2023/01/Status-of-Global-Christianity-2023.pdf)

Rebecca Lewis and Tim Lewis were raised in Latin America. They met and married when Rebecca's parents, Ralph and Roberta Winter, founded the US Center for World Mission (now Frontier Ventures) and Tim's parents, Norm and Anabeth Lewis, came to help. Moved by Dr. Winter's statistics, they did pioneering work among Muslim tribal groups, raising a team of forty adults and fifty-six children while having four children themselves. Tim helped to found the Frontiers mission organization and was later its third International Director. In 2018, Rebecca realized that clarity had been lost as to which people groups still had no indigenous movements to Christ. They subsequently identified which UPGs had no movements yet, naming them Frontier People Groups.

2

Following and Serving Jesus Globally

A Framework for Engaging with Our World

Kelly O'Donnell and Michèle Lewis O'Donnell

> Whoever serves me must follow me; and where I am, my servant also will be. My Father will honor the one who serves me.
> —John 12:26

> "Have you understood all these things [in the lessons of the parables]?" They said to Jesus, "Yes." He said to them, "Therefore every scribe who has become a disciple of the kingdom of heaven is like the head of a household, who brings out of his treasure things that are new and fresh and things that are old and familiar."
> —Matthew 13:51–52 Amplified

Life in our precarious, often perilous, yet precious world is tough, but throughout history, it has been much tougher for some people than for others. A case in point is the estimated 1.1 billion people living in multidimensional poverty (World Bank 2023); many of them belong to least-reached people groups. As people of faith or of no particular faith, we are all subject to the maims and moans of fallen creation. In the midst of life's adversities and traumas, Christians are called to participate in Christ's reconciliation and renewal of all things in heaven and earth (Col 1:20). And we await and yearn for our full adoption as the children of God (Rom 8:18–25)!

For the last twenty years, our work as psychologists in mission has increasingly taken us into various sectors (e.g., humanitarian, health, development, peace, human rights; international agencies and the United Nations). Central to our work has been a practical, strategic framework that we call Global Integration (GI) (Member Care Associates, Global Integration Overview).

GI is a framework for actively and responsibly engaging with our world, locally through globally, for God's glory. We seek to "integrate" our lives by connecting relationally and contributing relevantly on behalf of human wellbeing and the issues facing humanity and the planet, finding common ground for the common good. GI applies to individuals as well as to groups, organizations, and governments.

As the Scripture passages cited at the beginning of this chapter indicate, GI calls us to serve Jesus by following him wherever he goes—among all peoples and places—and to link new and old "treasures" (resources and directions) to share the good news and our good works. We do so in light of our integrity, commitments, and core values (e.g., ethical, humanitarian, human rights, faith-based).

We believe the GI framework is crucial for (a) member care/mission practice and direction; (b) colleagues working in different sectors and settings; and (c) all those who endeavor to live as global citizens with our common sense of belonging, identity, and mutual responsibility as humans. It is thus a mindset and a skill set, a perspective and a practice, for how we live and work in our world relevantly and righteously as followers of Christ, engaging in the seen and unseen realms with his authority, word, and power.

In this chapter, we discuss GI in terms of three directions for following and serving Jesus globally in mission for all peoples and all places: Humanity and Creation Care, Global Integrity, and Global Integrators. How can these GI directions apply to the church and mission community, to member care approaches across cultures, and to you and your organization? This chapter draws on our multi-sectoral and GI work in mission including our monthly *Global Integration Updates* (Member Care Associates, *Global Integration Updates*); two of our foundational articles (O'Donnell and Lewis O'Donnell 2017, 2020), as well as our more personal video account (O'Donnell 2022).

GI Direction One: Humanity and Creation Care

> Jesus called them together and said, "You know that those who are regarded as rulers of the Gentiles lord it over them, and their high officials exercise authority over them. Not so with you. Instead, whoever wants to become great among you must be your servant, and whoever wants to be first must be slave of all. For even the Son of Man did not come to be served, but to serve, and to give his life as a ransom for many."
>
> —Mark 10:42–45

> Leave no one behind. That defining principle of the 2030 Agenda for Sustainable Development is a shared promise by every country to work together to secure the rights and well-being of everyone on a healthy, thriving planet. But halfway to 2030, that promise is in peril. The Sustainable Development Goals (SDGs) are disappearing in the rear-view mirror—and with them the hope and rights of current and future generations. A fundamental shift is needed—in commitment, solidarity, financing and action—to put the world on a better path. And it is needed now.
> —UN Secretary-General António Guterres 2023, Paragraph 1.

A global effort is underway, spearheaded by the United Nations and its member states along with many international and grassroots organizations, to promote sustainable development and wellbeing for all people and the planet (United Nations 2015b). This effort is a major part of what we call *humanity and creation care*. The 2030 Agenda for sustainable development, adopted by world leaders and member states in September 2015, organized broadly around five overlapping areas: people, planet, prosperity, peace, and partnership. This effort calls on the world community to change its course drastically and to intentionally and accountably partner together in working toward peace, justice, prosperity, and the protection of the planet. As Christians, we have an unprecedented opportunity to become involved globally and to partner with others in such efforts.

Partnering in humanity and creation care is a core part of GI's emphasis on people of good will "finding common ground for the common good" and is reflected in the theological concept of the common grace of God available to all people. As people of faith, hope, and love who practice Christian spirituality, we embrace a foundational commitment to Jesus Christ that underlies all our partnering with secular organizations. We acknowledge the underlying reality of God and his redemptive purposes in Jesus Christ in dealing with the undermining reality of evil, sin, and brokenness (O'Donnell 2015).

Overview of Our Work

Our work in humanity and creation care is based primarily in Geneva, a strategic platform for "connecting relationally and contributing relevantly" as the GI framework emphasizes. It includes regular interactions with personnel and events around the United Nations, World Health Organization, international NGOs, and faith-based organizations. We regularly review materials from these sources and various news and information portals to inform our work and share them with colleagues (e.g., Justin Long's *Weekly Roundup*). We have found that GI is a key strategy to open new opportunities, thinking, relationships, and resources for member care and mission and efforts towards wellbeing for all people and the planet.

We disseminate information through two monthly updates which include news, perspectives, and resources (Member Care Associates, *Member Care Updates* and *Global Integration Updates*). We have also hosted many "Trio Gatherings" in our home for more informal and personal interaction with colleagues across sectors on topics such as integrity, poverty, peace, leadership, and work-life balance (Virtrios—Trio Gatherings).

Sample Topics of *Global Integration Updates*

- Why The "M" Word Matters: Missionaries and Development (January 2024)
- Universal Declaration of Human Rights: Dignity, Freedom, Justice for All (December 2023)
- Multidimensional Poverty: Ending Poverty in All Its Forms Everywhere (November 2023)
- Peace and Security: Staying Alive in Our World (September 2023)
- Being Inter-Faith-Based: Doing Better Together (April 2023)
- Developing Character Strengths: Being the Leaders Our World Needs (March 2023)
- Thinking Critically about Sustainable Development (February 2022)
- Planet SOS: The UN Climate Conference (November 2021)

We believe that a variety of people must be at the global tables and in the global trenches—and everything in-between—to research, shape, and monitor agendas, policies, and action. That includes people from all countries, sectors, and faith backgrounds who are informed, skilled, and dedicated to the common good.

As for the involvement of people of faith, it is estimated that 7.1 billion of the world's 8 billion people have a religious affiliation. That is truly the "majority world" in spiritual terms. Hence, people of faith should always be involved in influential fora on behalf of sustainable development and wellbeing for all people and the planet (e.g., Schliesser 2023). Here are ten suggestions for working across sectors in humanity and creation care, oriented for faith-based colleagues, for your consideration (Member Care Associates 2019).

**Connecting and Contributing Across Sectors:
Ten Suggestions for Faith-Based Colleagues and Organizations**

Faith is not simply a strategic *resource* to leverage for our important projects and agendas. Rather, faith is a fundamental *reality* that underlies all of life, including projects and agendas. Faith is not merely a *component* but often the *core* part of one's life and identity.

1. Prioritize and show up often at strategic events on humanity and creation care. Sometimes it is better to be on time than to be invited.
2. Be conversant with the terms, issues, major players, and main documents, and reference them freely. Get a grid to stay informed.
3. Be aware of mutual (mis)conceptions that can alienate everyone. Examples: proselytism, partiality, prejudices, paternalism.
4. Commit to mutual learning and mutual resourcing. It's a two-way or, actually, a multi-directional street. No one can do humanity and creation care alone.
5. Demonstrate relevance with action and research. This is how you "earn your stripes."
6. Develop personal relationships when possible, not just functional relationships.
7. Don't apologize for your faith and, in general, avoid emphasizing perceived weaknesses in others' faith or worldview.
8. One is not just a "faith-based" person but rather a fellow human who is a Muslim, Hindu, Christian, agnostic, atheist, "none," etc. Hold your head humbly and high.
9. Get dirty—it's a difficult world—but don't play dirty. Diligently maintain your moral health as you immerse yourself in the challenges of humanity and creation care.
10. Review "Charting Our Course Through the Sectors" for more ideas (O'Donnell 2013).

Some UN Efforts

Here are some of the UN's coordinated efforts to promote sustainable development and wellbeing for all people and the planet:

- 17 Sustainable Development Goals (SDGs) and their 169 Targets (United Nations 2015b)
- 196 States Parties adopted the Paris Climate Agreement at the UN Climate Change Conference (United Nations 2015a). It is the first multilateral, binding accord to combat and adapt to climate change.
- Five Core Responsibilities and their 24 Transformations for humanitarian action in the Agenda for Humanity (United Nations 2016)
- 23 Objectives in the *Global Compact for a Safe, Orderly, and Regular Migration* (United Nations 2018)
- Five priority areas in *The New Agenda for Peace* (July 2023), presented in the latest series of Policy Briefs that build upon the UN Secretary-General's *Our Common Agenda* (United Nations 2021)
- The Summit of the Future (May 2024) is a "once-in-a-generation opportunity to enhance cooperation on critical challenges and address gaps in global governance, reaffirm existing commitments including to the Sustainable Development Goals (SDGs) and the United Nations Charter, and move towards a reinvigorated multilateral system that is better positioned to positively impact people's lives." (See the Summit of the Future website, United Nations)

We encourage you to familiarize yourself with these efforts and the influential guiding documents and agreements, starting with the seventeen SGDs and their progress reports such as *The Sustainable Development Goals Report 2023* (United Nations 2023). Review these ambitious efforts to see how different countries, sectors, and colleagues are interacting with them. Consider applications for your own work and that of your organization as well as how you may already be interfacing with them, perhaps using other terms. Note that it can feel foreign and even overwhelming at first. But be persistent, pace yourself, and explore the SDGs together with others! As Teresa of Avila said, "Patience accomplishes all."

GI Clarifications

We understand that there are different perspectives about the United Nations, the "world community," the church and mission community's global roles, and concerns about compromise and syncretism. Here is how we respond to those concerns:

We affirm the combined efforts of [the humanitarian, development, and health sectors] and their dedicated personnel who take risks and make sacrifices often at great personal cost. However, we also appreciate informed critiques—such as aid and development being an industry, bureaucratic inefficiencies, private/corporate and geopolitical special interests, entrenched systemic and power inequalities, national sovereignty compromises, etc.—and know that there is much room for improvement in organizations, sectors, and the global community's efforts. The [major UN efforts such as the] 2030 Agenda, Mental Health Action Plan, and One Humanity, in our view, are crucial rallying and guidance points to truly make a difference regarding the horrific conditions affecting so many fellow humans (O'Donnell and Lewis O'Donnell 2017, 73).

GI in humanity and creation care is not about instigating and imposing a system of global governance, neutralizing national sovereignty, and ushering in an authoritarian world order. Rather, it is about fostering cooperation and good governance at all levels, from the local to the global. Nor is GI about pushing for human homogeneity, cultural conformity, or ethical relativism. Rather, it is about embracing our common humanity, prizing our rich variations, and engendering responsible lifestyles. GI is a framework to help us invest ourselves in fellow humans in every sphere of influence in which we live. For us, that means prioritizing unreached peoples and places, and doing so for God's glory (Lee 2024).

GI Direction Two: Global Integrity

> Your task is to be true, not popular. Your true being brims over into true words and deeds.
>
> —Luke 6:26, 45 *The Message*
>
> Let us strive for a culture of full integrity and transparency. We will choose to walk in the light and truth of God, for the Lord tests the heart and is pleased with integrity.
>
> —*Cape Town Commitment*, Lausanne Movement (2009, IIE.4)

Global integrity (GIn) involves living consistently in moral wholeness—with honesty, humility, and all the virtues—at all levels: individual, interpersonal, institutional, and international; across sectors and settings; local through global; systemic and structural. Maintaining integrity requires external moral referents—standards of virtue with accountability, not simply positive self-appraisals—to safeguard us from both blind and willful hypocrisy. The opposite of integrity is corruption: the distortion, perversion, and deterioration of moral goodness, resulting in the abuse and exploitation of people and the planet. We call it *integroty* (that is, rotten integrity). Like integrity, it also exists globally at all levels (based on our definition on the Global Integrity Day website's homepage).

GIn is not about imposing a moral code on others. Rather, it is about fostering moral dialogue, cooperation, and good governance at all levels, from the local to the global. Furthermore, GIn is not about pushing for human homogeneity, cultural conformity, or ethical relativism. Rather, it is about living in integrity at all levels by embracing our common humanity, prizing our rich variations, and engendering responsible lifestyles.

We like to refer to ourselves as "people of faith, hope, and love" and our organization as being "faith-hope-love-based." As people of faith who practice Christian spirituality, we are committed to acting with integrity as we engage responsibly with others in the local to global challenges facing our world, while holding firmly to our belief that we are in God's hands. We pray that God's purposes will be done on earth as they are in heaven; acknowledge that prayer, repentance, and relationship with God are key to human and planetary wellbeing; and live in hope for the time when God through Jesus Christ will intervene decisively in human history with righteousness and justice to restore all things. In the meantime, we seek to embrace lifestyles of integrity that prioritize a deep, practical love for truth, peace, and people, including willingness to acknowledge, resist, and confront evil in its many forms in the seen and unseen realms, starting with ourselves.

GIn Resources

Much of our material on GIn is listed and linked in the Global Integrity section of our main Member Care Associates website (Member Care Associates, Global Integrity). Kelly's video presentation at the United Nations during Geneva Peace Week 2018 reflects how we integrate GIn's main messages into our work (O'Donnell 2018). Additional materials include 25 weblog entries on global integrity (*CORE Member Care* 2016), our presentation at Gordon Conwell Theological Seminary, "Global Integration—Global Integrity: Applications for Christians in Leadership" (O'Donnell and Lewis O'Donnell 2018b), and our article in the *Lausanne Global Analysis*, "A Summons to a Global Integrity Movement" (O'Donnell and Lewis O'Donnell 2018a).

Some examples of significant efforts to promote integrity and confront corruption with which we are involved are the Lausanne Movement and World Evangelical Alliance's Global Integrity/Anti-Corruption Network, Faith and Public Integrity Network, PETRA People Network, and Global Integrity Day. We also regularly track and share about the work of Transparency International and the United Nations Office on Drugs and Crime. We encourage you to check out these strategic efforts.

Transformed People of Integrity

We support human efforts to act with integrity and do good—whether it be alleviating poverty among the estimated one billion urban slum dwellers, protecting the 1.5 billion people living in settings that are exposed to violence and conflict, or aiding the 360 million people currently needing humanitarian protection and assistance. We see these efforts as the *imago Dei* at work within the *missio Dei*, regardless of whether one believes in these things or not. Humans do good. However, we think humans do better when they include and honor God in the process. More specifically, we think we can do much better at transforming our world if God is included and honored in our efforts and if we start with transformation in our own hearts. The world will not be a sustainably better, transformed place unless better, transformed people of integrity make it so.

The despair and disillusionment that result from seemingly intractable problems such as corruption and the lack of integrity can also result in something positive. They can embody a crucial existential message about reality that can be revisited (i.e., explored and heeded) rather than resisted. They can point us to Someone who is bigger than ourselves, the Sustainable Development Goals, humanity, and our world—the knowable, Eternal One who is both in and beyond space-time and who loves us dearly. Global integrity can lead us into the path and the heart of the Creator.

GI Direction Three: Global Integrators

You are the salt of the earth. You are the light of the world.
—Matthew 5:13–14
We are a world in pieces. We need to be a world at peace
—UN Secretary-General António Guterres (2017)

Global integrators are people who use the GI framework to guide and goad their engagement in the world. They are learners and practitioners who call upon their best selves to link their skills, values, integrity, and relationships to positively impact their spheres of influence. As global citizens, global integrators galvanize their common sense of human belonging, identity, and mutual responsibility on behalf of human and planetary wellbeing (see Member Care Associates 2016 with its emphasis on education for global citizenship). Those who are Christians add the additional motivation and goal of being salt and light in the earth for God's glory as reflected in the prayer below.

> Lord of the universe, Lord of all nations, Lord of all peoples, to you all creatures will bow and acknowledge your goodness and wisdom and power and love through Jesus Christ and His shed blood (Revelation 4, 5). We acknowledge that we can do nothing without You (John 15) and that we as humanity are in desperate need of You (Psalm 130). You are our refuge and our strength in time of need and always (Psalm 48). We pray specifically that you would guide the efforts of the sustainable development goals, as the member states of the United Nations and the many organizations in civil society work to eradicate poverty, safeguard dignity and justice, protect your wondrous creation, and promote wellbeing for all. Use your people Lord to help shape this process and help us as we work together on behalf of our troubled world. Unless You build the house, Lord, we labor in vain (Psalm 127). Lamb of God You take away the sins of the world, have mercy on us. For Your glory. Maranatha. (*Brigada* 2015)

We believe it is important to further develop GI by organizing new coalitions of colleagues—global integrators—who are committed to GI and to crossing sectors on behalf of member care in mission (multi-sectoral member care). Specifically, there is a need to develop new entities and emphases that reflect global realities (issues, responsibilities, and opportunities), while still staying true to the member care core of focusing on the wellbeing and effectiveness of the diversity of mission workers and their sending groups. For more perspectives and examples, see the 25 weblog entries on Global Integrators (*CORE Member Care* 2015), as well as *Global Integration: Addressing the Pressing Issues Facing Our World* (O'Donnell and Lewis O'Donnell 2016a), *Multi-Sectoral Member Care: Engaging Our World as Global Integrators* (O'Donnell and Lewis O'Donnell 2016b), and *Engaging in Humanity Care: Stress, Trauma, and Humanitarian Work* (O'Donnell, Pidcoke, and Lewis O'Donnell 2020).

Following are seven practical directions and commitments for GI (based on O'Donnell and Lewis O'Donnell 2017). We encourage you to join with us and others who are committed to engage in GI by following and serving Jesus, bringing together new and old treasures (resources and directions) on behalf of all people and the planet. Global Integrators!

> **Directional Commitments for Global Integrators**
>
> - Commitment 1. We commit to diligently pursuing our own journeys of personal and professional growth—to grow deeply as we grow broadly.
> - Commitment 2. We commit to integrating the inseparable areas of our character (resilient virtue) and competency (relevant skills) with compassion (resonant love).
> - Commitment 3. We commit to going into new areas of learning and work: crossing sectors, cultures, disciplines, and comfort zones.
> - Commitment 4. We commit to embracing our duty to work in difficult settings, including those permeated by conflict, calamity, corruption, and poverty, as those in great need are often in places of great risk.
> - Commitment 5. We commit to maintaining clear ethical commitments and standards that guide our work, respecting the dignity and worth of all people.
> - Commitment 6. We commit to working with others to promote wellbeing and sustainable development, building the future we want and being the people we need.
> - Commitment 7. We commit to basing our work on the practice of fervently loving people—*agape*. Agape is the foundational motive and the ultimate measure of our GI work.

Summary Thoughts on Global Integration

GI is a grid to guide and goad our journeys into the all-encompassing *scope* of sharing the good news and good works among all persons and peoples, all places and spaces—into the *missio Dei*—as coworkers with God in restoring all creation to shalom in Jesus Christ—*"instaurare omnia in Christo"* (Eph 1:10). In our daily practice of Christian spirituality as people of faith, hope and love, GI is neither distracting nor discouraging. It can, however, be disturbing (and a challenge to our worldview) as it propels us into the realms of human misery, moral decay, planetary degradation, and spiritual warfare. Be encouraged, though, because through it all, we await the Blessed Hope (Titus 2:13), focusing on *Groom's Day*, not doomsday. Come, Lord Jesus!

Applications: Following and Serving Jesus Globally

Core Strategies

1. Actively refer to and use the Global Integration Framework to help you link your skills, values, integrity, and relationships as you follow and serve Jesus Christ for God's glory.

2. Embrace lifestyles of integrity that prioritize a deep, practical love for truth, peace, and people, including being willing to acknowledge, resist, and confront evil in its many forms in the seen and unseen realms, starting with ourselves.

3. Join with others to develop GI by organizing new coalitions (emphases and entities) of colleagues—global integrators—who are committed to GI and crossing sectors on behalf of member care in mission (multi-sectoral member care).

Core Resources

1. United Nations. 2015b. *Transforming our World: The 2030 Agenda for Sustainable Development.*

2. Kelly O'Donnell. 2013. "Charting Your Course through the Sectors."

3. Kelly O'Donnell. 2023. "Global Integration: My Journey into the *Missio Dei* Frontiers."

Reflection and Discussion

1. Describe how you are engaging with or want to further engage with any sectors in light of the 10 Suggestions for Connecting and Contributing Across Sectors.

2. What does it mean practically for you to be a "person of faith-hope-love"?

3. Review the seven "Directional Commitments for Global Integrators" and consider which ones are most relevant for you and any additional ones for your life and work.

References

Brigada. 2015. "Prayer for the United Nations." March 1. https://brigada.org/2015/03/01_15975.

CORE Member Care (blog). 2015. "Global Integrators." 25 weblog entries, January–December 2015. https://coremembercare.blogspot.com/search/label/global%20integrators.

CORE Member Care (blog). 2016. "Global Integrity." 25 weblog entries, January–December 2016. http://coremembercare.blogspot.com/search/label/global%20integrity.

Faith and Public Integrity Network. https://fpinetwork.org/.

Global Integrity and Anti-Corruption Network, Lausanne Movement and World Evangelical Alliance. https://www.globalintegritynetwork.org/.

Global Integrity Day. https://sites.google.com/view/global-integrity-day/.

Guterres, António. 2017. "We Must Not Sleepwalk into War, Secretary-General Warns in General Assembly, Citing Nuclear Peril, Terrorism, Inequality among Most Severe Global Threats." UN press release, September 19. https://press.un.org/en/2017/sgsm18693.doc.htm.

Guterres, António. 2023. "Progress Towards the Sustainable Development Goals: Towards a Rescue Plan for People and Planet." United Nations report, May. https://hlpf.un.org/sites/default/files/2023-04/SDG%20Progress%20Report%20Special%20Edition.pdf.

Lausanne Movement. 2009. *The Cape Town Commitment*. https://lausanne.org/content/ctc/.

Lee, Jason. 2024. "Untold Stories: The Intersection of Physical and Spiritual Health Among Frontier Peoples." *Lausanne Global Analysis* 13 (1). https://lausanne.org/content/lga/2024-01/untold-stories-the-intersection-of-physical-and-spiritual-health-among-frontier-peoples.

Long, Justin. "Weekly Roundup: What Happened in the Unreached World This Week and What It Means." https://www.justinlong.org/roundup-subscribe.

Member Care Associates. "Global Integration Overview." https://membercareassociates.org/global-integration/gi/.

Member Care Associates. "Global Integration Updates." https://membercareassociates.org/global-integration/gi-updates/.

Member Care Associates. "Global Integrity." https://membercareassociates.org/global-integrity/.

Member Care Associates. "Member Care Updates." https://membercareassociates.org/resource-updates/mca-resource-updates/.

Member Care Associates. 2016. "Global Citizenship." Global Integration Update 9 (June). https://us10.campaign-archive.com/?u=e83a5528fb81b78be71f78079&id=3e54230a8f.

Member Care Associates. 2019. "Being Faith-Based and Evidence-Based." Global Integration Update 35 (May). https://mailchi.mp/e8c785caf52d/global-integration-update-special-news-1376705.

O'Donnell, Kelly. 2013. "Charting Your Course Through the Sectors." In *Global Member Care, vol. 2: Crossing Sectors for Serving Humanity*, edited by Kelly O'Donnell and Michèle Lewis O'Donnell, 5–20. Pasadena, CA: William Carey Library. https://membercareassociates.org/wp-content/uploads/2018/01/Charting-Your-Course-through-the-Sectors-final-ODonnell-2013.pdf.

O'Donnell, Kelly. 2015. "Foundations and Worldview: The Centrality of Jesus Christ." *CORE Member Care* (blog) (November 26). http://coremembercare.blogspot.com/search?q=worldview.

O'Donnell, Kelly. 2018. "Health for Peace: Contributions from Peace Psychology." Presentation for Geneva Peace Week, November 7. PowerPoint at https://membercareassociates.org/wp-content/uploads/2018/11/ok-final-7-Nov-2018-Health-for-Peace-Contributions-from-Peace-Psychology-GPW-2018-ODonnell.pdf; video at https://www.youtube.com/watch?v=c7jMHkqvCxI&t=17s.

O'Donnell, Kelly. 2022. "Global Integration: My Journey into the Missio Dei Frontiers." Presentation to the Evangelical Missiological Society and International Society for Frontier Missiology, October 8. PowerPoint at https://membercareassociates.org/wp-content/uploads/2022/10/Global-Integration-Missio-Dei-Frontiers-ODonnell-8-October-2022-EMS-ISFM.pptx; video at https://www.youtube.com/watch?v=7UT68f6n5r0.

O'Donnell, Kelly, and Michèle Lewis O'Donnell. 2016a. "Global Integration: Addressing the Pressing Issues Facing Our World—Overview and Opportunities for Mental Health Professionals." *Christian Psychology Around the World* 8 (1): 191–194. http://emcapp.ignis.de/8/.

O'Donnell, Kelly, and Michèle Lewis O'Donnell. 2016b. "Multi-Sectoral Member Care: Engaging Our World as Global Integrators." *Journal of Psychology and Theology* 44 (1): 303–314. http://membercareassociates.org/wp-content/uploads/2016/12/ODonnells-2016-JPT-article-published-pdf.pdf.

O'Donnell, Kelly, and Michèle Lewis O'Donnell. 2017. "Well-Being for All: Mental Health Professionals and the Sustainable Development Goals." *Journal of Psychology and Christianity* 36 (1): 70–75. https://membercareassociates.org/wp-content/uploads/2017/03/format-single-space-MHPs-and-Sustainable-Development-Goals-JPC-Spring-2017-ODonnells.pdf.

O'Donnell, Kelly, and Michèle Lewis O'Donnell. 2018a. "A Summons to a Global Integrity Movement: Fighting Self-Deception and Corruption." *Lausanne Global Analysis* 7 (2). https://www.lausanne.org/content/lga/2018-03/summons-global-integrity-movement.

O'Donnell, Kelly, and Michèle Lewis O'Donnell. 2018b. "Global Integration-Global Integrity: Applications for Christians in Leadership." Gordon Conwell Theological Seminary (presentation May 17, 2018). https://docs.google.com/presentation/d/1C_Ltav17mZhlRLxQ1SA9DnfczUGdSAVn/edit#slide=id.p1.

O'Donnell, Kelly, and Michèle Lewis O'Donnell. 2020. "Following Jesus Globally: Engaging the World through Global Integration." *Lausanne Global Analysis* 39 (1). https://lausanne.org/content/lga/2020-01/following-jesus-globally.

O'Donnell, Kelly, Heidi Pidcoke, and Michèle Lewis O'Donnell. 2020. "Engaging in Humanity Care: Stress, Trauma, and Humanitarian Work." *Christian Psychology Around the World* 14 (May): 153–167. https://membercareassociates.org/wp-content/uploads/2020/08/Engaging-in-Humanity-Care-Stress-Trauma-and-Humanitarian-Work-final-version-for-CPAW-May-2020.pdf.

PETRA People Network. https://sites.google.com/site/petrapeople.

Schliesser, Christine. 2023. "On the Significance of Religion for the SDGs: An Introduction." New York: Routledge. https://library.oapen.org/handle/20.500.12657/61728.

Transparency International. https://www.transparency.org/.

United Nations. 2015a. "Paris Climate Agreement." UN Climate Change Conference. https://unfccc.int/process-and-meetings/the-paris-agreement.

United Nations. 2015b. "Transforming Our World: The 2030 Agenda for Sustainable Development." https://sdgs.un.org/2030agenda.

United Nations. 2016. "The Agenda for Humanity." One Humanity: Shared Responsibility (annex, 48–62). https://reliefweb.int/report/world/one-humanity-shared-responsibility-report-secretary-general-world-humanitarian-summit.

United Nations. 2018. "Global Compact for a Safe, Orderly, and Regular Migration." https://refugeesmigrants.un.org/sites/default/files/180713_agreed_outcome_global_compact_for_migration.pdf.

United Nations. 2021. "Our Common Agenda." https://www.un.org/en/common-agenda.

United Nations. 2023. "The New Agenda for Peace." Our Common Agenda: Policy Brief 9 (July 2023).

United Nations. "Summit of the Future." https://www.un.org/en/common-agenda/summit-of-the-future.

United Nations Office on Drugs and Crime. https://www.unodc.org/.

Virtrios—Trio Gatherings. https://sites.google.com/site/virtrios/.

World Bank. 2023. "Multidimensional Poverty Measure." https://www.worldbank.org/en/topic/poverty/brief/multidimensional-poverty-measure#:~:text=What%20is%20the%20Multidimensional%20Poverty,more%20complete%20picture%20of%20poverty.

Dr. Kelly O'Donnell, PsyD and Dr. Michèle Lewis O'Donnell, PsyD are consulting psychologists based in Geneva and the USA with Member Care Associates, Inc. (MCA). Their international and multi-sectoral emphases for consultation, training, and writing include member care, global mental health, integrity/anti-corruption, and sustainable development. Kelly and Michèle did their doctoral training in clinical psychology and theology at Rosemead School of Psychology, Biola University (USA). They have been representatives to the United Nations for the World Federation for Mental Health, and they have two wonderful adult daughters, Erin and Ashling. Links to their many resources are on the MCA website: https://membercareassociates.org/.

Into the *Missio Dei*

Promoting Wellbeing for All People and the Planet

David Johnston and Charlotte Johnston

> Today we are also taking a decision of great historic significance. We resolve to build a better future for all people, including the millions who have been denied the chance to lead decent, dignified and rewarding lives and to achieve their full human potential. We can be the first generation to succeed in ending poverty; just as we may be the last to have a chance of saving the planet. The world will be a better place in 2030 if we succeed in our objectives.
> —United Nations, *Transforming Our World: The 2030 Agenda for Sustainable Development* (2015)

In a time and a land where people knew much about shepherds and sheep, Jesus often used the metaphor of the shepherd to refer to himself. The Good Shepherd loves and cares for his sheep to the point of giving his life for them (John 10:11). In fact, this shepherd is on a mission: "I have other sheep that are not of this sheep pen. I must bring them also" (John 10:16). In one of Jesus's parables, the shepherd leaves the ninety-nine sheep to find the lost one (Luke 15:3–7). In mission circles, we use the Latin term *missio Dei* (mission of God) to describe how God is at work redemptively and broadly throughout the world—working through the Church and outside of the Church—and calling us to collaborate in his mission.

The image of the shepherd, which Jesus most certainly used with Psalm 23 in mind, also refers to the quality of life he wants to give us: green pastures, quiet waters, renewing our strength, and guiding our path. Jesus stated, "I have come that they may have life, and life to the full" (John 10:10). God's plan of salvation for a lost humanity from Genesis 3 to Revelation 22 includes repentance and faith, but also holistic flourishing, which—to a large extent—is available on this side of the New Jerusalem.

In this chapter, we highlight this notion of holistic flourishing in light of both the *missio Dei* and the global push to achieve the 17 Sustainable Development Goals (SDGs) by 2030 (United Nations 2015). We believe that God wants us to participate in this kind of global collaboration on behalf of all people and the planet. By doing so, we offer salt and light where it is desperately needed as we witness in word and deed to the precious values that will mark the coming Kingdom of God in the new heavens and the new earth (Rev 22).

Shepherding and holistic flourishing also apply to the disciples of Jesus who engage with God and others in mission, including those serving the least-reached people and places. What does wellbeing mean for people who serve in refugee camps, or in zones of conflict and war? To answer this question, we begin by recounting some of our own challenging life and mission experiences in the Middle East and North Africa (MENA) region, which helped to shape both our work strategies and our character development. These personal experiences over twenty years prepared us for and propelled us into the holistic *missio Dei*. We believe that beyond promoting explicitly Christian development and nongovernmental organizations (NGOs), the Church worldwide should strategically pursue a greater Christian presence in secular and global organizations and efforts.

As we write this chapter, representatives of all nations, large and small, are gathered in Dubai for what many call a watershed conference on climate change (COP28). The representatives continue to seek agreements and solutions to reduce the burning of fossil fuels, increase clean energy, and create a global fund that will compensate poor countries for their suffering from climate change—especially because these countries bear little or no responsibility for the problem. Several SDGs address this issue of climate justice. When it comes to matters of extreme poverty and egregious disparities between rich and poor, we are all stakeholders and must urgently work together.

We then illustrate these collaborative efforts by briefly describing three people who are working in global and international positions on behalf of the SDGs. They are examples of the growing number of believers from many nations who demonstrate Kingdom values in word and deed as they work alongside secular people and people of other faiths. Our understanding of member care must expand to include ways to further support believers who serve in such strategic secular settings.

Missiologist Al Tizon, who himself once planted a church in a dirt-poor squatter community in Manila, helpfully characterized the Great Commission as "the Whole Commission," meaning that the *missio Dei* aims to "reconcile all things in Christ" (Col 1:20). That reconciling work is in three dimensions: (a) reconciliation of people with God through Christ; (b) reconciliation between people, or peacemaking; (c) reconciliation of people with God and his creation, or healing creation (Tizon 2018). The "Prince of this world" (John 14:30) continues to sow chaos, death, and destruction in our world, but that is not the whole story. The Holy Spirit is also actively at work for reconciliation, wholeness, and peace. Our call is to join him as we are led, and this includes the realm of global engagement and cooperation (Johnston 2010).

Our Member Care Story

Member care had a powerful and positive impact on David and me while we were serving in particularly tense or violent settings. We lived in three different countries, and our exposure to member care evolved over the course of our time on the mission field.

Charlotte's View

David grew up as a mission kid in France, going to French schools. In 1978, after completing seminary, in 1978, he went to Algeria, where he worked as a pastor in an expatriate English-speaking church and then in a French-speaking church. After leaving my job as a bedside nurse in the US, I also went to Algeria, where I worked in the capital city of Algiers as the parish nurse and secretary. Caring for expatriates and discretely supporting the then-underground Algerian church filled our days and evenings.

When we married in 1986, neither of us was part of a mission organization. At our wedding, David's father took him aside and reiterated the mission agency's invitation for us to join. "You'll have a family to look after," he said with a smile. So, we accepted the invitation.

Later that year, we received our first visit from our mission's Africa team leader, during which our apartment was broken into spy-style while we were out sightseeing. Nothing was stolen (a truly suspicious situation in a socialist country with shortages of everything from butter to car parts and a thriving black market). But our guest's luggage had been rearranged and then relocked with the keys inside, and no money was stolen. Was the apartment now bugged? The church phone was already tapped and its mail was regularly opened. This was during the Cold War era. The Algerian secret police had been trained by the Soviet KGB, underground Algerian church leaders had been interrogated, and foreign workers were suspected of CIA connections. We soon learned that we were next in line to be expelled. "If you leave now, you can come back, but if you're expelled, you can never return," an elderly Algerian believer wisely counseled us. So we deliberately spoke on the telephone about our plans to leave Algeria. The police listening to this phone call got the message, and we were able to leave without expulsion.

With our agency's backing, in 1989 we went to Egypt, living alongside the Suez Canal. David taught in a church-run language school. We didn't have any mission team members with us, so we formed supportive relationships with workers from other agencies and members of the local church. We lived in a predominantly Muslim community and got to know many families. Life was calm until summer 1990, when the Gulf crisis erupted. By the time the US invaded the region in Operation Desert Storm, the canal had seen its share of warships heading to the Gulf under the cover of night. Every adult in the entire area was anxious, as they had experienced war with Israel less than a generation earlier.

As weeks passed, it became clear that Egypt was not at risk. School was back on course, but the other mission workers in our area had left months back and we missed them. We were later joined by young gap-year students sent by their churches, and we greatly enjoyed their fellowship. During the summer while school was closed, we would return to France to meet with Algerian believers, speak at summer youth camps, and get medical checkups for intestinal parasites. David's parents would host us and make sure that we regained our lost weight before going back to Egypt. We had two visits from our Africa team leader and one out-of-country conference during our three and a half years in Egypt.

Our mission leadership was very interested in partnering with churches of the West Bank to encourage and train their young people. Accordingly, in 1992, we moved to Bethany on the Jericho Road, just behind the Mount of Olives, with David teaching in Arabic at the Palestinian-founded Bethlehem Bible College. Again, we had no mission team members there, but we hoped to create a bridge for others to come and join us. The staff and students in Bethlehem inspired us by their example of living for Christ under Israeli military occupation. In Algeria, we had experienced a high degree of surveillance, and our time in Egypt was marked by seeing great poverty and by our proximity to the Gulf war. But during our three-plus years in the West Bank, we faced a new set of challenges. We observed violence and indignities, were subject to military curfews, and heard the sound of bullets during raids outside our building. The fact that the people around us had lived this way for years was hard to fathom.

In the West Bank, we met a variety of people from different mission agencies and NGOs. We learned that some agencies had extensive "member care" (a new term for us) and that NGOs usually had a hardship policy: if someone was assigned to an area with war zones, famine, disease, or refugee camps, for every six months they worked on site they would get one month off site and out of the country, without responsibilities.

The toll of living under military occupation, political tension, and frequent violence left David feeling tense and exhausted, though without a realization of how he was getting worn down. As a result, he would take risks, work long hours, and become impatient with our young children. I felt frayed as never before. We began to realize that we were falling apart. What we had done to cope in other contexts was not addressing our cumulative fatigue, so we began to strategize as best we could to take breaks, drawing inspiration from NGO policies. For instance, we would take our family on weekend trips to the local coast for a change of scenery. David and I tried to take turns each month going to a convent, where one of us would spend 24 hours on silent retreat while the other stayed home with the children. These activities were a financial stretch for us, and when we asked our mission's finance staff about possibly considering them a work expense, they were taken by surprise. It was a new idea for them.

Over the course of three and a half years, we had four team leader visits and one out-of-country conference with the Africa team. Apart from that conference, however, we did not leave Israel and Palestine at all until we traveled to the US in 1996 to visit supporters.

Our mission agency functioned largely in the US with a relatively small international division. We were receiving visits and attending regional conferences as staff from other geographic areas did. We were very grateful for that support. But no one else served in a conflict zone. Our mission leadership and we ourselves were largely unaware of how much we needed help until our stress level in the West Bank intensified.

When we came to spend a year in the US near the mission headquarters, the leadership arranged for our family to attend a five-day debriefing and reentry retreat for people from a variety of mission agencies. Topics such as reverse culture shock, PTSD, and marital and family stress were addressed with compassion and insight. David and I came away supremely grateful for this program. But that wasn't enough by itself. We decided to pursue follow-up counseling individually and as a couple. We also spent much of the following year resting and caring for our two children so that we could heal emotionally. Our agency made this possible, and it was a tremendous expression of member care back when the concept was still new.

David's View
I would like to point out three broad implications of our limited experience living as a couple and family in these contexts. As we continue to work and partner within the *missio Dei*, we understand that holistic wellbeing does not happen automatically or in a vacuum. This is also certainly true for Christian workers, who will always need some kind of intentional member care—self- and mutual care, sender and specialist care—adapted to their specific needs, regardless of their setting.

1. Moving to another country with a different culture, learning a new language and finding ways to serve in that new context will always be stressful. It's important to find good people to help guide and support us, including fellow believers.
2. Political instability and violence multiply the level of stress for individuals and have repercussions for marriages, families, and communities. The church and the mission community should try to better understand how to support local and international workers in these settings and should learn from research and best practices of secular development, humanitarian, and health sectors so as to mitigate the toll and help people thrive.
3. Human flourishing involves holistic wellbeing in the core areas of community, relationships of mutual care, and empathy in the context of a healthy planet. In the next section, we share how working to foster this flourishing for people and the planet is a way to anticipate and witness to the values of the coming Kingdom of God.

Holistic Flourishing and the Values of the Coming Kingdom

We began by quoting the parable of the Good Shepherd, which the apostle John wrote down after the destruction of Jerusalem's temple in AD 70. In the book of Revelation, an aging apostle John, now exiled to the island of Patmos, records a series of visions from God. Significantly, the last vision (in Rev 21–22) takes place after the last judgment. Creation is now completely renewed ("I saw a new heaven and a new earth"), and John sees "the holy city, the new Jerusalem, coming down from heaven like a bride beautifully dressed for her husband" (Rev 21:2 NLT). The focus on the city here is on its people, the church, the bride of Christ.

Here is another remarkable sign of God's creation made new. In this "new Jerusalem," we find the variegated hues of humanity and its many cultures not erased but enhanced:

> And the city has no need of sun or moon, for the glory of God illuminates the city, and the Lamb is its light. The nations will walk in its light, and the kings of the world will enter the city in all their glory. … And all the nations will bring their glory and honor into the city.
> (Revelation 21:24, 26 NLT)

Despite our sinfulness, God deeply loves each individual, family, village, town, city, ethnicity, and culture. Revelation 21 shows us that all the nations of the earth will gather in the New Jerusalem, which will sparkle like a diamond with many faces, like a prism refracting light in many glorious colors. This is the "glory and honor" that the kings and their people bring into the city. Each human grouping represents awesome cultural achievements and a wealth of human experience. Besides creation and individual people, God will have redeemed human cultures; all their art, communal cohesion, and politics will be cleansed from the darkness and corruption of sin.

In his last vision, which recalls the one in Ezekiel 47, John sees "a river with the water of life, clear as crystal" flowing from God's throne through the center of the main street: "On each side of the river grew a tree of life, bearing twelve crops of fruit, with a fresh crop each month. The leaves were used for medicine to heal the nations" (Rev 22:1–2 NLT). These are some of the characteristics of the future Kingdom of God: a just and equitable divine governance that allows for the flourishing of both nature and all his creatures; peace and harmony among all; ample provision to meet every need, including nourishment and healing; and finally, a synergy connecting all nations and amplifying the goodness of each one's contribution to the common good. Israel's prophets foretold many of these values, particularly justice and peace (e.g., Isa 2:1–4; 9:6–7; 42:1–4; 51:5–6; 54:14; Zech 9:9–10). This is the vision and these are the values that should be guiding our mission in the world today, as we align ourselves with the *missio Dei*. For many current and historical examples of the Church and mission at the forefront of development and human wellbeing, see "Rethinking Missionaries and Development" (Member Care Associates 2024).

Global Cooperation: The United Nations and the SDGs

In the ashes of two apocalyptic world wars, the United Nations was born. Its Charter proclaimed:

> We the peoples of the United Nations determined ... to save succeeding generations from the scourge of war ... to reaffirm faith in fundamental human rights, in the dignity and worth of the human person, in equal rights of men and women and of nations large and small, and to establish conditions under which justice and respect for the obligations arising from treaties and other sources of international law can be maintained, and to promote social progress and better standards of life in larger freedom. (United Nations 1945)

The United Nations is a complex institutional system designed to maximize the contributions of its nearly 200 member states to solving economic, social, cultural, and humanitarian concerns. It also has the greatest convening power and recognized authority to bring together nations, multilateral organizations, and a vast array of NGOs. The United Nations certainly has obvious flaws, and one of them stems from the unequal power gradient among nations, along with a constant jostling for power and influence in the world's political and economic arenas. Most notably, a veto by any one of the five permanent members of the Security Council (China, Russia, France, the United States, and the United Kingdom) can paralyze urgent humanitarian and security interventions. Yes, the Unted Nations' massive and unwieldy bureaucracy is vulnerable to inertia and corruption. Yet the work of the United Nations is irreplaceable. Many dedicated United Nations agencies and staff are involved in its peacekeeping forces in conflict zones, its proactive work in reducing conflicts by coaxing various parties to negotiate, its influential and skillfully performed coordination through many specialized agencies to deliver humanitarian aid in the wake of major disasters, its pooling of global expertise to combat climate change, and its construction of global plans to address global issues, the prime example being the 17 SDGs (Kennedy 2006).

The document that presented the SDGs and was signed by all nations in 2015 is called the 2030 Agenda. Its Preamble says, "We recognize that eradicating poverty in all its forms and dimensions, including extreme poverty, is the greatest challenge and an indispensable requirement for sustainable development." "All stakeholders"—nations and all multilateral and international bodies, including UN agencies, the larger NGOs that work officially alongside the United Nations and all other NGOs—"acting in collaborative partnership, will implement this plan." The Preamble adds, "We are determined to take the bold and transformative steps which are urgently needed to shift the world onto a sustainable and resilient path. As we embark on this collective journey, we pledge that no one will be left behind." Ending extreme poverty and hunger is about removing the obstacles faced by hundreds of millions of people worldwide so that "all human beings can fulfill their potential in dignity and equality and in a healthy environment."

Additionally, the SDGs make it clear that human wellbeing is realized in community. Comprehensive human flourishing requires all three pillars of development to be in place—namely, the social, economic, and political pillars for "peaceful, just and inclusive societies that provide equal access to justice and that are based on respect for human rights (including the right to development), on effective rule of law and good governance on all levels and on transparent, effective and accountable institutions" (paragraph 35). Here is the holistic framework outlined in the 17 SDGs:

Goal 1. End poverty in all its forms everywhere

Goal 2. End hunger, achieve food security and improved nutrition and promote sustainable agriculture

Goal 3. Ensure healthy lives and promote wellbeing for all at all ages

Goal 4. Ensure inclusive and equitable quality education and promote lifelong learning opportunities for all

Goal 5. Achieve gender equality and empower all women and girls

Goal 6. Ensure availability and sustainable management of water and sanitation for all

Goal 7. Ensure access to affordable, reliable, sustainable and modern energy for all

Goal 8. Promote sustained, inclusive and sustainable economic growth, full and productive employment and decent work for all

Goal 9. Build resilient infrastructure, promote inclusive and sustainable industrialization and foster innovation

Goal 10. Reduce inequality within and among countries

Goal 11. Make cities and human settlements inclusive, safe, resilient and sustainable

Goal 12. Ensure sustainable consumption and production patterns

Goal 13. Take urgent action to combat climate change and its impacts

Goal 14. Conserve and sustainably use the oceans, seas and marine resources for sustainable development

Goal 15. Protect, restore and promote sustainable use of terrestrial ecosystems, sustainably manage forests, combat desertification, and halt and reverse land degradation and halt biodiversity loss

Goal 16. Promote peaceful and inclusive societies for sustainable development, provide access to justice for all and build effective, accountable and inclusive institutions at all levels

Goal 17. Strengthen the means of implementation and revitalize the global partnership for sustainable development.

Connecting Mission and Member Care with Global Cooperation and Human Flourishing: Three Stories

Al Tizon's picture of reconciliation is particularly fitting in light of the apostle John's vision of the New Jerusalem. Justice and righteousness are the new characteristics of a redeemed humanity, and hence, its multiple nations and peoples with all their distinct cultures and leadership styles will live in peace in the presence of God and the Lamb. Why wouldn't God call some of his people to serve with these Kingdom values at the forefront of their hearts and minds at various levels of global cooperation today? We know some of the impact that Daniel—not to mention Joseph, Esther, and others—had as a top-level servant to multiple kings. Likewise, Eleanor Roosevelt, a devout Christian and arguably one of the most influential women in international politics of the twentieth century, was sent to the United Nations as a delegate to the General Assembly between 1945 and 1953. Many sources credit her with playing a key role in chairing the UN's Human Rights Commission and ably shepherding along with another Christian, Charles Malik, its diverse members in drafting and gaining approval of the Universal Declaration of Human Rights in 1948 against great odds (Nurser 2005; Smith 2018).

In a 2022 conversation with Christine MacMillan, a Canadian affiliated with the Salvation Army, I gained more insight on how faith-based and secular organizations can partner with the UN. MacMillan came to New York City to found the Salvation Army's International Social Justice Commission and rented office space just blocks from the United Nations headquarters.

After retiring from the Salvation Army, she served in various senior leadership positions for the World Evangelical Alliance (WEA) in relation to the UN. She currently chairs WEA's Global Task Force on Human Trafficking and represents the WEA at the United Nations. In a chapter she contributed to a book on the role of faith-based actors in and around the United Nations, she provided an illustration of how over 6000 NGOs have officially received "consultative status" in the United Nations system:

> The WEA holds Special Consultation Status in the Economic and Social Council of the UN (ECOSOC) which serves as the central forum for discussing international economic and social issues and formulating policy recommendations addressed to member states and the United Nations system. The WEA UN Team is a group whose mandate oversees the WEA's contribution within the UN by offering concrete proposals, while also serving as the liaison body between the UN and WEA's Networks, Global Partners, Regional and National Alliances, on behalf of the world's most vulnerable and marginalized communities. (MacMillan 2021, 280)

I have interviewed many other Christians in various United Nations or secular NGO contexts. Dorothy (name changed; original interview November 2022) is one example of Christians who see their involvement in global cooperation as a response to God's call to mission. This young woman participated in MacMillan's WEA United Nations intern program for university students. She received course credit at a Christian college for the internship. In her senior year, Dorothy was appointed as program coordinator. She and MacMillan recruited twelve interns that year, doubling the previous enrollment. The interns would meet with MacMillan every two weeks to discuss their readings and what they experienced at various UN meetings. As MacMillan told me, this process also entailed spiritual formation and helping students discover what areas of service interested them most. Dorothy was subsequently accepted into a master's program in international development in Europe. Students in this program can also receive official credit with the United Nations Systems Staff College.

When I interviewed a second time in June 2023, her group project had taken her to Mozambique, where her team studied a foundation that combined sustainable agriculture and operating a school for children in an isolated area. As of this writing, Dorothy has applied for a position with the United Nations High Commissioner for Refugees (UNHCR). She is open to serving elsewhere, but she prays for opportunities to serve the neediest in Christ's name and to be a light among colleagues at the UN or in a secular NGO. Dorothy's maturity spiritually, intellectually, and as a young adult navigating a future career is remarkable.

Another good example is Mijito, an Indian diplomat in his late thirties, whom I interviewed in June 2022. While in New York serving with India's permanent mission to the United Nations, he was assigned to the United Nations Security Council, as India was serving its two-year term leading that body. He told me how grateful he was for the Christian Embassy, a Cru ministry (formerly Campus Crusade for Christ) to people working at the UN. He found it encouraging to interact with other Christian diplomats from other nations and to learn ways to look at sensitive issues from a different perspective. During those two years, he traveled to Kinshasa, in the Democratic Republic of the Congo, and Bangui in the Central African Republic. Mijito stressed that in many situations, only the United Nations has the reach and resources to truly make a difference in many parts of the world. He shared with his pastor how easy it was to become cynical as one perceives that so many intractable problems remain unsolved due to political decisions made by powerful nations. The pastor counseled him to find joy in the little drops of good he can contribute, regardless of the ocean of suffering that persists. I am certain that God will greatly use Mijito wherever his career takes him.

Mijito's case shows how member care can support people engaged in global cooperation activities as Christians. Both his meetings with fellow believers through Cru and his pastor were conduits of encouragement and guidance in his journey. The global church should become aware of these opportunities to extend member care to Christians, people of other faiths, and those of no particular faith, so as to support them, guide them, and share Christ's love for them. We can have transforming impact with diplomats, administrators, and professionals in the towers of influence, just as with those who are in the "trenches" caring for the most vulnerable (Danieli 2001).

On this side of the new heaven and new earth, holistic flourishing will always be incomplete. But God is clearly at work. He is using many different instruments to bring the gospel to all peoples (Matt 24:14) and advance wellbeing for all people and the planet, working across sectors, countries, and cultures, even amid war and disasters (O'Donnell 2013). We pray that followers of Jesus who serve in this wider movement of global cooperation will find encouragement with other believers and truly be light and salt to those around them, stimulating a longing and hope for the kingdom to come. We also pray that many more Christian young people around the world will join them.

Applications: Into the *Missio Dei*

Core Strategies

1. When you pray for your regional and national leaders, pray also for leaders with global reach, including those in the United Nations system and other related NGOs.
2. Seek to widen the horizons of people in your family and church so that they may consider God's Kingdom purpose for all nations to come to know him and his desire for all people and the planet to flourish.
3. Find ways to encourage friends and Christians engaged in international work within the *missio Dei*, especially those who may have a limited access to supportive member care.

Core Resources

1. Read Al Tizon's *Whole and Reconciled* (2018) for a holistic view of mission and Glen Stassen's *Just Peacemaking* (1992) for a Christian ethicist's ten-step plan that has inspired many around the world.
2. Look at David's website (https://www.humantrustees.org), especially his posts under the category of "Religion and Global Society."
3. Global Integrity (Member Care Associates) lists many core resources produced over more than 15 years to promote moral wholeness from the individual through the international levels.

Reflection and Discussion

1. How can the apostle John's vision in Revelation 21–22 give new perspective and motivation for Christian mission today?
2. What did you learn about global cooperation in this chapter, and how might this knowledge inform your own prayers and actions?
3. What factors might help or hinder promising young Christians with a missional vision who are considering careers in the United Nations or with international NGOs?

References

Danieli, Yael, ed. 2001. *Sharing the Front Line and the Back Hills: International Protectors and Providers—Peacekeepers, Humanitarian Aid Workers, and the Media in the Midst of Crisis*. New York: Routledge.

Johnston, David L. 2010. *Earth, Empire and Sacred Text: Muslims and Christians as Trustees of Creation*. London: Equinox.

Kennedy, Paul. 2006. *The Parliament of Man: The Past Present and Future of the United Nations*. New York: Vintage Books.

Kirton, John, and Maria Larionova. 2018. "Accountability and Effectiveness in Global Governance." In *Accountability for Effectiveness in Global Governance*, edited by John J. Kirton and Maria Larionova, 3–22. New York: Routledge.

MacMillan, Christine. 2021. "Evangelicals Securing a Seat at the UN Table." In *Religious Soft Diplomacy and the United Nations*, edited by Sherie M. Steiner and James T. Christie, 279–295. Lanham, MD, and London: Lexington Books.

McArthur, John, and Krista Rasmussen. 2017. "How Successful Were the Millennial Development Goals?" *The Guardian*, March 30. https://www.theguardian.com/global-development-professionals-network/2017/mar/30/how-successful-were-the-millennium-development-goals.

Member Care Associates. "Global Integrity." https://membercareassociates.org/global-integrity/.

Member Care Associates. 2024. "Why the 'M' Word Matters: Rethinking Missionaries and Development." Global Integration Update (January 2024). https://mailchi.mp/455b691f706a/global-integration-update-special-news-13589728.

Nurser, John. 2005. *For All Peoples and All Nations: Christian Churches and Human Rights*. Geneva: WCC Publications.

O'Donnell, Kelly. 2013. "Charting Your Course Through the Sectors." In *Global Member Care, vol. 2: Crossing Sectors for Serving Humanity*, edited by Kelly O'Donnell and Michèle Lewis O'Donnell, 5–20. Pasadena, CA: William Carey Library. https://membercareassociates.org/wp-content/uploads/2018/01/Charting-Your-Course-through-the-Sectors-final-ODonnell-2013.pdf.

Smith, Harold Ivan. 2017. *Eleanor: A Spiritual Biography; The Faith of the 20th-Century's Most Influential Woman*. Louisville, KY: Westminster John Knox Press.

Stassen, Glen. 1992. *Just Peacemaking: Transforming Initiatives for Justice and Peace*. Louisville, KY: Westminster John Knox Press.

Tizon, Albert. 2018. *Whole and Reconciled*. Grand Rapids, MI: Baker Academic.

United Nations. 1945. "United Nations Charter." https://www.un.org/en/about-us/un-charter/full-text.

United Nations. 2015. "Transforming Our World: The 2030 Agenda for Sustainable Development." https://sdgs.un.org/2030agenda.

David L. Johnston, PhD. Growing up with mission parents in France, David served as a pastor and teacher in Algeria, Egypt, and the West Bank. He later completed a PhD at Fuller Theological Seminary and did research in Islamic Studies at Yale University and the University of Pennsylvania. Author of two books and peer-reviewed articles, he blogs at www.humantrustees.org.

Charlotte E. Johnston lived with a French family as a junior in high school and continued those contacts up into adulthood. She partnered with David in Algeria, Egypt, and the West Bank. Since returning to the United States, she has taken up again her pre-mission field career as a nurse. They have two adult children.

4

International Psychology for Mission and Member Care

Joyce Yip Green and Karen Brown

Member care over the past thirty-plus years has been a recognized and growing field supporting the wellbeing and effectiveness of mission workers across the globe. Fostering timely and culturally appropriate care for oneself and others and integration into new cultural contexts have been crucial for mission workers. International psychology (IP) provides a framework to support culturally relevant and effective member care practice and, more broadly, to facilitate meaningful interactions and collaborations with the communities in which mission workers serve. As IP practitioners, we are honored and delighted to be part of the increasing number of psychologists and colleagues from other disciplines who have been actively integrating their Christian faith and fields of professional practice on behalf of the global mission movement (Crawford and Wang 2016; O'Donnell and Lewis O'Donnell 2020).

Joyce: I have worked over the past thirty years in various capacities as a counselor, ministry leader, international psychologist, and professor across diverse communities internationally and in the United States, mostly in the Los Angeles area. In my role as a professor, I have organized intercultural and cross-cultural experiences involving students from the United States, Latin America, and Israel. Some of my most meaningful spiritual growth experiences have entailed working with the local church in supporting relocation efforts of Syrian refugees and participating in mission trips and field experiences to Asia, Europe, and Rwanda. As an international psychologist with a deep faith and commitment to linking faith and culture with mental wellbeing, I have seen how the IP framework and approach support a deeper connection and understanding between people and lead to greater spiritual, physical, and mental health.

Karen: I was born into a military family and was fortunate enough to spend the first fourteen years of my life traveling around the world with my parents. This experience fostered a lifelong love of all things cultural. Upon graduating from Kansas State University, I spent the next 26 years in the US Army, serving in such areas as counseling (spiritual, mental health, personal, and professional), mentorship, and advocacy efforts for soldiers and their family members around the world. I was licensed as a minister in 1997 and ordained as an elder in 2005. I have served in various areas of ministry including youth and adult choirs and worship teams, youth leader, Intercessory team, outreach coordinator, and Bible study or Sunday school teacher. Serving in the military has allowed me to share my faith in international spaces including the Middle East, Africa, Australia, Asia, the South Pacific, and across the United States. IP supports my passion for ministry in that its fundamental tenets align with the mission of the gospel: treating others with respect, advocating for human rights, embracing ethical, moral, and just ways, and being willing to walk alongside those in need.

This chapter introduces IP and explores how its principles can strengthen mission and member care practice. A key potential contribution consists of supporting mission and member care workers' greater self-awareness and understanding of how their culture and context impacts their interactions with others. IP principles can complement the cross-cultural training that mission workers receive and the cultural and ministry competencies that they continually develop. This exploratory chapter also embodies a commitment to reviewing member care practices and promoting mutual learning to better support mission workers (Camp et al. 2014; Schwandt and Moriarty 2008). Using an IP lens, we share examples of intercultural encounters where cultural awareness was lacking as well as ones in which attitudes and behaviors led to more meaningful exchanges between mission workers and the members of the communities they serve. We also include five applications of IP written for this chapter by S. Anand, a mission consultant and trainer living in Asia, and we finish with two brief examples of the IP-influenced training that we offer. Collaborating with mission and member care colleagues is key to applying IP principles well. Learning as IP practitioners always involves a dynamic process of receiving as well as sharing knowledge—a two-way street!

Defining the International Psychology Framework

The member care field has increasingly prioritized cross-cultural and contextual understanding and approaches to serve cross-cultural workers, moving away from Western models (Davis and Baraka 2021). This trend harmonizes well with the IP framework, which is based on multiculturalism and the understanding that Western psychologies can often discount non-Western traditions, belief systems, and global worldviews. IP incorporates a variety of culturally relevant perspectives in the development of decision making and problem solving, assessing and evaluating projects and programs, enhancing team-building skills, heightening awareness of cultural similarities, and increasing cultural intelligence.

IP practitioners work on issues and in settings at all levels, from global to local. They aim to identify communication gaps, evaluate current and evolving policies, and promote collaborative solutions designed to create and strengthen sustainable organizational models and goals, including all 17 of the United Nations Sustainable Development Goals (American Psychological Association 2022; Psychology Coalition at the United Nations; United Nations 2015). Along with these fundamentals of IP, three points of "being" are integral to the field: being culturally sensitive, contextually informed, and culturally relevant.

Cultural sensitivity requires a conscious effort to learn about a culture and setting and to be aware of any actions that may be considered culturally offensive. While it does not require a complete acceptance of behaviors that challenge one's own beliefs, it involves respect, consideration, recognition, and acknowledgment of the values, beliefs, and traditions of others. It calls for listening more than talking, observing more than showing, participating more than leading, and learning more than teaching.

To be *contextually informed* requires understanding the behaviors, traditions, and societal norms of the culture in which one is engaging. It involves seeking understanding of the concepts, practices, beliefs, and values that have been learned and transmitted across generations. IP understands cultural context as the influence of time, place, politics, community, power, and society on human development and behavior (Kim, Yang, and Hwang 2006). It holds that one must be continually learning because concepts, practices, beliefs, and values may change over time based on the results of technological advances, natural and human-made disasters, and/or increased interaction with other cultures.

Cultural relevance speaks to the provision of collaborative assistance that is appropriately designed to meet people's felt needs. It ensures that all helping efforts take into account existing cultural values, beliefs, and traditions and are based and grounded in meticulous and ethical research. Culturally relevant collaborations seek to find ways in which a culture is enriched and empowered rather than ways in which an outsider believes they can be improved. It considers how social, economic, political, and historical perspectives can be incorporated with the goals, cultural values, and beliefs of the community to support a harmonious and beneficial atmosphere for all involved.

Anand Application 1. Here we introduce the first of the five applications of S. Anand as mentioned above.

In the 1970s and 1980s, I started living and working among tribal communities on a volatile edge of the Muslim world. I saw hundreds of examples where *cultural sensitivity* (or lack thereof) either helped or hindered the understanding of the Good News. In the 1990s, we all were amazed at the sudden openness of the former Soviet Bloc countries, and I helped to train workers for various ministries there. Ministries that made an effort to be *contextually informed* by learning languages and cultures have borne more long-term fruit than those that tried to use short-cuts. In the last 25 years, I have continued to live among major unreached people groups, helping ministries to be *culturally relevant* and effective among them. Some ministries have felt led to take a more contextual approach (sometimes called an "insider movement"), leading to the creation of hundreds of house fellowships. We also have tried to apply these IP fundamentals as we developed discipleship apps to encourage deeper growth among believers. Whatever the geographic location, geopolitical developments, and technological advances, the role of the three IP principles described above is essential to our calling as ambassadors for his Kingdom.

Applying the Fundamentals of International Psychology

Four fundamental principles that guide IP are *advocacy, participatory action, acknowledging diverse perspectives,* and *operating in an ethical manner.* Mission work applies these IP fundamentals inherently but can become more effective by purposely employing them in all aspects of the work from start to finish.

Advocacy involves seeking greater public awareness and support for a particular cause and group—appealing to human rights, policies, action, justice, etc. As a core IP principle, it begins with seeing the inherent value in others, gaining a clear understanding of the issue(s), and then pursuing the intentional inclusion of individuals and communities. It respects diverse populations and communities and works to understand factors such as beliefs and traditions that can impact outcomes (Stewart 2021). It calls for an authentic interest in co-creating sustainable change that will empower and elevate communities for the betterment of all involved. Having cultural proficiency helps advocacy efforts to positively impact communities and individuals.

Applying IP in advocacy efforts means that programs should align with, generate, and promote ideas and actions that are specific to the issue, contextual to the population, and able to be maintained and sustained by the participants without outside assistance (Geller 2021). For example, I (Karen) am trained as a combat medic with a Westernized understanding of medicine. I was taught that the mind and the body are separate entities and must be treated separately. Working with Aboriginal people in Western Australia, I witnessed spiritual healings that baffled the scientific understanding of how modern medicine works. I then advocated on behalf of the Aboriginal community to be allowed to have faith healers included in treatment protocols. Flower essence healing protocols and mud bath soakings produced healing effects similar to those of chemical interventions when applied to chronic disease processes such as hypertension and diabetes. Community leaders and physicians met and discussed ways to work together, but it took many hours of advocacy work to get them to a point where they would listen carefully to each other and exchange information. Because I had collaborated with the Aboriginal community and had an understanding of modern medicine, I could bridge the cultural gap and bring the two communities together. The Aboriginal community members have since created a healing center that uses both modern and holistic medical protocols as options.

Anand Application 2. To keep national mission workers in the field long-term, advocacy in financial areas is often needed. Whether the nationals are bi-vocational, "raise support," or are salaried, there is a great need for advice and help in solutions that work in their settings. For example, IP skills can be used to advocate for training to improve workers' attitudes and skills in communication, fundraising, and planning for their family's future opportunities and expenses. Many national field workers need help to develop budgets and economical purchasing patterns for projects rather than resorting to short-term quick fixes. This training could include planning for a project's financial sustainability and long-range impact within the communities where they work. There can also be tension when big financial gaps exist between field workers and the leaders or consultants (e.g., in monthly salary levels, provisions for children's education, and other benefits).

Furthermore, if their organization does not have a retirement plan, then IP-informed advocacy (and mediation with ministry leaders) could help long-term workers buy land or housing and slowly develop these assets as part of their retirement strategy.

Similarly, *participatory action* means that mission workers act as stakeholders within the community to identify challenges and develop sustainable solutions. It means recognizing that solutions used elsewhere may not work everywhere. It means trusting community members and leaders and working alongside them to assist in determining what they perceive as the problem and the right solution for them. It means working to acknowledge and set aside any biases that may negatively influence how the mission is understood and accomplished. It ultimately means that you are a participant in the action and not always leading the action.

Participatory action is easier when one can acknowledge diverse perspectives. It sounds elementary to say that not everyone thinks the same way, but very often, we forget that basic principle. We are all products of our individual and collective experiences, and how we process those experiences, coupled with our cultural upbringing, determines our worldview. In turn, our worldview influences how we act, react, and interact with others.

Anand Application 3. A major issue for mission workers in honor- and shame-based cultures is forgiveness and reconciliation, especially among believers. Participatory action in this area can include building a bridge of connection between workers and mediating when invited to do so. Each situation is different, but the meeting might include prayer, identifying the power gaps, modeling humble apologies (that may look different from culture to culture), being careful with words that lead to loss of face, and building a proposal for future interaction that can offer a win-win dynamic. This IP principle can encourage people to actively define how they want to participate together—not just regarding the tasks but also in terms of relationships!

Acknowledging diverse perspectives is one way in which I (Karen) use IP perspectives in everyday life as I teach my children about relationships with others. I teach them that they must offer space and grace to those who respond to situations differently than we may expect.

I am reminded of a situation with a close friend involving his response to death and grief. In Louisiana (where I was born), when a loved one dies, our close-knit community celebrates with song, dance, and days of eating, drinking, and enjoying the presence of friends and family. Celebrations begin two to three days prior to the funeral and can last up to three days afterwards as we tell stories about our loved one, recounting the good as well as the not-so-good. For us, the extended event brings a sense of closure that would otherwise be missing. Those who are unable to attend the celebrations send letters and cards and (with modern technology) can now join via video platforms. In contrast, my friend was taught never to talk too much about a deceased person, as doing so was thought to disturb their rest and could potentially call them back as spirits. As we interacted, we were both very surprised at the other's understanding and participation in the cultural traditions involving death and grief. It took us a while to reconcile within ourselves why neither of us was "wrong" and how we could better understand and respect each other's traditions.

The above story was shared about an experience that occurred many years ago. Since then, I have learned how to lovingly discuss belief systems that may be different and even oppositional to my own. As a minister of the gospel and a practitioner of IP, I now have a better understanding of how to acknowledge the beliefs, values, and traditions of others while simultaneously sharing my own beliefs, values, and traditions from a biblical standpoint. Addressing beliefs that have been generationally and culturally grounded can be intimidating. However, establishing a point of connection is the first step in reshaping perspectives. When that connection is established, even if it occurs in a casual and fleeting moment, that open door is an opportunity to plant a seed.

Anand Application 4. How to facilitate *acknowledging diverse perspectives*, or even accepting diverse experiments in mission strategy, can be very important in contextualization efforts among cultures traditionally seen as resistant. Many times, apostolic workers take risks by sharing what they did and how their non-believing friends and relatives responded positively. But then they receive quick criticism of their experiment because they have deviated from the status-quo approaches used by various people and organizations. IP perspectives can protect or encourage apostolic experiments by helping everyone be more open to diverse perspectives and approaches. They can reinforce that it often takes months to assess whether an experiment is faithful to Scripture and perhaps years to see how fruitful an experiment can be in the long run.

Historically, the importance of *operating in an ethical manner* has often been unfortunately neglected amid work in international spaces, especially with indigenous population groups. In missions, ethical violations occurred at times because of misguided intentions to force people to embrace the gospel. This happened, for example, with the Aboriginal peoples in Australia. Mission workers were quick to disregard long-held traditions and belief systems of the local populace and watched as government policies and society pressures oppressed and marginalized entire communities. From our vantage point today, we understand (hopefully!) far better the importance of safeguarding the wellbeing and rights of both individuals and communities in which mission workers are involved. Furthermore, there is far more emphasis on intentionally embracing the tenets of equity and inclusion while rejecting unjust practices and systems. This means being accountable to others—such as to the "affected populations" in humanitarian work—and respecting the traditions, values, and belief systems of those with whom you work (CHS Alliance 2024). Currently, aboriginal family kinship groups are working with Australian governments to reconcile long-held mistrust between indigenous and non-indigenous population groups. In 2008, Prime Minister Kevin Rudd issued a national apology to the Australian and Torres Strait Islander First Nations communities, who were severely impacted by forced assimilation policies. This apology went a long way in helping communities through the healing process.

Anand Application 5. Most humans believe it is important to operate in an ethical manner, yet they may have mixed feelings about accountability. This IP principle can help mission workers achieve a healthy integration of accountability into the organization's goals (which usually demand key statistics) and ethical ways of treating workers and locals as humans and not just as numbers. If there is an undue or unethical pressure to produce favorable statistics and bigger numbers every year, then the quality of discipleship and leadership often declines and the virtuous foundation underlying the mission's original goals can be undermined. If accountability is too vague, then the organization will tend to have poor stewardship and, as a consequence, often fall short of its potential.

An Example from Haiti

Even when the best intentions regarding advocacy, participatory action, acknowledging diverse perspectives, and operating in an ethical manner are present, unfortunate events can occur. As an example, let us look at what happened after mission and humanitarian workers from all over the world arrived in Haiti to provide assistance after the devastating earthquake in 2010.

One mission group sent by an American church spent time in a Haitian community and provided much-needed comfort to the young people there. With great intentions, they planned a field trip to obtain shoes, clothing, and other resources specifically set aside for the children, gathered the children onto a bus, and drove across the city. As they traveled, the excitement of the children quickly turned to grief and mourning. Although the children had understood that an earthquake had occurred, they were unprepared to witness the widespread destruction and devastation that they saw while riding through areas that used to have homes, schools, and other familiar landmarks.

We do not wish to disparage the fine efforts of these mission and humanitarian workers, but we simply want to point out that regardless of the care we take to do the right thing, we can still sometimes come up short or encounter unforeseen consequences. This is where we have to reserve grace for ourselves and others, keep on learning, and remember that every day is a new day in which to do good.

Peace Work in West Africa through an IP Lens

Another example of IP principles in mission can be seen in the work of the Mendes brothers in West Africa. These award-winning musicians traveled extensively through West Africa, using the power of music to support peaceful solutions in war-torn areas. In one such area, the group was scheduled to perform but found themselves caught in the midst of an ongoing conflict that included three separate factions. As band members worked to set up equipment and perform sound checks, they noticed that three distinct groups had separated themselves from one another and refused to interact. The two band leaders discussed the situation with the other band members, who were also nervous about the tense and uncomfortable standoff. It was decided that the band would stay and perform as planned, as they had come a long way to provide music to isolated villagers who had not heard live music in many years.

After the group had played a few songs with very little interaction from the crowd, one of the brothers invited an elderly villager to dance and traded his brimmed hat for the local man's headwrap. The elderly villager joined the brother in dancing and quickly began teaching him some of the basic steps of a tribal dance. Other villagers joined in to help and soon most of the members of the villager's own group were dancing and enjoying themselves. Witnessing this, members of the two remaining groups cautiously began to thaw and dance along as well. Before long, all groups had apparently forgotten their differences and joined in the dancing. This shared experience led to a sharing of food and a marked decrease in the aggressive stances that had been seen previously, as the celebration lasted well into the night.

Unbeknownst to the band, the elderly villager was a local tribal chieftain who had been battling with the other two factions to maintain dominance in the area for quite some time. One of the factions involved was the local government, which was set to depose the chieftain and his rival and replace them both with someone chosen by the government. All three factions had tentatively agreed to a one-day cease-fire to allow villagers to enjoy the long-awaited festivities. The next day, the Mendes brothers brought all faction leaders to the table to discuss challenges that had heretofore seemed insurmountable. Referring to the previous evening's entertainment, the brothers reminded them that the groups were more similar than different and that they could amicably agree to disagree. In fact, they were reminded that differing perspectives, when acknowledged and respected, would bring about stronger and more collaborative solutions. Ultimately, the government backed off from installing its own leader and worked together with the village groups to create a form of government that provided benefit for all involved.

The IP principles used in that situation included participatory action, becoming involved with community members to advocate for peacebuilding, and being willing to act as a facilitator to achieve a common goal. The Mendes brothers and their band members used IP principles instinctively, even though they were not trained in the use of these principles. It is easy to identify IP principles in action when you know what to look for; many people use them daily. In our IP-influenced training and practice, we use various examples to identify and define those principles so that others—such as mission and member care workers—can apply them intentionally and daily.

Likewise, we believe it is important to learn from the wealth of experience already available in the world of mission to inform our own IP perspectives and practices. One major example is the values, approaches, and contributions of mission workers to community development (Misean Cara 2018; Woodberry 2018). Learning and collaboration are a two-way street that can help to bridge the historic gap between two diverse sectors: the development or humanitarian sector and the mission sector.

Reinforcing Intercultural Communication and Sensitivity

IP integrates personal and interpersonal awareness in interactions with others. This awareness is a key to effective intercultural communication and conflict resolution. Culturally competent mission and member care workers will be attuned to their own perspectives and values while remaining aware of the perspectives and values of others, and of how they use words to communicate their intentions. Understanding how language shapes the relationships between community members and mission workers is crucial.

For instance, in Rwanda in 2015, a group of American university students visited a youth center run by a local community leader. At the time, Rwanda had done away with the terms "orphan" and "orphanage," with their child welfare system moving toward reintegration and reunification of displaced street youth to their families. The youth center's mission was to provide education and housing to children who were living on the streets due to family poverty or illness. However, the American student administrator repeatedly referred to the youth center as an "orphanage" during a community meeting. After the first reference, the Rwandan community leader politely corrected the American administrator, explaining that the children were not orphans because they had families. After the third and fourth time, the Rwandan community leader's irritation was evident in his voice as he stated, "You keep referring to the center as an orphanage. I'd like to ask you not to refer to it this way, because we are a youth center and we work with the community to provide education and resources to improve opportunities for families to be strengthened and reunited." The lesson is clear: when community members feel as though mission workers understand them and their culture within the context of their sociopolitical and historical realities, they feel seen, heard, and more connected to the intention of the mission and can more readily collaborate. A corollary is also evident: when working across cultures and settings, you can expect to make mistakes, even if you try to minimize them, so you must be prepared to acknowledge and correct such mistakes when they are pointed out to you!

More Examples of Our IP Work

The importance of developing and maintaining culturally relevant perspectives and practices is common knowledge in mission. IP reflects and reinforces this focus and can be used to complement existing training. We have found that the fundamental principles of IP can be quickly taught and readily adapted to and applied by different groups of people.

I (Karen) have developed and continue to refine a training model on how to intentionally use IP in everyday life (Infinity LINC International). The C.O.U.R.S.E. training consists of six modules, taught over a six-week period. The letters in the name stand for cultural honesty, operating in context, understanding biases, recognition of others, self-reflection, and education/emulation. The program's intent is to enhance individual and collective awareness and provide techniques that assist in deepening inter- and intracultural skills. It seeks to increase one's capacity to understand their own limitations and be gracious with oneself so that one can better understand and show grace to others.

Another example is a two-week program that I (Joyce) facilitated in Mexico. The program brought together graduate art therapy students from the United States, Israel, and Latin America and focused on students' self-awareness, positioned them to learn from each other, and explored how art therapy is applied in the students' respective cultural environments. It is important for the participants to consider their different approaches and underlying assumptions about the work itself (Green, Metzl, and Treviño 2023). All students participated in daily personal and group reflections on the thoughts, beliefs, and assumptions they brought with them into each day. They were encouraged to dialogue openly about their reflections and to process together how they impacted one another while facilitating art therapy groups with the local Mexican community. The students also reflected on and listened to the different approaches to mental health care that their respective countries have adopted due to political and historic events. This reflective and experiential approach helped the students to connect more deeply with themselves and others, and then to focus on collaborative plans and actions for the day.

This IP-informed approach for art therapy students is similar to a strategy that I (Karen) learned in the military, known as after-actions review (AAR). The AAR is used by teams following an event, activity, or mission to discuss what was supposed to happen, what actually happened, and how the participants could improve on our collective actions (Henshaw 2021). I have used this approach following ministry conferences and workshops to review the events with the organizers—like a debriefing—with a view toward mutual learning, group cohesion, and improving future events.

Final Thoughts

Our IP lens and applications reflect similar efforts over the years by psychologists and colleagues from other disciplines who have been actively applying their professional knowledge to mission and member care. IP is a skill set and a mindset. It is a way of working and of being. It acknowledges the importance of culture and context in every interaction. It recognizes that social, spiritual, economic, historical, and political factors have combined to shape everyone's worldview, values, beliefs, and behaviors. It embraces humility that asks others what is needed rather than assuming that we have the best answers ourselves. IP principles can especially complement training programs and in-the-field strategies to help mission and member care workers better understand themselves and people in different cultures.

Applications: International Psychology for Mission and Member Care

Core Strategies

1. Encourage colleagues to apply their field of study and practice to mission and member care.
2. Integrate a practice of self-reflection before and during any engagement in activities that involve people from different cultures.
3. Seek to learn about the cultural contexts (social, political, historical, and environmental) of both mission workers and community members that could potentially impact mission and member care work.

Core Resources

1. Louis Hoffman. 2014. "Introduction to International Psychology" (video); American Psychological Association 2022. "Teaching International Psychology" (video).
2. Todd Henshaw. 2021. "After-Action Reviews: A Simple yet Powerful Tool."
3. Psychology Coalition at the United Nations.

Reflection and Discussion

1. Identify some instances in your work with others in which you related to them in a way that appeared sensitive or insensitive to their customs, traditions, or realities (that is, their cultural contexts).
2. Comment on which areas of the international psychology framework you have lived out and how they contributed to greater awareness and compassion.
3. Describe three practical ways in which IP can strengthen your work in mission or member care.

References

American Psychological Association, International Psychology Division. 2022. "Teaching International Psychology" (video), January 18. https://div52.net/webinars/#library.

Camp, Claire, Joy Bustrum, David Brokaw, and Christopher Adams. 2014. "Missionary Perspectives on the Effectiveness of Current Member Care Practices." *Journal of Psychology and Theology* 42 (4): 359–368.

CHS Alliance. 2024. *Core Humanitarian Standard*. https://corehumanitarianstandard.org/chs-revision.

Crawford, Nancy, and David Wang. 2016. "A Brief History of Psychology and Missions in *JPT*: Looking Back, Around, and Forward." *Journal of Psychology and Theology* 44 (4): 263–267.

Davis, Pamela, and Mandy Kellums Baraka. 2021. "What Mental Health Professionals Can Learn from Missionary Member Care: Ways of Thinking, Doing, and Being." *Journal of Psychology and Christianity* 40 (1): 29–39.

Eriksson, Cynthia. 2012. "Practical Integration in Cross-Cultural Member Care." *Journal of Psychology and Theology* 40 (2): 112–115.

Geller, Joanna. 2021. "Participatory Action Research and Evaluation." Organizing Engagement. https://organizingengagement.org/models/participatory-action-research-and-evaluation/.

Green, Joyce Yip, Einat Metzl, and Ana Laura Treviño. 2023. "International Online Art Therapy Education Program: Evaluating Cultural and Global Perspectives." *Art Therapy* 40 (2): 1–10.

Henshaw, Todd. 2021. "After-Action Reviews: A Simple yet Powerful Tool." Wharton Executive Education. https://executiveeducation.wharton.upenn.edu/thought-leadership/wharton-at-work/2021/07/after-action-reviews-simple-tool/.

Hoffman, Louis. 2014. "Introduction to International Psychology." https://youtu.be/HyLynM1RZao?si=JfhXuo-DuS9g8RLB.

Infinity LINC International. https://lincinternationalgroup.org/.

Kim, Uichol, Guoshu Yang, and Kwang-Kuo Hwang, eds. 2006. *Indigenous and Cultural Psychology: Understanding People in Context*. New York: Springer. https://indigenouspsych.org/Resources/Indigenous percent20and percent20Cultural percent20Psychology percent20- percent20Understanding percent20People percent20in percent20Context.pdf.

Misean Cara. 2018. "The Missionary Approach to Development Interventions (MADI): Conceptual Framework and Current Development Context." https://jliflc.com/resources/misean-cara-missionary-approach-to-development-interventions-madi/.

O'Donnell, Kelly, and Michèle Lewis O'Donnell. 2020. "Following Jesus Globally: Engaging the World Through Global Integration." *Lausanne Global Analysis* 9 (1). https://www.lausanne.org/content/lga/2020-01/following-jesus-globally.

Psychology Coalition at the United Nations. https://psychologycoalitionun.org/.

Schwandt, Joanne, and Glendon Moriarty. 2008. "What Have the Past 25 Years of Member Care Research Taught Us? An Overview of Missionary Mental Health and Member Care Services." *Missiology* 36 (3): 317–26. https://doi.org/10.1177/009182960803600304.

Stewart, Ada. 2021. "Cultural Humility Is Critical to Health Equity." American Academy of Family Physicians. https://www.aafp.org/news/blogs/leadervoices/entry/20190418lv-humility.htm.

United Nations. 2015. "Transforming Our World: The 2030 Agenda for Sustainable Development." https://sdgs.un.org/2030agenda.

Woodberry, Robert. 2018. "The World the Missionaries Made." Presentation delivered at the Center for Faith and Culture, Southeastern Baptist Theological Seminary, January 10, 2018. http://intersectproject.org/faith-and-economics/robert-woodberry-world-missionaries-made/.

Joyce Yip Green, PhD, is a professor and researcher at Loyola Marymount University. She also works in private practice as a licensed marriage and family therapist and board-certified art therapist. Her work focuses on supporting the mental health and wellness of individuals, families, and communities from an ecocultural and spiritual perspective.

Karen Brown, PhD, is a proud veteran of the US Army and an adjunct professor at the Chicago School of Professional Psychology, teaching in the Department of International Psychology (trauma track). She has been a licensed minister and ordained elder in ministry, both locally and internationally, for over twenty-seven years.

5

For All People and All Peoples

The Universal Declaration of Human Rights

Kelly O'Donnell

> All human beings are born free and equal in dignity and rights. They are endowed with reason and conscience and should act towards one another in a spirit of brotherhood.
> —Universal Declaration of Human Rights, Article 1

In this chapter, I invite you to review the Universal Declaration of Human Rights (UDHR) (United Nations 1948) and consider how its foundational principles are relevant for our world and for member care and mission. The importance we give to this document is reflected in its verbatim inclusion in each volume of the *Global Member Care* series.

> The [UDHR] is a milestone document in the history of human rights. Drafted by representatives with different legal and cultural backgrounds from all regions of the world, the Declaration ... sets out, for the first time, fundamental human rights to be universally protected and it has been translated into over 500 languages. The UDHR is widely recognized as having inspired, and paved the way for, the adoption of more than seventy human rights treaties, applied today on a permanent basis at global and regional levels (all containing references to it in their preambles). (United Nations)

I encourage you to read carefully and reflect on the UDHR. Afterwards, delve into the core materials in the Application section to explore ways to link human rights with member care and mission. In so doing, we believe that you will see how biblical values are pivotal for human rights and how human rights are embedded in good practice for member care and mission (O'Donnell 2011).

Highlighting human rights also requires acknowledging the challenges and failures of implementing the UDHR and human rights instruments and the need to balance human *rights* with human *responsibilities*. Sadly, there continues to be selective application and utter disregard of the responsibility to safeguard basic human rights. Humanity's virtuous qualities can easily become tainted by self-justification, intolerance, and the exploitation of others at all levels—individually, institutionally, and internationally. Nonetheless, my belief in the power of human rights embedded in divine and human love remains undaunted. I join with Martin Luther King Jr. (1964) in resolutely affirming that *"unarmed truth and unconditional love will have the final word in reality …* [and] *right temporarily defeated is stronger than evil triumphant."*

The Universal Declaration of Human Rights

Preamble

Whereas recognition of the inherent dignity and of the equal and inalienable rights of all members of the human family is the foundation of freedom, justice and peace in the world,

Whereas disregard and contempt for human rights have resulted in barbarous acts which have outraged the conscience of mankind, and the advent of a world in which human beings shall enjoy freedom of speech and belief and freedom from fear and want has been proclaimed as the highest aspiration of the common people,

Whereas it is essential, if man is not to be compelled to have recourse, as a last resort, to rebellion against tyranny and oppression, that human rights should be protected by the rule of law,

Whereas the peoples of the United Nations have in the Charter reaffirmed their faith in fundamental human rights, in the dignity and worth of the human person and in the equal rights of men and women and have determined to promote social progress and better standards of life in larger freedom,

Whereas Member States have pledged themselves to achieve, in co-operation with the United Nations, the promotion of universal respect for and observance of human rights and fundamental freedoms,

Whereas a common understanding of these rights and freedoms is of the greatest importance for the full realization of this pledge,

Now, therefore, the General Assembly,

Proclaims this Universal Declaration of Human Rights as a common standard of achievement for all peoples and all nations, to the end that every individual and every organ of society, keeping this Declaration constantly in mind, shall strive by teaching and education to promote respect for these rights and freedoms and by progressive measures, national and international, to secure their universal and effective recognition and observance, both among the peoples of Member States themselves and among the peoples of territories under their jurisdiction.

Article 1. All human beings are born free and equal in dignity and rights. They are endowed with reason and conscience and should act towards one another in a spirit of brotherhood.

Article 2. Everyone is entitled to all the rights and freedoms set forth in this Declaration, without distinction of any kind, such as race, colour, sex, language, religion, political or other opinion, national or social origin, property, birth or other status. Furthermore, no distinction shall be made on the basis of the political, jurisdictional or international status of the country or territory to which a person belongs, whether it be independent, trust, non-self-governing or under any other limitation of sovereignty.

Article 3. Everyone has the right to life, liberty and security of person.

Article 4. No one shall be held in slavery or servitude; slavery and the slave trade shall be prohibited in all their forms.

Article 5. No one shall be subjected to torture or to cruel, inhuman or degrading treatment or punishment.

Article 6. Everyone has the right to recognition everywhere as a person before the law.

Article 7. All are equal before the law and are entitled without any discrimination to equal protection of the law. All are entitled to equal protection against any discrimination in violation of this Declaration and against any incitement to such discrimination.

Article 8. Everyone has the right to an effective remedy by the competent national tribunals for acts violating the fundamental rights granted him by the constitution or by law.

Article 9. No one shall be subjected to arbitrary arrest, detention or exile.

Article 10. Everyone is entitled in full equality to a fair and public hearing by an independent and impartial tribunal, in the determination of his rights and obligations and of any criminal charge against him.

Article 11. (1) Everyone charged with a penal offence has the right to be presumed innocent until proved guilty according to law in a public trial at which he has had all the guarantees necessary for his defence. (2) No one shall be held guilty of any penal offence on account of any act or omission which did not constitute a penal offence, under national or international law, at the time when it was committed. Nor shall a heavier penalty be imposed than the one that was applicable at the time the penal offence was committed.

Article 12. No one shall be subjected to arbitrary interference with his privacy, family, home or correspondence, nor to attacks upon his honour and reputation. Everyone has the right to the protection of the law against such interference or attacks.

Article 13. (1) Everyone has the right to freedom of movement and residence within the borders of each state. (2) Everyone has the right to leave any country, including his own, and to return to his country.

Article 14. (1) Everyone has the right to seek and to enjoy in other countries asylum from persecution. (2) This right may not be invoked in the case of prosecutions genuinely arising from non-political crimes or from acts contrary to the purposes and principles of the United Nations.

Article 15. (1) Everyone has the right to a nationality. (2) No one shall be arbitrarily deprived of his nationality nor denied the right to change his nationality.

Article 16. (1) Men and women of full age, without any limitation due to race, nationality or religion, have the right to marry and to found a family. They are entitled to equal rights as to marriage, during marriage and at its dissolution. (2) Marriage shall be entered into only with the free and full consent of the intending spouses. (3) The family is the natural and fundamental group unit of society and is entitled to protection by society and the State.

Article 17. (1) Everyone has the right to own property alone as well as in association with others. (2) No one shall be arbitrarily deprived of his property.

Article 18. Everyone has the right to freedom of thought, conscience and religion; this right includes freedom to change his religion or belief, and freedom, either alone or in community with others and in public or private, to manifest his religion or belief in teaching, practice, worship and observance.

Article 19. Everyone has the right to freedom of opinion and expression; this right includes freedom to hold opinions without interference and to seek, receive and impart information and ideas through any media and regardless of frontiers.

Article 20. (1) Everyone has the right to freedom of peaceful assembly and association. (2) No one may be compelled to belong to an association.

Article 21. (1) Everyone has the right to take part in the government of his country, directly or through freely chosen representatives. (2) Everyone has the right of equal access to public service in his country. (3) The will of the people shall be the basis of the authority of government; this will shall be expressed in periodic and genuine elections which shall be by universal and equal suffrage and shall be held by secret vote or by equivalent free voting procedures.

Article 22. Everyone, as a member of society, has the right to social security and is entitled to realization, through national effort and international cooperation and in accordance with the organization and resources of each State, of the economic, social and cultural rights indispensable for his dignity and the free development of his personality.

Article 23. (1) Everyone has the right to work, to free choice of employment, to just and favourable conditions of work and to protection against unemployment. (2) Everyone, without any discrimination, has the right to equal pay for equal work. (3) Everyone who works has the right to just and favourable remuneration ensuring for himself and his family an existence worthy of human dignity, and supplemented, if necessary, by other means of social protection. (4) Everyone has the right to form and to join trade unions for the protection of his interests.

Article 24. Everyone has the right to rest and leisure, including reasonable limitation of working hours and periodic holidays with pay.

Article 25. (1) Everyone has the right to a standard of living adequate for the health and well-being of himself and of his family, including food, clothing, housing and medical care and necessary social services, and the right to security in the event of unemployment, sickness, disability, widowhood, old age or other lack of livelihood in circumstances beyond his control. (2) Motherhood and childhood are entitled to special care and assistance. All children, whether born in or out of wedlock, shall enjoy the same social protection.

Article 26. (1) Everyone has the right to education. Education shall be free, at least in the elementary and fundamental stages. Elementary education shall be compulsory. Technical and professional education shall be made generally available and higher education shall be equally accessible to all on the basis of merit. (2) Education shall be directed to the full development of the human personality and to the strengthening of respect for human rights and fundamental freedoms. It shall promote understanding, tolerance and friendship among all nations, racial or religious groups, and shall further the activities of the United Nations for the maintenance of peace. (3) Parents have a prior right to choose the kind of education that shall be given to their children.

Article 27. (1) Everyone has the right freely to participate in the cultural life of the community, to enjoy the arts and to share in scientific advancement and its benefits. (2) Everyone has the right to the protection of the moral and material interests resulting from any scientific, literary or artistic production of which he is the author.

Article 28. Everyone is entitled to a social and international order in which the rights and freedoms set forth in this Declaration can be fully realized.

Article 29. (1) Everyone has duties to the community in which alone the free and full development of his personality is possible. (2) In the exercise of his rights and freedoms, everyone shall be subject only to such limitations as are determined by law solely for the purpose of securing due recognition and respect for the rights and freedoms of others and of meeting the just requirements of morality, public order and the general welfare in a democratic society. (3) These rights and freedoms may in no case be exercised contrary to the purposes and principles of the United Nations.

Article 30. Nothing in this Declaration may be interpreted as implying for any State, group or person any right to engage in any activity or to perform any act aimed at the destruction of any of the rights and freedoms set forth herein.

Applications: Human Rights in Member Care and Missons

Core Strategies

1. Use the lens of human rights to explore some of the challenges and opportunities for incarnating the gospel among least reached peoples and places.

2. Identify a human rights area that interests you and learn more about it. For example, see the *Member Care Updates* that relate human rights to good practice (December 2023), children (November 2022), human trafficking (December 2020), and persecution (December 2020) (Member Care Associates) as well as "Human Rights and Psychological Ethics" (Gauthier 2022).

3. Prioritize reading stories by people and organizations who are working effectively in human rights areas, including their personal struggles and successes. Explore ways to connect and contribute!

Core Resources

1. Organizations. Office of the High Commissioner for Human Rights (United Nations); Religious Liberty Commission (World Evangelical Alliance).

2. Books and articles. Nelu Burcea and Liberato Bautista. 2023. *Shaping a World of Freedoms: 75 Years of Legacy and Impact of the Universal Declaration of Human Rights*; John Nurser. 2005. *For All Peoples and All Nations: Christian Churches and Human Rights*; Janet Epp Buckingham. 2023. "Exploring the Intersection of Faith and Universal Freedoms: Evangelical Christians and Human Rights"; Wilfred Wong. 2002. "Human Rights Advocacy in Missions."

3. Additional human rights instruments. Organization of African Unity, *African Charter on Human and Peoples' Rights* (1981); Asia Meeting of the World Conference on Human Rights, *Bangkok Declaration on Human Rights* (1993); League of Arab States, *Arab Charter on Human Rights* (2004).

Reflection and Discussion

1. Consider these five applications of the UDHR Preamble for member care and missions (adapted from ODonnell 2011, 192). Note that both rights and responsibilities are emphasized.

    a. We recognize the dignity and equality of our staff and of the people who are the focus of our services. The pursuit of freedom, justice, and peace is a responsibility that is reflected in our core values and goals.

    b. We promote friendly relations, social progress, and better standards of life within our organizations and within the people that are the focus of our services.

    c. We are gravely concerned ("outraged" in the Preamble) when basic rights are disregarded within our organizations and within the people who are the focus of our services. We seek to protect people's rights and we oppose ("rebellion" in the Preamble) those entities that stifle freedoms of speech and beliefs and freedom from fear.

d. We reaffirm our ongoing commitment to basic human rights in both our organizations and the people who are the focus of our services.

   e. We are willing to prudently make sacrifices in order to safeguard and promote the rights and well-being of vulnerable people, including mission/aid personnel and the people whom they serve.

2. How do human rights provide a foundation for our responsibility to manage and support our mission staff, including internationals, nationals, locals, volunteers, and their families?

3. How do human rights provide a foundation for our responsibility in mission work to help vulnerable populations, including those who have experienced human rights abuses?

References

Asia Meeting of the World Conference on Human Rights. 1993. *Bangkok Declaration on Human Rights.* https://www.hurights.or.jp/archives/other_documents/section1/1993/04/final-declaration-of-the-regional-meeting-for-asia-of-the-world-conference-on-human-rights.html#_edn1.

Burcea, Nelu, and Liberato Bautista, eds. 2023. *Shaping a World of Freedoms: 75 Years of Legacy and impact of the Universal Declaration of Human Rights.* New York: UNEQUAL World Research Center. https://unequal.world/books/.

Epp Buckingham, Janet. 2023. "Exploring the Intersection of Faith and Universal Freedoms: Evangelical Christians and Human Rights." In *Shaping a World of Freedoms: 75 Years of Legacy and Impact of the Universal Declaration of Human Rights*, edited by Nelu Burcea and Liberato Bautista, 161–171. New York: UNEQUAL World Research Center. https://unequal.world/books/.

Gauthier, Janel. 2022. "Human Rights and Psychological Ethics: Working Together for a Better World." Webinar from Global Network of Psychologists for Human Rights, September 21, 2022. https://www.youtube.com/watch?v=VBMHpfs_-cI&t=1373s.

King, Martin Luther, Jr. 1964. "Martin Luther King Jr. Acceptance Speech—The Nobel Prize." https://www.nobelprize.org/prizes/peace/1964/king/acceptance-speech/.

League of Arab States. 2004. *Arab Charter on Human Rights.* https://www.icj.org/wp-content/uploads/2014/10/Arab-Charter-on-Human-Rights.pdf.

Member Care Associates. "MC Updates—Special News." https://membercareassociates.org/resource-updates/mca-resource-updates/.

Nurser, John. 2005. *For All Peoples and All Nations: Christian Churches and Human Rights*. Geneva: WCC Publications.

O'Donnell, Kelly. 2011. "Extending the Foundations of Good Practice." In *Global Member Care, vol. 1: The Pearls and Perils of Good Practice*, 186–205. Pasadena, CA: William Carey Library.

Organization of African Unity. 1981. *African Charter on Human and Peoples' Rights*. https://au.int/en/treaties/african-charter-human-and-peoples-rights.

United Nations. 1948. "Universal Declaration of Human Rights." https://www.un.org/en/about-us/universal-declaration-of-human-rights.

United Nations. Office of the High Commissioner for Human Rights. https://www.ohchr.org/en/ohchr_homepage.

Wong, Wilfred. 2002. "Human Rights Advocacy in Missons." In *Doing Member Care Well: Perspectives and Practices from Around the World*, edited by Kelly O'Donnell, 477–488. Pasadena, CA: William Carey Publishers. https://passionexchange.files.wordpress.com/2008/10/doingmembercarewell.pdf.

World Evangelical Alliance. Religious Liberty Commission. https://religiousfreedom.worldea.org/.

Kelly O'Donnell, PsyD, is a Licensed Clinical Psychologist (California) based in Geneva and the USA with Member Care Associates, Inc. (MCA). His international and multi-sectoral emphases for consultation, training, and writing include member care, global mental health, integrity/anti-corruption, and faith-based contributions to sustainable development. Kelly did his doctoral training in clinical psychology and theology at Rosemead School of Psychology, Biola University (USA). https://membercareassociates.org/.

PART 2
Staying the Course in the Regions

Samuel Girguis & David Tan, Consulting Editors

Introduction to Part 2

It is amazing to see how the principles and strategies of member care are being contextualized all over the world! I (Samuel) am an Egyptian-American psychologist trained in the United States who has worked in several different cultural contexts, including Cambodia (Chang et al. 2020), the Philippines (Barrozo et al. 2023), and Lebanon (manuscript in process). It has been an incredible privilege to work together with ministry leaders, healthcare providers, and community members in these contexts. I have also seen firsthand the toll that doing Kingdom work can take.

In the Philippines, I worked alongside organizations focused on sex trafficking, seeking to eliminate the evil practice through legal means. Their work also sought to support the survivors, often young women, who experienced the terrible impact of sex trafficking. This difficult work can easily lead to burnout, vicarious trauma, and secondary traumatic stress. My team and I had an opportunity to interview Philippine mental health professionals and ask what sustains them in doing this work. Overwhelmingly, the responses pointed back to experiencing strength and support from God, their families, and their organizations. These sources of strength and support were deeply connected to their cultural identities and environment.

In Lebanon, I collaborated with Christian ministries serving the huge influx of refugees from Syria during the civil war. There is a long history of tension between Syria and Lebanon due to past conflict and occupation. In my interviews of the Lebanese Christian teachers and aid workers, it was remarkable to see how their Christian faith, family support, and organizational support sustained them in their work. The themes were similar but looked very different in these two cultural contexts.

David Tan is the other consulting editor for part two. He reviewed and gave important input on all five chapters. Unfortunately, due to health reasons he was not able to actually co-author this introduction with me. David has been active in pastoral ministry and mission for over four decades. He was the co-founder with Wilson Phang of the Asia Member Care Network (AMCN), which began in 2008 in collaboration with Barnabas International, Heartstream Resources in the USA and New Zealand, and The Well in Thailand. There have been seven AMCN consultations. The most recent consultation (2023) offered workshops, pastoral reflections, and informal interactions to share "stories, strategies, and struggles" related to doing member care in Asian settings. The focus remained on Asian mission workers, including those in international teams, as well as on workers from the rest of the world ministering in Asia. Both AMCN and Part Two of this book have similar goals and contributions as they share lessons in developing more contextualized and comprehensive member care to support fellow Asians and inform the larger global member care community.

Since the more systematic development of member care started in the early 1990s, there has been a growing recognition of the importance of including different cultural perspectives in member care practice. Member care colleagues around the world, who are interspersed among the rich mosaic of cultures and peoples, have so much to offer each other. This is the incredible value of Part Two: as a multi-national and multi-cultural body, we are committed to listening to one another with respect and humility for mutual learning and support as we collaborate in the church's work among unreached people groups throughout the *missio Dei*.

In 2005, journalist Thomas Friedman wrote a popular book, *The World is Flat*. Friedman asserted that technology fueled globalization, which created a more equitable playing field for many across the globe. Since the publication of Friedman's book, there indeed have been many advancements globally. We have also witnessed upheavals in communities around the world that challenge globalization and the notion that "a rising tide lifts all boats" (a saying popularized by John F. Kennedy). Grassroots movements in low-income to high-income countries have pushed back, seeing globalization as an exploitative tool of ongoing colonialism and plutocracy (those with wealth and power). These movements sometimes call for a reclamation of identity that is not marred by the negative aspects of globalization. One cannot help but wonder whether globalization in the twenty-first century is a cure or a curse.

Perhaps what is missing in this dichotomous questioning of globalization's value is a failure to understand that two seemingly opposite perspectives can both be true. As it pertains to member care, how do we glean valuable lessons in different mission contexts and apply these lessons to unique and complex settings? How do we draw from good practices without giving in to overly simplistic universal formulas? How do we acknowledge the good work that has been done but also the mistakes? We believe that the essential ingredient to maintain a complex view of the issue is rooted in understanding the beautiful tapestry of context, in all its varied and interactive threads, including the cultural, organizational, and historical. It is in specific contexts that member care concepts can be explored for their relevance and member care approaches can be evaluated, possibly adapted, and implemented.

Introducrion to Part 2

Overview and Perspectives

Part Two of this volume builds on foundational work from previous decades, such as the 15 chapters on Regional Insights and Issues in *Doing Member Care Well* (O'Donnell 2002) and the chapter on Listening to our Global Voices in *Global Member Care, vol. 1* (O'Donnell 2011). It highlights several examples of how more contextualized member care is being developed and practiced by various Asian senders and colleagues in China, Korea, the Philippines, Indonesia, and India. The five chapters are by individuals who have firsthand experience in the challenges of contextualizing both mission and member care to support godly, resilient, and effective cross-cultural workers. They have learned from Western approaches and then have respectfully gone on to use research and practice-based evidence to develop and contribute their own contextually sensitive training and strategies as part of the global member care knowledge exchange.

Chapter 6 by Rainbow Cai and Raymond Yang, provides reflections and strategies for holistically supporting the growing number of Chinese mission workers. The authors consider historical realities for Chinese mission and several areas that impact Chinese mission workers: mission development stages; Chinese culture and values; the relationship between agencies, sending churches, and mission workers; understanding host cultures; and mission workers' traits. Their recommendations are informed by their own personal ministry as mission workers, counselors, and leaders as well as by interviews with many Chinese cross-cultural workers regarding the types of training, adjustment challenges, and care they have experienced.

Chapter 7 by Steve Sang-Cheol Moon and Mary Hee-Joo Moon, draws from the authors' years of experience in supporting Korean mission workers to highlight the importance of contextualization in member care. They discuss several dynamics, both positive and negative, that are specific to the Korean Christian context (and the overall Korean context) and how these should influence the ways in which member care is provided to Korean mission workers. Some Korean mission workers, for example, have had an inordinate drive to work (task orientation) and high expectations for themselves and from others that led to neglecting the importance of self-care and resulted in burnout and family conflicts. The consistent message throughout this chapter is that Korean missions need to adjust policies, programs, resources, and approaches for member care in line with both the home and host cultures of mission workers.

Chapter 8 by Grace Margaret Alag and Jorge de Ramos, discusses caring for overseas Filipino workers (OFWs) who are working and ministering in two Middle Eastern countries and Hong Kong. The authors share their own histories and how they found themselves supporting and encouraging OFWs in these different cultural settings. They highlight the variability of training and skill among the OFWs themselves and how best to care for their diverse needs. This chapter is especially relevant in view of the massive human diaspora, voluntary and involuntary, that will only increase in the foreseeable future. The reality of so many people being on the move and relocating will provide many new opportunities for the church and mission community to minister to these people—including unreached groups—and to support Christian workers among them.

Chapter 9 by Traugott Boeker, Hanni Boeker, and Hendry Pangaribuan, recounts the careful and systematic development of member care in Indonesia by an interagency team of Indonesians and the two expatriate authors. The chapter captures the cultural humility of the authors as they collaboratively encouraged Indonesian "senders" and "goers" to develop member care approaches, trainings, and principles that both honor and challenge cultural norms. Readers will appreciate the helpful tools and processes that were developed over a 10-year process. The lessons learned for the Indonesian mission movement can have many positive applications for colleagues in other countries.

Chapter 10 by Isac Sounderaraja and Lancelot Paul, identifies specific needs and resources for member care in the challenging contexts of India. It draws upon the research and experiences of two large umbrella organizations: the India Missions Association and Missionary Upholders Trust. The authors address the holistic challenges (physical, emotional, and spiritual) as well as practical realities (e.g., children's education, bereavement, and retirement) that Indian mission workers and their families experience. It is encouraging to read the many examples of collaborative member care by which sending groups are supporting the estimated 60,000 Indian Christian workers who are involved in cross-cultural mission among the country's more than 4,700 people groups!

Final Thoughts

The five chapters in Part Two provide helpful tools and ideas on developing member care in specific cultural contexts. We hope that they will stimulate additional research and writing on how to do mission training and offer member care support embedded in specific cultural values and practices. Most importantly, we hope that the chapters will inspire readers to consider how to advance the work of God through healthy and effective staff who are living and working among the world's least-reached peoples and places.

References

Barrozo, Deborah, Samuel Girguis, Robin Blair, and Jenss Chang. 2023. "Examining the Understanding and Practices of Self-Care Among Philippine Helping Professionals." *International Perspectives in Psychology: Research, Practice, Consultation* 12 (2): 112–122. https://doi.org/10.1027/2157-3891/a000076.

Chang, Jenss, Robin Blair, Michelle Tran, Samantha Meckes, Alexander Jun, Samuel Girguis, and Katharine Putman. 2020. "Perspectives of Cambodian (Khmer) Youth Victims of Sex Trafficking on Trauma Symptomatology and Healing: A Qualitative Study." *Journal of Ethnographic & Qualitative Methods* 5 (1): 17–33. https://www.researchgate.net/publication/354254520_Perspective_of_Cambodian_Khmer_Youth_Victims_of_Sex_Trafficking_On_Trauma_Symptomology_and_Healing_A_Qualitative_Study.

Friedman, Thomas. 2005. *The World Is Flat: A Brief History of the Twenty-First Century*. New York: Picador.

O'Donnell, Kelly, ed. 2002. *Doing Member Care Well: Perspectives and Practices from Around the World*. Pasadena, CA: William Carey Library. https://passionexchange.files.wordpress.com/2008/10/doingmembercarewell.pdf.

O'Donnell, Kelly, ed. 2011. *Global Member Care, vol. 1: The Pearls and Perils of Good Practice*. Pasadena, CA: William Carey Library.

Samuel M. Girguis, PsyD, is a licensed psychologist who specializes in child/adolescent trauma and resilience. He is currently the department chair and director of the Doctor of Psychology Program at Azusa Pacific University. Before coming to Azusa Pacific, Samuel worked with children and adolescents impacted by trauma at Children's Hospital Los Angeles. In his work in Cambodia and the Philippines, he partnered with organizations focused on human trafficking and sexual exploitation. His work in Lebanon has focused on supporting aid workers caring for refugees from Syria.

David Tan, DMin, served for over forty years in pastoral ministry and has lived and worked on three continents. For the past twenty years, he has provided member care for Asian workers on the field. In 2008, he co-founded and helped launch the Asian Member Care Network. His passion is to encourage mission colleagues and provide soul care within the member care movement. David is also trained in spiritual direction and in supervision of spiritual directors.

6

Supporting the Wellbeing and Effectiveness of Chinese Mission Workers

Rainbow Cai and Raymond Yang

With the growing enthusiasm and involvement of Chinese churches in cross-cultural missions, more attention has been paid to Chinese cross-cultural mission workers' spiritual, psychological, physical, and relational wellness. This chapter considers the member care needs of Chinese mission workers and practical ways to support their wellbeing and effectiveness. We first introduce the history of Chinese mission work and discuss Chinese mission workers' perspectives on member care. Next, we highlight several areas that impact Chinese mission workers: mission development stages and characteristics of each stage; Chinese culture and values; the relationship between agencies, sending churches, and mission workers; understanding host cultures; and mission workers' traits. We close with reflections and applications, including equipping emphases; motivations for mission; and resources to help mission workers care for their own physical, spiritual, emotional, and social needs.

Our perspectives are influenced by the many Chinese cross-cultural mission workers we have interviewed, including the participants in Rainbow's doctoral research (Cai 2020a). Rainbow focused on how Chinese mission workers understand cross-cultural missions and member care, so as to explore ways to help those sent from China. She interviewed twenty-five participants, ranging in age from 35 to 55, who represented more than eleven cross-cultural field locations and had been serving for between 2.5 and 12 years. We share some of her research's implications for member care throughout this chapter. We also feature many representative issues for Chinese mission workers throughout the chapter via the story of a married couple, Peter and Lisa.

Introduction

China and India have the largest world populations, each with over 1.4 billion people (Worldometer). The Christian population in China is estimated at 50 to 130 million people; the estimates vary widely because of differences in sources and methods used (Yang 2018). Christianity in China has experienced an amazing revival over the past four decades, with a significant increase in believers. The number of Chinese Protestants has grown by an average of 10 percent annually since 1979 (McPherson 2018). Yang Fenggang, a Chinese scholar at Purdue University, predicted that China would have more Christians than any other country in the world by 2030 (Phillips 2014).

In recent years, Chinese Christians have become increasingly active in international missions, and some people believe that the 21st century will be the century of Chinese missions. China started mission work late, but it still has a history of nearly 100 years. The "Mission China 2030" project held its first mobilization conference in Hong Kong in 2015. The project's goal is to see the Chinese church send 20,000 mission workers into the world by 2030, especially to the Middle East and Central Asia. In addition, the Back to Jerusalem (BTJ) movement has gained renewed vigor over the past 30 years. Its vision, birthed among Chinese Christians in the 1920s, is to fulfill what they believe is their integral role in the Great Commission. BTJ suggests that Christianity developed from Jerusalem and circled the whole earth in 2,000 years, and that now it is time for the Chinese church to finish the circle of world mission back to Jerusalem, especially by serving among unreached peoples.

Chinese Workers' Global Sending History: Three Movements

There have been three movements in the modern mission history of China. We are encouraged that in spite of the many challenges, God has been using Chinese to do his mission. As a Chinese proverb says, "Lessons learned from the past can guide one in the future" (前事不忘, 后事之师).

There have been three major mission-sending evangelical movements in China. The first such indigenous movement started in the early 20th century. In 1901, Uong Nai-siong (黄乃棠) took the gospel to Chinese and other ethnic groups and built the largest Christian church in east Malaysia (Chan 2013). Another Chinese mission worker, Choe Sing Huen (朱醒魂), started churches among the Vietnamese in Cholon, a neighborhood of Saigon in Vietnam. Some Chinese mission agencies were founded during that time, such as

Chinese Christian Crusade (中华基督徒布道会), Northwest Spiritual Society (西北灵工团), Preaching the Gospel to All Places Society (传遍福音团), and Christian Native Evangelistic Crusade (中华传道会). This era ended when the Communists took over China in 1949 (Hattaway 2003).

The second Chinese mission movement began in the mid-1990s. Three leading house church figures, Brother Yun, Peter Xu Yongze, and Enoch Wang, made the Back to Jerusalem (BTJ) vision well-known and turned it into a mission movement (Hattaway 2003). The goal of BTJ was to send 100,000 Chinese mission workers by 2013. Though the goal was not reached and the movement peaked and waned, Chinese overseas missions continued (Kam 2013; Shi 2016).

The third Chinese missions movement is more reflective and realistic regarding the goals and status of Chinese mission work. Mission workers and organizations began to realize their need for additional resources. The church is expecting a more credible and sustainable mission to emerge from these reflections. However, the concept and practices of member care are still in the initial stages of development.

Chinese Mission Workers' Perspectives on Member Care and the Status Quo

In the past fifty years, many Western mission professionals and psychologists have developed strategies to help Western mission workers improve their effectiveness and sustainability in cross-cultural ministry. Member care is understood as needed in different ways throughout the mission worker life cycle. This understanding has not yet been mainstreamed into Chinese mission strategy—but we believe this situation can and will change!

Peter, a mission worker with more than twenty years of experience, has a long-established support group around him. When asked if they had heard of the concept of member care, he responded:

> Most of the Chinese churches and mission workers do not even know the need for or existence of member care. They even believe that asking for help is a sign of weakness; especially to some people, seeking counseling is considered a sign of not being spiritual or having little faith. Member care can sometimes be viewed as lacking faith or as a secular service.

Lisa, Peter's wife, stated that mutual support groups are most helpful in the face of the various challenges that affect mission workers' finances, their marriage, and their children's education. People can share resources, information, and sometimes training opportunities through a support group.

Lisa added, that after a long time away from home, her relationship with the sending church was weakened and their support gradually decreased. However, she mentioned some churches in Wenzhou that maintained a more systematic and continuous vision for the mission. The mission workers they sent could regularly return for retreat, reequipping, and care.

Member care resources in the Chinese language and written by Chinese authors are limited. Some organizations are trying to translate Western materials. For instance, ChinaSource recently published a series of 25 translated articles on Chinese cross-cultural mission workers' member care (Chang and Fulton 2022). The good news is that Western member care models can be excellent references for Chinese member care practitioners to learn from as they create a contextual member care model for Chinese mission workers. Some Chinese sending churches have begun to adapt Western models to train member care facilitators, which provides structures and directions for the churches in China. A special website—"Running to Win: Resources for Chinese Workers"—went live in 2005 (China Member Care). A second and more recent website is "Resources for Workers and Senders" (China Member Care). Chinese workers have increased access to helpful resources online, including opportunities for participating virtually in mission-related events.

We are encouraged to note the growing number of online opportunities and resources by and for Chinese mission workers and senders. A main illustration is the migration of care-giving services, such as counseling, to the online realm in response to the COVID-19 pandemic. Chinese churches have adopted platforms like Zoom to provide virtual services, and a considerable number of Christians are proficient with the software. This creates the prospect for Chinese mission workers to participate in virtual support groups and avail themselves of essential information and resources, aligning with Shi's (2000) proposal for online training, coaching, and counseling services for mission workers in China.

Issues that Impact the Wellbeing and Effectiveness of Chinese Mission Workers

In this section, we discuss five major issues that impact the wellbeing and effectiveness of Chinese mission workers: (1) mission development stages, (2) Chinese culture and values, (3) the relationship between agencies, sending churches, and mission workers, (4) understanding host cultures, and (5) mission workers' skills.

1. Mission Development Stages in China

Chinese cross-cultural mission is still at the toddler stage. Mission workers are full of passion and curiosity regarding mission, but they have more enthusiasm than resources or equipment, which leads to high demands on the mission workers and low support or understanding. Rainbow's study indicates four typical characteristics of this developmental stage.

Limited in experience and highly passionate

According to the interviewees, most Chinese mission workers were inexperienced and seemingly expendable. They were highly passionate about sacrificing themselves for the gospel when they were sent, but usually that sentiment did not last long. An interviewee told us he was one of 50 young mission workers sent out from house churches. When he arrived on the mission field, he realized he did not know how to live there. He was willing to die for the Lord but did not know how to live for him. He felt lost in the challenging learning and adjustment process for a long time.

The mission workers' maturity should be considered as much as their calling. He told us a story about George, who attended a mission conference ten years ago when still a new believer. He was deeply moved by the message that "it was time for Chinese Christians to rise and pay the mission debts after the Western mission workers had sacrificed so much in China." He and his girlfriend joined an Asian mission agency and were quickly sent to the field. But they soon burned out because they rushed into service without a proper understanding of cross-cultural missions. They concluded that zeal without strategies and preparation resulted in the early end of their mission. Peter admitted that many mission workers like them left the mission field earlier than planned, and that some of the deaths there could likely have been prevented.

Unclear plans versus new plans

Some interviewees stated that when the short-term mission plan contradicted the long-term mission strategy, the mission suffered. A local mission leader in China shared one such story. Her organization leader in America asked the long-term mission team in China to organize an English summer camp to share the gospel during a politically sensitive time. She reported on the situation, but the leader told her to proceed regardless of the risk. Her team had to obey and tried their best to follow the request. But the police quickly found them and monitored them the whole time. They failed to accomplish the mission.

Some mission workers and organizations do not actually have a plan. Tim was recruited by a mission team with 30 other people after he graduated from seminary and was given a few months of training. Then, the team was sent out. Tim was confused because he did not know what to do next. He said the training was not systematic, and the teachers did not have cross-cultural mission experience. Some mission leaders believed it was an expression of faith for them to do mission work without a plan. They encouraged the mission workers to cross into the new field by themselves, like crossing a river step by step by probing for stones on which to stand. But Peter argues that the river can be too wide and the stones to step on might not even exist.

A restrictive religious law enacted in 2018 has largely limited local church activities and pushed one large church (5000 members) to step out and develop new missions elsewhere. After learning about previous failures, the church started taking new approaches. Sam, the senior, shared that they have called back their pioneer mission workers and allowed them to have a retreat at their home church, work on a slower schedule, and receive training in areas such as theology, culture, and work skills.

Low-budget and non-viable tentmaking approaches
This third characteristic of the current developmental stage is that mission organizations demand too much from mission workers and give them too little support. Peter believed that the main reasons why mission workers left their ministry were low financial support and high demands regarding the number of converts. For instance, Greg joined an Asian mission agency for eight years. He was sent into the mission field with a meager living budget. His leader told him and his wife that a simple life allowed them to fully depend on God and learn to be submissive in suffering.

The tentmaking mission strategy has been widely discussed in mission literature. Half of the participants in Rainbow's research were tentmakers. This group struggled with balancing ministry and family needs, especially financial needs. Pastor Sam adjusted the church's mission approach to send mission workers back into the field with better work skills. This was an intentional strategy so that workers and families would have less stress and more balanced lives. During our interview, John (one of the church's sent mission workers) shared the financial struggles he faced due to the low support budget. Two years later, he reported that he had developed a small business to sell local produce in his hometown. He has solved the financial problem and has a better connection with the local people.

More mission workers, few trainers and mentors
There is a lack of consistent and timely input from experienced colleagues who can function as role models, trainers, and mentors for mission workers. Lisa, a leader of a mission team of thirty members, said, "Having a mentor to help us when we encounter spiritual warfare is crucial. During such times, we need assurance and confirmation of our calling." However, finding experienced teachers and seasoned mentors is hard at this developmental stage. As Peter urged, "We need more 'bridges'—I mean the trainers and mentors who can integrate both cultures to help cross-cultural mission workers."

The good news is that after thirty years of mission experiences, more trainings for new generations in mission are available, based on past experiences and failures. Some mission advocates and trainers, for example, are facilitators for the "Perspectives on the World Christian Movement" course. In this course and in other trainings, they spend time covering the need for member care.

2. Chinese Culture and Values: Honor/Shame Culture
The second developmental area relates to culture and value issues. During our interviews, we noticed that the word *shame* arose frequently. The mission workers believe that understanding the characteristics of honor/shame cultures is significant for understanding themselves.

There are many ways to define shame and honor. One definition of honor is "the value of a person in his or her own eyes (that is, one's claim to worth) plus that person's value in the eyes of his or her social group. Honor is a claim to worth along with the social acknowledgment of worth" (Malina 2001, 30). Shame can be defined as "a negative public rating: the community thinks lowly of you. You are disconnected from the group" (Georges and Mark 2016, 16). Shame culture affects mission workers in the following ways.

Honor/shame culture and funding
In Chinese culture, it is shameful to ask for money. Peter said that in Chinese culture, fundraising is almost like begging for food, which is one of the most shameful things possible. One mission worker told us that he had to leave the field at one point because he ran out of money after working there for seven years. He decided to work for two years to make money before returning to the field. He said, "Taking money from others is like receiving alms from them. I don't know why I can't do that. It is hard to describe that feeling."

Honor/shame culture and identity
Identity is a multi-layered and complicated concept. In Chinese culture, identity involves a person's occupation and how other people view you. In our conversations with the mission workers, *identity struggle* was mentioned frequently. For Western mission workers in China, obtaining visas so as to gain a legitimate status can be relatively easy, and they are usually welcomed in China just because they are "foreigners." When they return to their home countries, finding a job or taking further education is usually not as difficult.

In contrast, Chinese mission workers are in quite different situations. Peter explained, first, most mission workers in China are poorly educated. Mission work is not an acceptable profession in many countries. The term "mission worker" is unfamiliar to most Chinese, including Christians. Therefore, most mission workers have difficulty explaining their occupation to their relatives, friends, and the local people they serve. Second, obtaining a visa for valid reasons and staying legally in a Muslim country is another challenge. Third, when mission workers return to China, it is hard to find jobs, for various reasons. There are no mission-related jobs in China, and their work experience as mission workers won't help them find a job. Furthermore, they cannot put mission experience in their resume for security reasons in China.

Honor/shame culture, parenting, and children's education
Among all the interviewees' concerns, children's education was the biggest. A father said he told her daughter, "If you could not get into a college, you would shame your parents, your God, and our prayer and financial supporters." When it was time for children to enter high school, they had to leave the mission field. Otherwise, it would be almost impossible for their children to catch up with the Chinese school system or pass the exam to enter college in China. Due to the enormous cost, very few mission workers in China would consider sending their children to study abroad. Moreover, no proper school was available in the mission field. Ben explained, "Most of our mission workers went to Muslim areas. The only choice for their children would be Muslim schools. The parents do not know what to do, or sometimes they neglect their children's education." A mission worker told us, "We lived in a remote area. We did not know how to teach our older son. Therefore, he was not able to finish high school. Because of this, there is no way that he would make it into any college. So we sent him to a non-accredited Christian school for further education. Although this school is not a real college, it is probably the best option since he is too young to be sent into society now. We do not know the next step in his life."

*Honor/shame culture affects how mission workers cope
with their stresses and pain*

Chinese believe people should not wash their (figurative) dirty linen in public. Not surprisingly, a mission worker told us that he would not describe his stress to another person if he could not trust that person, because he didn't want his image or his leader's reputation to be ruined. He continued, "I know a man who spoke of his weakness and was called back by the church for not being spiritual enough."

The shame culture affects how other Christians view mission workers' emotional stress. Peter was deeply hurt once by the people he served, and it was hard to stay in that place. But he could not tell anyone about his pain, for two reasons. First, he was afraid that people from his home church would think that his own immaturity caused this hurt. Second, he feared that the church counselor would question his qualifications as a mission worker. These factors contributed to his eventual and lengthy burnout, marked by ongoing distress and lack of support.

The Chinese church expects mission workers to be strong in facing *any* challenge. Susan shared that when she did not meet this expectation, she found it difficult to return to her home church. She lamented, "If mission workers take a break, they may lose financial support."

3. The Relationship between Agencies, Sending Churches, and Mission Workers

Forming strategic relationships, the third developmental area, is a prominent issue between church, agency, and mission workers. Interviewees felt especially pained in situations where they had to choose between their church and their agency—for example, if the church and the agency disagreed on mission objectives or strategies. In other cases, workers had to choose to whom they were primarily committed, and eventually, they had to end one or the other affiliation. Among the twenty mission workers we interviewed, four left the church for the agency, seven left the agency because of the power struggle between the church and the agency, and some were still caught in between.

Mission workers were thus often sandwiched between the tensions of churches and agencies. We believe harmonious relationships would be achievable if churches and agencies humbly prioritized common ground through adopting a broader perspective on the Kingdom of God.

4. Understanding Host Cultures

The fourth developmental area involves learning the new culture. Living a cross-cultural life can be exciting and challenging but also overwhelming without adequate preparation. Preparation to understand the new culture(s) and language(s) is essential. "A Bible school in China at one point even arranged Arabic-language courses in response to the students' overwhelming interest in mission to Muslims" (Brandner 2023, 356). In addition, most Chinese cross-cultural mission workers serve in developing countries and remote areas, especially Muslim areas, where the living environment can be impoverished and dangerous and where evangelism is restricted and risky. Hence, preparation to anticipate such conditions is essential.

Host cultures have enormous impact on mission workers' spiritual, physical, and interpersonal lives and personal wellbeing. Failing to follow the local culture's norms will make mission workers stand out in negative ways and will hinder them from evangelizing the people in that culture. It took Peter years to learn the host culture and its taboos. He recognized that the more he knew, the more he realized he was just a beginner. He stated, "We were so used to living in a no-boundary life with many more personal freedoms; especially when we became Christian, we cared less about cultural taboos … [so] if we do not pay attention, we can easily break their taboo."

Current Chinese cross-cultural study

Most of our interviewees reported their limited knowledge of the host culture, and none of them had experienced people teaching them. They had to navigate their cross-cultural lives themselves, sometimes at a painful cost.

Lisa, Peter's husband, said that at first, she refused to learn the local language. But soon she realized that "It is impossible to build trust and intimate relationships without speaking their language." Accordingly, she decided to learn the language. Lisa admitted, "Initially, I did not like their language and didn't want to learn it. I didn't like the way they treated women and children, and I always wanted to see them get 'saved' in hope that they would rebel against their culture."

The more mission workers know about people of different cultures, the less likely they are to suffer severe culture shock. Lisa stated, "I wanted to share the gospel with the local people, but I didn't understand their culture or their religion. I suffered a lot in vain. If I had learned it before arriving, I would have had a better transition." Lisa and Peter agreed that knowing local people's culture, customs, and taboos is essential for mission workers.

Lisa added, "If I could do it again, I would like to build better relationships, participate more in the community, do what people like to do, and learn more about their religious practices. I want to learn their language and know how to survive in a strange environment."

5. Mission Workers' Skills
The fifth developmental area involves workers' skills. The workers we interviewed faced similar challenges in a variety of cross-cultural settings, including spiritual warfare, an unknown culture, taboos, dangerous environments, food adaptation, and shame. Some thrived while others struggled. We believe that the following factors made the difference.

Theological knowledge and skills
Few people in China studied theology between 1950 and 1980 because no formal theological training existed. The Chinese government allowed "freedom" of Christian worship in 1980, but the Chinese church still faces the limitations regarding Christian education, including training in missiology.

However, most interviewees either underwent Chinese government seminary or underground seminary training. Four interviewees who joined a Western mission agency had more than four years each of formal seminary education. They indicated that the knowledge and skills gained from theological education are critical for church development and cross-cultural missions.

English language skills
Cross-cultural mission workers lived in an unfamiliar land as strangers, and they needed to connect with more experienced mission workers for guidance. In the international context, most resources are Western; therefore, knowing the English language can be a bridge for them to connect with those resources.

Jane met many other mission workers at international and largely English-speaking mission conferences. She attended a group therapy workshop and felt it was beneficial, especially when she realized that many others had similar experiences. However, she could not have benefited from that opportunity without her English language skills.

Chinese cross-cultural mission is still in an early stage and in need of both Chinese and international mentors and role models for its maturation. English language skills allowed people like Jane to connect with Western mission workers who could share their years of mission experience, insights, wisdom, and practice.

Applications: Supporting Chinese Mission Workers

Our interactions with mission workers show that in many cases (although certainly not all cases) Chinese understanding of mission and member care is very limited. As a movement, we need to slow down and focus on learning what cross-cultural mission entails in general and then the essential competencies and strategies needed in specific situations. We use two well-known Chinese proverbs to encourage mission workers, churches, and agency leaders to take the necessary time and effort to improve their practical understanding of mission and member care: "Haste makes waste" and "A beard well-lathered is half shaved."

We are encouraged by some of the shifts in understanding we are seeing and are cautiously optimistic that contextualized member care will take root in Chinese mission to the unreached. To achieve important shifts in member care, we urge mission leaders and mission workers alike to take time to learn, observe, and be equipped in the following areas.

Core Strategies

1. *Relevant training*

   Train bridgers. Send people to experienced international mission agencies to study, and ask the agencies to train them as bridgers who can integrate and contextualize their models with the current Chinese situation.

   Provide multi-dimensional and tailor-made training. The scope of the training received determines mission workers' abilities. Although theological training is essential, training in interpersonal skills, survival skills, and cross-cultural living is equally important. Tailor-made training is based specifically on where mission workers are going and what kind of ministry they will do.

2. *Personal equipping*

   Pursue personal development. Mission workers need to consider their personal and career development. They could take counseling courses and psychological tests to explore their personality and character strengths, study the language, get more training in areas related to mission and tentmaking, and develop interpersonal and conflict management skills.

   Make a long-term financial plan. Mission workers must budget and reserve funds for important items such as trips home, their children's education, retirement, and unexpected issues. We are called to be good and faithful stewards of God's resources—for the long-term.

Being wise with planning and financial reserves does not contradict faith in God.

Embrace the importance of self-care and mutual care. Self-care and mutual care are not a luxury. They are fundamental to the wellbeing and effectiveness of workers—and they are thoroughly biblical! Mission workers can learn to have some of their needs met in different ways in their new cross-cultural settings and to take better care of themselves physically, mentally, spiritually, and relationally. We believe that "resting well," maintaining a healthy connection with God and people, and encouraging family members and fellow workers day after day (Heb 3:13) are just as important as the "ministry" itself!

3. *Mission Motivations*

   Although one's personal calling is essential, having the right motivation for missions is also vital. When agencies try to mobilize churches and mission workers, they should explain to their audiences the blessings and challenges of cross-cultural ministry. This includes counting the cost of being mission workers, along with the kinds of suffering and stresses that they and family members accompanying them could encounter.

Core Resources

1. Hong Kong Association of Christian Missions. "Missionary Care." (宣教士关怀).
2. Cai, Rainbow. 2020b. "Chinese Missionary Experience: A Step Towards a Contextualized Member Care Model for Chinese Missionaries" (summary of Rainbow's doctoral dissertation).
3. Kingdom Sources for Christ. (让我们彼此相爱, 认识华人宣教士关顾).

Reflection and Discussion

1. Identify some of the main challenges and hindrances for Chinese missions, especially among unreached peoples.
2. What are some important member care strategies to support the wellbeing and effectiveness of Chinese mission workers?
3. Review the various resources and references in this chapter. List a few that you want to explore further.

References

Brandner, Tobias. 2023. "Chinese Missionaries in Cross-Cultural Overseas Mission: Emergence of a New Missionary Nation?" *International Bulletin of Mission Research* 47 (3): 356–369. https://doi.org/10.1177/23969393221138714.

Cai, Rainbow. 2020b. "Chinese Missionary Experience: A Step Towards a Contextualized Member Care Model for Chinese Missionaries" (summary of Rainbow's doctoral dissertation). https://drive.google.com/file/d/1v1jDRy3820H60rSBRPYH2L_KnD6U7yu9/view.

Cai, Weihong. 2020a. "Chinese Missionary Experiences: A Step Towards a Contextualized Member Care Model for Chinese Missionaries." PhD diss., Biola University (Order No. 27962647). Available from ProQuest Dissertations and Theses Global (2403987138). https://www.proquest.com/pqdtglobal/docview/2403987138/4291E057F6D446D2PQ/1?accountid=8624.

Chang, Ruth, and Brent Fulton. 2022. "Member Care Is Part of the Mission." *ChinaSource*, September 12, 2022. https://www.chinasource.org/resource-library/articles/member-care-is-part-of-the-mission/.

China Member Care. "Resources for Workers and Senders." https://sites.google.com/view/chinamembercare/home.

China Member Care. "Running to Win: Resources for Chinese Workers." https://chinamembercare.com/en/index.html.

Georges, Jayson, and Mark D. Baker. 2016. *Ministering in Honor-Shame Cultures: Biblical Foundations and Practical Essentials*. Westmont, IL: InterVarsity Press.

Hattaway, Paul, Brother Yun, Peter Xu, Peter Yongze, and Enoch Wang. 2003. *Back to Jerusalem: Three Chinese House Church Leaders Share Their Vision to Complete the Great Commission*. Westmont, IL: InterVarsity Press.

Hong Kong Association of Christian Missions. "Missionary Care." (宣教士关怀). https://hkacm.net/s_missionary-care/.

Kingdom Sources for Christ. (让我们彼此相爱，认识华人宣教士关顾). https://www.shen-guo.org/intro-to-chinese-missionary-care-s.html.

Malina, Bruce. 2001. *The New Testament World: Insights from Cultural Anthropology*. Louisville, KY: Westminster John Knox Press.

McPherson, Marisa. 2018. "Christianity in China." Council on Foreign Relations, October 11, 2018. https://www.cfr.org/backgrounder/christianity-china.

Phillips, Tom. 2014. "China on Course to Become 'World's Most Christian Nation' within 15 Years." *Telegraph*, April 19, 2014. https://www.telegraph.co.uk/news/worldnews/asia/china/10776023/China-on-course-to-become-worlds-most-Christian-nation-within-15-years.html.

Shi, Si. 2016. *Effects of Mission Sending Practice on Sustainable Deployment of Chinese Medical Missionaries* (Unpublished doctoral dissertation). Fuller Theological Seminary, California.

Shi, Qi. 2020. "Don't Leave, Stay Strong: Enabling Chinese Mission Workers to Thrive in the Context Where They Serve." PhD diss., School of Intercultural Studies, Fuller Theological Seminary. (See the condensed version from January 2024 including contact and website information here: https://drive.google.com/file/d/1omOXjpF-O8hYpFiSmVGTgQVXOkAo0No7/view?usp=sharing.)

Worldometer. "Top 20 Largest Countries by Population." https://www.worldometers.info/world-population/#top20.

Yang, Xiaoli. 2018. "The Rise of the Middle Kingdom: Reflections on Chinese Indigenous Mission Movement." *Australian Journal of Mission Studies* 12 (1): 37–43. https://theglobalchurchproject.com/middlekingdom/.

Rainbow Cai, **PhD,** studied intercultural education at Biola University. She has been a licensed counselor in China since 2003.

Raymond Yang, PhD, studied educational studies at Biola University. He has been a licensed counselor in China since 2008. Rainbow and Raymond married in 1995 and have run a counseling center in China since 2003. They have two sons who are currently working in the US.

Contextualizing Member Care

Lessons from Counseling Korean Mission Workers

Steve Sang-Cheol Moon and Mary Hee-Joo Moon

In this chapter we discuss how policies and programs for member care in missions need to follow the missiological principle of *contextualization*. Different social, cultural, and organizational settings, for example, must be considered in the development of relevant member care practices. Indeed, the importance of contextualization has been asserted in many ways over the last several decades as member care has developed and spread globally. In general, progress has been observed in member care by many Majority World leaders and specialists who initially learned member care from Western models. However, these efforts still need to go beyond simply learning from the West. Within Korean missions—one the largest mission movements globally—it is necessary to adjust policies, programs, resources and approaches for member care in line with both the home and host cultures of mission workers. Interspersed with our perspectives, we overview several significant needs identified in our experience of counseling Korean mission workers.

Characteristics of Home Culture Affecting Korean Mission Workers

Reflecting the cultural norms of Koreans in general, Korean churches are both relationship-oriented and task-oriented. Traditionally, the cultural expectations of Korean society and churches have been relationship-oriented. But over the years, modernization has dramatically changed the cultural landscape. With this coexistence of opposite norms and expectations in Korean culture, complex cultural dynamics affect mission workers' understanding of what their senders and funders expect—which could, in turn, be quite different from the cultural expectations of the people they are serving in their host country.

In many cases, we have seen how the *relationship-oriented* aspect of Korean culture and churches functions in a positive way. When mission workers are in a crisis due to natural disasters, terrorism, or abduction, their churches tend to respond with proper remedies and follow-up programs in accordance with their contingency plans. Financial aid for the mission workers' psychological treatment and counseling services is provided willingly. Church members show hospitality to workers who are suffering through a crisis. Such compassionate support for them and their families has been considered normative among Korean churches in general.

The relational dynamics of Korean mission workers tend to be more complex and subtle than those of Western counterparts, characterized by more hierarchical understandings of interpersonal relationships. The rigid understanding of senior-junior relations among workers stands in the way of their lateral thinking because the vertical understanding works negatively among workers even within the same mission agency or denomination. We have observed clashes of different perspectives and expectations between senior and junior mission workers. This characteristic of collective culture demands more caution, and thus people are afraid of sharing their feelings when they face such problems. Concerns about misunderstandings prevent them from sharing their negative feelings, which accumulate and can lead to psychological burnout. Conflict with fellow workers has been one of the leading reasons for attrition in Korean missions (Moon 2015, 137; Moon et al. 2015, 104). This phenomenon continues to be observed even in this globalized age.

Contemporary Koreans tend to also be *task-oriented*, with social pressures for achievement and successful performance driving this trend. The church culture wherein Korean mission workers interact with their senders and supporters has been affected, to a significant degree, by the standards and expectations of society. The mindset of the church growth movement, which emphasizes numerical growth, still lingers as an essential part of ministry dedication. Evaluation of services from a managerial perspective can be intimidating and can impede efforts at member care on the part of mission workers and mission leaders.

Some cases of burnout among Korean mission workers reveal the negative impacts of task orientation on their overall health and that of their families. The drive to work, often while neglecting the importance of self-care, can result in family conflicts as well as burnout. One of us (Steve) is a good example of recovery from neglecting self-care and the resulting burnout that he experienced at age 40. Mary was instrumental in facilitating his restoration process in collaboration with other specialists. Now we are grateful to be used in the ministry of healing and restoration for other mission workers and their children.

Relational and task orientations (including internal and external expectations) can thus have both positive and negative impacts on mission workers' lives and need to be understood for developing contextualized member care. This need also applies to contextualizing member care in other cultures.

Contextualizing Member Care Programs

Korean member care ministries are indebted to Western specialists for developing the foundational philosophy and mindset of member care as well as for their professional knowledge and expertise in the initial developmental stage. Marjorie Foyle, Laura Mae Gardner, David Pollock, Lois Dodds, Kelly and Michèle O'Donnell, and Karen Carr have contributed significantly to the development of member care ministries through their seminars and publications for Korean mission leaders and workers. It has been a pleasure for us to meet and work with these dedicated member care professionals over the course of many years! Building on this globally shared foundation, our member care programs have moved forward with the emergence of Korean member care specialists and the input of Korean mission workers and their families, which has contributed to raising the overall relevance of member care practices. More contextualized approaches and programs are needed, however, by sending groups and in collaboration with others.

Awareness Programs for Sending Churches

Various mission awareness programs are offered by mission agencies and local churches in Korea. The main purpose of such programs is to facilitate Christians' participation in mission activities as either a future worker or a supporter. A growing number of churches and mission agencies emphasize the importance of member care through their programs. But others are still emphasizing the need for what we believe can be an unhealthy "heroic" sacrifice by workers. More must be done to raise the awareness of member care issues among sending churches in Korea.

Short-term mission programs by Korean churches should likewise highlight the need to care for mission workers and their families and resist the excessive and unhealthy expectations often placed on workers and families to be super-spiritual and always strong while not dealing with their personal weaknesses realistically. Field-based outreach programs should highlight the vulnerable realities of mission life that require empathetic listening and observation. The face-saving culture of Confucian tradition seems to hinder openly acknowledging the realities of life in missions. This cultural background calls for nuanced approaches in contextualizing awareness programs in such a way that they may not only be culturally relevant but also transform existing cultural frameworks.

An example of such a field-based program can be found in several local churches. We have appreciated how some church members spend their vacation time in the field helping mission kids (MKs) to familiarize them with the Korean language and history. Visiting teachers try to make up for the MKs' weaknesses in various subjects so that they can prepare well for the university entrance exams. The volunteer teachers effectively address the idiosyncratic Korean realities that demand diligent, focused efforts by both mission parents and children, considering that the Korean educational system drives a high level of competition among students. With this kind of support, more Korean MKs will enjoy a smoother reentry into the Korean educational system and Korean society in general.

Training Programs for Member Care Workers
In Korea, training for member care workers has been largely dependent on the academic degree programs of Christian universities, several of which offer doctoral programs in counseling psychology. But the particularities of member care for mission workers do not seem to be professionally addressed in these degree programs, with only general psychological treatments applied in counseling services for workers. The specific issues and challenges of mission life should be studied, with help from the theories and treatments of cross-cultural psychology.

The Korean Member Care Network (KMCN) has been offering a training program since 2021 with Steve having served a term as program director and Mary serving as one of the speakers. The program is composed of three curricular stages that aim to equip potential member care workers with basic mindsets and skills to care for mission families. People interested in learning more about member care have received this training. Notably, some field workers have also joined this online training program as preparation to serve as caregivers for younger and less experienced workers in the field.

Korean mission work is characterized by an emphasis on frontier missions that require great sacrifice and commitment on the part of workers. For example, a 2012 survey reported that 41 percent of Korean missionaries were involved in frontier missions. A 2008 survey found that over 42 percent of Korean missionaries were working in either the Islamic bloc (23.2 percent) or China or other Communist countries (19.4 percent) (Moon 2016, 39, 41). The hostage incident involving Korean Christians in Afghanistan in 2007 also illustrated the potential dangers faced by Korean mission workers in creative access nations (Moon 2016, 96, 108, 243–250). In view of this major and bold mission commitment, more adapted approaches and caregivers are needed for mission workers and families in these particularly stressful and isolating contexts. The example of KMCN's training program illustrates growing awareness of the need for member care among frontier mission workers and staff members of mission agencies. In this training program, books by Western experts have been used effectively, sharing a sense of continuity in learning how to do member care and crossing barriers of cultures and organizations. Two translated books were used for this program: *Doing Member Care Well* (O'Donnell 2002) and *Trauma and Resilience* (Schaefer and Schaefer 2016).

The training provided by KMCN intentionally incorporates a discussion session after the lecture on each day of the online program. The discussion topics and questions effectively address many specific realities and issues that Korean mission workers and their children face. The shared experiences and insights of the Western-influenced and other international authors were helpful in dealing with those issues, but the participants also wanted to probe in-depth the particularities of Korean realities in these challenging contexts, interacting further with Korean specialists in member care. This kind of interaction helped to contextualize member care strategies (including mutual care, self-care, and specialist care) and enabled a healthy sense of balance between global and the local perspectives in pursuing excellence in member care services.

Debriefing Programs for Mission Workers

The Korean missions circle is also indebted to Western specialists and their organizations in terms of developing further its debriefing programs adapted from Western models. Korean mission agencies initially used Western programs for debriefing but later contextualized and optimized the debriefing programs to reflect the specific needs and requests of Korean mission workers.

Mary's doctoral dissertation was devoted to developing a debriefing program for a small, homogeneous group setting of Korean mission workers that could run for three days (Moon 2018). Not only field workers but also member care specialists gave feedback in the process of developing this program. Its effectiveness was measured in terms of raising the sense of spiritual wellbeing, with tests being administered before and after the debriefing program. The results of the measures verified the effectiveness and durability of the treatment (Moon 2018). More important than these experimental findings are the actual responses from mission workers who have participated in this program. Korean mission workers in the Philippines, Malaysia, and other countries, as well as member care specialists, are using this program in their ministry contexts according to the guidelines provided by the leader workshop and the manual. To date, this debriefing program has been used mainly by member care specialists, but it could also be used by peer mission workers in mutual care systems.

Korean mission workers tend to depend too much on specialist or professional care, not recognizing the need for self-care and mutual care (Moon 2016, 131). Many care issues could and should be addressed through mutual care. To facilitate mutual care among workers, peer debriefing should be facilitated. Korean mission workers need to overcome the baggage of a face-saving culture that inhibits the free flow of sharing emotional burdens and frustrations. They can do so through peer debriefing programs as well as through encouraging informal, supportive relationships for mutual support.

In some cases, however, mission workers who have had traumatic experiences may need to request a debriefing offered by a specialist instead of by a leader of the mission agency. That is because trauma healing may demand professional expertise and a clear understanding of confidentiality. Moreover, in the case of other traumas caused by interpersonal conflicts, organizational management, or high levels of stress in general, mission agencies and sending churches are often part of the problem. Consequently, the neutral perspective of external specialists is needed to address such situations.

When intervening in traumatic incidents, debriefers and counselors need to figure out the best timing for interventions. Sometimes the earliest possible intervention is not helpful because trauma specialists need to wait and watch how those who experienced the trauma are going through the processes of stabilization and normalization after their traumatic experience.

Further efforts to provide contextualized and optimized services are needed in trauma care and debriefing programs, building on the accumulated and shared foundation of expertise in member care services.

Contextual Issues Identified Through Counseling Cases

Korean mission workers' overall tendency to be task-oriented regarding their personal and psychological problems is addressed in counseling cases more often than other issues. The inner being of Korean mission workers tends to be suppressed by external expectations. These cultural and structural expectations must be more deeply understood to develop healthy ways to alleviate the pressures that work against their wellbeing and effectiveness as mission workers.

Psychological Traits and Ministry Expectations

Our general sense is that many Korean mission workers come from dysfunctional family backgrounds, that many of them have a dramatic experience of conversion, and that this experience can lead to a passionate commitment to mission service in later years. When they face stressful situations in the mission field, however, the workers' unresolved family of origin and psychological problems often surface as they experience conflicts with their spouse, children, or coworkers who frustrate them. Sometimes their childhood experiences with their parents or authority figures are reflected in their relationships with the pastors of the sending church or leaders of the sending agency.

The idealized images that mission workers themselves often embrace, as mentioned earlier, can hinder them from living their lives confidently, because those images force them to abide by the expectations of the churches or others. This in turn leads to a conflicted and hypocritical life without consistency of self-identity as well as to burnout (Kyong-Jin Cho 2020). The dissonance between expectations and realities is at the root of the problem in many cases.

Further exacerbating this cultural trend, supporting churches tend to view mission workers as highly dedicated and mature Christians. When church leaders see them making mistakes or wrong decisions, they find it hard to forgive them and sometimes decide to terminate their support. Knowing this, mission workers usually try to appear as if all is fine, for fear of making mistakes. Many try to contain their difficulties within themselves, which creates immense internal stress.

Conflicting Cultural Expectations of the Host and Home Cultures
The cultural characteristics of the host country sometimes restrict freedom to engage in social activities that are accepted in the home country. This clash of cultural expectations is most explicit in Islamic countries.

Female mission workers (both single and married), for instance, find it hard to travel or work outside by themselves. In many cases, they must be accompanied by male colleagues to be safe and culturally relevant. Single female workers are reluctant to ask for a male worker's help when needed. Sometimes, local female friends can help a female mission worker in a relevant way, but such help is not always available.

Teenagers can freely walk around outdoors in Korea, and public transportation and security are safe and stable. Young people can play with their friends outside their home. In many mission fields, however, MKs face restrictions of their freedom because they depend on their parents for rides to visit or meet with their friends. This kind of limitation tends to constrain their growth as independent persons, and when they enter university in Korea or the United States, suddenly they are expected to figure out ways to live independently. The pressures of entry into a third country or reentry into the home country frustrate them even more, with the clashes of cultures and the culture shock that often ensue. These are hard realities and not just theoretical problems facing many MKs. Published stories and verbal accounts of adult MKs often testify to how they overcame these challenges in their process of entry and reentry.

Conflicting Perspectives of Mission Workers and Their Children
In our experience, Korean mission workers can tend to send a signal to their children that they should become independent both psychologically and financially as early as possible. MKs know this expectation of their parents, but their environments may not work positively to make independence possible. Many parents send a double message by overly controlling the educational path of their children. Therefore, this conflicting expectation results in a low level of autonomy among MKs even when they become adults.

Korean MKs can feel pressure to avoid freely expressing their difficulties in matters of adjustment at school or peer relationships, among others. They also can be very hesitant to freely share their wishes and desires for themselves because they know their parents are depending on others' support for their livelihood and ministry. In many mission families, ministry needs are prioritized over family needs, which also intimidates MKs into not voicing their needs. In some cases, MKs even find it hard to identify what they want and need before sharing it with others because they have suppressed these thoughts for such a long time. After an extended period of suppression and silence, some older teens begin to question and be at a loss about what to do about the problem in their lives that originated with their parents' decision to become mission workers.

In many cases, MKs, especially those who attend boarding school, tend not to share what they feel deeply with their parents. They communicate only superficially and do not express the deep psychological conflicts present in their inner being.

Mutual Care and Confidentiality
In the collective cultural setting of Korea, confidentiality (i.e., protecting and not sharing personal information) is not valued sufficiently. Often, transparency is emphasized so strongly that confidentiality is sacrificed for it. Christian leaders try to know what is going on among people, but sometimes they do not pay attention to the cultural value of confidentiality among the younger generations in the contemporary Korean society.

In the mission field, Korean mission workers find it hard to share their frustrations and difficulties with colleagues, for fear that their story will leak out. Such fear gets in the way of mutual sharing and care and tends to aggravate the problem, causing it to develop into a more serious one later. In some cases, Korean workers spend extensive time pursuing healing and restoration. If a mode of mutual care could be modeled and cultivated among workers in the field, much of the pressure would be eased before it could become serious.

Sometimes mission workers are concerned about the counseling report on them that will be provided to the executives and other leaders of their mission agencies. Counseling reports need a strict boundary of confidentiality within a mission agency so that only a small number of leaders known to the counselee are able to refer to them. Any records of counseling interactions must also be kept secure, as is required in professional counseling practice. A trusting relationship among the people involved and a sense of psychological safety within the mission agency must be ensured for the workers who receive counseling services.

Cultural Differences in the Self-Care of Mission Workers
Many Korean mission workers seem to feel a certain level of guilt about self-care. They tend to think they should not spend money for family travels or purposes other than ministry obligations, and they also feel guilty or

uncomfortable about having a time of rest and restoration. To many Korean workers, having a furlough is considered a luxury.

Experienced Western experts have shown that it is both wise and realistic to balance work and rest. A balanced posture is best reinforced by modeling from top mission leadership right through the mission agency's system. Such a perspective would support the health and soundness, in both body and soul, of workers who are vulnerable to workaholism and the unresolved chronic stress that leads to burnout.

Conclusion

This summary of the psychological issues faced by Korean mission workers reminds us that overall cultural characteristics and contextual dynamics impact the practice of member care for workers. These phenomena are not simply psychological matters related to individual mission workers; they also need to be understood in light of the broad cultural and intercultural dynamics of the places where they work. Therefore, contextualized approaches of member care services are crucial, and there should be more efforts to optimize programs and services of debriefing, counseling, and training, taking into consideration this principle of contextualization. Building on the shared expertise of member care efforts at the global level, member care specialists and workers need to go the extra mile to develop and provide services based on in-depth understanding of the cultural and psychological dynamics of mission service.

The complicated challenges of member care in mission cannot be resolved solely by the efforts of counselors; rather, they require the orchestrated efforts of all people involved in mission movements to transform restrictive cultural frameworks and mindsets. Overall awareness of member care issues must be raised among churches and mission agencies in Korea.

In this ever-globalizing world, a *glocal* perspective for member care (that is, combining the global and local) will be increasingly relevant. As we have shared and illustrated throughout this chapter, context-specific realities and issues should be reflected in member care policies and practices, building on the globally accumulated body of knowledge and expertise. This perspective is ultimately rooted in an incarnational approach to gospel ministry, as exemplified by the apostle Paul: "To the weak I became weak, to win the weak. I have become all things to all men so that by all possible means I might save some. I do all this for the sake of the gospel, that I may share in its blessings" (1 Cor 9:22–23).

Applications: Contextualizing Member Care for Koreans

Core Strategies

1. Plan and run an awareness seminar on member care for mission workers, inviting leaders of local churches.
2. Invite mission workers and/or MKs to a listening session hosted by your mission agency or local church and encourage them to share freely their burdens and suggestions for member care. Then, involve adults and youth in a co-creative process to find solutions to meet the expressed needs.
3. Provide mission workers and MKs with information on available debriefing and counseling services offered by member care organizations.

Core Resources

1. Jonathan Bonk, ed. 2013. *Family Accountability in Missions: Korean and Western Case Studies*.
2. Korea Member Care Network. This website offers important resources on networking and collaboration for member care. Introductory information and materials on member care organizations and their ministry programs are available.
3. Wonsuk Ma and Kyo Sung Ahn, eds. 2015. *Korean Church, God's Mission, Global Christianity*.

Reflection and Discussion

1. How can we help mission workers to balance work and rest in the mission field? List three practical ways that are relevant for your setting(s).
2. How can we encourage MKs to be more autonomous in their decision making and be themselves as they grow? Discuss how this can be an important part of their development and well-being, instead of being perceived as primarily a "Western" cultural value.
3. How can we raise the awareness of member care issues for mission workers among pastors and church leaders? Identify a few challenges and suggestions given in this chapter.

References

Bonk, Jonathan, ed. 2013. *Family Accountability in Missions: Korean and Western Case Studies*. New Haven: OMSC Publications.

Korea Member Care Network. https://kmcn.or.kr/.

Kyong-Jin Cho, Hannah. 2020. *Understanding Burnout Recovery Among Native-Born Korean Missionaries*. Eugene, OR: Pickwick Publications (summary article: https://krim.org/cmt-17-5-1/). https://ebooks.faithlife.com/product/193659/understanding-burnout-recovery-among-native-born-korean-missionaries.

Ma, Wonsuk, and Kyo Sung Ahn, eds. 2015. *Korean Church, God's Mission, Global Christianity*. Oxford: Regnum.

Moon, Mary Hee-Joo. 2018. "Yungjuk Anyunggam Jeungjin Eul Uihan Sunkyosa Jipdan Simli Debriefing Program Gaebal: Kidokkyojuk Iyagichiryo Kwanjumesu" (Program Development for Group Psychological Debriefing to Raise the Sense of Spiritual Well-being for Missionaries: From the Perspective of a Christian Storytelling Therapy). PhD diss., Torch-Trinity Graduate University, Seoul, South Korea.

Moon, Steve Sang-Cheol. 2015. "Missionary Attrition in Korea: Opinions of Agency Executives." In *Too Valuable to Lose: Exploring the Cause and Cures of Missionary Attrition*, edited by William D. Taylor, 129–142. Pasadena, CA: William Carey Library.

Moon, Steve Sang-Cheol. 2016. *The Korean Missionary Movement: Dynamics and Trends, 1988–2013*. Pasadena, CA: William Carey Library.

Moon, Steve Sang-Cheol, Chaneui Park, Kyungsup Shin, Mary Hee-Joo Moon, and Nansook Cho. 2015. *Hankuk Sunkyosa Member Care Kaesun Bangan* (Ways to Improve Member Care for Korean Missionaries). Seoul: Korea Research Institute for Mission.

O'Donnell, Kelly, ed. 2002. *Doing Member Care Well: Perspectives and Practices from Around the World*. Pasadena, CA: William Carey Library. https://passionexchange.files.wordpress.com/2008/10/doingmembercarewell.pdf.

Schaefer, Frauke C., and Charles A. Schaefer. eds. 2016. *Trauma and Resilience, A Handbook: Effectively Supporting Those Who Serve God*. Frauke C. Schaefer, MD, Inc. http://www.traumaresilience.com/.

Steve Sang-Cheol Moon, PhD, studied Intercultural Studies at Trinity Evangelical Divinity School. He is the Founder and CEO of the Charis Institute for Intercultural Studies and professor and director in the PhD program in Intercultural Studies at Grace Mission University.

Mary Hee-Joo Moon, PhD, studied Christian Counseling at Torch-Trinity Graduate University. She is president and CEO of Eirene Counseling and professor and director in the PhD program in Counseling Psychology at Grace Mission University.

Steve and Mary are married and blessed with two grown children (one married daughter and one son) and one grandson. They live in Seoul, South Korea. Their passion is to continue to serve as wounded healers for mission workers and their children in the years ahead.

> # 8

Ministry in the Diaspora

Supporting Philippine Christians in the Middle East and Hong Kong

Grace Margaret Alag and Jorge de Ramos

The *World Development Report* estimates that there were around 281 million international migrants (i.e., people living in a country other than the one in which they were born) in the world in 2020, which equates to 3.6 percent of the global population. This total is 128 million more than in 1990 and over three times the estimated number in 1970 (International Organization for Migration 2022). There are also over 117 million displaced or stateless people in 134 countries or territories (United Nations High Commissioner for Refugees 2023). Understanding the shifts and emerging trends in migration and displacement helps us make sense of the changing world and plan for the future. It also helps us in strategizing how we live and work among unreached peoples.

In this chapter, we share some of our experiences supporting Christian Overseas Filipino Workers (OFWs) located in two countries, in the Middle East (Grace) and in Hong Kong (Jorge). Most of these workers relocate for economic reasons and need supportive care. Most also desire to be salt and light as Christians. First, Grace describes her transition from her member care focus on Filipino and other mission workers to also include identifying and ministering to the needs of OFWs. Her work over the past 10 years, although fraught with expected and unexpected challenges, has opened many new opportunities for ministry in the Middle East and beyond, including co-founding Heartstream Resources in the Philippines. After that, Jorge discusses the partnership between a mission agency and his sending church to establish a business-as-mission enterprise that placed OFWs in Hong Kong. He describes the holistic care emphasis of the business plan—from recruitment to returning home—and some of the struggles and successes in providing such care.

The human diaspora will only increase in the coming years and decades. The church and mission community will thus continue to have many new opportunities to build relationships with and minister among diaspora people and to support Christian workers among them.

The 2022 survey of OFWs estimates that 1.96 million Filipinos worked abroad during the period from April to September 2022 (Philippines Statistics Authority 2023). This number has steadily increased. In his article, "Modern Filipino Diaspora," Daniel Anne Nepomuceno (2009) indicated that this scenario, according to a report by the Philippine Institute for Development Studies (PIDS), reflects the global contemporary diaspora. Citing the PIDS study (2008), he explains that the modern diaspora involves migration to another country for economic reasons. It also more broadly relates to the movement of any population sharing common ethnic identity who was either forced to leave or voluntarily left their settled territory and became residents in areas often far removed from their former land.

Grace's Crossing into the Middle East: New Cultures, Less Structure, New Priorities

In 2013, I became one of this growing number of OFWs as a dependent spouse of a Filipino engineer working in the oil and gas industry in the Middle East. In this chapter, I share my unique perspective as a Filipina, informed by my journey as a global worker, who is also a member care practitioner and advocate. My journey in member care, published by *Asian Missions Advance* (Alag 2022), tells how God moved me from serving in church ministry to serving cross-cultural workers through member care.

I was so excited to move to the Middle East and join my husband! We had been apart for seven years and had seen each other for just one month each year. Yet I was also filled with questions about how I would continue to pursue my calling to member care. Transitions, setting up a new life, cultural adjustments, and learning new rules of living overwhelmed me. My previous yearly visits helped me understand many aspects of Islamic life, but there were still many norms that I learned only through cultural immersion.

As I transitioned from a highly structured work and ministry environment, my first struggle was having far less structure for my day. My days, weeks, and months used to be well-defined with meetings, teaching schedules, seminars, and events in different areas. Now my world and work were much less structured. I became a spouse first and a person in ministry second. Later, within a few months of relocating, I became the partner development coordinator for a popular Christian television program, the mother company of the training organization which I had served for twelve years. My role was to promote its ministries, invite new partners, and organize events for our president and his ministry team in our first host country.

Yet in my heart, the desire to continue caring for global workers continued unabated. Many of these workers were in the 10/40 window countries where I had helped to deploy them. This was my life call, my passion. How would I pursue my call and passion where I was? What did member care look like for me in the Middle East and for these global workers in Asia, Africa, and other locations? I thank God for the technology that kept me in touch with many of them via emails, Facebook, Messenger, Skype, and (later) Zoom.

Transitions into Two Middle Eastern Countries in Ten Years

Transitions in the inner core
"Who am I now?" I wondered. For twelve years, I carried a card that introduced me according to my position and function in my organization. Now, I was a dependent spouse doing ministry from home.

How could I begin to serve both Christian and non-Christian OFWs? Integration as a couple into a faith community was the priority. We made new friends, joined a Bible study and fellowship group that met weekly, and regularly attended worship services. We discovered a vibrant Christian presence in the two nations where we lived and worked, which allowed gatherings even though in a controlled manner. Lois and Larry Dodds, in their paper "Am I Still Me? Changing the Core Self to Fit a New Cultural Context" (2003), helped me grapple with the question, "Who am I now?" It spoke loudly to my struggles in identity and loss of self-esteem, which resulted from the loss of familiar reference groups and relationships. Their paper explores the reason for and the process of change, and it suggests strategies for shoring up the shifting self.

I had to give up the urge to conduct seminars about member care. I discovered that almost no one knew what member care was all about, even among the pastors and church leaders. So I felt I was back to ground zero in doing any member care–related trainings.

Grief and loss
Here, I will take a moment to look back at my days of preparation prior to transitioning into the Middle East. I experienced grief that could not find proper expression due to my many responsibilities and things I wanted to accomplish. Preparing for the transition included selling my home, which involved numerous details of how to dispose of precious furniture and store personal belongings. Then in January 2013, the year of my move to the

Middle East, we lost my older sister to chronic kidney disease. There were layers upon layers of grief. I felt like the psalmist who said in anguish, "Deep calls to deep in the roar of your waterfalls; all your waves and breakers have swept over me" (Ps 42:7). It was so hard to handle the tragic loss of my dear sister while trying to navigate all the practical and emotional challenges of preparing to move!

My husband and I also experienced how difficult it was to grieve from a distance when we lost close relatives. This was especially hard because we could not go home to pay our respects due to work and financial constraints.

Challenges for OFWs
In both Middle Eastern countries, the OFWs have varying skills, educational attainment, and professional levels. Christian faith communities reflect a similar variety. I love the merry mix of my *kababayan* (compatriots) in Bible study groups and services. I met household workers who are church leaders. They study God's word diligently, learn how to share the gospel, and grow to lead various ministries. They are the best evangelists as they can reach and connect with nationals in their own homes. Many of them, I discovered, were professionals and teachers in the Philippines but were driven to seek work overseas, mostly as domestic helpers, to earn more money for their families. Employers strongly preferred Filipinos because of their education, ability to understand and speak English, good hygiene, and amiable and caring dispositions. These qualities endeared them to the families they served.

Filipinos were also the preferred nationality for hospitality services and sales. Most Filipino workers were hard-working and resilient, with great perseverance. Their hopes were anchored in providing for the education of their children. However, this dynamic also brought about a tendency to give everything to their children in order to make up for their long daily absence from home. They worked hard to buy designer clothes, brand-name shoes, and the newest mobile phones for their families. Sadly, the families did not fully appreciate the sacrifices needed to make these things possible. I met workers with huge debt problems, reflecting the need for financial literacy education.

Another common OFW life challenge was their visa situation, which was dependent on the company or employer and the job offered. Many times, the contract they signed in the Philippines was not for the job they ended up doing. Not having any alternative, they would stay and accept their situation and the low salary. The church to which I belong is composed of migrant workers and served by migrant workers as well. They have full-time jobs so that they can stay in the country and serve the church, but these demands have had an impact on their work-life balance. Just as traditional harvest workers experience stress, struggles, and sacrifices, or what I call the three S's, so do OFW tentmakers in the Middle East. Perhaps a handful of workers have received formal ministry schooling, and thankfully, formal programs are being offered online or in person in Middle Eastern countries. But the problem is the lack of time for such studies.

OFWs in general do not have their families with them, due to the various rules and laws governing who qualifies to apply for residence visas for their families. This creates the emotional cost of being away from one's family. I met some OFWs who had two families, the legal one back home and another partner in the host country. Sadly, even Christian OFWs are tempted in this area. This practice is highly prohibited in the host country, but they found ways to circumvent the laws.

I believe the dilemma of so many social, emotional, spiritual, and moral problems relates to the limited discipleship that those who professed to be Christians received in the homeland prior to their migration. If they became Christians in the Middle East, then the challenge concerned their discipleship in the host country. Some factors, such as the spiritual, moral, and emotional state of their marriage and family before migration, motives for migrating, and preparation for service or work, also had great impact on their overall adjustment and thriving. The three-volume series *Global Servants: Cross-Cultural Humanitarian Heroes* (Dodds, Gardner, and Chen 2011) provides very helpful information in preparing and caring for global workers. I apply their concepts to the lives of the general expatriate population, both within and outside Christian faith communities.

Flowing into OFW Care
I learned that it took one or two years of developing relationships before one could do any significant ministry with OFWs. In both Middle Eastern countries, having weekly Bible studies and fellowships in small groups allowed my husband and me to get to know people in a deeper way. They shared their struggles at work, concerns with family members who were mostly in the Philippines, decision-making difficulties, relationship problems, and conflicts. Sharing in the context of studying God's word allowed us to interact about our personal journeys, both successes and failures. Informally, they would seek us out for counseling on work or life issues. My husband's involvement with basketball teams allowed him to develop friendships further. He and I saw clearly that forming relationships was the key. I learned that conducting seminars was not the priority. I simply had to live with and

be one of them, be a learner, listen, and open my eyes to the realities of life overseas. I was no different from them. I relished the times when I listened to stories from those who have worked in the host country for up to 30 years. They had different experiences and realities; some were blessed with benevolent employers but, sadly, many were not. Being among them as one like them soon resulted in their discovery that I actually had Bible training and could lead Bible studies effectively.

Being vulnerable was another key to acceptance. Though we were both older than most, we did not try to claim an expert role or superior wisdom. We also shared our failures and mistakes in life choices. Many times, OFWs shared their wisdom in navigating life struggles. Caring by listening without judgment was something they were hungry for. We declared our home to be "your home away from home," often inviting them for dinner. In church, we preferred to play a "Barnabas" role instead of taking on formal church leadership.

I gained deeper understanding that being a faithful *presence* had a more lasting impact than one's expertise or knowledge, biblical or otherwise. Of course, all of one's life experiences help to shape one's sharing and teaching. But in forming long-lasting relationships, our availability, non-judgmental listening ears, and tangible ways of caring such as sharing meals meant so much more. I also thank our mentors in spiritual direction, colleagues from Heartstream, New Zealand who imparted to us their program for practicing the various spiritual disciplines, which complemented my spiritual formation focus in my doctoral program. We were able to conduct a special gathering—the Retreat in Everyday Living program—in our first host city with some 30 participants. Through it all, the Heartstream philosophy of ministering to the whole person has been my guide for the past 23 years in member care. The focus on being rather than doing was a major shift in my member care approach. I invited participants to embrace a lifestyle of member care and minister from the overflow of their life in Christ rather than treating it as just an activity in their organization, so that they could take this lifestyle wherever the Lord takes them in their journey.

Recognition and Broader Scope

After two years of integration in the first host country, I was invited by the associate pastor of our church to become a part of the pulpit ministry. My assignment was to preach once a month and to be open to invitations from their outreaches in the country's six major cities. In our second country, I have also been invited to teach and preach in Bible studies and churches.

Expanding to other churches' invitations
In addition to our local church, my involvement as partner development coordinator opened relationships with other churches. Consequently, I received invitations to preach, conduct seminars, and facilitate spiritual retreats. Friendships with pastors and their wives developed beyond just serving as preacher or teacher. Again, we spent time listening to them and their ministry concerns, including various issues related to their children, leadership, and relationships. We have forged friendships that last to this day.

Referrals of difficult cases
One reality that ministers in both host nations faced was the lack of Filipino professional counselors. Although there were practicing mental health professionals working with the expatriate community, none were Filipino. Moreover, OFWs showed great reluctance to approach them also due to the preconceived notion that seeing them, in spite of confidentiality, might somehow show up in their employment record and be viewed negatively by their companies. Furthermore, many pastors were reluctant to handle difficult cases because they were not trained in counseling. Through informal referrals, some cases were brought to my attention as pastors sought help and direction. I had to define my role not as a professional counselor but as someone who was willing to listen and help people construct a healing strategy. I discussed options with them, including online counseling if viable. I also encouraged seeing professional mental health practitioners, especially in cases of intended or attempted self-harm by loved ones. One other opportunity was to help organize basic counseling seminars in two major cities, bringing together church pastors and workers from different churches.

Blessings and opportunities
Although civil society organizations and government entities are responding to the various concerns of the Filipino expatriate community, there remain huge gaps in addressing their spiritual and emotional needs. Thus, the opportunities to expand member care and reach OFWs, especially in crisis situations, are great. The challenge has been to define one's boundaries in such a vast ocean of need. In our first city of residence, I was able to establish a connection with the Philippine embassy, which allowed access to the Filipino "distressed wards" under their care. "Distressed ward" is the preferred term for people who seek shelter in the embassy to escape difficult or abusive employment situations, mostly involving domestic helpers. The ambassador

in the first host country was active in involving the faith community to care for distressed wards. There were tangible needs but also needs for emotional and spiritual healing. I encouraged visits by our counseling team from the Christian television network's prayer counseling center. As a result, hundreds of distressed wards were ministered to. In our current city, a similar arrangement is yet to be accomplished, but initial contact has been made with an embassy official. This is taking member care beyond church walls.

My member care work also includes traditional harvest workers and tentmakers around the world through my leadership in Heartstream Philippines. Through Zoom technology, we conduct webinars and even spiritual retreats for workers in the Philippines, Asia, and the Middle East. I have also ministered to "intentional" and "accidental" tentmakers in both countries. Intentional tentmakers are those who purposely migrate, work in their professions, and serve the churches' mission or church planting objectives. Accidental tentmakers are people already in the country before becoming strong Christians; as they grow in their Christian faith, they feel led to serve in evangelism and mission. Some were accountants, engineers, and highly skilled construction workers.

Confronting so much need in the many aspects of OFW life, I am reminded that I cannot be the sole problem solver. I have avoided claiming to be the person with all the resources and answers. The Member Care Model developed by Kelly O'Donnell and David Pollock (O'Donnell 2002) served as a template for me from the very start. Developing networks and discovering specialists in various fields have been essential and helpful steps in referring people.

My prayer focus is for the Lord to raise up individuals and groups around the world who want to become equipped in member care. I am blessed to see people express a serious interest in being mentored in member care. For example, I trained seventeen young professionals in active listening and levels of debriefing in my first host country. I contextualized the principles of member care to serve as a bridge to also sharing the Good News. Not all trainings bore fruit, but I looked at them as planting seeds of member care that would grow somehow as the Lord worked in their lives. In the Philippines, I continue to offer online training in member care skills to various groups.

"Most of all, make me faithful to the vision you have given me, so that wherever I go and whomever I meet, I can be a sign of your all-renewing love. Amen" (Nouwen 2023).

Jorge's Story and Ministry: Member Care Among OFWs in Hong Kong

There are approximately 2.7 million households in Hong Kong. Half of this population can afford to employ domestic helpers in their household. There are now around 200,000 Filipinos among Hong Kong's 330,000 foreign domestic workers (Government of Hong Kong Special Administrative Region Census and Statistics Department). This provided the opportunity for us—a partnership between a mission agency and my sending church—to establish a business-as-mission enterprise to serve OFWs in Hong Kong. An employment agency for domestic workers was consequently established. The business plan emphasized holistic member care for OFWs from recruitment to returning home.

Recruitment, Training, and Pre-Departure Orientation

During the initial online meeting with both the employees and employer, we first needed to address the anxiety in both parties. Much of the anxiety comes from fear of the unknown.

The next stage is the training and orientation of OFWs. We have to comply with government regulations and standards for training foreign domestic workers. We do this by partnering with a Philippine government-accredited institution in order to ensure that enhancements to the basic training curriculum are included.

We enhance the usual training with relevant teachings from the Bible. The Bible teachings aim at encouraging trainees toward personal resilience by utilizing spiritual exercises such as prayer, devotions, and understanding the gospel message. During the training, we build camaraderie and mutual support among the trainees. Other training enhancements include language learning and cultural orientation along with practical household work skills.

Volunteers from the church community provide prayer support for the trainee OFWs until they leave to work abroad. The relationships are maintained using social media.

Upon mutual signing of the work contract, the necessary procedures with the Philippine Overseas Employment Agency are expedited and accomplished. This is done by partnering with a government-accredited placement agency sending Filipinos overseas.

Arrival Orientation and Care

We meet clients upon their arrival at the Hong Kong airport. We assist OFWs as they apply for a Hong Kong ID card and take additional medical tests required by some employers. We help them set up their mobile phones, learn the city's transportation system, and know what to do in case of sickness or other emergencies. Along the way, we establish closer personal ties with them.

We also offer OFWs additional post-arrival orientation seminars that we call the *Tagumpay* (Victory) class. This is an enhancement to the Philippine government-mandated Post-Arrival Orientation Seminar (PAOS), offered at the Philippine consulate.

Tagumpay Classes

Tagumpay classes consist of five sessions covering issues faced by OFWs in Hong Kong. The first letters of the session titles spell the word *buhay* (life). They include *Bigyan Halaga ang Buhay* (Give Value to Your Life), about self-esteem and encouraging self-care; *Ulayaw sa Kalungkutan* (Companion in Times of Loneliness), on coping strategies in handling homesickness; *Halaga ng Pamilya* (Caring for Your Family), about maintaining family life over a long distance; *Abot Kaya ang Pangarap* (Reaching for Your Dreams), on identifying and setting personal goals including financial goals and plans to achieve it; and *Yaman na Tunay* (Real Riches), emphasizing the riches found in Jesus Christ who gives true meaning to life.

Embedded in the learning activities of the sessions are spiritual disciplines of prayer, devotions from the word, and sharing. We encourage the *Tagumpay* class members to become small group communities of care who are eventually led and mentored by a volunteer leader who is a follower of Christ and well-adjusted to OFW life in Hong Kong.

Church as Community

The small groups gather during weekends for worship, fellowship, and mutual encouragement. These have become core activities for the church community. Baptism and breaking of bread to remember Christ are celebrated in these groups.

On occasion, we provide special seminars on how to minister to others, sharing the gospel, discipling others as followers of Christ, and even mission education. This increased awareness on missions causes the participants to channel their love for family into concern for their spiritual well-being as well. The believers become motivated to share the gospel with their non-believing family members.

Much of pastoral care consists of debriefing sessions with these OFWs, especially among recent arrivals. Aside from obvious homesickness and cross-cultural adjustment issues, personal and family issues compound their anxieties.

Many female OFWs left home to escape serious dysfunction in their marriage and family life. We have grieved with these women over their failed marriages, or upon learning that their teenage children have fallen into problems commonly associated with parental absence, such as rebellious behavior, failing in school, gender dysphoria, unwanted pregnancy, drug abuse, and even criminal acts.

The weekly Bible studies conducted by caring and spiritually mature OFWs address many of these issues and demonstrate the operation of God's grace in their chosen lifestyle. Guidance is also needed in the matter of choosing one's life partner.

Challenges over the Years

A business enterprise with an expressed Kingdom purpose such as ours can expect to face spiritual opposition. My wife and I finally returned home after four years of serving in Hong Kong, as we felt the need to care for our own growing children and their schooling in the Philippines. Fortunately, I was able to recruit a fellow pastor to take on the responsibilities and tasks that I left behind in Hong Kong. He arrived with his wife and two young daughters in 2014 to minister to the OFWs.

Sadly, in 2016, tragedy struck. The older daughter fell to her death in an office building. This event brought debilitating grief to the new pastor and his family. Grief support came from many sources, and they were able to keep going in ministry.

In the following year, a series of sexual scandals committed by the Western mission worker who served as managing director of the enterprise was exposed. This resulted in a divorce with his wife. We separated from the company, as he insisted on keeping it for himself. This resulted then in the loss of significant funding for the local church for the support of the pastor and his family.

After a year of dealing with the repercussions of that scandal, in 2018 the pastor suffered a brain aneurysm. The stroke affected his speech and some cognitive functions. This unfortunate event served to accelerate the plan for the church to decentralize ministry activities. This meant gathering and meeting the members who were OFWs in small groups in the park in various districts of Hong Kong and gathering as a large group only on special occasions. Through this small-group system, the local church of OFWs thrived. However, this growth was challenged when the political conditions in Hong Kong induced frequent rioting on the streets. Public gatherings even in small groups were banned. Moreover, in 2020 the COVID-19 pandemic lockdowns further prohibited gatherings. Many employers did not allow their domestic workers to leave home. This caused grief and demoralization among the OFWs. We shifted our mode of serving these OFWs by using social media facilities like Facebook Messenger and Zoom.

Travel to and from Hong Kong opened up in 2023. But the pastor contracted a vicious viral infection that quickly grew into life-threatening pneumonia. As of this writing, he is in good health and back to his level of functioning prior to the infection.

Definitely, the powers of evil are operating to keep the work of God's Kingdom from advancing. The OFW church community dwindled in number as many returned home or took jobs in another country. Finances dwindled as well. And worse, many stumbled back into their old way of life due to the scandal. But there remains a faithful remnant, struggling but maturing in their faith and moving forward.

Prepare Well and Care Well

The business of the placement agency seems to continue to profit and thrive. But the church decided to sever the partnership with the agency, despite the loss of financial subsidy from the company and ministry opportunities with the company's OFW clients.

We learned two main lessons over time, with regard to the business and ministry model partnership we had adopted. These lessons can be helpful for other Christian ministries working among diaspora communities.

1. The business enterprise should be clearly delineated within the mission agency. The enterprise was formed when the mission agency was eager to get involved in doing business as missions. There were no policy guidelines in place on how this strategy should be implemented. There were also no prior agreements on handing ownership and control over to the business enterprise, and even closure, if necessary, especially for extreme conditions where the enterprise had departed from its core values.

2. More pastoral workers are needed to help in managing difficult issues and crises. Additional people within the church were needed to help the pastor discipline erring members and process the sexual scandal with church members. The pastor, with his own family still debilitated by grief and infirmities, had to bear the bulk of the burden of helping the church heal. Other ministers were ready to come and assist, but lack of financial support and the complications of acquiring visas for Hong Kong kept these mission workers at home.

The conditions of the ministry in Hong Kong are sadly in dire straits but our attitude through it all is expressed well in this Psalm: "We put our hope in the LORD. He is our help and our shield. In him our hearts rejoice, for we trust in his holy name. Let your unfailing love surround us, LORD, for our hope is in you alone" (Ps 33:20–22 NLT).

Applications: Supporting Filipino Christians in the Diaspora

Core Strategies

1. **Building community.** Faithful presence occurs through small groups or communities of care that are centered on God's word, spiritual disciplines, and learning activities. The ability to build and maintain good friendships and live out the tenets of the Kingdom of God in this context enabled the OFWs to face and overcome seemingly insurmountable personal and communal challenges.
2. **Partnering.** With the whole person in mind, purposely foster relationships with an interdisciplinary network of helpers, agencies, and specialists. No single entity can cover all member care needs. Utilizing government services like health services, social services, and the police combined with services provided by the church community and other institutions like schools, or community clubs proved to be timely and valuable in certain situations.
3. **Training and equipping.** A main strategy is to train and equip OFWs so that they can engage in self-care and even thrive in their jobs in the Middle East and Hong Kong. This type of discipleship focused on developing resilience and navigating life and work challenges. Training in basic ministry skills helped them minister to others and among people of different cultures.

Core Resources

1. Lois Dodds and Laura Mae Gardner. 2011. *Global Servants: Cross-Cultural Humanitarian Heroes*, vols. 1–3.
2. Lois Dodds and Larry Dodds. 2003. "Am I Still Me? Changing the Core Self to Fit a New Cultural Context."
3. Sadiri Joy Tira and Juliet Uytanlet. 2020. *A Hybrid World: Diaspora, Hybridity, and Missio Dei.*

Reflection and Discussion

1. Identify the main challenges and struggles that member care staff experienced in the Middle East and Hong Kong, as described in this chapter.
2. What key member care strategies for OFWs were shared? What might be relevant to your situation?
3. List a few lessons from this chapter that could inform the church and mission community's ministry among diaspora peoples. How might these apply to your context?

References

Alag, Grace Margaret. 2022. "My Journey in Member Care." *Asian Missions Advance* 76 (Summer): 13–15. https://www.asianmissions.net/asian.

Dodds, Lois, and Larry Dodds. 2003. "Am I Still Me? Changing the Core Self to Fit a New Cultural Context." Paper presented at the American Association of Christian Counselors World Congress, Nashville, Tennessee.

Dodds, Lois, and Laura Mae Gardner. 2011. *Global Servants: Cross-Cultural Humanitarian Heroes*, vols. 1–3. Heartstream Resources, Inc. https://www.heartstreamresources.org/shop.

Government of Hong Kong Special Administrative Region—Census and Statistics Department. https://www.censtatd.gov.hk/en/scode500.html.

International Organization for Migration. 2021. "World Development Report 2022." https://worldmigrationreport.iom.int/wmr-2022-interactive.

Nepomuceno, Daniel Anne. 2009. "Modern Filipino Diaspora." *Popular Economics* 27 (March).

Nouwen, Henri. 1972. "With Open Hands." *Lectio 365* (October 16, 2023).

O'Donnell, Kelly. 2002. "Going Global: A Member Care Model for Best Practice." In *Doing Member Care Well: Perspectives and Practices from Around the World*, 13–22. Pasadena, CA: William Carey Publishers. https://passionexchange.files.wordpress.com/2008/10/doingmembercarewell.pdf.

Philippine Statistics Authority. 2023. 2022 Survey on Overseas Filipinos (Final Result). Reference No: 2023-321 (October 11, 2023). https://psa.gov.ph/statistics/survey/labor-and-employment/survey-overseas-filipinos.

Siar, Sheila. 2008. "Diaspora: Explaining a Modern Filipino Phenomenon." Philippine Institute for Development Studies, *Economic Issue of the Day* 8, nos. 4 and 5 (June 1, 2008). https://www.pids.gov.ph/publication/economic-issue-of-the-day/diaspora-explaining-a-modern-filipino-phenomenon.

Tira, Joy Sadiri, and Juliet Uytanlet. 2020. *A Hybrid World: Diaspora, Hybridity, and Missio Dei*. Pasadena, CA: William Carey Publishers.

United Nations High Commissioner for Refugees. 2023. *Global Appeal 2024*. https://reporting.unhcr.org/global-appeal-2024-6383.

Grace Margaret Alag, DMin, currently serves as President and CEO of Heartstream Resources Philippines, Inc. Grace received a master's degree in leadership from Azusa Pacific University, USA. She has been married for five years to Jose Rosiler Alag, an engineer and safety manager in an oil and gas company.

Jorge de Ramos, DMin, serves as the Senior Pastor of Capitol City Baptist Church in the Philippines. He is the former mission director of the Conservative Baptist Association of the Philippines. Jorge received a MDiv degree from Asian Theological Seminary in Quezon City, Philippines. He and his spouse, Bolen Jopson, are blessed with five now-adult children and two grandchildren.

9

Developing Member Care in Indonesia

Collaborations with Goers and Senders

Traugott Boeker and Hanni Boeker with Hendry Pangaribuan

This chapter tells how the concept and practice of member care began to take root in the Indonesian mission movement over an initial period of ten years. What obstacles were encountered? What helpful tools and processes did the inter-agency team of Indonesians and two expatriates discover along the way? What lessons were learned and what remains to be done?

In recent years, member care has left its mark on the Indonesian mission movement. At the end of 2023, the national director of the Indonesian Peoples Network (IPN), the network of Indonesian agencies and churches that focus their efforts on reaching Indonesia's more than 164 Least-Reached Peoples and Places (LPPs, comprising at least 178 million people), wrote, "Churches and institutional leaders who have participated in the member care training have greatly improved in their member care function as senders. …Since its inception 10 years ago, Member Care Indonesia (MCI) has made a great contribution to accelerating the fulfillment of the Great Commission among the LPPs of Indonesia" (Bagus Surjantoro, email to authors, November 10, 2023). How did this come about?

Sovereign Foundations

Roughly since the early 1990s, mission awareness has grown among the churches in Indonesia through wide use of mission courses. LPPs were identified, their needs assessed, outreach intensified, and a national prayer network was born.

Political realities caused the number of expatriate mission workers to shrink gradually, their role largely shifting from frontline work to consulting and equipping Indonesian cross-cultural goers mainly through training in church planting and disciple making.

The first member care consultations were held in Jakarta in 2004 and 2005 followed by a website with member care resources in Bahasa Indonesia (Indonesia Member Care 2005–2024). Sadly, their impact on the Indonesian mission movement was limited.

Toward the end of 2012, we (the Boekers) returned to Indonesia wanting to work alongside the Indonesian church in outreach to LPPs. Twenty years before, we had trained pastors and goers at the Indonesian Bible Institute for fourteen years, emphasizing outreach to LPPs.

Could our twenty years of national and international mission leadership and member care experience since leaving Indonesia be of value? We had been exposed to global mission developments and growth, including South Korea and Brazil as new sending countries—both thriving and struggling. Might there be a place for us to encourage churches and agencies in Indonesia to become healthy sending agents, to learn about preventive member care, and to avoid high levels of attrition?

As we listened to leaders and cross-cultural workers, we heard heartbreaking, credible stories of how workers felt misunderstood, left alone to face the challenges of cross-cultural ministry among LPPs, under intense pressure to produce results, and still inadequately supported despite their senders' success in raising substantial funds for them. Ultimately, far too many goers were leaving the field prematurely and broken. One question kept nagging us: how can we continue to call young people into cross-cultural ministry when there is no nurturing support base—a home where they can experience love and be prepared for their calling, and from which they can be sent, supported, and welcomed back? Our resolve was strengthened to take steps to share our heavenly Father's heart not only for LPPs, but also for his messengers.

National Member Care Consultations

Church Focus

We knew that for any work of God in Indonesia to be effective, it must be done in the national language of Bahasa Indonesia, *owned by Indonesian churches, and ultimately led by Indonesians*. To introduce Indonesian Christian leaders to member care, we encouraged several leaders to attend the 2012 Global Member Care Network Conference in Chiang Mai, Thailand. At the end of the conference, the Indonesian contingent spontaneously indicated, "We need a conference like this in Indonesia!"

Immediately planning started for a member care consultation in Indonesia the following year (2013) with Laura Mae Gardner as keynote speaker. We were amazed when 103 leaders, board members and staff from 30 Indonesian sending agencies and 17 different denominations convened. In small groups, they shared experiences, discussed case studies, and brainstormed how to apply the concepts of member care to their situations—"a new way of looking at mission," they said. One mission leader confessed, "I have sinned by sending workers abroad without good preparation and then forgetting them in the field, leaving them to fend for themselves." Subsequently, he and others invited us to train and coach their agency in applying a structure and ethos for member care.

"We Need More!"
Participants agreed that more such events were needed to introduce the concept of member care to many more mission and church leaders. Thus, another consultation was held again with Laura Mae Gardner as presenter. Meanwhile Indonesian practitioners had reviewed her teaching notes and case studies from an Asian perspective as well as additional materials addressing some of the major issues facing field workers, such as loss and grief, family and ministry tensions, conflict, crisis, and moral dilemmas. As a result the first member care text in the Indonesian language was created (Gardner 2014).

As member care appeared to gain traction, the organizing committee decided that the next consultation would be presented in the national language by a team of Indonesian practitioners, with the Boekers as coordinators. Ah Kie Lim, then YWAM International Member Care Director, was invited as Asian specialist trainer.

This time even more participants from sending churches and agencies as well as theological institutions attended. Also, other professionals such as doctors, counselors, psychologists, and human resource managers were invited to raise awareness of how much they can contribute to the health, resilience, and effectiveness of Indonesian intercultural workers. Shortly after the event, reports began circulating on how the action plans were being put into practice.

The "Barnabas Team"–Shaping Member Care Indonesia

"Twelve Disciples"
Since returning to Indonesia with a vision for member care in 2012, we had this prayer in our hearts: "Lord, give us a learning community of 12 disciples who can learn from us and we from them and who will carry this forward!"

Indeed, after the third national consultation, God brought together a group of key people from different Indonesian ethnic and church backgrounds: pastors, experienced goers, counselors, sending agency workers, and a doctor—all of whom wanted to be a "Barnabas" to the goers among LPPs. Adopting the name "Barnabas Team," this core group has gradually grown to twenty members who share, brainstorm, pray, and strategize together. This interaction is crucial to fostering unity, mutual learning, and creativity.

In our desire to equip Indonesian leaders in member care, we identified experienced couples and singles, primarily from our team, and encouraged them to pursue advanced training in counseling, an important aspect of member care. In addition to giving them a solid foundation for their member care ministry, this advanced study has proven to be life-changing for all of them.

Discerning Powerful Obstacles

As Barnabas Team members reflected upon their conversations with senders and goers, powerful obstacles preventing member care being widely adopted in Indonesian missions surfaced. Here are five of them:

1. "All is well, why bother?"—hard facts needed!

At a team meeting, a senior team member, himself a goer, sighed in frustration, "The senders are not convinced of the need for member care. We need to create a crisis, then maybe they will listen and act!" Another replied, "The crisis has been there for a long time in every organization, but no one dares to talk about it!" Then someone else concluded, "We need to do a nationwide survey of the member care needs of Indonesian cross-cultural workers!" And so, we went to work!

The results of this study, based on 260 respondents out of the more than 700 cross-cultural workers serving among the 164 Indonesian LPPs, documented the alarming phenomenon of attrition. In days to come, these results would drive home the reality that the case for member care was based not on anecdotal evidence but on hard facts (MCI and IPN 2015).

2. Business mindset

Increasing numbers of Indonesian Christian businesspeople want to be involved in mission. However, their business practices, emphasizing cost-effectiveness, and their ethnic identity, can sometimes inadvertently influence their approach to mission in ways that contradict the way of Christ. Typical business concepts include:

- Missions must bring tangible benefits to the church.
- Often social action is seen as identical with mission.
- Priority mission fields are areas or ethnicities that will produce converts quickly, while LPPs are usually avoided for a variety of reasons.
- Capable individuals, some of them with a strong burden for mission, are often placed in church ministry while those deemed less capable (and without an interest in mission) are released to LPPs.
- Mission workers are often recruited from Indonesian ethnic groups that are economically disadvantaged—due to their perceived robustness and cost-effectiveness despite their minimal education. This can lead to multiple problems and contribute to the lack of high regard for mission workers.
- The prevailing attitude toward relations with the goer is typically of a boss-employee nature, prioritizing accountability over care.
- When problems arise or desired results are not achieved within a few years, agencies often resort to dismissing workers without proper debriefing or abandoning projects altogether. One consequence is that dedicated workers with a strong call to an unreached people group continue working independently, which creates its own set of problems.
- Proper care for and preparation of workers are viewed as unnecessarily costly and time-consuming.

A compassionate member of the Barnabas Team commented, "It's not that they don't want to care, they just are not self-aware and don't know how to care."

3. Shame culture
There is a high expectation to conform to common norms, as any deviation brings shame upon the individual, their family and community. This makes it difficult for both senders and goers to admit to the struggles, crises, and failures they are experiencing.

4. Church culture
Seniority, hierarchy, fear of losing face, high regard for "servants of the Lord," and success-oriented ministry are powerful—though often unrecognized—paradigms in many Indonesian churches, similar to the Korean situation as described by Bonk (2019). The biblical concept of sabbath is almost nonexistent. Church mission departments are generally seen as a necessary part of the church structure. Sadly, the positive potential of this organizational

structure is often not realized because any church elder—often from the business community—may be assigned to lead the mission department and rarely do they have direct mission experience or even a specific passion for mission. These paradigms, along with frequent changes in leadership, are formidable barriers to sustainable member care processes.

5. Unbalanced mission strategy

In the passionate pursuit of the initial goal of "reaching as many unreached people groups as possible in as short a time as possible," the ultimate biblical goal of "presenting everyone mature in Christ" (Col 1:28) and the realization that "the messenger is the message" are often neglected. The spiritual, physical, emotional, and social well-being of workers and new converts is sacrificed because of a preoccupation with tasks, performance, and finances (Gardner 2018, 59–62). Workers who have never themselves experienced care and nurturing from their senders, are not equipped or motivated to relate to their converts in a nurturing way.

These were and still are some of the key issues to address in our desire to give member care its rightful place in the Indonesian mission movement.

Equipping Senders and Supporters to Care for Their Goers: The Member Care Training Course (MCTC)

Rather than continuing with the consultation format, one team member suggested developing a training course with all the basic aspects of member care that sending churches and agencies need to know. Another leader stated, "mission courses have convinced many churches that they need to get involved in missions; now your teaching on member care is the logical next step in showing churches *how* to send and support those whom the Lord has called to go." The team accepted the challenge and began gathering materials and real-life situations from Indonesian workers' frontline experience for developing the Member Care Training Course (Boeker and Boeker 2024).

Definition of Member Care

Standing on the shoulders of many others, we developed and worked from the following concise definition of member care:

> By member care we mean the ongoing effort—of coming alongside, equipping, and restoring cross-cultural messengers so that they remain healthy, resilient, effective, and glorifying God in their life and ministry as they take the gospel of Christ to the least-reached. This begins with recruitment and continues until ministry completion.

Member Care Formula

The constant call to "keep it simple and memorable!" eventually led us to "5-3-5," our "Member Care Formula" which answers the three fundamental questions about implementing member care:

- **What goals does member care aim to achieve?** *Goers growing in five-fold resilience: spiritual, physical, emotional, creative and mental, social.*
- **When should member care be provided?** *Throughout the three stages of a goer's life and ministry: preparation, on-field, and reentry/home assignment.*
- **Who is responsible for making member care a reality?** *Five sources: the Master, self, the community in the field, the senders (church and agency), and the specialists.*

This Member Care Formula serves as the organizing framework for the course.

Relevance of the Member Care Formula

As the MCTC progressed, it became clear how relevant the 5-3-5 layout was to the Indonesian situation:

- **Five aspects of resilience.** Senders are generally aware that *spiritual* resilience is important for the goer. However, the vital role of the other four aspects of resilience is greatly underestimated. A weakness in *any one* of these five aspects can be the cause of a goer's downfall (Horsfall and Hawker 2019).
- **Three stages of the life and ministry of a goer.** The preparation stage tends to receive the least attention, followed by the reentry phase. Senders don't realize that failure and early return from the field are often rooted in inadequate selection and preparation. Few appreciate that special attention from the sender during reentry can redeem an "unsuccessful" term in the field.
- **Five sources of member care.** Learning about the five (not one!) sources of member care encourages senders and opens their minds to ways of sharing responsibility that they might not have seen before.

This 5-3-5 layout has also made it easier for everyone to understand, remember and teach the key concepts of member care. Every single aspect of the Member Care Formula is being expanded and illustrated with real-life situations throughout the MCTC.

Course Elements that Contributed to Effectiveness

Biblically based

Since member care was not only a completely new concept to most Indonesian Christians but also went against the grain of accepted culture and church policy, we concluded that every aspect of member care had to be solidly based on the word of God. Here are some of the paradigms in the minds of Indonesian churches and agencies that made them hesitant to consider the concept of member care:

- "Member care is a Western concept! Asians see things differently!"
- "Member care is driven by psychology—not biblical truth!"
- "Isn't God caring for his servants in the most perfect manner? Member care seems to imply that this is not enough!"
- "Member care slows down the speedy evangelization of the least reached!"

Nothing short of a solid biblical foundation for every aspect of member care will convince Asian Christian leaders and mission workers that member care is vital for an Asian mission movement to thrive. For example, a large, downloadable banner of some 30 New Testament characters who actively supported missions was created to illustrate the very practical forms of biblical member care.

Linking member care to reaching the least reached

Often, churches were eager to learn about member care, as it was an intriguing new concept not heard of before. However, this did not mean that they understood what mission was all about, let alone the need to focus mission on the LPPs. Therefore, the first session in each MCTC is devoted to God's priority to reach the LPPs. This focus also has a significant impact on how certain topics are presented in the MCTC.

Focus on the "Father heart" of God

Each day of MCTC begins with approximately 45 minutes called "Intimate with the Father"—a time of reflection on a passage of Scripture. As preaching often focuses on what God *expects of us*, we invite participants to see how the Father and Jesus graciously *care for and about us* sinful people before they ever expect anything from us. A guided, contemplative approach (e.g., lectio divina, personal "entering into a story," memorizing, and acting out the word) to selected passages of Scripture is a new experience for most participants, but it is deeply moving and effective in sowing the seeds of a caring attitude. As one leader of an underground church network in China commented after a member care seminar, "We have a theology of suffering, but we don't have a theology of care." Participants often share how this time has touched them in deep ways.

Touching emotions
The mission challenges identified in our survey are made real through a series of dramas with deeply moving scenes depicting the life and ministry of a young family and a single worker during the three stages of their calling as cross-cultural workers with an unreached people group. City pastors and their congregations begin to feel the need to care for workers in domestic LPPs. A much-loved theme song, specially composed by a Barnabas Team member, completes the emotional learning and always brings tears to participants' eyes.

Time for personal reflection
Since everything in the MCTC is designed for personal application and implementation after the course, it is important to provide regular opportunities to stop and reflect. Therefore, at the end of each session, we reserve time for each participant to record in their workbook (a) two lessons from this session that were particularly important to them and (b) how they can apply this learning to their member care practice.

Printed manual
Participants receive a printed manual containing the outline and detailed explanations, including illustrations, discussion questions, and appendices with checklists. One mission leader said, "The checklists alone made the course worthwhile." There are reading assignments (Gardner 2014; Horsfall and Hawker 2019) as well as application tasks for their goers.

Goal-oriented selection of participants
Every training invitation emphasizes that churches and organizations should send at least two or three participants, preferably leaders. This makes it easier to implement what is learned.

Make the most of group work
To maximize interaction and cross-fertilization, participants are seated in groups of three to five people, sometimes with mixed backgrounds (pastors, mission agency leaders and staff, theological schools, professionals, church members, field workers), sometimes with the same roles in different denominations or agencies. People who often don't have much contact with each other get to know, appreciate, and learn from others, including those who may have been viewed with suspicion.

As a fruit of the dramas, case studies, and biblical teaching, difficulties, and crises in doing mission are brought out into the open without fear of shame or blame. Rather, a shared sense emerges of being in the same boat and of gaining hope through a model of love and workable strategies.

Maximize implementation potential
In the evening, participants from the same setting or organization meet in affinity groups to compare notes from the personal reflection time. They discuss what their church or agency needs to do in terms of member care. The final session of the MCTC, when participants meet again in affinity groups, is devoted to creating a specific member care action plan for the church, agency, or individual participant.

By the end of 2023, nearly 2,000 participants from 150 agencies, 100 denominations, and 20 theological schools in Indonesia had completed the MCTC.

Member Care Providers Ask for Advanced Training

As more people became convinced that member care was a necessary part of mission, a need developed to further equip caregivers for ministry to field workers. Observation and research among goers led to the conclusion that the type of care that goers most miss and desire is being listened to. Leaders must take the time to listen. But what (male) leader would be willing to take a course in listening skills?

"Barnabas Training"

For this reason, it was decided to offer "Barnabas Training" in debriefing and coaching, because these topics, unbeknownst to many leaders, have listening skills at their core. A growing understanding and personal experience of the powerful effects of asking good questions and then listening, rather than telling or preaching at the goer, has revolutionized the leadership approach of many in the mission community. These two courses have become a staple of MCI training for those who have successfully completed the MCTC.

It was only logical to develop further advanced "Barnabas Training" courses, such as Understanding Personality Type, S.H.A.P.E. (Spiritual gifts, Heart, Abilities, Personality, Experience), and Conflict Resolution in a Team. Training modules on issues of mission families and children are planned.

A seed starts to sprout
The long process of working together as the Barnabas Team, training churches and agencies, and not giving up on networking began to bear fruit as member care was put on the map in Indonesian missions.

Leadership transition

After six years of pioneering MCI with the Barnabas Team (2013–2018), we (the Boekers) announced that after four more years we felt it would be time for us to leave Indonesia. Not that there was no more work to be done, but we felt that if we stayed, we might hinder the Barnabas Team from fully owning this movement. The team responded by asking us to train them as member care trainers who would eventually feel able to conduct the MCTC on their own.

We prayed that God would prepare people who would be willing to serve as leaders with enough time for a smooth transition. After another two years, this prayer was wonderfully answered when the whole team confirmed the leadership of Pastor Hendry Pangaribuan who had actively participated in the Barnabas team from the start.

We also established a new structure with three ministry divisions: training (with a focus on senders), counseling and retreats (with a focus on goers), and mobilizing and equipping regional member care hubs. The new leadership and structure turned out to be the foundation for further expansion.

Going online

The COVID-19 pandemic in March 2020 challenged us to be flexible. We would have to either restructure the course for online delivery or abandon it.

Although face-to-face interaction would be lost, online courses offered many advantages, most notably that mission-minded people from all over our far-flung archipelago of more than 5,000 kilometers could participate without having to worry about expensive airfare and accommodation costs. In this way, in 2021, 330 participants completed the 15-hour online member care training.

Video and online resources

Roleplays needed to be turned into videos. We discovered gifted videographers on the Barnabas Team. A pastor turned case studies into scripts for several videos and directed the filming with volunteers from her church; another team member, a medical doctor, continues to produce videos with his colleagues.

Effective use of virtual breakout rooms

Virtual breakout rooms with carefully assigned participants have become an effective way to break through the anonymity of the Internet and ensure quality face-to-face communication and cross-fertilization as an essential element of learning that lasts.

Entering seminary

MCI now teaches a two-credit required online course on member care at a theological seminary. Future pastors need to know how to lead their church in caring for their goers.

Multiplication of trainers

The online format also allowed more people to participate as presenters as well as breakout room facilitators. This meant that we had to develop a 30-hour "training of trainers" for 20 dedicated alumni—a significant investment in expansion!

As it turned out, the restrictions of COVID-19 and going online became a multiplication tool for member care in Indonesia.

Directly Serving the Needs of Goers

Also, during COVID-19, some members of the Barnabas Team began to feel that it was not enough to equip senders in member care while waiting and hoping that they would meet the needs of their goers. As a result, we introduced additional new features.

"Casual Chat"

Frontline workers felt isolated and depressed when face-to-face contact was severely restricted for about two years during the pandemic. During that time, a bimonthly informal meeting for field workers via Zoom, called the "Casual Chat," was born. To ensure that field workers feel free to share openly, registration is very strictly monitored. Participants must be recommended by someone known to MCI, and leaders are not allowed to attend. These informal gatherings, with a focus on personal sharing in smaller virtual breakout groups, are greatly appreciated. Goers are encouraged as they feel that "I am not alone" and "I am not the only one going through this!" Out of these meetings have come online peer mentoring groups, the "Friends Traveling Together." The results of a straw poll conducted during a Casual Chat on what causes stress in goers were shared with leaders to help them better understand their goers.

All present and former participants in the "Casual Chat" get a monthly short biblical devotion, "A Glass of Cool Water," via WhatsApp to encourage them on their often-challenging journey.

Affordable counseling

Through these ministries, trust began to grow, and goers started to admit their deep needs, prompting MCI to offer professional, one-on-one counseling.

A Christian lady offered rooms in her home to host individuals and couples in need of counseling. In particularly serious cases, a member of the counseling team attempts to visit those in need, which sometimes involves air travel. However, most counselees are served remotely. Funding this ministry remains challenging. One of the counselors is supported financially by her home church. Another group of Christians has begun sending regular funds to cover the counseling fees of workers who are unable to pay.

Real retreats

Most Indonesian churches and agencies organize "retreats" for their workers, but these events are usually packed with training, planning, and strategizing. As a result, most field workers have never experienced a retreat that focuses on time alone with God and with each other, personal rest and relaxation, renewal, and refreshment. Planning and conducting such revitalizing retreats have become part of MCI's ministry. Some agencies have begun to request MCI retreats for their goers. Funding is a challenge because the goers lack resources for travel. Some organizations have considered providing funding, but only if training is included, which MCI tries to avoid so as not to compromise the nature of the retreat. Fortunately, some funding from outside Indonesia has been instrumental in making these retreats possible.

Member care training for goers

Some senders who felt blessed by the MCTC urged us to share the biblical and practical concepts of care with their goers. This request resulted in the delivery of "Timothy Training" specifically for field workers, focusing on the five aspects of resilience, as well as master care, self-care, and community care. The response from senders and goers has been positive. Goers feel refreshed and equipped to nurture themselves as well as understanding more fully their responsibilities to their senders.

Rest homes and member care centers

Two couples from the Barnabas Team are now taking first steps in a faith project to provide homes where goers can rest and recuperate. The need for such homes is great in many parts of Indonesia.

How to Get the Leaders on Board

Leaders have a right to know who and what is influencing their members. Sheep stealing among agencies is a sad reality, and money often plays a big role in this dynamic.

Turn suspicion into trust

Having leaders in our ranks means that the Barnabas Team is aware of these dynamics and is therefore highly committed to transparency and to building bridges between goers and senders. We know that if MCI listens to and prays with a worker, let alone supports them medically or financially, this could cause a loyalty conflict. Therefore, leaders are usually involved before one of their workers is served by MCI.

"Leaders' Forum"

How can we keep leaders informed and positive about member care when most of them will not want to attend a full member care training, nor will they likely serve as a caregiver? We met this need by holding half-day "Leaders' Forum" seminars that address member care topics of particular relevance to leaders. To ensure that leaders want to come and feel free to share their opinions, it proved wise to limit attendance to leaders only and to have expert input on such topics as the following:

- "Crisis in the Field: How to Prevent and Deal with It"
- "So Few Workers: Can We Afford to Be Selective?"
- "Models for Financially Supporting Field Workers"

Developing such topics for leaders has helped to create an awareness of and a more positive disposition toward member care.

Impactful mentoring

After many years of input from MCI, several churches have asked for ongoing mentoring from Barnabas Team members as they begin to create a member care policy for their church, form support groups for each of their goers, and develop a curriculum for preparing goers. Such paradigm shifts in churches have required significant, patient input from MCI.

Contribution of expatriates

In several areas of Indonesia, well-integrated expatriates play an important role in modeling, encouraging, and actively supporting member care for Indonesian goers in the ministries to which they belong. These senior expats can also provide a much-needed shoulder to cry on, especially for leaders and member care providers who sometimes feel traumatized by the actions and attitudes of both goers and senders.

Member Care for Each Province

Every one of Indonesia's thirty-eight provinces has LPPs and goers. Therefore, MCI's long-term goal has been to make sure that goers have access to member care within their province—an ambitious goal in view of the vastness of the country.

Thanks to the longstanding collaboration between MCI and the IPN, a breakthrough toward this passionate goal was achieved in 2023 through the formation of several regional IPN member care working groups. It will be MCI's special role and privilege to assist these groups in developing appropriate strategies and equipping them for their task.

In summary, there is much to praise the Lord for, but even after 10 years, many of the obstacles described above still exist. The Indonesian mission movement is vast, and with ever-changing leadership, raising awareness of the need for member care and equipping senders to provide it remains an urgent priority.

Applications: Member Care in Indonesia

Core Strategies

1. Ask multiple people in a varied group (e.g., senders, goers, member caregivers) to identify current stressors and causes of attrition. Explore dominant cultural paradigms that can help or hinder relationships between senders and goers.

2. Work with local goers and senders to develop a practical curriculum for contextualized preventive member care. Focus on training and equipping local sending units to care for their mission workers, modeling an ethos of care throughout the training and follow-up. Base every aspect of member care on biblical principles and examples, to demonstrate what biblical member care looks like and why it is an essential requirement, not an option.

3. Prioritize building relationships and trust with senders and goers. Don't be discouraged by initial disinterest or even resistance. The ultimate goal is systemic change in sending organizations, which will result in administration and policies that reflect the Father's heart. Be prepared for the long haul.

Core Resources

1. Laura Mae Gardner. 2018. *Healthy, Resilient, and Effective in Cross-Cultural Ministry*
2. Tony Horsfall and Debbie Hawker. 2019. *Resilience in Life and Faith*
3. Traugott Boeker and Hanni Boeker. 2024. *We'll Never Let Go of That Rope*

Reflection and Discussion

1. What three insights stand out for you from this chapter? Why?
2. Based on the Indonesian experience, how could your approach to member care and mission change?
3. Who are the people who could help to implement a culture of care in your organization? In what ways do they need to be supported and equipped?

References

Boeker, Traugott, and Hanni Boeker. 2024. *We'll Never Let Go of That Rope! A Member Care Training Course Manual for Churches and Agencies in Newer Sending Countries.* Developed for course participants. (contact: traugotthanni@gmail.com)

Bonk, Jonathan J., ed. 2019. *Missionaries, Mental Health, and Accountability*. Pasadena, CA: William Carey Publishing.

Gardner, Laura Mae. 2014. *Sehat, Tangguh, & Efektif dalam Pelayanan Lintas Budaya*. Yogyakarta Indonesia: Katalis. (Published in English in 2018 as *Healthy, Resilient, and Effective in Cross-Cultural Ministry: A Comprehensive Member Care Plan*. Condeo Press.)

Horsfall, Tony, and Debbie Hawker. 2019. *Resilience in Life and Faith: Finding Your Strength in God*. Abingdon: Bible Reading Fellowship.

Indonesia Member Care. 2005–2024. https://sites.google.com/site/indonesiamembercare.

Member Care Indonesia and Indonesian Peoples Network. 2015. "Survey of Indonesian Cross-Cultural Workers Among UPGs 2015." Unpublished research paper. (contact: traugotthanni@gmail.com)

Traugott Boeker and Hanni Boeker (from Germany and Switzerland, respectively) have served with WEC International since 1978 in Africa, Europe, and Asia in theological education, national and international leadership, and member care/third culture kid care. They spent ten years with Indonesian practitioners developing Member Care Indonesia (MCI), an inter-agency network focused on equipping churches and agencies in preventive member care. Currently they assist emerging sending nations with member care training.

Hendry Pangaribuan (Indonesia) was an engineer with Indonesia's state-owned oil company before pioneering missions among unreached people groups. He is now a mission pastor, associate director of the Indonesian Peoples Network (IPN), and the leader of Member Care Indonesia (MCI). He is married to Isabella, and they have three children.

10

Doing Member Care Well in India[1]

Isac Soundararaja and Lancelot Paul

In this chapter, we present an overview of needs and resources for member care in India. Over the past 20 years, various studies have assessed the challenges and wellbeing of mission workers and their families in India. This article is informed by several such studies. We specifically focus on mission workers whose organizations are members of the India Missions Association (IMA) and Missionary Upholders Trust (MUT).

The first part of this chapter explores challenges and needs for Christian workers and their families as well as for retired Christian workers. The second part deals with how member care is being facilitated in the partnership between IMA and MUT. We use the term "Christian workers" to refer to Indian cross-cultural workers serving in India's multicultural society. These workers and their families often serve in extremely difficult places, and there are increasing collaborative efforts to support their work among unreached peoples by providing quality member care.

Part One: Perspectives on Member Care in India and Why Does Member Care Matter?

In India, over 60,000 Christian workers are involved in cross-cultural mission among the country's more than 4,700 people groups, most of which are unreached with the gospel. Thousands of workers from south central and northeast India are moving into the central and northern parts of India, where the majority of the unreached people groups reside. The diverse challenges and unmet needs of these Christian workers and their children are significant and need to be addressed holistically.

Many words can be used to describe member care: friendship, encouragement, affirmation, help, fellowship, as well as sharing, communicating, visiting, guiding, comforting, counselling, and debriefing. Christian work-

---

[1] The first part of this chapter includes material adapted from the article "From Ministry Call to Home Call: The State of Member Care in India" in *Evangelical Missions Quarterly* (Soundararaja 2022). Used by permission.

ers are on the frontlines of a spiritual war between the powers of good and evil, and their battles are fierce. They need trusted and competent support staff engaged in member care, people with whom they can share their inner battles, because they are literally in a war with the forces of hell.

"Member care is important not because missionaries necessarily have more or unique stress, but rather because missionaries are strategic. They are key sources of blessing for the unreached" (O'Donnell 2002, 21). God is concerned for mission workers and their families. Quality member care protects and promotes their health and resiliency. It is the foundation of a God-pleasing strategy in missions. So many times, we have seen how Christian workers who lack a solid caring network in their mission organization and church end up carrying excessive burdens that negatively impact their work-life balance, wellbeing, and effectiveness. "Carry each other's burdens, and in this way you will fulfill the law of Christ" (Gal 6:2). Mission workers need others (and each other) for supportive mutual care and to ensure that their needs are met. Togetherness increases strength and reduces vulnerability, especially when the enemy attacks.

Member Care Challenges and Unmet Needs in India

The following discussion summarizes many of the unmet personal and family needs of cross-cultural mission workers in India. It is based on several sources: Isac's experience in the last 23 years with MUT; a study identifying the stress factors of Christian workers in India (Samuel 2012); a study of the challenges of Indian MKs (Solomon 2015); and a study of the challenges and needs of retired workers (Sudhakar 16th June 2016). Other sources include Rajendran (2002) and Amalraj (2008a, 2008b) as well as the REMAP study, in which top reasons for leaving mission service were reported to be inadequate commitment, disagreement with the agency, immature spiritual life, problems with peers, and lack of home support (Brierley 1997, 94).

Physical Challenges

- Health: Mission workers may suffer major illnesses such as cardiac arrest or cancer. Others experience prolonged health issues such as diabetes, hypertension, high cholesterol, respiratory problems, or renal failure.

- Bereavement: Some mission workers face deaths in their family, and others lose their dear ones early in life.

- Unexpected crises such as sudden deaths in one's extended family, loss of property due to natural calamity, or persecution.

Emotional and Spiritual Challenges

- Levels of spiritual and emotional maturity may vary across team members of the same organization.
- The temptations placed before each Christian worker differ. But because the enemy (devil) knows who is weak and in what areas, workers may succumb to temptation easily and quickly.
- Many struggle with fears, others feel lonely, and still others cannot bear pain or suffering.
- Some are highly sensitive while others shared living with past hurts.
- Some do not have clarity regarding their life purpose; others struggle because of faulty teaching they received before they joined the mission.
- The fruit of the Spirit is minimal or not very evident in some people's lives.
- Denominational differences can bring disunity; some people exhibit pride and arrogance over such differences.
- Unlearning bad habits can be difficult for some members.

Challenges in Christian Workers' Married Life

- Many mission couples have serious relationship struggles. The normal struggles of married life are compounded by high levels of stress and, in many cases, by the lack of companionship and love from their children, who are attending boarding school.

Challenges Posed by Retirement

- More than 2,000 Christian workers retired from various missions in India over the past 10 years. But retirement presents another significant challenge for Christian workers, particularly when the sending organization has not adequately prepared them for this transition. Consider for example the Christian worker who had terminal cancer. While his wife was staying at the mission rest house, their mission suddenly served them a retirement notice! They were devastated because they had not planned for this eventuality. Missions and churches must take the problems around retirement seriously. There is a growing recognition of the role of sending organizations in preparing their workers for retirement and offering supportive care during retirement.

Challenges of Mission Children (MKs)

There have been various efforts to identify and address the challenges of Indian MKs since 2004. At the MUT Member Care Consultation in Bangalore (2012) a report was presented for discussion and decisions to address the challenges and needs of the Indian MKs (Paul 2012). The main concerns expressed in this study were the socio-emotional and relational challenges of MKs. A follow up study (Solomon 2015), presented at the 2016 MUT Member Care Consultation in Coimbatore, revealed there were few changes in the reported challenges of Indian MKs. However, these two studies helped MUT and some of the mission organizations to specifically focus on these challenges and address the needs in the context of retreats, counseling sessions, online meetings, and visits with MKs in their schools and colleges. Such efforts enabled the caregivers to provide meaningful care and support to the Indian MKs. Like all children, Christian workers' children desire to be with their parents and to enjoy personal parental care. But the call to cross-cultural mission often requires children to be separated from their parents at a very early age (sometimes before age five), mainly due to their educational needs. Those who live in hostels or at boarding schools miss their parents' love. Since the 1980s, most Indian cross-cultural workers have placed their children in boarding schools. An estimated 100,000 MKs born to Christian workers' families are living in India today.

The following challenges and needs persist among Indian MKs and require further interaction for developing better care.

- Families spend very limited time together over the course of a year (usually only one to three opportunities), in addition to having limited or no phone contact between visits. Whether for reasons of neglect or ministry commitments and requirements, many children have believed that their parents did not care about them or have abdicated their nurturing responsibilities to the school, where they may not feel loved by the staff. For some, emotional and psychological struggles ensue from the long separation, including depression and anxiety.

- Parents who greatly miss their children may be tempted, in their anxiety and desire to show their love, to do anything to please their children at every reunion. They pamper them to the extent that the children become spoiled.

- MKs can feel deprived when they compare their lives to those of Christian children whose parents have secular jobs. These other

children may seem to benefit from a good education, comfortable life, consistent parental care, and love and care from extended family that mission children may lack.
- Many MKs openly say that they would never become Christian workers. Some may even start to accuse and hate God and their parents.
- Some MKs become rebellious and even go astray. Parents may feel helpless, depressed, and unable to do ministry work properly.
- MKs in boarding schools often lack life skills to cope with adverse situations. One study, which assessed MKs in the higher secondary grades of a boarding school, found that they were weak in their ability to cope with day-to-day challenges in the areas of relationships, loneliness, management of time, and finances (Jeyarani 2023).

Better News for MKs and Their Families

In contrast to some of the concerning trends described above about Indian MKs, a recent study by MUT revealed some positive changes in the emotional and spiritual development among older MKs (Lancelot 2023). Over the years, boarding schools have become better equipped and produced more successful and professional MKs. Currently, a couple of boarding schools have strong alumni organizations that continuously support their schools by enhancing infrastructure, such as by updating kitchen facilities, improving cleanliness on the school premises, and mentoring younger MKs. In general, much more care is now provided by boarding schools, mission agencies, and sending churches. Boarding schools play an active role not only in academic and spiritual areas, but also in raising awareness of job opportunities in India and abroad. As a result, among older boarding students, fewer problems seem to be arising because of their separation from their parents.

The MUT study utilized an online questionnaire sent to 80 Indian MKs who studied at boarding schools and colleges in Tamil Nadu. The study included both quantitative and qualitative measures. The key findings, though limited in scope, point to some positive changes in addressing longstanding challenges. To understand if this positive trend is more general, additional research is needed with all ages of MKs and at additional locations. Findings included the following:

1. 70.2 percent of respondents indicated that they were not negatively affected by the absence of their parents during their study at the boarding school.

2. 74.3 percent indicated that they did not lack faith.
3. 73.8 percent expressed their desire to continue seeking spiritual and emotional support.
4. 63.6 percent responded positively that they had overcome a problem with self-esteem.
5. 61.2 percent have stated that their studies were not financially burdening their parents.
6. 64.1 percent said that they do not want to be "unequally yoked in marriage" with people of other faiths.
7. 56.7 percent said they were careful about keeping their life holy to avoid falling prey to lust.
8. 65.2 percent indicated that they were confused about the future and do not know what to do next.
9. 70.4 percent indicated that they had difficulty in choosing the right course of study.
10. 77.5 percent indicated that they faced financial burdens in their current studies and/or regarding pursuing further study.

Additional issues from the MUT study included the following:

- 95 percent of the MKs surveyed were concerned about socioeconomic challenges and unemployment. Most lacked financial resources to cover the steep cost of higher education after their parents had already spent a few thousand rupees each year for their earlier school education. When they start their university studies or professional courses, they have to expend a large amount of money, which puts tremendous pressure on both the parents and the children. This can lead to interpersonal conflicts and sometimes a test of faith.

- MKs reported common teenage problems. However, very few MKs in this study suffered from lack of faith or fear of facing life challenges.

- MKs in boarding school missed their parents' emotional and spiritual nurture, especially from their mothers.

- About 60 percent of the MKs talked infrequently to their parents and felt neglected by them.

Member Care in India

In the context of these ongoing challenges, God enabled the IMA to take action to address the unmet needs of Christian workers and their families. The seed for the IMA's involvement in member care ministry sprouted in the1980s. In the 1990s, the IMA developed a partnership with MUT. In 1996 and 2000, a consultation was held with IMA member missions and with MUT, particularly to address bereavement issues and the health challenges of Christian workers in India. MUT came forward to facilitate meeting these needs. Subsequently, in 2012 a landmark book with over 50 chapters, *Member Care in India: From Ministry Call to Home Call*, was published and widely read in India and internationally (Manoharan et al. 2012).

As a result of the IMA's partnership with MUT, member care has been provided to at least 2\76 missions, representing about 23,522 Christian workers. However, as many as 55,000 cross-cultural workers still have limited or no access to needed member care. It is discouraging to hear both church and mission leaders say, "God will help you; he will be there for you!" It is true that God will take care of us, but Christian workers also need to know and experience visible care and support from their own mission organization. We also often hear people say, "The Christian workers are our heroes," but in reality, the attitude of the mission organization and the church toward workers can be discouraging and even detrimental. "Many organizations do not have a care department to focus on their leaders and staff," explains Pramila Rajendren (2020). We need to see a major effort by mission organizations and sending churches to build teams and structures that can facilitate member care.

A God-honoring and caring organizational culture is the most important part of member care and is foundational for the care system itself. As Brenda Bosch, an international member care consultant, has told us, "It is crucial that mission agencies and their leaders and members create a work and family environment for Christian workers where they are valued above their manpower, contributions toward work objectives, and achievements."

Local supporting churches also need to participate because holistic care for Christian workers and their children is the mutual calling of churches and mission organizations. When they stand together with mission workers to support them holistically in the context of sacrifice, stressful work and prudent risk, there is less chance of burnout or attrition. Belonging to these types of caring communities is essential to help Christian workers function as salt and light for God's glory in places where Jesus is not known.

Part Two: Missionary Upholders Trust

Missionary Upholders Trust (MUT) was formed in 1993 by the late J. J. Rathnakumar as an offshoot from Missionary Upholders Family (MUF). The close association of the people involved in MUF with their Christian workers helped us understand the various difficulties that workers and their families faced. Although some needs were met by their own organizations, the mission workers had to largely fend for themselves.

Our initial focus was on providing calamity relief to bereaved mission families (IMPACT), rest houses, and medical help. Additional projects such as Master Health Checkup (MHC), Love Your Brother (LYB), Scheme for Missions Linked to Evangelism and Help (SMILE), Crisis Relief Support Scheme (Good Samaritan Fund), Mission Kids Welfare (assistance for higher education), Retired Missionary Welfare (shelter assistance), and personal development programs for mission workers and spouses have been included. As of August 2023, about 169 missions covering approximately 15,207 Christian workers have joined MUT's IMPACT scheme and about 8,315 Christian workers from 107 organizations have joined MUT's SMILE Scheme. The following are some details regarding MUT's core strategies and resources for member care.

1. Rest and Recuperation. In Mark 6:31, Jesus says to his disciples after their challenging time of ministry, "Come with me by yourselves to a quiet place and get some rest." Likewise, after a busy ministry season, it is important for the servants of God to take time to rest, relax, and renew their body and soul. MUT has established rest houses for Christian workers to spend quality, quiet time alone (as individuals or couples) or with their children, away from their field commitments, and to receive affordable medical attention as needed. These rest houses are located in close proximity to Christian hospitals such as Christian Medical College in Vellore, Tamil Nadu; Christian Fellowship Hospital in Oddanchatram, Tamil Nadu; and Asha Kiran Hospital, Lamtaput, Odisha. All these rest houses are fully furnished with multiple kitchen facilities and a chapel. Dedicated and committed teams of volunteers and caregivers manage these facilities and provide in-house care.

2. Bereavement Care. Inter Mission Plan of Assurance during Calamity Times (IMPACT) is a contributory scheme through which all members contribute toward providing financial assistance to a bereaved mission worker, pastor, or family members upon the death of a member. Apart from financial assistance, continued care and counseling support are provided to these families by volunteers. Periodic retreats are conducted in regional languages for bereaved families as a group so that they can strengthen and encourage one another. Bereavement counseling and crisis debriefing are also offered.

3. Health Care. Master Health Checkups are available for mission workers periodically at subsidized rates. These checkups can go a long way in identifying hidden problems and preventing serious complications as well as in supporting healthier lifestyles and behaviors. In partnership with Christian hospitals across the country, programs such as "Love Your Brother" and "Helped to Help" provide medical assistance to mission workers dealing with major illness or accidents or needing lifelong treatment. Some financial assistance is provided from the members' contributions and from donations to the "Friends of MUT."

4. Crisis Care. Mission workers are not immune to serious crises such as theft, loss of property and injury due to natural calamities, road traffic accidents, persecution, death of loved ones, sudden illnesses, and health and financial concerns for parents. At crisis junctures, MUT tries to provide care through its volunteers and financial assistance in practical, albeit small, ways through its *Good Samaritan Fund*.

5. Care for Retired Mission Workers. Once a career mission worker, always a mission worker! When mission workers retire, the member care provided by the mission agency slowly (or quickly!) diminishes, since the agency's primary focus tends to be on active mission workers. This can cause tremendous stress along with the process of disengaging from the usual routines of ministry, adjusting to a new location and environment, and managing older-age health issues and loneliness. MUT organizes writing workshops to train mission workers in recording their experiences, so as to encourage both themselves and younger generations. In addition, some financial assistance is provided for health care and crisis situations. Shelter homes are available at the Oddanchatram Campus in Tamil Nadu for those who do not have a place to live. Annual retreats and regional meetings are held for fellowship. MUT volunteers also call or visit retired mission workers for friendly conversation.

6. Care for MKs. MUT organizes retreats for MKs and pastors' children in different regions, catering to multiple language groups. These retreats give MKs a platform to express their needs, support one another, and understand and value their parents' ministry. After the retreat, volunteers continue to listen to, mentor, counsel, and guide the MKs. The 2023 MUT survey of MKs found that most of them faced severe financial challenges in pursuing higher education due to their parents' low income. Limited financial assistance is provided to member missions for MKs pursuing higher education. It is expected that MKs, once they have completed their studies and secured employment, will repay the money in monthly instalments, as a gesture of gratitude, which MUT then uses to bless other MKs.

Prioritizing Member Care

In the midst of various challenges and the needs of Christian workers in Indian missions, God raised members of his church in the 1980s to stand in the gap, advocating for and facilitating member care in India. Many of these individuals and groups were from the secular work world and had little grasp of member care initially. One such individual was J. J. Ratnakumar, a company CEO who resigned to become involved full-time in member care and founded MUT. Stanley Chellappa, an engineer by profession, started a member care organization called Christian Comforting Ministries, which provides financial assistance to Christian workers and their families during times of crisis or bereavement. This ministry is also involved in counseling and prayer mobilization for member care in Indian missions. Through the efforts of such individuals, member care in India has steadily developed among sending and supporting groups (especially churches) with important accompanying shifts in mindsets and in resource allocation. One example is the 700-plus supporting families (upholders) in MUT who volunteer for various aspects of caring for Indian mission workers and their families.

After thirty years of facilitating member care in Indian missions to over one-third of the mission community, we know that collaborative and intentional efforts are crucial. Much progress has been achieved! Nonetheless, additional areas must still be addressed to strategically shape and support member care in India. Here are some of them:

- Continue to develop member care ministries and organizations, especially considering the many unmet needs and the increasing number of Christian workers. For some examples, see Rajendran (2002, 85–86).

- Conduct a comprehensive study of the current challenges and needs of Christian workers in India. This study would focus on the impact and types of care, gaps in care, and recommendations for further developing member care.

- Develop a new paradigm and emphasis to facilitate care among mono-cultural workers (i.e., those working among their own socio-cultural communities). There are an estimated 700,000 mono-cultural workers in the remote villages and hills of India. We know of no adequate member care programs among this group of workers.
- Provide member care training within and for mission-sending groups. This reflects the need for senders to take ownership of responsibility and resource development and not to primarily outsource care to others. Member care should be part of the values and policies of mission organizations.

IMA and MUT are in complete agreement that prioritizing member care helps to safeguard and strengthen mission workers and their ministry among unreached peoples. K. K. Rajendran (2002, 85) affirmed this point in his foundational article on member care:

> In the IMA, we realized that India will never hear about and respond to Christ unless there is healthy care of Christian workers. Therefore, the need of member care for Christian workers has become critical to take the gospel forward. The IMA, in conjunction with other groups, is working to help develop an ethos of member care within missions today. We want to support mission leaders and sending groups as they care for their people. Our approach is becoming more proactive, and there are many opportunities which we believe the Lord is giving us. We fully expect to see Christian workers become more effective as we work together to nurture them and their families for the long-haul. And we fully expect a splendid harvest of people for the Lord as a result of their commitment and care for Christian workers.

Applications: Doing Member Care Well in India

Core Strategies

1. Stay aware of the spiritual nature and warfare involved in mission among the unreached, as well as the member care needs of Christian workers and their families.
2. Encourage sending agencies and sending churches to prioritize both the wellbeing and effectiveness of their workers and to continue to provide and develop training and member care collaboratively with others.

3. Sacrifice, suffering, and risk have always been part of taking the gospel to the unreached. Support mission workers and their families as they grow in resilience, faith, and love for one another; in mutual support with colleagues; and above all in their relationship with Jesus Christ!

Core Resources

1. Training Programs. Learning and upgrading skills is an ongoing process in mission life. Various life skill programs on interpersonal relationships, team building, spiritual vitality, enhancement, marriage enrichment, and inner healing are offered by and through MUT and IMA. Check the MUT and IMA websites for news, updates, and other information.

2. Publications. Various books published by member care specialists have addressed challenges for Christian workers in India. The most comprehensive one is *Member Care in India: Ministry Call to Home Call* (Manoharan et al. 2012). MUT also produces a magazine, *Care and Serve*, two times each year with updates on programs, projects, services, and events.

3. Counselors. Indian missions have a growing body of trained counselors who specialize in cross-cultural mission. These counselors also conduct workshops and programs to address issues for Christian workers such as parenting, emotional needs of MKs, marriage, pre-marital preparation, and stress and trauma. One example is the trauma care resources offered by the Trauma Healing Institute (https://traumahealinginstitute.org/) to address grief, loss, recovery, and post-traumatic growth for Christian workers and their families.

Reflection and Discussion

1. The authors describe many challenges and struggles for Indian mission workers. Which ones are most relevant for your context?

2. In what ways are these challenges and struggles being addressed and even turned into opportunities for fruitful ministry? List some examples.

3. Describe some of the main directions for member care in India and any possible hindrances to their realization.

References

Amalraj, John. 2008a. "From Statutory Welfare Measures to Member Care." In *Worth Keeping: Global Perspectives on Best Practice in Missionary Retention*, edited by Rob Hay, Valerie Lim, Detlef Blöcher, Jaap Katelaar, and Sarah Hay, 196–198. Pasadena, CA: William Carey Library.

Amalraj, John. 2008b. "One Vision to Reach the Lost at Any Cost." In *Worth Keeping: Global Perspectives on Best Practice in Missionary Retention*, edited by Rob Hay, Valerie Lim, Detlef Blöcher, Jaap Katelaar, and Sarah Hay, 268–269. Pasadena, CA: William Carey Library.

Brierly, Peter. 1997. "Missionary Attrition: The ReMAP Research Report." In *Too Valuable to Lose: Exploring the Causes and Cures of Missionary Attrition*, edited by William Taylor, 85–103. Pasadena, CA: William Carey Library.

Christian Comforting Ministries. https://christiancomfortingministries.com/?fbclid=IwAR0VX-dZ-8xqi5df4Itbgw1G35fZslMpLq7FheOAcYWc1IydukXo62sbxnE.

India Mission Association. https://imaindia.org/.

Jeyarani, Joyce. 2023. "Correlates of Life Skills and Wellbeing among Higher Secondary Students at Santhosha Vidyala, Tirunelveli—An Empirical Study." PhD diss., Department of Social Work, Bishop Heber College.

Manoharan, J. N., Jacob Ninan, J. J. Rathnakumar, and Isac Soundararaja, eds. 2012. *Member Care in India: Ministry Call to Home Call*. Vellore, India: Missionary Upholders Trust. http://mutindia.org/publication.html. (Hardcopies available for purchase at mut.vellore@gmail.com.)

Missionary Upholders Trust. http://mutindia.org/.

Missionary Upholders Trust. *Care and Serve.* http://mutindia.org/publication.html.

O'Donnell, Kelly. 2002. "Going Global: A Member Care Model for Best Practice." In *Doing Member Care Well: Perspectives and Practices from Around the World*, edited by Kelly O'Donnell, 13–22. Pasadena, CA: William Carey Library. https://passionexchange.files.wordpress.com/2008/10/doingmembercarewell.pdf.

Paul, Lancelot. 2023. "The Current Challenges of the Indian MKs." Unpublished research, Missionary Upholders Trust. (Contact author for more information: jplance@gmail.com.)

Paul, Polly. 2015. "Missionary Kids—Uncared People Group?" In *Ministry Call to Home Call*, edited by J. N. Manoharan, Jacob Ninan, J. J. Ratnakumar, and Isac Soundararaja, 167–175. Vellore, India: Missionary Upholders Trust.

Rajendran, K. 2002. "Care for Christian Workers in India: Dark Obstacles and Divine Opportunities." In *Doing Member Care Well: Perspectives and Practices from Around the World*, edited by Kelly O'Donnell, 77–86. Pasadena, CA: William Carey Library. https://passionexchange.files.wordpress.com/2008/10/doingmembercarewell.pdf.

Rajendran, Pramila. 2020. "Setting Up a Care Department in an Organization." Miila Consulting, June 30, 2020. https://www.miilaconsulting.com/post/setting-up-a-care-department-in-an-organization.

Samuel, Anand. 2012. "Stressors of God's Chosen People." In *Ministry Call to Home Call*, edited by J. N. Manoharan, Jacob Ninan, J. J. Ratnakumar, and Isac Soundararaja, 57–67. Vellore, India: Missionary Upholders Trust.

Solomon, Daniel. 2015. "The Study on the Challenges of the MKs in the Boarding School and Colleges in Tamil Nādu." Unpublished research, Missionary Upholders Trust.

Soundararaja, Isac. 2022. "From Ministry Call to Home Call: The State of Member Care in India." *Evangelical Missions Quarterly* 58 (2). https://missionexus.org/from-ministry-call-to-home-call-the-state-of-member-care-in-india/.

Sudhakar, Juno. 2015. 2016. "The Study on the Challenges and Needs of the Retired Christian Workers in India." Unpublished research, Missionary Upholders Trust. (For more information contact: mut.vellore@gmail.com.)

Isac Soundararaja, PhD, serves with India Missions Association as its General Secretary. He became a Christian at age nineteen. He has held various responsibilities in missions in India, including specialized teaching in cross-cultural communication, facilitating non-formal theological training for rural church planters, and working in member care initiatives. generalsecretary@imaindia.org.

Lancelot Paul, PhD, was a researcher with the government of India. Based in Bangalore, he is actively involved with church ministry, missions, and member care. Presently he serves as the President of Missionary Upholders Trust. jplance@gmail.com.

PART 3
Staying the Course in the Sectors

Michael Pollock & Timothy Sanford, Consulting Editors

Introduction to Part 3

Michael: I spent my formative years in Kenya as part of a mission family and then in several US states. I have worked in international missions for over 30 years, educating, coaching, debriefing, and training third-culture individuals, families, schools, and organizations working in different international sectors. My wife (Kristen) and I raised three children in China for nine years, where I was an international school principal and TCK development leader. I also served as director of Interaction International for almost three years and established a hub of international TCK caregivers in 2019 to facilitate global networking. Together with Ruth Van Reken, I revised and updated *Third Culture Kids: Growing Up Among Worlds* (3rd edition, 2017), which Ruth had originally co-authored with my late father, David Pollack.

I served for two years on the board for Families in Global Transition (FIGT), another good example of an organization networking across sectors that is highly relevant for mission and member care. One of the many resources on its website is an annotated list of over 80 books—written and/or recommended by FIGT members—related to international transition and expatriate life for people and families in different sectors.

Currently, I direct Daraja, an organization that serves the needs and potentials of cross-cultural and mobile families, couples, and individuals across the globe with a focus on TCKs. I am also the co-founder of the International TCK Conference (ITCKC), which convened for the first time in 2023 in Thailand. This conference brought together colleagues from various sectors who are involved in TCK work. One special emphasis was on equipping under-resourced regions and inspiring the next generation of TCK caregivers.

Timothy: I was raised as a TCK in Ecuador in the early 1960s. My earliest memories are of life in South America; when I was told we'd be returning to the United States, I felt I was going to a foreign country. Landing in the suburbs of the US Midwest was a radical culture shock after the jungles and mountains of Ecuador.

Like many TCKs, I have always gravitated towards other TCKs. Once I began working as a licensed professional counselor, I applied my clinical expertise to helping mission organizations support their member families and TCKs specifically. Many of these TCKs experience not only multiple cultures while growing up, as I did, but also multiple sectors in terms of the diversity of positions, jobs, and advanced degrees through which they engage local and global problems. Their skill sets, forged through cross-cultural living and transitions, are often well suited for recognizing novel, inclusive, empathic, and culturally sensitive approaches to problem solving.

In 2022, I was asked by a law firm, Telios Law, to participate in a restorative justice gathering for TCKs from Japan. Venturing into the legal sector with my clinical skills brought a greater appreciation for the potential of multi-sectoral collaboration.

Overview and Perspectives

Working cross-culturally is a core part of mission and member care (training strategies and incarnational lifestyles) and increasingly involves engaging with different sectors (e.g., humanitarian, development, and peace). Part Three explores connecting and contributing to different sectors. The five chapters build upon the 35 chapters in volume 2 of the *Global Member Care* Series (*Crossing Sectors for Serving Humanity*) and in particular on "Charting Your Course Through the Sectors" (O'Donnell 2013) and "Sector Connectors: Families in Global Transition" (Van Reken, Bushong, and Quick 2013).

Staying the course across sectors is critical to the message and ministry of Jesus the *global* Messiah. That message includes the pervasiveness of the Kingdom of God, the inclusiveness of Christ's ministry, and the new commandment that we love one another. This love that seeks the good of others is not meant to be limited by any confines. Its global focus encompasses the whole of humanity and the many diverse ways to do ministry within the *missio Dei*.

In this third part, the authors take a hard look at ministry in five sectors that might not fall easily into "missions" categories. They challenge us to consider the issues and care perspectives involved as well as overlooked and even blind spots in our vision of ministry and member care. We are invited to see the needs and the beauty of both individual human beings and communities regardless of their experiences with mental health and trauma, corruption and exploitation, climate and environmental degradation, and human abuse and trafficking. And we are invited to open our eyes, and to see the many fields that are ripe and ready for harvest (John 4:35).

Chapter 11 by Emily Hervey and Dean Mellerstig, take us into the field of global and community mental health care. First, we see their formative experiences and the needs they encountered in missional settings, regarding both the victims of displacement and trauma and the people ministering to those victims. The authors discovered that in creating a holistic and cohesive program to address mental health needs, they had in hand a solid, spiritually rich, and grounded approach that could be multiplied. The curriculum and training process are outlined, along with the vision for multiplication. The importance of defining trauma culturally and contextualizing training and care are emphasized. At the heart of this approach is the privilege and power of bringing people to Jesus for healing.

Chapter 12 by Kelly and Michèle Lewis O'Donnell, focuses on understanding, preventing, and confronting the many facets of corruption with integrity, skill, and solidarity. A particular focus is the importance of humility in acknowledging our own tendencies toward self-justification and rationalizations and when correcting unethical practices or situations. The case study digs deeply into the widespread and long-term impacts of failure to confront and amend fraud in the mission community. The authors spur us on to take the necessary steps, as quickly and thoroughly as possible, to identify problems and make redress. The process of identifying and addressing corruption must be approached with prudence and the support of others, considering the cultural components, the needs of victims, and the importance of putting safeguards in place for organizations and their staff. The authors finish with an earnest appeal to embrace integrity at all levels—individual, institutional, and international—by walking in the light and joining in a global movement for integrity. As C. S. Lewis wrote in *The Case for Christianity* (1943), "We all want progress, but if you're on the wrong road, progress means doing an about-turn and walking back to the right road; in that case, the man who turns back soonest is the most progressive."

Chapter 13 by Jenny Smith, tells her personal story of suffering a life-altering injury and consequent disabilities. She explores the role of people with disabilities in ministry and how that understanding may inform the ways in which we minister *to* and *with* the disability community. She emphasizes that solid teaching is based upon lived experience—we must own an understanding and practice if we are to share it with others. Just as Jesus used the foolish of the world to shame the wise, we find that the "less able" among us have much to teach the "abled" if we work to make room at the table for them. Culture has a powerful impact on how ability and disability are perceived and approached. Therefore, it is imperative to cultivate an awareness of our own perceptions and judgments about disability and of the cultural views and practices where we minister and develop partners.

Chapter 14: Debbie, David and Jamie Hawker, and Biniam Guush, take on a controversial topic: the human causes and consequences of climate change. By engaging in a biblical view of creation and stewardship and pairing it with the unfolding crisis of climate change, they raise crucial questions. These questions not only concern Christians' responsibility to care for our planet, but also how to show empathy and compassion toward those whose lives are increasingly impacted by rising seas and weather anomalies. Global climate change is an important subject in the far-flung places where many minister, but it also needs attention in the places and economies with greater resources that are more able to respond flexibly to emerging conditions. The authors encourage us to view climate change as an issue of justice with important implications for our choices, behaviors, and lifestyles in mission and member care.

Chapter 15 by Timothy Friesen, shines light on the massive reality of human trafficking and bringing hope to the victims of these dark assaults against humanity require international, multi-sectoral collaborations. This chapter shows how member care plays a strategic role in an international justice mission's fight against human trafficking. The author describes that organization's development of a comprehensive model to support staff care and resilience as well as to mitigate the risks of vicarious trauma, compassion fatigue, and burnout. The chapter is a cutting-edge case study detailing member care structures, practices, and services for people working in one of the most psychologically challenging and potentially traumatizing contexts. We can glean much from this model of care in contexts where trauma and the abuse of human rights are everyday realities.

Final Thoughts

We want to remind everyone of the importance of words and of a "people first" approach to dignity. Using terms like "people in migration," "laborers without documentation," and "children who have been trafficked" orients us less toward unhelpful labels and more toward God's person-centered view of fellow humans. We want to see and affirm the inherent value, strengths, and glory along with the needs and struggles of each person. Thus, when we cross sectors in mission and member care, it matters how we think and talk, and make budget and policy decisions about, the *persons* in our spheres of ministry.

We have also come to recognize that our "mission" involves more than only our primary "job." It also includes caring attitudes and behaviors toward all people with whom we come into contact: not just family, friends, staff, and volunteers, but also migrant workers, taxi drivers, urban professionals, or the rural poor. In other words, God brings many people across our paths who are part of our mission for living out the Kingdom. We need reality checks and accountability to stay focused on this broader Kingdom mission. This perspective reflects the message of Part Three. There are sectors—such as health, anti-corruption, disability, environment, and protection—full of challenges, opportunities, and *people* waiting for us. They too can be part of our Kingdom work. What are we waiting for?

References

Families in Global Transition. Online Bookstore. https://www.figt.org/Online_Bookstore.

International TCK Conference. https://itckc.global/.

O'Donnell, Kelly. 2013. "Charting Your Course Through the Sectors." In *Global Member Care, vol. 2: Crossing Sectors for Serving Humanity*, edited by Kelly O'Donnell and Michèle Lewis O'Donnell, 5–20. Pasadena, CA: William Carey Library. https://membercareassociates.org/wp-content/uploads/2018/01/Charting-Your-Course-through-the-Sectors-final-ODonnell-2013.pdf.

Pollock, David, Ruth Van Reken, and Michael Pollock. 2017. *Third Culture Kids: Growing Up Among Worlds*, 3rd ed. London: Nicholas Brealey.

Van Reken, Ruth, Lois Bushong, and Tina Quick. 2013. "Sector Connectors: Families in Global Transition." In *Global Member Care, vol. 2: Crossing Sectors for Serving Humanity*, edited by Kelly O'Donnell and Michèle Lewis O'Donnell, 21–36. Pasadena, CA: William Carey Library.

Michael Pollock, MEd, is an adult TCK (Kenya/US), coach, and consultant. Co-author of *Third Culture Kids: Growing up Among Worlds*, 3rd edition (2017), he trains, speaks, and writes on third culture issues, advocating for broader and more informed care. After spending nine years in China, he founded and leads Daraja (www.darajatck.org), a nonprofit organization focusing on TCK care. Michael and his wife Kristen are parents of three adult TCKs.

Timothy Sanford, MA, LPC, is a licensed professional counselor and an ordained minister. He is currently the clinical director of counseling services at Focus on the Family (USA) (www.focusonthefamily.com/). Tim is a TCK, works with TCKs, and is the author of *I Have to be Perfect (and Other Parsonage Heresies)*, a book for children of pastors and mission workers. Tim and his wife Becky have two grown daughters and reside in Colorado, USA.

11

Mental Health as Mission

Our Journey into Trauma Training and Care

Emily Hervey and Dean Mellerstig

Encountering trauma is unavoidable in our world and in missions, whether we are simply building a relationship with an individual from a broken, abusive home or managing humanitarian operations for entire populations devastated by war, upheaval, or a natural disaster. Many mission workers are ill-equipped to help others and are personally impacted by vicarious trauma from the stories they hear (Bagley 2003). In this chapter, we explore means of addressing trauma and discuss how, in our work in Africa and the Middle East, we have equipped local pastors, lay leaders, and volunteers to experience healing and serve others better through intensive five-day workshops. Churches remain a central part of society and missions, with pastors often bearing the weight of hearing stories of trauma. Trauma-informed training and support for senders, mission workers, disciples, churches, and communities are crucial. It is part of an expanding initiative to promote mental health.

Participating in the Global Mental Health Initiative

The inclusion of churches, civil society organizations, and local communities in global mental health efforts is consistent with a broad concern to promote holistic wellbeing on a worldwide scale. One description of Global Mental Health (GMH) states:

> GMH is a growing domain of study, research, and practice which promotes equitable mental health and wellbeing for all—locally through globally. It is international, interdisciplinary, culturally relevant, and multi-sectoral; emphasizes the right to health and equity in health; encourages healthy behaviors and lifestyles; is committed to preventing and treating mental, neurological, and substance use conditions (MNS) especially for vulnerable populations (e.g., in settings of poverty, conflict, calamity, and trauma) and in low- and

middle-income countries; and seeks to improve policies and programs; professional practices and research; advocacy and awareness; and social, structural, systemic, and environmental factors that affect mental health and wellbeing. (GMH–Map 2023)

GMH moves beyond the Western mindset of relying on specialized professionals to address mental *disorders and conditions* and seeks to engage society on a broader scale to promote mental *wellbeing*. This effort is included in the Sustainable Development Goals (United Nations 2015), both directly in the third goal (on promoting health and wellbeing for all) and indirectly as part of other goals and their targets (Rich and O'Donnell 2023). The World Health Organization's (WHO) leadership and participation in the GMH effort to expand resources and promote equity in health care led to the development of the *Comprehensive Mental Health Action Plan 2013–2030* (WHO 2021), with similar objectives, including "more effective leadership and governance for mental health; the provision of comprehensive, integrated mental health and social care services in community-based settings; implementation of strategies for promotion and prevention; and strengthened information systems, evidence and research" (p. v). The ongoing challenges and positive outcomes of practical efforts around the world were presented in the *World Mental Health Report: Transforming Mental Health for All* (WHO 2022). The accounts of successful undertakings have inspired additional creative, culturally appropriate initiatives. WHO has dozens of other evidence-based resources available free online; two widely used examples are the *mhGAP Intervention Guide for Mental, Neurological, and Substance Use Disorders in Non-Specialized Health Settings* (2016) and *Psychological First Aid* (2011).

Trauma Involvement for the Church and Missions

Trauma is not a new concept or a new issue, but awareness regarding its occurrence and effects has exploded over the last fifty years. Indeed, trauma has coexisted with persecution throughout the history of the church. From the very beginning, all followers of Jesus were called to count the cost, take up their crosses, and lay down their lives. These requests are not to be taken lightly! But how well do we equip and enable mission workers to deal with the suffering—including from mental health conditions and trauma—that they encounter among others and in their own lives in field locations?

Indeed, mental health problems, including trauma, create a distinctive mission field. As Mwiti and Smith (2018) wrote:

There is a growing global mental health movement around the world today; and the global church is beginning to recognize mental health problems, which are the leading cause of disability worldwide—more disabling than such conditions as heart disease, stroke, or diabetes—as a major ministry priority. … The lack of attention to this important issue both by the church and secular society has left thousands of people with mental health problems stigmatized, judged as spiritually deficient, and sometimes, in the case of major mental illness, locked up and even chained in institutions where they are exposed to poor living conditions, sexual and physical abuse, and neglect. Those with mental health problems have poorer health care, diminished human rights, and higher mortality. They comprise one of the largest mission fields for the church worldwide.

The reality, particularly in low to middle-income nations, is that current mental health care resources do not meet existing needs, especially in areas of high trauma. In places of high conflict and/or persecution, serving as a mission worker can be particularly stressful or even traumatizing, so member care is critical. At the same time, mission workers capable of addressing trauma may be scarce in such demanding regions. There is a great need to equip the local communities with trauma-response tools applicable to both Christians and non-Christians. One example of trauma training and care from a Christian perspective is the "Trauma Healing" resources, including a book authored by mission workers in Africa, used for training in dozens of countries, and translated into over 200 languages: *Healing the Wounds of Trauma: How the Church Can Help* (Hill et al. 2015).

As the Global South becomes a growing source of mission workers, the communities being reached are also the ones sending others out (Zurlo, Johnson, and Crossing 2020). As sending groups and mission structures multiply throughout Africa, South America, and beyond, those coming from areas with high rates of post-traumatic stress disorder (PTSD) often need to find healing themselves before they are sent out. They also need to be equipped to help others. With this in mind, we have developed *The Tree of Life: Finding Healing and Growth in Jesus* (ToL) as an interactive workshop and have implemented it in several countries around the globe.

Emily's Story

After growing up on three different continents (in Chile, the USA, and Kazakhstan), I've maintained a fairly mobile, cross-cultural lifestyle.

But today's mobility for me heavily corresponds with areas in need of trauma response care, such as Nigeria and northern Iraq, not usually places where one would plan a vacation. While pursuing my doctorate in clinical psychology from 2007 to 2012, with the intent to serve as a member care provider, I also received training in addressing trauma. I started using these skills when deploying with the Green Cross Academy of Traumatology to various natural disasters. After graduation, I served as a psychologist for mission workers at a counseling center in Kenya. I came to recognize trauma as a common theme on the mission field, for both the workers and those whom they serve.

About ten years ago, I returned to the United States, exploring next steps, considering long-term plans, and asking God for direction. Instead, I kept hearing, "Wait … wait on the Lord." I had an opportunity to compile what I had been discovering about how frequent and prevalent trees are in Scripture, and about how their growth amidst life's storms parallels human experience. The Bible starts in Genesis and ends in Revelation with the tree of life, and the pages in between are full of psalms, prophecies, proverbs, pictures, and parables related to trees, about everything from roots to fruits.

At that time, I had not yet conceived the workshop that would emerge with the integration of inner healing and efforts to equip leaders globally. As I began teaching at a seminary in Nigeria in 2014, I came to realize that member care was critical not only for international mission workers, but also in caring for and equipping national workers. The material that came out of that season of waiting was first implemented and refined in Nigeria, working directly with pastors, students, and frontline workers in regions controlled by Boko Haram. The need for trauma care was obvious, and thus this emphasis was integrated into the program. Along the way, I met a fellow missions-minded traveler, Dean Mellerstig, who is now my husband and partner in ministry.

Dean's Story

I grew up in a home that supported missions and went with the whole family on a mission trip when I was in high school. In college, I engaged in cross-cultural ministry in Mexico, doing building projects and vacation Bible school, and tutored underprivileged kids in the inner city of a metropolis. After universy, God directed me to seminary, where I studied spiritual formation from 1994 to 1996. During this time, God revealed his love for me and shifted my motivation from satisfying myself to wanting to share God's love with others.

I became a youth pastor and also earned an MDiv degree while overseeing a college group from 1999 to 2002. Then I ministered in a Chinese church. As my next step, God guided me into itinerant missions. I went to remote places in the world to provide theological training for pastors at conferences, seminaries, and Bible schools (2009–2016). My journey in mental health as mission began after I started dating Emily. We met at a seminary in Nigeria, where I was teaching theology and she was teaching psychology. In talking with each other, we realized that we shared a love of Jesus, a desire to help others, and a nomadic lifestyle.

In 2016, we went to Iraq and saw firsthand the conditions of people who had been displaced by the Islamic State of Iraq and the Levant and were living in tents in camps for internally displaced persons. We interacted with the Yazidis, a group that follows a syncretized form of Christianity and Islam. By one count, they have experienced seventy-four genocides throughout their history. What a multi-generational trauma that needs to be addressed!

There is such a great need for trauma care in our world. In Africa especially, I have seen firsthand how trauma stems from sources such as conflicts, poverty, political corruption, and natural disasters. Because there is so much trauma and so few resources to help people heal, I felt compelled to make a difference by doing whatever I could. Having seen the effectiveness of the Tree of Life workshop, I realized the strategic nature of helping hurting individuals gain a clearer picture of who God is, finding healing in encounters with him, and becoming equipped to help others find healing in Jesus.

The Program: The Tree of Life

When we were developing the biblical basis for the program, the tree was a central metaphor, representing who we are and how we grow. Just as a tree receives life through the light of the sun and water to grow, so we receive life through Jesus, the light of the world, and living water welling up inside of us, the Holy Spirit. As a tree absorbs nutrients from the soil, so we receive the word of God as a source of truth to help us put down healthy roots.

Our roots, which begin forming at the very beginning of life, influence how well we grow and how secure we are against the storms of life. Our relational roots form from our early relationships and influence the relational patterns we establish as adults. Our emotional roots can lead to a secure identity and healthy resiliency, or to distorted belief systems and unresolved trauma and loss. Our spiritual roots can allow us to be immersed in and dependent on

God's love, grounded in faith, and secure in eternal hope, or they can lead to a distorted perception of God and a superficial view of religion.

The metaphor continues by noting that the story of a tree's life is recorded in the rings of an ever-expanding trunk, with its hidden memories of flourishing or drought. The knots in the wood record where a branch was broken off, a record of trauma or loss that has left either a story of healing or mark of decay. While talking about the storms of life we present the concept of trauma, describing human reactions on an immediate and long-term basis, and giving practical tools for providing psychological first aid and recognizing PTSD symptoms. *Complex trauma* is also touched on with discussion of abuse (resulting from exposure to severe and pervasive trauma over time and often affecting emotional regulation, identity and sense of self, and relationships), similar to the disease that can affect the core of the tree.

Finally, a tree's constant maturation process corresponds with our sanctification in love for God and for others. We grow in our love for God through the integration of our heart, soul, mind, and strength. We relate to others through our branches, sharing the fruit of love and its characteristics of joy, peace, patience, kindness, goodness, faithfulness, gentleness, and self-control in our interactions with others.

Added to the tree metaphor is the discovery of growth and healing, centered on the Giver of Life. The primary practice now incorporated into the program is an inner healing process called the Immanuel Approach (Lehman 2016). This approach centers on the promise of Christ's presence at all times, whether we are experiencing joy or enduring sorrow and fear. The primary goal is intimacy with Jesus, beginning by connecting with him in our joyful memories and experiencing his presence in the here and now. When we are securely attached to him, we can also find healing when going back to painful memories and encountering his presence there. The Immanuel intervention specifically starts with joyful memories, connecting with Jesus and then proceeding to encounter him in painful memories. It seeks to transform traumatic memories that usually trigger negative emotions such as fear, anger, sadness, and shame into memories of experiencing the healing and truth provided by Jesus. Although the facilitator plays an important role in directing the wounded person to Jesus, the emphasis is on Jesus himself who brings transformation and healing. What differentiates this from other inner healing models is the emphasis on connecting with Jesus, first in the joyful memories and present time, establishing a secure connection and safety nets to avoid retraumatization.

One woman, with the help of a facilitator, started by recalling a joyful memory of her baptism at a young age. While remembering this experience, she saw Jesus smiling at her. In the present room, she encountered Jesus close by, and he reminded her of his forgiveness for her sins and his unconditional love for her. Then she recalled a painful memory of her abusive father, a man whom she deeply hated; this destructive relationship contributed to her mistrust of men. There Jesus showed himself to be present, weeping with her and reminding her of his deep love for her. Jesus invited her to release her bitterness, to forgive as she had been forgiven. She described a weight being lifted, her anger being replaced by peace and joy. This experience represented a critical shift in her healing journey and has made possible her effective ministry to others.

During the ToL seminar, participants not only have opportunities to identify and address such deep wounds and unhealthy relational patterns, all the way from roots to recent storms, but also practice forms of intimacy with Jesus, starting with joyful memories and later encountering Jesus in their painful memories. Not only are they the recipients of these interventions, but they also learn how to guide others through the same process. This process is simple, and the main role of the facilitator is to keep directing the person back to Jesus to find truth and love, healing and wholeness.

There isn't room to solve every problem and heal every wound during a typical five-day workshop. But again, we, the trainers, are not the ones doing the healing! Jesus does it! We get to start the ball rolling, praying that participants will continue to grow in their intimacy with Christ and to help each other do the same. We seek not only to teach concepts and facilitate healing, but to equip participants to develop skills that they can take home and implement in their families and communities. During the final session we have participants gather in groups based on geographical locations to set goals and make specific plans on how to support one another when doing interventions, practice with each other, and keep each other accountable.

As with GMH interventions, this program was not meant to be developed in the West and transplanted into other cultures. The very first implementation of the curriculum was in Nigeria, working with an organization focused on the persecuted church. Constant feedback and eventually co-facilitating with a Nigerian allowed us to make modifications and ensure that the material was understandable, relatable, and relevant. The beauty of the tree metaphor is that trees are globally symbolic yet extremely diverse across climates and ecosystems. Patterns of roots and growth are consistent across cultures, while the sources of harm to a tree, such as natural disasters or human-caused damage, are just as diverse as the forms of trauma we experience, ranging from earthquakes to abuse to wars. The use of the word "trauma" varies from one region to another, with some languages not even having a direct translation, so we include discussion of the concept as it relates to that context. We highlight the global reality of suffering, including the theological questions attached, and create space to explore the theology of suffering. The most transcendent factor is the reality that God is the source of life and healing. *How* people experience his presence is very diverse, but *whom* they encounter remains the same.

Research Outcomes

To test the effectiveness of the program, measurements of trauma symptoms and spiritual wellbeing were administered at the beginning and end of the program, along with open-ended questions. The primary intention was to assess whether ToL was making a difference in the lives of participants and how it could be improved. Small changes were made along the way, and then a formal program assessment was completed using data gathered from three groups in Nigeria in 2020 (prior to the COVID-19 pandemic). Results were published in Hervey (2023). In 2021, another study was conducted in Nigeria with a broader group of participants, followed by research in Kenya for a doctoral dissertation (Bresser 2022).

All three studies found that symptoms of PTSD were significantly reduced among all groups, but the impact of the intervention was particularly evident for those who initially had the most severe symptoms. The outcomes were particularly impressive in Kenya, where 80 percent of participants began with likely cases of PTSD; after the program, that number dropped to 20 percent. The third study included long-term outcomes, with measures taken nine months later. Although the number of responses was unfortunately small, within that group the number of symptoms continued to decline, except for those who experienced an additional distressing event; for them, the symptoms returned, demonstrating the need for follow-up care to address new sources of trauma.

The measures of spiritual wellbeing included awareness of God, disappointment with God and realistic acceptance (two related measures), and instability. In all three studies, there was an improvement in awareness of God, but the difference was not statistically significant for two studies, likely because of the high initial scores. Similarly, there was a decrease in instability for all groups, with statistically significant change in two of them. Realistic acceptance and disappointment both improved significantly in the first two studies, and both showed a small improvement in the third, though it was not statistically significant.

Looking more deeply into the effect of the Immanuel approach, participants were asked if they had an encounter with Jesus and, if so, how it impacted them. In the 2021 cohort, five of the 98 participants referred to a positive spiritual experience that occurred earlier in their lives, while the rest all reported having a positive experience of encountering Jesus during the program. Many gave more specific descriptions, the most dominant theme being an influence on their perception of and/or relationship to Jesus, including a greater awareness of his presence (e.g., "The encounter calmed me down and gave me assurance of his presence and provision"), increase in trust (e.g., "It actually influenced me greatly as my heart was strengthened to trust his presence always and never to be afraid of anything"), and a transformation of memories (e.g., "Recalling the joyful past and Jesus's presence was helpful to bring release from past painful events and its memories").

There were numerous reports of a decrease in negative emotions (e.g., pain, fear, bitterness) and an increase in positive emotions (e.g., joy, peace, gratitude, freedom). Some also mentioned the significance of personal growth (e.g., "It helps me to forgive more easily and have more desire for prayer, studying the word of God, fellowship with other believers, and a high desire for reaching out to people with the word of God") and helping others (e.g., "Whoa! In so many ways, through my experience of encounter, I received a tool to carry on with what I am supposed to do, how I am supposed to live and act, and what will help me be able to reach others for the Lord—helping others connect with Jesus"). Participants' descriptions suggest that both spiritual growth and emotional transformation are prominent outcomes. The increased intimacy with Jesus can have both positive immediate effects and long-term changes in outlook and lifestyle. Habitually finding security in his presence contributes to greater resilience when encountering future suffering and trauma.

Implementation Strategy
Two key facets of strategy in our program are sustainability and multiplication. To make the ToL workshop sustainable, ownership must be adopted by local hosts, who from the beginning are asked to determine who the participants

should be, manage logistics, and determine how the costs of conducting the program will be covered (through either individual registration fees or sponsorship by a church or organization). We go only when and where we are invited, with leaders present who recognize the need and are ready to invest their time and resources to equip people to meet that need. That investment results in an interdependent relationship, avoiding too much dependence on us. It also means allowing local partners to share in the financial responsibility by working out how they want to pay for participants' workbooks, the venue, and room and board. Our donors cover our international transportation while local partners take care of our local transportation.

We print the workbook in the country hosting the training to reduce the production cost and make future self-sufficiency more feasible. The revenue from the material published (the workbook, the instructor's manual, and the accompanying Bible studies) helps fund translation into the dominant local language. There is nothing like having the workbook translated into another language to take us out of the equation.

In an effort to multiply ToL, we have two levels of training: introductory and advanced. The first is a five-day intensive workshop in which the participants increase their intimacy with Jesus; learn, experience, and implement the Immanuel approach; and establish a theological grounding. We cap the number of participants at fifteen because we wish to offer supervised practice of the Immanuel approach.

There are essentially three outcomes for the participants in the first workshop: receiving, giving, and training. All participants encounter Jesus, receive healing, learn the Immanuel intervention, and personally benefit from the experience, but some do not utilize the tool at their disposal. The givers receive and see the value of facilitating the Immanuel approach for others; they go on to use the tool, facilitate Jesus's healing of wounds, and experience the joy of seeing God at work in others' lives.

Some participants continue to facilitate the Immanuel intervention and seek to take it a step further to help others learn how to do so. We require future trainers to report on ten Immanuel interventions they have facilitated. Doing so increases the likelihood that the trainees will encounter situations that call for troubleshooting; working through these situations helps them develop confidence in their ability to teach others. For this group, we return and conduct a four-day advanced training, which teaches them how to deliver the workshop, including reviewing the material in the training, supervising practice of skills to ensure competence, and providing feedback as they present the content. In a best-case scenario, advanced graduates teach an introductory workshop themselves while we coach them to become better instructors. However, it is often difficult for students to devote so many days in a row to this endeavor; therefore, we often must hold the introduction at a later date and have the advanced graduates receive training on how to be better trainers at that time.

Locations of Focus

Emily's early focus around 2012 on helping mission workers deal with their own trauma expanded to helping both expatriates and nationals from a faith-based approach, while equipping both groups to help others. In Nigeria, we have worked with the local church and organizations. There has been ongoing violence in the north (from Boko Haram) and middle belt regions (due to conflict between Muslim herders and Christian farmers), with a recent dramatic growth in kidnappings for ransom. Mission workers are scarce, mental health care is very limited (0.07 practicing psychologists per 100,000 people; WHO 2006), and the rates of PTSD are very high. A study conducted in Jos, where we've done many ToL programs, found a 46.1 percent rate of PTSD (Tagurum et al. 2015), with even higher rates further north, such as 78 percent for internally displaced people living in camps in Maiduguri (Aluh et al. 2020). Churches remain a central part of society, with pastors bearing the weight of hearing stories of trauma. As a result, our work there has been equipping local pastors, lay leaders, and volunteers with intensive five-day workshops that help them encounter healing and equip them to help others.

Kurdistan, in northern Iraq, has also become an area of focus for us. Because of the greater attention from the West, there are an abundance of NGOs with international funding and quite a few workers. But the rate of exposure to trauma is extremely high, particularly with the thousands of displaced people still living in camps, where overall feelings of hopelessness have contributed to high rates of suicide. Anyone working there must be equipped to respond to trauma and to wrestle with the realities of suffering. Our recent faith-based training has been predominantly with workers who wish to help those who are hurting around them, while also dealing with their own exposure to trauma. It is clearly necessary to equip local NGO staff who provide much of the psychosocial care in camps, a need just as real as medical care and provision of food. Although most of these groups are not believers, as there are very few in the region, they have a heart for the hurting in their own community and want to be better equipped to care for others and themselves. This is an example of mental health as mission, building relationships with those who have open hearts and reflecting the love of the ultimate Healer.

Another example is our trip in the summer of 2023 to Uganda. We were invited by an agency with a sending hub in Uganda. Their mission workers are involved in ministries from the inner city of Kampala to war-torn South Sudan. They work with individuals from very difficult backgrounds, some of whom have been changed by Jesus and are now part of the mission. Former prostitutes, for instance, now minister in challenging neighborhoods in Kampala. The agency recently identified the need to help these local mission workers recover from trauma so that they can be more effective in the field, leading to their invitation for us to provide the ToL in Kampala. In the anonymous feedback forms, many expressed appreciation, with comments such as this one: "This training helped me to realize that I also had trauma within me that I had not paid attention to. It's so helpful that it deals with you at first before you use it as a tool to heal other people's hearts." In a follow-up virtual meeting several months later, we heard stories of implementation in the field, including transformational experiences.

Conclusion

Over the years, our life experiences and ministry practices have highlighted the reality that suffering is a practical and theological issue that all mission workers and sending groups must wrestle with. God's heart for the vulnerable is evident throughout Scripture, and showing his love to those hurting in emotional and spiritual ways is just as critical as providing physical resources. We need to explore and develop culturally appropriate forms of response, both in terms of preparing mission workers to help the hurting and to equip nationals to minister to their own neighbors and send out their own mission workers. Cultural sensitivity has long been emphasized in missions, and it must be equally central in mental health care. Just as church-planting and disciple-making movements are strategic for multiplication, so mental health care and trauma response need to go beyond individual intervention to effectively provide care for the many communities that are hurting. Using resources such as ToL, with its multiplicative model, can help us move across cultures, facilitate healing, and prepare mission workers, pastors, and lay leaders to address multiple levels of trauma. Let us continue, as followers of Christ around the globe, to be equipped and to become equippers in mental health and trauma care!

Applications: Mental Health as Mission

Core Strategies

1. A cross-cultural, holistic model: integrate spiritual, emotional, physical, and relational healing and growth. An illustrative metaphor such as a tree can be understood across all cultures and remembered easily.

2. Sustainability: promote ownership by local sponsors from the beginning to ensure future independent implementation of resources and training.

3. Multiplication: train future trainers, providing supervision, feedback, and advanced training to equip them to be the next instructors. Support translation into local languages so that the instruction can be shared more broadly.

Core Resources

1. Contact the authors' website for more information on ToL and other resources, including the ToL Bible study series (www.emilyhervey.com), and email us if you are interested in hosting ToL training (familiesworldwide@gmail.com).

2. Karl Lehman. 2016. *The Immanuel Approach: For Emotional Healing and for Life*; Patricia Velotta. 2011. *Immanuel: A Practicum Immanuel Approach* website, www.immanuelapproach.com.

3. Resources related to Global Mental Health: Global Mental Health Action Network, Humanitarian Disaster Institute, Mental Health and Substance Use (WHO), and Mental Health Innovation Network.

Reflection and Discussion

1. In view of the high rates of trauma exposure, especially in newer sending countries, what can be done to address mission workers' past trauma before they enter the field?

2. Think about contexts where mental health is not recognized as a high priority. How can programs like the Tree of Life be introduced in a way that promotes a more holistic approach to preparing for the mission field?

3. Which GMH resources listed in this chapter would you like to explore? How can they support the church and mission community in preventing and addressing mental health issues and trauma? How might the situation be different in different cultural contexts?

References

Aluh, Deborah Oyine, Roland Nnaemeka Okoro, and Adamu Zimboh. 2020. "The Prevalence of Depression and Post-Traumatic Stress Disorder among Internally Displaced Persons in Maiduguri, Nigeria." *Journal of Public Mental Health* 19 (2): 159–168. https://doi.org/10.1108/JPMH-07-2019-0071.

American Bible Society. "Trauma Healing." https://ministry.americanbible.org/trauma-healing/trauma-healing-resources.

Bagley, Robert W. 2003. "Trauma and Traumatic Stress among Missionaries." *Journal of Psychology and Theology* 31 (2): 97–112. https://doi.org/10.1177/009164710303100202.

Bresser, Kristen. 2022. "A Quantitative Study of a Faith-Based Trauma Healing Intervention among Kenyans." PhD diss., Regent University. https://www.proquest.com/dissertations-theses/quantitative-study-faith-based-trauma-healing/docview/2645791129/se-2.

Global Mental Health Action Network. https://unitedgmh.org/global-mental-health-action-network.

GMH-Map. 2023. https://sites.google.com/site/gmhmap/.

Hervey, Emily. 2019. *The Tree of Life: Finding Healing and Growth in Jesus: Instructor's Manual*. Worldwide Writings.

Hervey, Emily. 2023. "Spiritually Oriented Trauma Healing in Nigeria: A Program Evaluation to Assess Trauma-Symptom Reduction and Spiritual Growth." *Journal of Psychology and Theology* 51 (3): 412–428. https://doi.org/10.1177/00916471221150402. (Pre-print version: https://emilyhervey.com/made-by-emily/articles/.)

Hill Margaret, Valerie Hill, Dick Baggé, and Pat Miersma. 2015. *Healing the Wounds of Trauma: How the Church Can Help*. Philadelphia: American Bible Society. https://bibles.com/product/categories/christian-books-and-resources/healing-wounds-trauma-how-church-can-help-north-american-edition-pod.

Humanitarian Disaster Institute, Wheaton College. https://www.wheaton.edu/academics/academic-centers/humanitarian-disaster-institute/.

Immanuel Approach. https://www.immanuelapproach.com/.

Lehman, Karl. 2016. *The Immanuel Approach: For Emotional Healing and for Life*. Immanuel Publishing.

Mental Health Innovation Network (MHIN). https://www.mhinnovation.net/.

Mwiti, Gladys, and Bradley Smith. 2018. "Turning the Church's Attention to Mental Health: Binding Up the Brokenhearted." *Lausanne Global Analysis* 7 (6). https://lausanne.org/content/lga/turning-the-churchs-attention-to-mental-health.

Rich, Grant, and Kelly O'Donnell. 2023. "Global Mental Health." In *Oxford Bibliographies in Psychology*, edited by Dana S. Dunn. New York: Oxford University Press. https://drive.google.com/file/d/1xXpYV4Yzw0uKQ0YseGHqnnVvmAg8Bg3K/view.

Tagurum, Yetunde Olubusayo, Oluwabunmi Oluwayemisi, Chirdan Taiwo, Danjuma Ayotunde Bello, Tolulope Olumide Afolaranmi, Zuwaira Ibrahim Hassan, and Christopher Yilgwan. 2015. "Prevalence of Violence and Symptoms of Post-Traumatic Stress Disorder among Victims of Ethno-Religious Conflict in Jos, Nigeria." *Journal of Psychiatry* 18 (1): 1–6. https://doi.org/10.4172/Psychiatry.1000178.

Velotta, Patricia. 2011. *Immanuel: A Practicum*. This Joy! Books. https://immanuelpracticum.com/book/.

World Health Organization. Mental Health and Substance Use. https://www.who.int/teams/mental-health-and-substance-use/.

World Health Organization. 2006. "WHO-AIMS Report on Mental Health System in Nigeria." https://cdn.who.int/media/docs/default-source/mental-health/who-aims-country-reports/nigeria_who_aims_report.pdf?sfvrsn=6bd16cef_3&download=true.

World Health Organization. 2016. *mhGAP Intervention Guide for Mental, Neurological, and Substance Use Disorders in Non-Specialized Health Settings*, version 2.0. https://www.who.int/publications/i/item/9789241549790.

World Health Organization. 2021. *Comprehensive Mental Health Action Plan 2013–2020*. https://www.who.int/publications/i/item/9789240031029.

World Health Organization. 2022. *World Mental Health Report: Transforming Mental Health for All*. https://www.who.int/teams/mental-health-and-substance-use/world-mental-health-report.

World Health Organization. 2011. "World Vision, and War Trauma Foundation." *Psychological First Aid: Guide for Field Workers*. http://apps.who.int/iris/bitstream/10665/44615/1/9789241548205_eng.pdf.

Zurlo, Gina A., Todd M. Johnson, and Peter F. Crossing. 2020. "World Christianity and Mission 2020: Ongoing Shift to the Global South." *International Bulletin of Mission Research* 44 (1): 8–19. https://doi.org/10.1177/2396939319880074.

Emily Hervey and Dean Mellerstig met on the mission field when both were teaching at a seminary in Nigeria. Now they serve globally as a couple, combining Emily's background as a clinical psychologist and field traumatologist and Dean's experience as an itinerant pastor and teacher. They co-facilitate faith-based workshops for trauma healing. Emily serves as an assistant professor, develops and evaluates trauma training programs, and deploys in response to disasters. Dean enjoys getting to know people and writing about their experiences. When in the USA, they generally travel around in an RV. They can be reached by email at familiesworldwide@gmail.com or via the website www.emilyhervey.com.

12

Being a Prophetic Voice in Mission[1]

Living in Integrity and Confronting Corruption

Kelly O'Donnell and Michèle Lewis O'Donnell

Do not fear. These are the things which you should do: speak the truth to one another; judge with truth and judge for peace in your courts. Also let none of you devise evil in your heart against another, and do not love perjury, for I hate all these things, declares YHWH. ... Therefore, love truth and peace.

—Zechariah 8:14–19, excerpts

Corruption is criminal, immoral and the ultimate betrayal of public trust. ... We must hold leaders to account. ... A vibrant civic space and open access to information are essential. And we must protect the rights and recognize the courage of whistleblowers who expose wrongdoing. ... As an age-old plague takes on new forms, let us combat it with new heights of resolve.

—UN Secretary-General António Guterres 2020

This chapter explores the reality of corruption in our world and the resilience and integrity needed to disrupt it. The mission community is not immune to the destructive impacts of corruption from both inside and outside its ranks.

In the first section of this chapter, we discuss several key concepts from our work over the past twenty years to promote integrity and confront corruption (based on O'Donnell and Lewis O'Donnell 2018). As both Christians and psychologists, we reflect on the nature of integrity and corruption, highlighting the challenges and tactics of dysfunction, deviance, and self-deception. In the second section, we share excerpts from a composite case study of a mission family who refused to ignore an international fraud that was affecting many mission organizations and

---

[1] This chapter is an adapted case study from our chapter, "Loving Truth and Peace," that was used with our permission in, *Family Accountability in Missons* (2013).

personnel (based on O'Donnell and Lewis O'Donnell 2013). This case study should inspire colleagues in the member care and mission community to reflect on the ethical quality of their lives, and to develop good governance in their work marked with accountable management and verifiable transparency (O'Donnell and Lewis O'Donnell 2017). The third section presents a global summons to colleagues and organizations in the international mission community to live in integrity and to collaborate resolutely toward a global integrity movement, marked by righteousness and relevance. Reviewing the suggested resources and participating in the annual Global Integrity Day can support our call to be a prophetic voice in mission and to engage in the seen and unseen realms with the authority of Jesus and the power of the Spirit. We are the light—or the darkness—of the world.

Our Capacity for Integrity and Corruption

Integrity means living consistently in moral wholeness. Its opposite is corruption: the distortion, perversion, and deterioration of moral goodness, resulting in the exploitation of people and the planet. Living in global integrity is essential for sharing the good news and good works among all peoples. It is also requisite for fostering sustainable development and transformation, health and wellbeing, and peace and security in our world. Integrity is not easy, it is not always black and white, and it can be risky.

Have you ever wondered how much integrity you have? If you are like most people, then your response is a definite "lots!" Yet, despite our character strengths such as courage and compassion, our self-appraisals of integrity can be seriously influenced by our own self-serving distortions, by which we rationalize inconsistencies between our purported values and our actual actions. Kelly has written a personal account about his own self-deception and need for correction (O'Donnell 2011).

Manipulating Virtue and Vice

We have been challenged over the years by the sixteenth-century treatise on power by Niccolò Machiavelli, *The Prince*. Machiavelli resolved to develop a reasoned argument for leadership that was practical and reality-based, and not simply idealistic or solely virtue-centered. In his view, power could be "legitimately" unencumbered by ethical values.

Especially illuminating for organizational management was a core principle from Chapter 15: "A man who wishes to act entirely up to his professions of virtue soon meets with what destroys him among so much that is evil. Hence it is necessary for a prince wishing to hold his own to know how to do wrong, and to make use of it or not according to necessity."

Machiavelli's work has had major influence on the "realpolitik" thinking that has impacted governance practices for the last five centuries. Such thinking has also crept into the mission community, undermining the global integrity that is so desperately needed in our world today (O'Donnell 2016).

Exposing Dysfunction and Deviance
Unfortunately, we can all be seriously duped and disabled by Machiavellian-type people and processes (Luke 16:8). We call these situations *DD realities* (or DD for short): personal and organizational dysfunction (distortion of reality for one's own ends) and deviance (exploitation of others for one's own ends). The New Testament uses various terms to describe evil people *within* the church and warns us not to be naïve (see O'Donnell 2008).

DD is often disguised as "virtuous" or "necessary for the greater good." In organizations, managing DD is especially tricky when there is insufficient understanding, accountability, or political will to resolutely enforce good practice standards. Above all, DD is reinforced when people compromise their integrity by looking the other way, rationalizing their responsibility, and ultimately becoming polluted themselves (see Prov 16:2; 25:26).

Tactics for Combating DD
Here is a tool to help you recognize the presence and progression of DD in organizational settings. These five tactics can overlap. The grid (adapted from O'Donnell 2012) can also be used as a mirror to examine your own integrity.

- **Deny**. Conceal DD. "Don't ask about problems (even obvious ones), don't talk about problems, and don't rock the boat" is a pervasive, core, unwritten rule.
- **Downplay**. Minimize DD's negative impact. State that it is probably "normal." Relational unity and conformity trump truth and genuine relationships.
- **Distract**. Distract from the real DD issues. "Feign pain" and get sympathy; or admit that something is "not exactly right" and refer to problems as being largely a matter of having different perspectives or preferences, thereby implying its merely a matter of having to "agree to disagree."
- **Discredit**. Belittle those who point out or inquire about DD. Silence them. Instill an atmosphere of fear of reprisals and intimidation to prevent people from speaking up or calling for good practice.

- **Destroy**. Demolish people's reputations, contributions, relationships, and wellbeing. Use half-truths, spin, lies, rumors, threats, false accusations, and dismissals. Reap the benefits of control, position, respect, status quo, and revenue streams.

Practicing Self-Deception
Cognitive dissonance is a powerful concept from social psychology that can help us to understand our propensity to deceive ourselves while still believing we are living in integrity (Jer 17:9). It refers to the self-serving rationales we use to calm our disturbing, internal incongruence and harmonize discrepant thoughts about ourselves—who we want to be versus who we actually are (O'Donnell 2017). Tavris and Aronson (2007, 2, 9–10) shed light on how these moral maneuvers help us feel good about ourselves:

> Most people, when directly confronted by evidence that they are wrong, do not change their point of view or course of action but justify it even more tenaciously. Even irrefutable evidence is rarely enough to pierce the mental armor of self-justification. … Yet mindless self-justification, like quicksand, can draw us deeper into disaster. It blocks our ability to even see our errors, let alone correct them. It distorts reality, keeping us from getting all the information we need and assessing issues clearly. It prolongs and widens rifts between lovers, friends, and nations. It keeps us from letting go of unhealthy habits. It permits the guilty to avoid taking responsibility for their deeds.

Bad Leaders Are Bad News
Self-justification to minimize cognitive dissonance is a big reason why any leader can become a bad or Machiavellian leader. One international survey assessing the experiences and views of Christian leaders identified three main categories of negative characteristics among fellow leaders: "Prideful, always right, and always the big boss; lack of integrity, untrustworthy; harsh, uncaring, refused to listen, critical" (Overstreet 2010).

Robert Sternberg's extensive psychological research consistently finds that bad leaders see themselves as being above accountability—"Ethics are for other people." They do not avail themselves of needed input from others to complement, balance, and correct themselves. They lapse into an unrealistic and often disguised sense of omnipotence, inerrancy, unrealistic optimism, and invulnerability. And they become entrenched in their ways, even when it is obvious to others that they are digging a bigger pit of mistakes into which they and others will fall (summarized in O'Donnell 2011, 144–145).

Tactics for Feigning Integrity
The following four tactics illustrate what *not* to do when we are asked to give an account for a possible mistake or misconduct. Use this tool also as a mirror into your own life and integrity.

- **Distance yourself from the issue.** Dodge, reword, or repackage it. Obfuscate the facts; talk tentatively or vaguely about concerns or "mistakes in the past." Disguise any culpability.
- **Appeal to your "integrity" and to acting with the "highest standards."** Point out your past track record and your current contributions and emphasize that you are doing your best. Punctuate it all with the language of transparency and accountability without demonstrating either.
- **State that you are being attacked and being treated unfairly, and that people don't understand.** Remind people that leadership is hard and full of ambiguities and tough choices. Mention other people's problems; question their motives and credibility.
- **Hold out until the uncomfortable stuff goes away.** Sack staff but don't change the system. Maintain your self-interests, lifestyle, affiliations, and illusions of moral congruity. Remember, you are special. Cognitive dissonance applies to others but not to you.

A Case Study in Confronting Corruption in Mission

We turn now to a composite case study in mission that illustrates many of the concepts and issues discussed so far. The focus on a larger case of corruption is not meant to obscure the destructive reality of many "smaller" types of corruption that plague church and mission communities globally. As you will see, corruption is often closer to our home and work than we think!

At the heart of this case is the Pace family, four resilient people who refused to ignore an international fraud in the mission/aid community. Names and other identifying details have been changed, and some information is presented in a composite form. This is a wakeup call on the reality of corruption in our midst and the resilience and integrity needed to confront it with others. See the original source (O'Donnell and Lewis O'Donnell 2013) for more commentary and resources to strengthen individual and organizational integrity. Especially noteworthy are the quotations from *Transparency: How Leaders Create a Culture of Candor* (Bennis et al. 2008).

Waking Up
"You were formerly darkness, but now you are light in the Lord; walk as children of light" (Eph 5:8 NASB). It was unbelievable and utterly disconcerting. Could respected and trusted mission leaders *really* act so uncharacteristically? Could the nefarious face of fraud *really* go undetected by seemingly mature, Spirit-led believers, hiding for years behind a mask of benevolence in the Christian mission/aid community? Would good people *really* deal with corruption by rationalizing their responsibility to help, protecting themselves and their livelihoods, and tolerating the discrediting and dismissal of their fellow colleagues who confronted it? Could resilient evil (complicity, cover-ups, and cowardice) *really* win the day over resilient virtue (perseverance, honesty, and courage)? The answer, sadly, can be a resounding "yes."

Alejandro (Alex) Pace, a respected, middle-aged Asian leader known for his tireless efforts to create mission/aid networks on behalf of the poor, was ejected from the organization to which he had belonged for fifteen years. A trio of organizational leaders informed him that he had a mental disorder and was responsible for a long history of broken relationships, that he had willfully disregarded the instructions of his organizational leaders, and that he needed psychiatric care and spiritual direction. Pace—along with his wife, by default—was dismissed, his services were neither endorsed nor recommended, and no appeal against his dismissal was permitted. Almost all communication was by email. With no warning, donor funds for the Pace family ceased to be passed on to them.

Prior to his dismissal, Alex Pace and Chandra, his wife of seventeen years, had asked to meet with senior leaders of the organization to discuss the impact of a long-running, international, multi-million-dollar fraud in the church and mission communities that had just become public. The fraud was essentially a Ponzi scheme, with payments made to earlier investors coming from subsequent investors' capital, rather than from earnings gained from the capital investment itself. The scheme, available only privately, had been sold to people in Christian ministry with guarantees that their capital would be protected, that they would receive a 10 percent annual return on their investment, and that the fund would make an additional donation to a charity. The scheme had been presented in a low-key manner as a special opportunity for mission workers and for the Kingdom of God.

Their request for a meeting denied, the Paces continued, along with others, to request organizational disclosure and independent review. Well-informed and committed to the organization's health, the Paces were typecast as disloyal problem makers. Was their real transgression that they knew too much about the fraud (firsthand as investor-victims), were too influential, and could create instability in the organization by calling for transparency and accountability?

Rising Up
"And do not participate in the unfruitful deeds of darkness, but instead even expose them" (Eph 5:11 NASB). The accusations justifying the Paces' dismissal sounded convincing, and the mission's leaders claimed they had also received letters of complaint about Alex that had to be kept anonymous for reasons of confidentiality. These charges rapidly unraveled, however, and in their place criminal investigations focusing on Christian mission leaders and organizations came to light. Nevertheless, organizational guidelines for handling complaints were still circumvented, there was a lack of due process, and ultimatums were delivered when there had been no violation of organizational rules or moral failure.

Despite deep organizational and mission/aid loyalties, the Paces' friends, family, sending churches, and long-term donors, as well as several close colleagues in the organization, were not misled by the accusations and held their ground. They not only had known Alex and Chandra personally for many years but also were concerned that their dismissal had taken place in the context of an international fraud that had a serious impact on many organizations. Yet the organization remained silent regarding the fraud's impact, either positive or negative, on their projects and personnel, thereby missing the opportunity to conduct the necessary intensive postmortem review.

Wising Up
"So then, be careful how you walk, not as unwise people but as wise, making the most of your time, because the days are evil" (Eph 5:16–17 NASB). Notwithstanding the ongoing support they received, Chandra, Alex, and their two adolescent sons, Nate and George, were entering a very dark period. Confronting corruption takes time and skill. It also compounds the normal adjustment challenges that couples and families face, and it can take a toll on the mental health of those involved. In spite of what they knew to be true, the Paces began to wonder if some of the accusations and half-truths were accurate, as there was some connection to their attempts with others to resolve relational discord in another setting. Additionally, they were

experiencing the lingering, pervasive hold that dysfunctional organizational systems can have on their members (e.g., group conformity and "group think"), a hold that can undermine members' critical evaluation and spiritual discernment. The desire to remain part of one's mission family (seeking unity and belonging at all costs), the desire to trust leaders and believe the best about them (pleasing surrogate parents), and a fear as to how one might make a living outside of the organization (dependence on the organizational system or "family") can all facilitate succumbing to group think.

As they helped to spearhead a call for transparency and accountability, Alex and Chandra found themselves embroiled in a trying five-year period marked intermittently by despair, disillusionment, and a sense of betrayal. The protracted experience led to self-doubt and deep soul-searching. Were they truly committed to serving Jesus with integrity, regardless of the cost? There were many sleepless nights punctuated with pervasive entreaties of "How long, O Lord?" Chandra suffered chest pains, apparently caused by stress. A substantial amount of their professional and personal time was devoted to supporting a government investigation, distracting them from their usual work of networking and advocacy on behalf of the poor. Discouragement lurked as a fifth, unwanted member of the family. How might their experiences affect the boys' understanding of God's goodness and justice? Did their family have the resilience to continue to pursue justice? Twice their car was tampered with in such a way that there could have been a fatal accident. Many times, they were excluded or disinvited from interagency and regional mission gatherings. Three other groups of which they were a part followed the lead of their former mission organization and dismissed them. Colleagues who had appeared to be friends now kept their distance.

The Paces endeavored to maintain a balanced perspective by getting regular input from those to whom they were accountable (their sending churches) and by recognizing the spiritual dimensions of the situation. They sought to maintain, in their words, a "tender heart" and a "strong mind" in the face of bullying while they sought to confront organizational misconduct. They were also keen to avoid bitterness, to maintain their bodily health through exercise and sound nutrition, and to experience beauty daily with gratitude. Scripture provided strength to persevere and offered mirrors for self-awareness. The Paces were also inspired by secular and Christian writings and by models of faith and courage provided by historical heroes. They were sustained in the long haul by their faith in God; their commitment to loving truth, peace, and people; and their understanding of human behavior, as well as by close lifelong friends and supportive exhortations from their two sending churches: "Stay the course" and "Help to bring the fraud into the light."

Only in retrospect is it evident that the Pace family became more resilient through their experiences of adversity. Existing family strengths were reinforced, and their compassion for others and sensitivity to issues of social justice were heightened. Characteristics often associated with people who flourish can be identified in the Paces, such as the presence of positive emotion displayed in happiness and life satisfaction, as well as in their living lives of engagement, relationships, meaning, and achievement. These years were a growing season for the fruit of the Spirit (Gal 5:22–23) and the fruit of the light (Eph 5:9) in all their lives. The boys felt that their parents modeled a healthy spirituality, demonstrating that one could struggle honestly with one's faith in the midst of adversity. Both boys also specifically described a sense of stability in their home life and the family's shared sense of hope in spite of hardship.

Powering Up

> Finally, be strong in the Lord and in the strength of His might. Put on the full armor of God, so that you will be able to stand firm against the schemes of the devil. (Eph 6:10–11 NASB)

The Paces' case is not uncommon. No one can escape exposure to fraud's far-reaching toxins, including people and organizations in the faith-based community. Prudently confronting corruption and the unspeakable evils within one's spheres of influence is truly a form of being salt and light in this world (Matt 5:13–16); in these matters, ordinary folks can act heroically. As Aleksandr Solzhenitsyn stated in his 1970 Nobel Prize address, "And the simple step of a simple courageous man is not to partake in falsehood, not to support false actions! Let [the lie] enter the world, let it even reign in the world—but not with my help" (Solzhenitsyn 1970, section 7).

The multi-million-dollar international fraud in this case study has affected many organizations, people, and projects. An initial professional review carried out by a business consultant explored its impact on the church and mission community, including dismissals, responses, and lessons learned. A network was formed for mutual support and to share information with the public. Governments began to investigate. Alex and others testified at a court case that revealed gross, longstanding fraud. In the meantime, media reports were published in several countries, accompanied by calls for assistance from victims and from members and donors of affected organizations. Public court records shed light on forms of involvement and the flow of money. Yet limited help was offered or action taken by the church and mission communities, an unsettling fact that called their reputation into question. Nonetheless, Alex and Chandra, along with others, continued to confront the protracted corruption and wrongful dismissals, using websites, blog sites, and podcasts to share information and call for contrition and change. In the process, they shared many pro-integrity and anti-corruption resources to further educate the international church and mission community.

A Summons to Live in Global Integrity

Corruption preys on the poor, with estimates of over one trillion dollars being siphoned each year from countries in development (ONE 2014). Within the worldwide church, an estimated $86 billion is stolen via "ecclesiastical crime" (Zurlo, Johnson, and Crossing 2024). For additional perspectives on integrity and corruption in mission, see Baker and Hayward (2010).

Corruption is not just about financial fraud (Transparency International, Glossary). It also manifests as "bribery, law-breaking without dealing with the consequences in a fair manner, unfairly amending election processes and results, and covering mistakes or silencing whistleblowers (those who expose corruption in hope that justice would be served)" (Time and Date). In the humanitarian sector, corruption extends into "nepotism/cronyism, sexual exploitation and abuse, coercion and intimidation of humanitarian staff or aid recipients for personal, social or political gain, manipulation of assessments, targeting and registration to favor particular groups, and diversion of assistance to non-target groups" (Feinstein International Center et al. 2008).

Fortunately, the deluge of scandals can sensitize us to the grim realities of widespread financial deception, exploitation, and abuse of power. Also helpful for raising our awareness and spurring action have been the United Nations (2015) Sustainable Development Goals, which prominently include anti-corruption targets such as "Substantially reduce corruption and bribery in all their forms" (Target 16.5) and "Develop effective, accountable and transparent institutions at all levels" (Target 16.6).

To combat corruption, it is imperative to understand that the fundamental struggle is against world forces of darkness and spiritual forces of wickedness (Eph 6:12). Hence prayer, spiritual disciplines, the word of God, and lifestyles of integrity are crucial. Let us do all we can to take greater precautions as we learn about the alluring schemes of corruption concocted by humans and the evil one, and to develop ways to deal at all levels (i.e., local through global) with facets of corruption in our midst, including in our own hearts.

Our Resources
In addition, it is valuable to keep abreast with the experiences and resources of other sectors. For example, two Christian networks which we are actively involved with are the Faith and Public Integrity Network and the Global Integrity Network, connected with the Lausanne Movement and World Evangelical Alliance. You will find many of our materials in the Global Integrity section of our main website (Member Care Associates), including a core list of Lausanne Movement materials (O'Donnell and Lewis O'Donnell 2022a) and multi-sectoral materials (O'Donnell and Lewis O'Donnell 2022b). Over the past decade, we have also developed websites, blog sites, and podcasts that provide current news and resources on integrity and corruption, with a primary focus on a major international fraud that continues to negatively affect the international church and mission community (e.g., Into Integrity; PETRA People Network).

Another substantial way to support global integrity is to engage with colleagues via Global Integrity Day (GID) and to take advantage of its many resources. We launched GID on June 9, 2020 as a positive day to reflect, teach, and collaborate on ways to integrate integrity in all we do throughout the entire year. It is a *strategic day* to promote (a) cultivating lifestyles, cultures, and systems of integrity from the individual through the international levels; (b) joining together to understand and address the causes and consequences of corruption in its many forms; and (c) working toward just and equitable societies marked by wellbeing for all people and for the planet.

A Summons to a Global Integrity Movement
We believe that our common identity and shared responsibility as Christians who are global citizens can be leveraged to *integrate integrity* into the individual, interpersonal, institutional, and international levels, and everything in-between. This is *global integrity*. We believe it is a propitious season to invest in integrity worldwide (O'Donnell 2016).

We envision a growing, sustainable global integrity movement, a collaborative platform for promoting integrity and combating corruption at all levels. It would include sharing and developing tools to encourage integrity, virtue, and ethics; understand and prevent corruption in different cultural contexts; and foster healing to both victims and perpetrators alike. We call upon righteous and relevant people, committed to Jesus Christ and the good news, to work together resolutely and across sectors on behalf of the wellbeing of all people and the planet. As the Global Integrity Day website states, "Make every day an integrity day! … Be the people we need—build the world we need!"

Global integrity requires ongoing, honest reflection at all levels. Like the character and virtue in which it is embedded, it is refined in the cauldron of life's tough challenges and choices. We live in integrity with prophetic voices to speak into the seen and unseen realms, with the authority of Jesus and the power of the Spirit. We are keys to influencing moral wholeness for a whole world. We are the light—or the darkness—of the world.

Applications: Being a Prophetic Voice in Mission

Core Strategies

1. Cultivate a life of integrity by connecting with trusted others for mutual support and accountability.
2. Explore your own vulnerability to temptation, including propensities to distort information and to justify mistakes and misdeeds.
3. Keep current with multi-sectoral resources on integrity and anti-corruption to support being a prophetic voice, and discuss the content of these resources with colleagues, friends, and family.

Core Resources

1. Reality DOSE website, featuring "Wise Doves and Innocent Serpents?," an overview article on dysfunction and deviance in mission (in twelve languages).
2. Global Integrity Day website: Resources and engagement around the annual day for integrity (June 9) and throughout the year.
3. Member Care Associates "Global Integrity" website: Core resources that we have produced over more than fifteen years.

Reflection and Discussion

1. Identify some of the main challenges presented in this chapter with regard to living in integrity. Which ones are most relevant for you and your setting(s)?
2. Using the composite case study as a springboard, describe any experiences with corruption that you have had or witnessed within mission. What have been some helpful or unhelpful responses?

3. Comment on some ways to build resilience in mission as workers deal with adversity, including corruption. What safeguards, training, or resources are needed?

References

Baker, Dwight, and Douglas Hayward, eds. 2010. *Serving Jesus with Integrity: Ethics and Accountability in Mission*. Pasadena, CA: William Carey Library.

Bennis, Warren, Douglas Coleman, James O'Toole, and Patricia Biederman. 2008. *Transparency: How Leaders Create a Culture of Candor*. San Francisco, CA: Jossey-Bass.

Faith and Public Integrity Network. https://fpinetwork.org/.

Feinstein International Center, Humanitarian Policy Group, and Transparency International. 2008. *Preventing Corruption in Humanitarian Assistance: Final Research Report*. https://www.transparency.org/files/content/pressrelease/Humanitarian_Assistance_Report.pdf.

Global Integrity Day. https://sites.google.com/view/global-integrity-day/.

Global Integrity Network. Lausanne Movement—World Evangelical Alliance. https://www.globalintegritynetwork.org/.

Guterres, Antonio. (2020, October 15). "Statement on Corruption in the Context of COVID-19." United Nations. https://www.un.org/en/coronavirus/statement-corruption-context-covid-19.

Into Integrity (blog). https://intointegrity.blogspot.com/.

Machiavelli, Niccolò. 2015. *The Prince*. http://www.gutenberg.org/files/1232/1232-h/1232-h.htm.

Member Care Associates. "Global Integrity." https://membercareassociates.org/global-integrity/.

O'Donnell, Kelly. 2008. "Member Care: Tares, Tears, and Terrors." *CORE Member Care* (blog), November 6. http://coremembercare.blogspot.fr/search/label/na percentC3 percentAFve.

O'Donnell, Kelly. 2011. "Good Leaders Live in Reality." In *Global Member Care, vol. 1: The Pearls and Perils of Good Practice*, 144–145. Pasadena, CA: William Carey Library.

O'Donnell, Kelly. 2012. "Wise Doves and Innocent Serpents?" In *Member Care in India: Ministry Call to Home Call*, edited by J. N. Manoharan, Jacob Ninan, J. J. Rathnakumar, and Isac Soundara Raja, 111–126. Vellore, India: Mission Upholders Trust. https://membercareassociates.org/wp-content/uploads/2017/11/Wise-Doves-and-Innocent-Serpents-ODonnell-India-MC-book-2012.pdf.

O'Donnell, Kelly. 2016. "Global Integrity: Moral Wholeness for a Whole World" (25 blog entries in 2026), *CORE Member Care*. http://coremembercare.blogspot.fr/search/label/global percent20integrity.

O'Donnell, Kelly. 2017. "Integrity and Accountability for United Nations Staff: Navigating the Terrain." *UN Special* 767 (March): 40–41. https://www.unspecial.org/2017/03/integrity-and-accountability-for-un-staff/.

O'Donnell, Kelly, and Michèle Lewis O'Donnell. 2013. "Loving Truth and Peace: A Case Study of Family Resilience in Mission/Aid Corruption." In *Family Accountability in Missions: Korean and Western Case Studies*, edited by Jonathan Bonk, 175–186. New Haven, CT: OMSC Publications. https://membercareassociates.org/wp-content/uploads/2017/11/Loving-Truth-and-Peace-Mission-Aid-Corruption-ODonnells.pdf.

O'Donnell, Kelly, and Michèle Lewis O'Donnell. 2017. "Moral Care: Resources for Living in Integrity." *Member Care Update* 97 (May). https://mailchi.mp/ab8a9a78444d/moral-care-member-care-update-may-1263961.

O'Donnell, Kelly, and Michèle Lewis O'Donnell. 2018. "A Summons to a Global Integrity Movement: Fighting Self-Deception and Corruption." *Lausanne Global Analysis* 7 (2). https://www.lausanne.org/content/lga/2018–03/summons-global-integrity-movement.

O'Donnell, Kelly, and Michèle Lewis O'Donnell. 2022a. "Living in Global Integrity: Moral Wholeness for a More Whole World." In *Essays on Holistic Biblical Ministries*, edited by Reuben van Rensburg, Zoltan Erdey, and Thomas Schirrmacher, 335–354. Bonn: Culture and Science Publishers. https://www.bucer.de/fileadmin/dateien/Dokumente/Buecher/978–3-86269–236–1_Festschrift_Manfred_Kohl.pdf.

O'Donnell, Kelly, and Michèle Lewis O'Donnell. 2022b. "Multi-Sectoral Resources: Pro-Integrity and Anti-Corruption." https://membercareassociates.org/wp-content/uploads/2022/02/Living-in-Global-Integrity-chapter-Multi-Sectoral-Resources-Feb-2022.pdf.

ONE. 2014. "Trillion Dollar Scandal Report." https://www.one.org/us/stories/trillion-dollar-scandal-the-biggest-heist-youve-never-heard-of/.

Overstreet, Jane. 2010. "We Have a Problem! But There Is Hope. Results of a Survey of 1,000 Christian Leaders from Across the Globe." *Cape Town 2010 Congress*, Lausanne Movement. https://www.lausanne.org/content/we-have-a-problem-but-there-is-hope-results-of-a-survey-of-1000-christian-leaders-from-across-the-globe.

PETRA People Network. https://sites.google.com/site/petrapeople.

Reality DOSE! Dysfunction, Deviance, and Discipline. https://sites.google.com/site/mcaresources/.

Solzhenitsyn, Aleksandr. 1970. "Nobel Lecture in Literature." The Nobel Prize. www.nobelprize.org/nobel_prizes/literature/laureates/1970/solzhenitsyn-lecture.html.

Tavris, Carol, and Elliot Aronson. 2007. *Mistakes Were Made (but not by me): Why We Justify Foolish Beliefs, Bad Decisions, and Hurtful Acts.* Orlando, FL: Harcourt.

Time and Date. "International Anti-Corruption Day." https://www.timeanddate.com/holidays/un/international-anti-corruption-day.

Transparency International. "Anti-Corruption Glossary." https://www.transparency.org/glossary.

Transparency International. "What Is Corruption?" https://www.transparency.org/what-is-corruption.

United Nations. 2015. "Sustainable Development Goal 16." https://www.un.org/sustainabledevelopment/peace-justice/.

Zurlo, Gina, Todd Johnson, and Peter Crossing. 2024. "Fragmentation and Unity." *International Bulletin of Mission Research* 48 (1): 43–54. https://www.gordonconwell.edu/wp-content/uploads/sites/13/2024/01/Status-of-Global-Christianity-2024.pdf.

Kelly O'Donnell, PsyD, and Michèle Lewis O'Donnell, PsyD, are consulting psychologists based in Geneva and the USA with Member Care Associates, Inc. (MCA). Their international and multi-sectoral emphases in consultation, training, and writing include member care, global mental health, integrity/anti-corruption, and sustainable development. Kelly and Michèle completed their doctoral training in clinical psychology and theology at the Rosemead School of Psychology, Biola University (USA). They have been representatives to the United Nations for the World Federation for Mental Health, and they have two wonderful adult daughters. Links to their many resources are on the MCA website: https://membercareassociates.org/.

13

Room at the Table

Welcoming People with Disabilities in the Church and Missions

Jenny Smith

Disability. The word may evoke feelings of pity, a fear of doing or saying the wrong thing, or inspirational images of a child with a disability overcoming obstacles. It can create an us-and-them mentality. However, nearly one in six people in the world's population is disabled (WHO 2023), and the disabled community is the only minority group that anyone may join at a moment's notice. That includes you. Yes, *you*.

A disability is a physical or mental condition that makes it difficult for a person to perform certain activities of daily living and to interact with the world around them. According to the Convention on the Rights of Persons with Disabilities (CRPD, Article 1), "Persons with disabilities include those who have long-term physical, mental, intellectual, or sensory impairments which in interaction with various barriers may hinder their full and effective participation in society on an equal basis with others" (United Nations 2006, Article 1).

Disabilities may be present at birth (e.g., cerebral palsy, spina bifida, Down syndrome), sustained in an injury (traumatic brain or spinal cord injuries), or associated with a long-term progressive disease (multiple sclerosis or Parkinson's disease). Depression, diabetes, cancer, and heart disease are among the top ten causes of disability worldwide. Not all disabilities are visible; conditions such as autism, learning disabilities, chronic pain, Crohn's disease, Long COVID, and mental illness also qualify.

With nearly 1.3 billion people with disabilities in the world (WHO 2023), one would think that the church and mission organizations should be intentional in employing and ministering to people with disabilities. But are we?

In this chapter, I discuss the unique advantages and challenges people with physical disabilities experience as they minister in a cross-cultural context. I explore the responsibility of the global church and mission organizations in ministering to the disabled community and successfully involving people with disabilities in cross-cultural ministry. Finally, I look at the biblical mandate to welcome the disabled community and how to meet their physical, social, and emotional needs.

My Story

At age 16, I became a statistic. I had been a competitive gymnast from an early age. On a hot and humid summer morning, I was outside tumbling. I hadn't noticed that the grass was wet with the morning dew. As I launched myself into a back flip, my feet slipped on the wet grass. I didn't have enough height or rotation to make it back around to my feet. In a fraction of a second, my forehead hit the ground and my body crumpled. I was on my stomach, face-first in the grass. I heard a popping sound upon impact.

I had sustained a C6–7 spinal cord injury that left me paralyzed from the chest down and without the use of my hands. Immediately, I entered the world of disability.

The months and years that followed my injury included relearning how to sit, roll over, push a wheelchair, brush my teeth, brush my hair, hold a fork to feed myself, and pick up a cup to drink. I was dependent on others for many of my basic needs.

However, disability also has an emotional, spiritual, and financial impact that I did not anticipate and that the church and mission community often overlook. Emotionally, I floundered. I lost my identity as a gymnast. My ability to express emotions through playing piano and physical exercise was gone.

Spiritually, I had a strong foundation of faith, but I also had unanswerable questions. If so many people were praying for me, and if Jesus had healed others, then why was I not healed? Financially, I was more fortunate than most. My family was well-supported by the community, and my grandmother moved in to help so that both of my parents could continue working. Thirty-four years after my injury, my life is still impacted by the emotional, spiritual, and financial realities of disability.

How We View Disability

Historically, the disabled community has been the recipient of ministry. Disability ministries in churches, therapy centers, and medical clinics are designed to meet the physical needs of underserved people. But how often are people with disabilities invited (or allowed) to serve in their community and the church? This general lack of invitation to serve stems from how the church and society view disability.

The *medical model* of disability views disability as a defect that needs to be cured or managed. If a disability isn't cured, then it's assumed that a person's quality of life is inferior to that of non-disabled people.

The *social model* of disability states that the inability to participate in the community is due to social and physical barriers and negative or derogatory attitudes (see CRPD, Article 2). In this view, disability is not what is primarily disabling—societal barriers are—and the solution is to fix society and its surroundings (e.g., by enabling access to buildings and changing negative stereotypes), not the person.

A *moral model* argues that sin, karma, or the actions of the person or their family cause disability. This model of disability results in stigma, shame, and blaming the disabled person. Interestingly, we often see a spiritualization of disability in Christian circles, with clichés like "God chooses his strongest warriors to bear the heaviest burdens." Other responses, such as "All things happen for the good," may be rooted in biblical truth yet lack empathy and understanding of the experience of disability.

The default view of many people in the church is a combination of the medical and moral models of disability. The person needs to be healed, cured, have more faith, pray harder, or turn away from sin. If you don't believe me, ask anyone with a disability if a well-meaning stranger has ever prayed for their healing. The message this action can send is strong: disabled people are not whole in their current state. We are not strong enough with a disability. We do not have enough faith if we have a disability. We cannot accomplish enough with a disability.

A Calling to Ministry

During one of my internships for my master's degree in counseling psychology in 1998, I met two interns from Poland. I began asking David and Magda questions about people with disabilities in their country. In my naiveté, I assumed that people received help for their basic needs—like a wheelchair—as I had after my spinal cord injury.

I quickly learned that many people lacked wheelchairs and other mobility aids, not just access to education, transportation, and medical care. David and Magda told me about an organization that distributed wheelchairs in Poland.

That sounded like something I would love to do, but I was a busy graduate student. One year later, I read in the weekly bulletin at church that a man from our congregation was going to Afghanistan to distribute wheelchairs. I got his contact information and gave him a call.

Tim shared with me his passion for Afghanistan, a country many North Americans like me hadn't heard of before September 2001. After so many years of war, many people needed wheelchairs, but few were available. He offered to put me in touch with the organization if I was interested. Several weeks later, the vice president of the organization called me. He explained how they collected, refurbished, and shipped the wheelchairs, after which they would send a team to properly fit each chair for the recipient. I asked, "How can I help?"

"We're going to Mexico. Why don't you come with us?"

I nearly choked. *Me? Go out of the United States? That's impossible*!

I can tell numerous stories about how that trip changed my life, but this is the one where God showed me he could use me in a unique capacity.

One evening, as we ate at an outdoor restaurant, an older waitress came to our table. She asked the president of the organization if I'd be willing to talk with her husband, who had suffered a stroke several months prior. She wanted me to share my hope with him.

A thousand thoughts rushed through my mind. *What do I have that can give him hope?* Yes, I understood the hopelessness and frustration that occur after a disability, but I had access to resources that he couldn't even imagine. I pushed myself over to this man, praying for wisdom as I went.

I sat face-to-face and chair-to-chair with this gentleman in his late sixties, who acknowledged my approach with a crooked grin and nod of his head, cradling his useless left arm in his lap. I told him the story of my injury. I spoke in Spanish and used an interpreter when my Spanish failed me. I then shared my hope.

"Hebrews 6:19 says, 'We have this hope as an anchor for the soul, firm and secure.' When everything around me was changing after my injury, God was the one I knew I could count on. He was always there. *He* is my hope and my strength."

With tears in his eyes, the man nodded with understanding. I asked if I could pray with him. Reaching out his right, non-paralyzed hand to me, he said, "*Sí, por favor.*"

Yes, a non-disabled person could have spoken those same words. The same truth. The same hope. But not with the shared experience of disability.

For the next eight years, I worked in Mexico, Afghanistan, Costa Rica, and El Salvador. On these two- to three-week trips, I hired local women to assist with my personal care. While I'd prefer not to need assistance with personal care, I built relationships that my non-disabled coworkers couldn't build. I learned the language and culture more quickly and had opportunities for spiritual conversations.

People with disabilities have a role in the mission field. My role looked different from that of my non-disabled coworkers, but it was no less important. I was no less called by God … until I wasn't.

Supporting Others through Member Care

I had resigned from my position distributing wheelchairs. I desperately wanted to work in Afghanistan full-time. But God had other plans.

For the next thirteen years, I served in member care at a sending organization's home office. When I said yes to the job, I knew I'd need to ask for some accommodations. I was going into an office with set hours of 9am to 5pm. With a knot in my stomach, I requested a thirty-two-hour workweek with two days working from home. I wanted—needed—to maintain my health. Thankfully, the organization was willing to accommodate me.

Through emails and video calls, I listened to and encouraged my mission coworkers as I heard the loneliness of being half a world away from friends and family, the frustration of learning a second language, and the joy when a friend decided to give her life to God. I educated new workers on the stressors of cross-cultural life—including culture shock, team conflict, the importance of self-care, and how to avoid burnout—and helped them navigate the never-ending transitions of life overseas.

None of these skills are directly related to my disability. Yet I came to realize that many of my coworkers struggled with the loss of identity, independence, and relationships. They had to learn new ways of living and how to adapt to challenging conditions. Oddly enough, these are the same issues I've had to work through over the past few decades, just in a different capacity.

Considerations for Disabled Workers, Churches, and Sending Organizations

God has used people with disabilities throughout the Bible. Moses had a speech disorder (Exod 4:10). Jacob limped (Gen 32:31). David was prone to depression. Paul was … well, I'll let the scholars debate that topic. Varying disabilities, yet God used each of them. In our human wisdom, would a church committee or sending organization have rejected Moses, David, Jacob, and Paul for cross-cultural service because of their disabilities?

Yes, working with a disability—especially in countries with limited accessibility, medical care and psychosocial support—has a unique set of challenges. But this shouldn't be an automatic dismissal. First, in the United States, Europe, and Australia, laws exist to protect the employment opportunities of people with disabilities. Second, and more importantly, Paul clearly states that the church is a body in which even its "weaker" and "less honorable" parts are indispensable (1 Cor 12:23). Finally, Matthew 28:19–20 contains no clause that excludes people with disabilities or allows them to opt out of the Great Commission.

Barry Funnell, a paraplegic from South Africa, successfully served as a Bible translator in Malawi and Tanzania. Hannah, with a hearing loss, learned a South Asian language and flourished in ministry. Parents of children with developmental, intellectual, or learning disabilities successfully serve when sufficient supports are in place.

I am *not* arguing, however, that every person with a disability or parents with disabled children who apply to become global workers should be sent or that they should stay in the field after the onset of a disability.

Sometimes, the host country's prevailing cultural and religious views on disability may hinder fruitful ministry. While serving in Nepal, John Trotter progressively lost his sight. He eventually left the field. Trotter stated:

My [mission] service in Nepal became overshadowed by the broader society's perception of what the blind should or should not do. People regularly attempted to carry me as I walked down the road, questioned me about whether God cursed me in a former life or if I had bad karma, or advised me on medical treatment. (Trotter 2022, 55)

In retrospect, part of the reason I gave up the desire to serve in Afghanistan full-time was that I knew it would require an abundance of financial, emotional, and physical resources. In addition, I slowly realized that my presence could be a distraction or place others at risk when Westerners began to be targeted.

How Can We Send Well?

One of my job responsibilities in member care was to serve on the applications committee. A family with several young children felt called to a remote location. As I read their application, I discovered that two of their children had significant physical disabilities. That wasn't the *main* problem, though.

The parents' nonchalant attitude about the lack of health care that would be available to them concerned me, as did the over-spiritualization of "God will take care of our kids. In addition to the normal hardships that third-culture kids (TCKs) experience, I believed the lack of physical resources would add to an already difficult childhood and adolescence for TCKs with disabilities. In this situation, I sensed the parents were placing a desire to serve God before their primary calling of providing for their children's basic needs. While this is a topic that needs to be addressed in depth, it is not within the scope of this chapter.

What about other disabilities—the ones mission committees call "red flags"? Depression, anxiety, dyslexia, PTSD, ADD/ADHD, addiction. Good reasons exist for these conditions to be a concern. Instead of rushing to judgment, however, we need to ask, "Is this applicant qualified and a good fit for this position?" If so, the next question should be "How can we accommodate you to allow you to flourish in ministry?"

The CRPD (Article 27) recognizes the right to work and prohibits discrimination based on disability. In addition, it promotes reasonable accommodations to ensure equal enjoyment of human rights for persons with disabilities (CRPD, Article 2). Seventy-seven countries in the world have legal provisions requiring employers to provide reasonable accommodations to their employees (Heymann, Wong, and Waiseth 2021). Churches and mission organizations need to offer reasonable accommodations to potential staff and workers with disabilities.

What reasonable accommodations might churches and organizations consider when someone with a disability plans to go overseas? Well, the worker is the primary person to answer that question. Each person is unique and has different needs. Below are some practical tips from my own experience.

- Technology: How can technology enable people to do their job successfully?
- Location: Is it possible to live in an area with greater access to the resources the worker might need? Is working remotely possible?
- Travel: Will more frequent returns to their home base or a secondary location be allowed for any medical issues that cannot be handled in the field or via telehealth?
- Finances: Does the worker have the flexibility to increase the amount of financial support needed for ongoing medical expenses?

With accommodations, I can travel to faraway locations. But this includes extra layovers with a hotel, a travel companion to help with my physical needs (e.g., bathrooms on planes are not accessible), and an itinerary that considers my physical needs. This is more expensive than purchasing the cheapest fare with a half-hour layover. On the other hand, I know my expenses could be less in many countries due to group health insurance rates or socialized medicine, the lower cost of hiring a personal care attendant, and—depending on where I am serving—a lower cost of living.

One argument I often hear is that sending—or going—with a disability is too risky. Yet risk is inherent for every person on planet Earth. We praise and admire the bravery of the first global workers who packed their belongings in a casket, knowing they would not return alive to their home country. If we argue that it's too risky for a disabled person to serve, then are we not arguing that there is an inherent difference in strategic value between non-disabled and disabled people?

However, the risks need to be acknowledged and discussed openly. On one trip to Afghanistan, everyone caught a bad respiratory virus, which was especially difficult for me since I can't cough well. When a group experienced a bad case of food poisoning in Mexico—well, consider dealing with diarrhea when you don't have control of your bowels. When I was traveling to Europe after the 2016 Brussels airport bombing to provide member care at a conference, my friend and travel buddy frankly asked, "What should I do if a bombing happens?" "Run," I responded. I wanted her to know she was not responsible for my safety.

I traveled as prepared as possible for the what-if scenarios concerning my health and safety. The people whom I was with knew my strengths and the risks. And they welcomed me to serve alongside them.

We should expect people with disabilities to be serving. Paul Lindenwood—a wheelchair user with limited dexterity and communication who spent nine years in rural Kenya—asks, "Do we simply accept [people with disabilities], saying, 'Well done for getting this far'? Or should we *expect* to see them, and ask where they are when they don't appear?" (Deuel and John 2021, 75).

If people with disabilities aren't serving, we need to ask ourselves why. Have the church and the mission community welcomed people to both serve and be served? Maybe, but not very effectively.

Welcome at the Table?

At Church

Jesus tells a parable about a man who invited many guests to a dinner. The people he invited had excuses and didn't come. So, the host told his servant, "Go out at once into the streets and lanes of the city and bring in here those who are poor, those with disabilities, those who are blind, and those who are limping" (Luke 14:21 NASB).

How can we apply this parable to the global church and missions?

If and when people with disabilities are invited to an event, has the location been chosen with them in mind? Unfortunately, the church has historically left people with disabilities out. One example occurred in the United States when churches fought to be excluded from their legal obligations under the Americans with Disabilities Act (ADA) of 1990. Religious entities are exempt from Title III of the ADA that requires businesses and nonprofits to be accessible to people with disabilities. Why? Because many pastors and church representatives thought modifying buildings for the disabled community would cost too much. Ramps, bathrooms, wider doors, interpreters for the deaf, and wheelchair-accessible seating are thus not *required* in churches or mission organizations. In some cases, however, costs can be a reasonable concern (e.g., for small churches with limited income needing to make major modifications). Nevertheless, the disabled community still gets the message loud and clear: we aren't worth the cost.

Yes, giving access to people with a variety of disabilities takes time, money, and a different way of thinking. But if we truly believe that every person is made in God's image, then we must give them access to our churches and our ministries. For example, is the location of a small group of believers accessible to those with mobility issues? Is an interpreter provided for the deaf community? Are you willing to take the time and effort to learn how to interact with people with intellectual disabilities, autism, or learning differences? If no one with a disability is in the community of faith where you serve, are you willing to seek them out? If the WHO (2023) statistics are accurate and fifteen percent of the people you minister to don't have a physical, mental, or intellectual disability, then where are they?

In Missions

Sending organizations and member care providers need to have the same mentality of expectancy when it comes to employing, sending, and serving disabled workers and/or their disabled children. Our home offices, retreats, and conferences need to keep accessibility in mind—not only for disabled workers and their children, but for the aging population of global workers who may struggle with mobility, hearing loss, or other disabilities.

Meeting the Needs of the Disabled Community

As global workers, we need to ask if we are meeting the disabled community's needs. As I look back on the ministry of providing wheelchairs, I wonder if we were adequately serving people with disabilities and their families.

I remember a mother with three severely physically and intellectually disabled children. We provided new wheelchairs designed to grow with the children and last for years in the rough terrain. When I saw the mother a year later, none of the children were in their chairs. She had sold them. This mother didn't need wheelchairs for her children as much as she needed the ability to support and feed her children. We had met a need, but not the most urgent one. Did we even ask?

The plea of the disability rights movement in the 1970s in the United States—and the theme of the first International Day of Disabled Persons (2004)—was "Nothing about us, without us." This statement is every bit as true today as we reach out and include people with disabilities.

Physical and Social Needs

Throughout the New Testament, we see examples of a twofold process by which Jesus both cures a physical impairment and ministers to the spiritual, emotional, and social aspects of life. The woman who touched the edge of Jesus's cloak was healed of her chronic hemorrhaging (Mark 5:25–34). She no longer experienced the discomfort and fatigue, or the shame and social isolation that her condition carried (Lev 15:25–27). Jesus cured the woman physically, but just as importantly, he healed her status in society.

In Matthew 8:1–4, we read of a man with leprosy who asks Jesus to "make me clean." Jesus cures the leprosy and tells the man to present himself to the priest. Jesus's willingness to cure the man precedes the man's restoration into his social and spiritual community. Jesus focuses on not only the physical cure but the social, emotional, and spiritual state as well.

We want to minister to the disabled community with Jesus's holistic concern for people's physical, social, spiritual, and emotional wellbeing. How can global workers provide community support and heal social isolation by including people with disabilities in all areas of life? Begin by asking the community about the following:

- Access to public buildings and transportation (see CRPD, Article 9)
- Access to adequate housing (see CRPD, Articles 19 and 28)
- Access to mobility aids (see CRPD, Article 20)
- Access to education (see CRPD, Article 24)
- Access to employment opportunities (see CRPD, Article 27)
- Access to health care (see CRPD, Article 25)
- Access to recreational activities (see CRPD, Article 30)

How can global workers come alongside people with disabilities to advocate for equal access to education, remove physical barriers in society, and change prevailing attitudes in the culture? Advocacy can be a lonely and tiring endeavor that usually takes years, if not decades. If the church and mission community help people with disabilities to have access to the world around them, the world will notice.

Emotional and Mental Health Needs
Rates of depression and anxiety are high among people with disabilities. This is usually due not to the disability itself but to the lack of social interaction that people with disabilities often experience. A study by the US Centers for Disease Control reported that adults with disabilities are more than four times more likely to experience frequent mental distress, defined as fourteen or more mentally unhealthy days out of the past thirty days (Cree et al. 2018).

In addition, people with disabilities may experience trauma because of their injury or ongoing medical procedures. Both acute and cumulative trauma affect people's hopes and expectations for the future. Many people with disabilities may believe they won't experience the typical milestones of life in education, relationships, or work and volunteer opportunities (Center for Substance Abuse Treatment 2014). A life without hope or positive expectations for the future could certainly explain increased rates of depression and anxiety.

Transition
One day, I was sitting in front of the computer attending a training about TCKs when I was struck by the similarities between living cross-culturally and living with a disability. I subsequently adapted models of cross-cultural debriefing and transition and developed a workbook called *The Journey: Discovering Emotional and Spiritual Health after Disability* (Smith 2024).

People with acquired disabilities have to learn a new language, one full of medical terminology. Many people lose close relationships when spouses abandon a marriage or when they can no longer participate with friends in their former activities. Traditions—like getting up early on Christmas morning or preparing a large meal for a special celebration—are lost. Each day can feel overwhelming. Life is difficult and requires more energy, and everything we do takes longer. It takes time to understand and manage government assistance, healthcare, and transportation. The transition can be chaotic as one seeks to resettle physically, emotionally, and spiritually into a new way of life.

Moving Toward Inclusion and Belonging
One major objective of the church and mission communities should be creating a sense of belonging for people with disabilities. What does belonging look like? Erik Carter (2016) describes the characteristics of a community where people with disabilities experience a sense of belonging. These qualities include being present, invited, welcomed, known, accepted, supported, cared for, befriended, needed, and loved.

In Australia, Missions Interlink is instructing sending organizations on how to facilitate the call of people with disabilities in mission work. The Shine Ministry, a disability ministry at Southeast Christian Church in Louisville, Kentucky (USA), welcomes people with intellectual and developmental disabilities into its community and provides age- and developmentally appropriate ways for people with disabilities to hear the gospel. The Shine Ministry also provides opportunities to serve in the Shine Cafe, which supports a sense of inclusion and belonging. At national and international levels, CBM Global advocates for inclusive education, health care, and disaster relief for people with disabilities.

We can see examples of churches and organizations creating inclusive opportunities for people with disabilities. I challenge all of us to embrace and act on the Lausanne Movement's *Cape Town Commitment* (2010), which calls us to "encourage church and mission leaders to think not only of mission among those with a disability, but to recognize, affirm and facilitate the missional calling of believers with disabilities themselves as part of the Body of Christ."

Conclusion

Paul states, "Now you are the body of Christ, and each one of you is a part of it" (1 Cor 12:27). As the global church and mission community, let us work together, in unity, through the Holy Spirit. We are neither Jews nor Gentiles, slave nor free, *disabled nor abled*. We are one in Christ and dependent on one another. We have different roles, none more important than the other. Whether God calls us to go or stay, preach or pray, serve or be served, let us remember that God created *every* man, woman, and child in his own image (Gen 1:27).

Applications: Disabilities in the Church and Mission

Core Strategies

1. Develop a theology of disability (see resources below).
2. Become familiar with the United Nations Convention on the Rights of Persons with Disabilities.
3. Create inclusion and belonging for people with disabilities in the global church and in mission organizations.

Core Resources

1. David Deuel and Nathan John. 2021. *Disability in Mission: The Church's Hidden Treasure*.
2. Lamar Hardwick. 2021. *Disability and the Church*.
3. Wheaton Center for Faith and Disability.

Reflection and Discussion

1. Have you ever considered the fact that you are a just a moment away from being disabled? How would a disability impact your identity, income, marriage and relationships, independence, or relationship with God? Would a disability change your calling?
2. Does your church or mission organization see only the *disadvantages* of people with disabilities in ministry (e.g., physical or mental health factors, financial impact, security concerns), or does it also acknowledge the advantages (e.g., resilience, ability to adapt, ability to relate to those who hurt) that people with disabilities have?
3. How can the church and mission organizations be intentional in reaching the largest minority group in the world? How can the church and mission organizations accommodate and creatively engage people with disabilities in the Great Commission?

References

Carter, Erik, Elizabeth Biggs, and Thomas Boehm. 2016. "Being Present versus Having a Presence: Dimensions of Belonging for Young People with Disabilities and Their Families." *Christian Education Journal*, 13 (1): 127–146. https://doi.org/10.1177/073989131601300109.

CBM Global. https://cbm-global.org/.

Center for Substance Abuse Treatment. 2014. *Trauma-Informed Care in Behavioral Health Services*. Rockville, MD: Substance Abuse and Mental Health Administration. https://www.ncbi.nlm.nih.gov/books/NBK207191/.

Cree, Robyn A., Catherine A. Okoro, Matthew M. Zack, and Eric G. Carbone. 2020. "Frequent Mental Distress among Adults, by Disability Status, Disability Type, and Selected Characteristics—United States, 2018." *Morbidity and Mortality Weekly Report* 69, no. 36 (September 11, 2020): 1238–1243. https://doi.org/10.15585/mmwr.mm6936a2.

Deuel, David, and Nathan John. 2021. *Disability in Mission: The Church's Hidden Treasure*. Carol Stream, IL: Hendrickson Publishers.

Heymann, Jody, Elizabeth Wong, and Willetta Waisath. 2021. "A Comparative Overview of Disability-Related Employment Laws and Policies in 193 Countries." *Journal of Disability Policy Studies* 33, no. 1 (April 17): 25–34. https://doi.org/10.1177/10442073211006396.

Lausanne Movement. 2010. *The Cape Town Commitment*. https://lausanne.org/content/ctc/ctcommitment#p2–4.

Missions Interlink. https://missionsinterlink.org.au/.

Shine Ministry. https://www.southeastchristian.org/ministries/deaf-and-disabilities-ministry.

Smith, Jenny. 2021. *Live the Impossible: How a Wheelchair Has Taken Me Places I Never Dared to Imagine*. Louisville, KY: Significant Publications.

Smith, Jenny. 2024. *The Journey: Discovering Emotional and Spiritual Health after Disability*. Louisville, KY: Significant Publications.

Trotter, John. 2022. "Transforming Frames of Marginalization." *Evangelical Missions Quarterly* 58, no. 4 (October 2022).

United Nations. 2006. Convention on the Rights of Persons with Disabilities. https://www.un.org/development/desa/disabilities/convention-on-the-rights-of-persons-with-disabilities/convention-on-the-rights-of-persons-with-disabilities-2.html.

Wheaton Center for Faith and Disability. https://www.wheaton.edu/wheaton-center-for-faith-and-disability/.

World Health Organization. 2023. "Disability." https://www.who.int/news-room/fact-sheets/detail/disability-and-health.

Jenny Smith, MEd, has a master's in counseling psychology from the University of Louisville and has been in ministry for over twenty years. She ministers to people with chronic physical conditions to support and encourage their holistic health. She also advocates for including persons with disabilities in churches and mission agencies.

14

Climate and Environmental Issues
Code Red for Member Care and Mission?

Debbie Hawker, David Hawker, Jamie Hawker, and Biniam Guush

Stephen, a mission worker in Asia, was reprimanded by his team leader for preaching a sermon on creation care and climate change. He talked to a member care provider about his frustration.

Isabella, a worker in Latin America, was distressed about team conflict over environmental issues. Her organization had introduced a Creation Stewardship policy, which was viewed as controversial by some team members.

Hannah, a teenager in a mission family, became upset on returning to her parents' home culture, where she learned about climate change at school. "We are destroying the world and no one in our mission even cares about this!" she told her counselor. "What's the point of going on?" Two weeks later, she attempted suicide.

Environmental issues are being raised more and more frequently in member care consultations. This should not surprise us, as these issues are receiving increasing attention in society generally and from humanitarian organizations. The United Nations has warned of a "code red" for humanity's survival due to climate change. Air pollution kills nearly seven million people a year (Ritchie and Roser 2021). Plastic pollution and biodiversity loss are among the other environmental issues causing serious concern.

In this chapter, we introduce various voices to help us understand why environmental and climate concerns raise important issues of ethics and human flourishing that we should consider in our mission and member care work. We then discuss responses to these concerns along with ways to take action.

Listening

Listening to Third Culture Kids (TCKs) and Mission Kids (MKs)

> A study of 10,000 people aged 16 to 25 in 10 countries found that 84 percent reported being at least moderately worried about climate change, 75 percent were frightened about the future, and 39 percent said they were hesitant to have children because of climate change. (Hickman et al. 2021)

TCKs spend a significant part of their formative years living outside their parents' home culture. They often take on the values and concerns of the host culture and other third-culture friends. In many host cultures, climate change is a visible and experiential threat. TCKs may have witnessed the effects of extreme temperatures, droughts, floods, wildfires, hurricanes, famine or insect plagues. They know that their local friends are at risk because of climate change, and they want to do what they can to reduce the risks. Teenage TCKs often hold strong views. Like Hannah, they can become upset if their family or mission community does not seem to care about these issues. These young people want us to listen to them. So, let's listen to 16-year-old Jamie Hawker—one of this chapter's authors—speaking from his generational perspective:

> The United Nations has declared that we are in an era of "global boiling." It is now virtually impossible for us to stay under the 1.5°C temperature rise target set in Paris in 2015. We are not even remotely on track for an agreement we made less than a decade ago, an important target to ensure that humans, plants and animals can go on living despite the increasing population, demand for food and constant development in technology. Wow! I think that sums up the current problems. We humans are the ultimate procrastinators. We become so distracted by everything else that we forget how much is at stake if we don't tackle climate change. Our politicians have set disappointing targets. I've seen 2070 as the deadline for some climate targets, by which time there may be more plastic in the sea than fish (World Economic Forum et al. 2016, 29).
>
> Let's go back a couple of years. In 2021, in a speech before the Glasgow COP26 meeting, I said that there was no vaccine for climate change. I said that if we do nothing to keep to our target, the world would become unrecognizable: unrecognizable through deadly wildfires, unrecognizable through violent and frequent thunderstorms, unrecognizable through new records for wind speeds and snowfall and

unrecognizable because many regions would be too hot for humanity to survive. Well, I think that's starting to happen.

A couple of years ago, when we were still getting out of a pandemic, I didn't think these changes would happen so soon. But as I write this in August 2023, we have just seen a convergence of many extreme climate events including wildfires in Greece, Portugal, and Hawaii. All three are popular tourist destinations that now have permanent scars. Meanwhile, deadly typhoons have derailed plans for a Scout jamboree in South Korea. Southern Europe became unbearable, not just with wildfires but with Spain and Italy being drenched in deadly heat. In Mexico, over 100 people died due to temperatures soaring above 50°C (122°F). Worldwide, July 2023 was the hottest month ever on record.

Extreme weather events may become steadily worse and may spread to additional densely inhabited areas, displacing countless people. According to UNICEF (2023), over 43 million children have been displaced by weather-related events in the last six years. It is of course hard to predict the future, but if it gets so bad that temperatures rise 4°C above pre-industrial levels, Antarctic and Arctic ice sheets could melt and many humans will move towards the poles. Asia, Africa, Southern Europe, Latin America, Australia and the Caribbean could all become largely uninhabitable.

I know there are other threats in this world. I sympathize with those living in war zones or under dictatorships. Poverty is a massive struggle needing solutions. And the world has many more challenges, from hunger to homelessness to abuse to rape. But no other issue is quite like climate change which has the potential to affect the greatest number of people, especially the people who contribute to it the least. Barring extinction scenarios like a nuclear holocaust, none of the other issues is likely to affect as many people as climate change, especially the people who have the least.

Listening to the Cultures with Which We Engage

As Jamie reminds us, climate change particularly impacts low-income countries, which include many of the countries where mission workers serve.

The study by Hickman et al. (2021) cited above involved 1,000 young people from each of ten countries, including Brazil, India, Nigeria, and the Philippines. In every country, there was widespread concern about climate change.

We provide member care for people in Ethiopia and Chad, among other places. What do people from these countries think about climate change? Let's hear from Biniam, another of this chapter's authors:

> I am from Tigray in the northern part of Ethiopia. The people worked hard to make their environment a better place, for instance by conserving water to cultivate land. But now there is war and genocide which have wiped out all the progress they made in the last 20 years. The war has driven deforestation. People are cutting down trees because they have been cut off from any other option for cooking fuel.
>
> Climate change has caused difficulties in Ethiopia. There is not much rain, which means that crops fail. The food that remained was eaten by locusts in many places. That was also related to climate change. Now there is starvation.

Issa is from Chad, where temperatures have been rising and rainfall decreasing. In the last 50 years, over 90 percent of Chad's largest lake has disappeared. Chad experiences droughts, floods and famine. Issa explains further:

> Chad is one of the poorest countries in the world, despite its diverse natural resources. All the villagers depend on cultivation. In recent years, due to climate change, they are paying very dearly. Often the bushes catch fire, and the seasons no longer respect their times. Chad experiences droughts, floods, and famine. All this has very negative effects on villagers and their animals. We are asking humanitarian organizations to support us in this great challenge that is beyond our capacity to address.

A survey of 30,000 people in twenty-eight countries (YouGov 2019) found that at least 94 percent of people in every nation believe that climate change is happening. Most people believe that climate change will cause the destruction of cities due to rising sea levels, seriously damage economies, lead to large numbers of climate refugees, and cause wars.

A larger survey of nearly 110,000 adults from 192 countries and territories found that the majority are worried about climate change. For example, 95 percent of those in Mexico and 93 percent in Chile and Portugal expressed concerns (Leiserowitz et al., 2022). Mission workers are surrounded by people who are deeply distressed by climate change.

Listening to Data and Scientists

Ninety-seven percent of climate scientists agree that humans are making the Earth warmer (Cook et al. 2016). NASA and *Our World in Data* summarize some of the evidence that convinces them. For instance, in the last century, both levels of carbon dioxide (which traps solar heat in the atmosphere) and global temperatures have risen rapidly and far above previous fluctuations (graph taken from Hawkins 2020 and used with permission).

In the graph below, the eruptions refer to large volcanic eruptions. The Maunder Minimum refers to a period in which sunspots were exceedingly rare. The black area shows the median temperature change (compared with the year AD 1). The gray area illustrates the highest and lowest temperature changes.

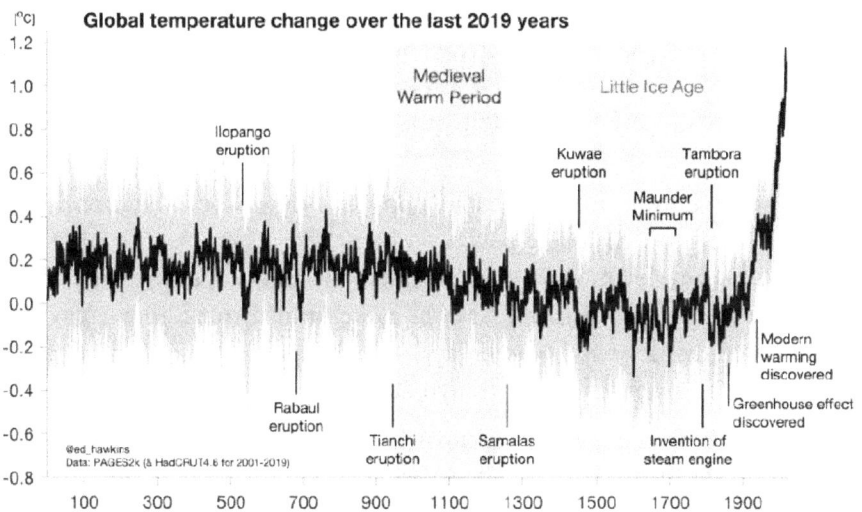

Listening to Those with Whom We Disagree

The percentage of people who do not believe in climate change is 1 percent or less in most Asian countries, 2 percent in the United Kingdom, 5 percent in Australia, and 6 percent in the USA. However, among American evangelical Protestant Christians it rises to 32 percent (Pew Research Center 2022).

Why might some evangelical Christians, for example, be less likely than the general public to believe in climate change or less inclined to do anything about it? Views and myths are often aligned with politics and amplified by the echo chambers of social media. Some may distrust science and/or the way it has been applied. Some may tolerate the destruction of the earth because they believe it will hasten the time when Christ returns and create a new heaven and earth. Others may see the end of the world as a matter in God's hands, not to be influenced by human activity. Some may view this world as not our home and destined for destruction and may thus be less motivated to care about it. Still others may interpret God's command to humans to subdue and rule over the earth as giving us permission to exploit the earth for human benefit, with little consideration for the consequences. There are also people from many faiths or no particular faith who believe climate change exists but is not primarily caused by humans. For more information related to this view see the Cornwall Alliance.

The Hebrew text (Gen 1:28) carries the idea of stewardship, responsibility, and caring for God's land as tenants. The Bible tells many stories in which God's decisions about ending civilizations are influenced by humans. And never mind the end of the world—if current trends in rising temperature continue, the environmental destruction carried out by some countries, in particular high-income nations, will be responsible for prematurely killing around a billion people in low-income countries over the next century (Pearce and Parncutt 2023).

In multi-cultural mission teams, opposing views about environmental issues can lead to division, especially when these issues are the subject of sermons or team devotional times. Stephen and Isabella, at the start of this chapter, illustrate this tension. As well as cultural divides, there may also be a gender divide, with women typically being more concerned about environmental issues than men (Kalyn 2023).

Listening to Different Ways of Expressing Faith
When we published *Changing the Climate* (Hawker, Hawker, and Hawker 2021), we were criticized online by someone who claimed that environmental activities are a distraction from sharing the gospel. But in our experience, talking about caring for creation has helped us introduce biblical teaching to people who had previously shown little interest in the Bible. Jamie's friends, teachers, and extended family members requested copies of our book, which includes teaching from many Bible passages. We had opportunities to share our faith at secular meetings and in the media.

Surveys of young Christians in the United Kingdom, Canada and Australia have found that they are very concerned about climate change and believe that Christians should be responding (Tearfund and Youthscape 2020; Tearfund 2022; Tearfund and A Rocha 2023). A lack of response has caused some to disengage with the church. Laura Hancock of Youth for Christ says:

So many young people today aren't asking "Is faith in Jesus real?" but "Will faith in Jesus make a difference?" The clear cry from this research is that our faith should not only make a difference to our lives, but to our planet. (Tearfund and Youthscape 2020)

Listening to God's Word
There are at least seven biblical reasons to care for creation:

1. Out of respect for our Creator (Gen 1)
2. Because God cares about creation (Ps 50:10–11)
3. As an act of love for our neighbors worldwide and future generations (Mark 12:31; Phil 2:4), who face devastating consequences if we fail to do so
4. Because God cares about justice (Prov 29:7) and the ecological crisis is severely unjust
5. Because God commands us to care for the earth (Gen 2:15)
6. As an act of witness (Matt 5:16)
7. As an act of unity (Ps 133:1)

In addition, caring for the environment is part of building resilience, as our resilience is influenced by our environment. Member care practitioners help mission workers build resilience. It is hard to thrive in a fragile environment that is too hot or too cold, highly polluted, or at risk of flooding or burning, or when our food supply is destroyed, or when our children are afraid about the future because of environmental damage. If we care about people, we must care about the environment.

Responding

Response to Eco-Anxiety and Conflict
Whatever our own views may be, we must listen to the mission workers we seek to support and try to understand their perspective. When conflict is reported, we can encourage those involved to listen to the other view and to try to understand where the other person is coming from. Sometimes mediation sessions may be necessary.

Some people may want help in dealing with their anxiety, grief, anger, shame, or guilt feelings about the climate crisis. They might find it helpful to be guided in lament. "Climate-aware therapy" is an emerging field of psychological therapy that deals with mental health issues related to the climate emergency.

Lise Van Susteren says that because of climate change, "some people are frozen by worry and don't leave the house; others are depressed or angry. Climate distress can exacerbate already-present anxiety and depression in people who have been diagnosed with it. Climate distress can affect relationships, job performance, and your sense of the future" (Kalyn 2023).

Pointing people toward resources, groups, or actions can help them feel less isolated. Action reduces the sense of helplessness and hopelessness associated with despair (and, for people like Hannah in the opening account, suicidal ideation) (Weber and Constantino 2023).

Jamie wrote over 130 tips in our book to help people act, turning hopelessness to hope. Resources such as our book have been used by groups and teams to aid discussions about what the Bible says about creation care.

Response from Christian Denominations and Mission Organizations
More and more Christians are uniting in caring for creation. In 2006, nearly 100 key evangelical leaders signed a document entitled "Climate Change: An Evangelical Call to Action." Since then, many denominations have endorsed climate action, from Southern Baptists to Vineyard churches, from the Roman Catholic Church to the Salvation Army, and from the Methodist Conference to the Anglican Communion. Churches across the denominations have signed up to become "eco-churches."

In 2012, the Lausanne Movement met in Jamaica for a consultation on creation care and the gospel. The participants reached two primary conclusions: (1) creation care is a "gospel issue within the lordship of Christ" and (2) we are facing a pressing, urgent crisis that must be resolved in our generation. They issued a creation care call to action, which included the statement that: "environmental issues represent one of the greatest opportunities to demonstrate the love of Christ and plant churches among unreached and unengaged people groups in our generation. We encourage the church to promote 'environmental missions' as a new category within mission work" (Lausanne Movement 2012, point 5).

When Jamie was 12, he wrote to short-term mission agencies to encourage them to reflect on how they could minimize their negative environmental impact. Global Connections, the United Kingdom network of mission agencies, responded by holding an online conference, which was attended by over 100 people representing dozens of mission agencies. Ideas included setting up short-term mission projects among international migrants in our home country, including students, refugees, and diaspora communities, rather than traveling abroad on short-term trips that can sometimes amount to "voluntourism." The Global Connections commitment to best practice in short-term mission added a section on climate change to be adhered to by all mission agencies, "to ensure the church or agency adopts a considered and responsible approach to climate change" (Global Connections 2023).

Some mission agencies focus primarily on caring for creation (e.g., A Rocha). Others include environmental mission activities (such as reforestation projects, clean energy and rainwater harvesting tanks) among a wider range of activities. A growing number of mission organizations have developed creation stewardship policies (e.g., Baptist Missionary Society 2022; OMF International 2023; Tearfund 2023; World Relief 2022).

Response from Member Care
All around us, people are taking action to care for the environment. There are daily press reports on these issues. Schools are registering as "eco-schools" with "eco-clubs." Festivals offer compostable toilets and attempt to go plastic-free. Employers encourage people not to print documents unless absolutely necessary, and they encourage environmental champions and recycling schemes. Banks have stopped sending paper statements. Universities offer courses related to climate change across several disciplines. Many universities in the United Kingdom encourage at least one-fifth of psychology students to choose a research project related to environmental issues (British Psychological Society 2023). Community volunteers pick up litter, clean beaches, maintain community gardens, run repair shops, and prevent food waste by distributing surplus food from supermarkets. Online groups facilitate the giving away or selling of used items so that they do not go to landfill sites. Homes have solar power and heat pumps. Churches and mission organizations are starting to respond in many of these ways.

Nearly all the groups we belong to are taking action to reduce carbon emissions. Psychologists are using their skills to tackle the climate emergency at many levels (Whomsley 2021). Member care groups, however, seem to be a notable exception. We love our member care colleagues, who are some of the kindest people we have ever met. But as a group, we in member care (including ourselves) have been slow to take steps to care for creation. *Does member care not care?*

For instance, some member care meetings still provide plastic bottles of water, whereas in secular meetings people bring reusable bottles. When we questioned this practice, we were told, "You can recycle the bottle." This response misses the point that it is better to reduce plastic (and other disposable products) than to recycle.

Response When Traveling

One way in which we can reduce our individual carbon emissions is to fly less. Many of us travel around the world frequently to provide member care and to attend meetings. We fly in to provide member care, for instance, after a natural disaster. But what if all these flights contribute to climate change and the risk of more disasters?

Many secular conferences encourage participants to travel by rail instead of air when possible, or they offer the option to join online. When we suggested this for a gathering of hundreds of member care practitioners who were planning to fly across the world for a few days, the idea was dismissed. We were told that others were not as bothered by climate change as we were.

In truth, we also felt less bothered by climate change too until ten years ago. We loved flying to different cultures to spend time with people. We thought it would not make any difference if we were not on the plane, as the plane would still fly. But the weight of every person (and their luggage) on a flight increases the emissions as more fuel is burned. In contrast, as more people model the decision to not fly, fewer flights take off. Tens of thousands of people have pledged not to fly and many more have reduced their number of flights. Only about 3 percent of the world's population take regular flights (Timperley 2020). But our impression is that most member care practitioners are frequent flyers and see no problem with flying as often as we want.

The early mission pioneers managed flight-free mission, as did Jesus and the apostles. Frequent flying is a recent phenomenon. Our own family crossed the oceans by boat in the 1950s and 1960s, between the United Kingdom and New Zealand (in the case of David's aunt) and Jamaica (Debbie's parents, who hand-washed their baby's diapers on the ship). At that time, few people would have dreamed of flying, and all diapers were reusable.

Crossing continents without flying is still possible today. Most asylum seekers, like Biniam, travel long distances by land and sea.

In 2015, Jonny Burgess traveled by ship for fourteen days from England to Senegal, then took a bus to the Gambia for his mission placement. Jonny recommends traveling by sea to allow time to process emotional goodbyes; to have time to prepare for the transition to a new place; and to provide quality and quantity time to pray, meditate on God's word, and reflect. This method of travel offers environmental as well as spiritual and emotional benefits of slow travel. His blog might inspire others to consider this mode of travel (Burgess 2015).

Jonny got this idea from others who went to South America by boat. We know a mission family who traveled by boat from Brazil to the United Kingdom in 2016 after completing six years of mission. Such choices are not as rare as might be imagined.

John Barclay, a TCK specialist who now lives in Australia, also tries to limit his travel-related carbon emissions. He told us:

> During our twenty-eight years in Asia, our only family transport was two-wheelers—we chose not to own a car. I try to travel by road or train whenever possible; that's not difficult in India and Nepal. Recently I decided not to go to a member care conference in New Zealand; I didn't think my flight there was justified, but we sponsored someone from Papua New Guinea to attend instead. When I need to travel internationally, I try to combine trips and use train travel whenever possible. I am about to go to Thailand and India on a single trip. I will travel by train from Chiang Mai to Bangkok instead of flying, and my preferred mode of travel in India is always on a train. (Barclay 2023)

Debbie, David, and Jamie have also traveled by train from Chiang Mai to Bangkok. We took a sleeper train, which took about 18 hours due to a delay. We thoroughly enjoyed the experience and saw a lot more of the country than we would have done from the air. We have taken even longer train journeys in India, singing "Amazing Grace" to fellow passengers who asked for a song along the way. This experience was far more enjoyable than flying. Our World In Data provides useful comparisons of the carbon footprint of various forms of travel (Ritchie 2023).

Taking More Action

Taking Action to Love Sacrificially

Many member care workers enjoy traveling to experience varied cultures and meet people. That is not a bad thing. For our family, not flying has been one of the most difficult changes we have made. But we believe that if we really care about the people who live in different lands, we should pay attention to the impact that our carbon emissions have on them. For example, a 17-year-old in Samoa says:

> Climate change is a day-to-day thing for people in Samoa. As a teenager growing up, it is my reality to see cyclones, flash floods, general flooding in the area we live in, droughts and all sorts of extreme weather. … My wish for the world is that everyone can concentrate on [limiting the

temperature rise to 1.5 degrees] because that is the only way our Pacific islands can survive. (Global Witness 2017)

In 1990, when Debbie first went to Africa, everyone in her mission organization was asked to sign a contract agreeing not to drink alcohol and not to be alone with a member of the opposite sex apart from their spouse, so as not to offend African Christians or risk being accused of misbehavior. Today, might we consider signing a pledge to try to reduce our carbon emissions, to help protect people who are suffering due to climate change?

Taking Action to Reduce Travel Emissions

We are not saying everyone must stop flying. There might be good reasons for taking a flight. But if we all took slightly fewer flights, we could make a significant difference—vastly more than we can achieve by recycling more or by changing to low-energy lightbulbs (Wynes and Nicolas 2017).

Here are some questions for those in mission to consider:

- When could we meet remotely (speaking and training over the internet)?
- Can we arrange and attend local or regional member care meetings rather than international ones?
- Can we choose venues accessible by public transport?
- How necessary is this journey?
- Could someone more local provide the input we are offering? Can we train more local people to provide member care?
- Is there an environmentally friendly way to travel (e.g., by train, bus, or boat)?
- If we fly, can we take a direct flight rather than several flights? And can we check which airline produces the least carbon emissions (Atmosfair 2018)?
- Can we reduce or offset our carbon emissions (e.g., by contributing to projects that help absorb carbon dioxide)?

If we tell other people that we are reducing our flights and why, we can make an even bigger difference. "Making it known that you're someone who's given up flying for climate reasons can start to have a statistically significant impact on the amount that people around you fly" (Timperley 2020).

Low-carbon member care is possible. During the COVID-19 lockdowns, flights stopped and member care took place remotely. People soon became accustomed to this method. Some people preferred it as care could be provided more quickly.

Other Actions to Make Member Care and Mission More Sustainable
To do member care ethically and to live justly, we can also consider these questions:

- Can we reduce the amount of single-use plastic at our events (e.g., encouraging reusable water bottles, cups, cutlery, and plates, or recycling name badges)?
- How can we reduce waste, including food waste?
- Can we offer locally produced food and plant-based options?
- Can we use an energy provider which uses sustainable energy?
- Can we use an ethical bank which lends to organizations which make a positive impact on the environment?
- What impacts (positive or negative) do our choices have on the planet, people with fewer resources than ourselves, and future generations?
- Can we become more informed and climate-aware as member care practitioners?
- Does our group have a creation care policy?
- Can we help others (including the mission workers we support) to do what they can to reduce their carbon footprint and care for the environment?

Being Hopeful and Responsible

Jamie says, "There is still hope. Always. Although we won't meet the 1.5-degree target, we can still try to go as low as we can. We can take steps to reduce our own carbon emissions. Slowly, that could make an impact if we all worked together."

To be good stewards of the earth that God created, let us all listen and respond. In this way, we will show Hannah and all young people like her—along with the mission community itself and the people with whom we are ministering—that we truly care for the earth and are willing to make sacrificial changes in our lifestyles.

Applications: Climate and Environmental Issues

Core Strategies

1. Anticipate and provide a means for mission workers and their children to raise environmental issues. Consider how your organizational ethos can help to facilitate this.
2. Regularly review and reduce the carbon emissions of your member care work.
3. Encourage your organization to produce a creation care policy.

Core Resources

1. Debbie Hawker, David Hawker, and Jamie Hawker. 2021. *Changing the Climate: Applying the Bible in a Climate Emergency*. Many chapters explore the complexity of issues only mentioned or briefly discussed in this chapter. There is also a chapter on hope.
2. Kyle Meyaard-Schaap. 2023. *Following Jesus in a Warming World*.
3. Lalbiakhlui Rokhum, Jasmine Kwong, and Dave Bookless. 2023. "Climate Crisis and God's Creation." *Lausanne Global Analysis*.

Reflection and Discussion

1. Watch Katharine Hayhoe's short films on Christianity and climate change (Hayhoe 2021). Discuss the questions at the end of each film.
2. Pray for the people of Tigray, Chad, Samoa, and other regions where climate change is causing mass suffering.
3. What actions are you taking to care for creation? What else would you like to do?

References

Atmosfair. 2018. "Airline Index." https://www.atmosfair.de/en/air_travel_and_climate/atmosfair_airline_index.

Baptist Missionary Society. 2022. "BMS World Mission Policy for Creation Stewardship." September 2022. https://www.bmsworldmission.org/wp-content/uploads/2023/08/2022.10-Creation-Stewardship-policy.pdf.

British Psychological Society. 2023. "A Focus on Environmental Change." *The Psychologist*, September 2023: 8.

Burgess, Johnny. 2015. "Unusual Journeys 1: The Boat." *Serving and Surfing* (blog). October 30, 2015. http://servingandsurfing.blogspot.com/2015/10/unusual-journeys-1-boat.html.

Cook, J., et al. 2016. "Consensus on Consensus: A Synthesis of Consensus Estimates on Human-caused Global Warming." *Environmental Research Letters* 11, no. 4 (April). https://iopscience.iop.org/article/10.1088/1748-9326/11/4/048002.

Cornwall Alliance. https://cornwallalliance.org.

Global Connections. 2023. "Short-term Mission Commitment to Best Practice." https://globalconnections.ams3.digitaloceanspaces.com/files/New_CBP_HistoryChanges_for_2023.pdf.

Global Witness. 2017. "Climate Change on the Front Line: Why Marginalized Voices Matter in Climate Change Negotiations" (blog). August 9, 2017. https://www.globalwitness.org/en/blog/climate-change-front-line-why-marginalized-voices-matter-climate-change-negotiations/.

Hawker, Debbie, David Hawker, and Jamie Hawker. 2021. *Changing the Climate: Applying the Bible in a Climate Emergency*. Abingdon: Bible Reading Fellowship.

Hawkins, Ed. 2020. "Open Climate Science." *Climate Lab Book*. https://www.climate-lab-book.ac.uk/2020/2019-years/. Creative Commons. https://creativecommons.org/licenses/by-sa/4.0/.

Hayhoe, Katharine. 2021. "Christianity and Climate Change." Series of 9 films. https://www.tearfund.org/campaigns/christianity-and-climate-change-film-series.

Hickman, Caroline, et al. 2021. "Climate Anxiety in Children and Young People and Their Beliefs about Government Responses to Climate Change: A Global Survey." *The Lancet, Planetary Health* 5 (12): E863-E873. https://www.thelancet.com/journals/lanplh/article/PIIS2542-5196(21)00278-3/fulltext.

Kalyn, Wayne. 2023. "Weathering the Weather: Climate-Aware Therapist Q&A." *Psycom*, April 7. https://www.psycom.net/anxiety/climate-change-anxiety-irl.

Lausanne Movement. 2012. "Creation Care and the Gospel: Jamaica Call to Action." https://lausanne.org/content/statement/creation-care-call-to-action.

Leiserowitz, Anthony, et al. 2022. *International Public Opinion on Climate Change, 2022*. New Haven, CT: Yale Program on Climate Change Communication and Data for Good at Meta. https://climatecommunication.yale.edu/wp-content/uploads/2022/06/international-public-opinion-on-climate-change-2022a.pdf.

Meyaard-Schaap, Kyle. 2023. *Following Jesus in a Warming World*. Downers Grove, IL: IVP.

OMF International. 2023. "Creation Care." https://omf.org/what-we-do/creation-care/.

Pearce, Joshua, and Richard Parncutt. 2023. "Quantifying Global Greenhouse Gas Emissions in Human Deaths to Guide Energy Policy." *Energies* 16 (16): 6074. https://www.mdpi.com/1996-1073/16/16/6074.

Pew Research Center. 2022. "Religious Groups' Views on Climate Change." https://www.pewresearch.org/religion/2022/11/17/religious-groups-views-on-climate-change/.

Richie, Hannah. 2023. "Which Form of Transport Has the Smallest Carbon Footprint?" Our World In Data (August 30). https://ourworldindata.org/travel-carbon-footprint.

Ritchie, Hannah, and Max Roser. 2021 revision. "Air Pollution." *Our World in Data.* https://ourworldindata.org/air-pollution.

Rokhum, Lalbiakhlui, Jasmine Kwong, and Dave Bookless. 2023. "Climate Crisis and God's Creation." *Lausanne Global Analysis* 12 (6). https://lausanne.org/content/lga/2023–11/climate-crisis-and-gods-creation-calling-global-christian-leaders-to-act.

Tearfund. 2022. "They Shall Inherit the Earth." https://assets.tearfund.org.au/files/Tearfund_Climate-Report_Summary-for-Church-Leaders.pdf.

Tearfund. 2023. "Environmental and Economic Sustainability." https://www.tearfund.org/about-us/annual-report/environmental-and-economic-sustainability.

Tearfund and A Rocha. 2023. "For All the Earth." https://www.creationcollective.ca/wp-content/uploads/2023/04/Tearfund-A-Rocha- percentE2 percent80 percent93-Climate-Change-Survey-Report_Digital-1-min-min.pdf.

Tearfund and Youthscape. 2020. "Burning Down the House." https://youthscape.ams3.cdn.digitaloceanspaces.com/documents/Burning-down-the-house.pdf.

Timperley, Jocelyn. 2020. "Should We Give Up Flying for the Sake of the Climate?" February 19, 2020. https://www.bbc.com/future/article/20200218-climate-change-how-to-cut-your-carbon-emissions-when-flying.

UNICEF. 2023. "Children Displaced in a Changing Climate." https://www.unicef.org/reports/children-displaced-changing-climate.

Weber, E., and Sarah Constantino. 2023. "All Hearts and Minds on Deck: Hope Motivates Climate Action by Linking the Present and the Future." *Emotion Review* 15 (4): 293–297. https://doi.org/10.1177/17540739231195534.

Whomsley, Stuart. 2021. "Five Roles for Psychologists in Addressing Climate Change." *European Psychologist* 26 (3): 241–248.

World Economic Forum, Ellen MacArthur Foundation and McKinsey & Company. 2016. *The New Plastics Economy Rethinking the Future of Plastics.* https://emf.thirdlight.com/file/24/_A-BkCs_skP18I_Am1g_JWxFrX/The percent20New percent20Plastics percent20Economy percent3A percent20Rethinking percent20the percent20future percent20of percent20plastics.pdf.

World Relief. 2022. "World Relief's Commitment to Environmental Stewardship." https://worldrelief.org/blog-world-reliefs-commitment-to-environmental-stewardship/.

Wynes, Seth, and Kimberly Nicholas. 2017. "The Climate Mitigation Gap: Education and Government Recommendations Miss the Most Effective Individual Actions." *Environmental Research Letters* 12 (7). https://iopscience.iop.org/article/10.1088/1748-9326/aa7541/pdf.

YouGov. 2019. "Most People Expect to Feel the Effects of Climate Change, and Many Think It Will Make Us Extinct." https://today.yougov.com/politics/articles/25263-global-climate-change-poll?redirect_from= percent2Ftopics percent2Fscience percent2Farticles-reports percent2F2019 percent2F09 percent2F16 percent2Fglobal-climate-change-poll.

Debbie and David Hawker are clinical psychologists based in England. They specialize in supporting mission workers and their families around the world, as well as supporting refugees.

Jamie Hawker, age sixteen at the time of writing, received a Diana Award for his environmental activities. Together, the Hawkers wrote *Changing the Climate: Applying the Bible in a Climate Emergency* (2021).

Biniam Guush, a teacher in his twenties, fled Ethiopia because of genocide and threats to his own life. Since seeking asylum in England, he has received a BBC "Make a Difference" award for his extensive volunteering.

15

Staff Care in the Fight Against Human Trafficking

Timothy Friesen

This chapter focuses on the development of a comprehensive staff care model for members of a justice organization that works globally to eradicate human trafficking through rescuing and rehabilitating victims and prosecuting offenders. Justice workers are at risk for the effects of vicarious trauma, compassion fatigue, and burnout. Therefore, it is critical to develop a continuum of services to provide support for them and build resilience. As an external staff care consultant, I will share my experiences of facilitating staff care for members of a global justice organization.

We are called to bring light into the darkest places of this world, where evil prevails in the victimization of vulnerable children, youth, and adults. While living in Chiang Mai, Thailand from 2001 to 2007, I consulted with a faith-based justice organization whose mission was to rescue victims of sex trafficking. The field director requested that I meet with his team to share strategies on combating the stress and trauma associated with the work of investigating, rescuing, prosecuting, and rehabilitating victims of sex trafficking. This initial strategic meeting launched my work as a staff care consultant.

According to the International Labor Organization (2022), there are 27.6 million victims of human trafficking, among whom 3.3 million are believed to be children. The human trafficking business generates an annual income of $150 billion. Violence, dislocation, and exploitation of the global poor provide an ideal market for human trafficking.

After assisting the team in Chiang Mai, I subsequently (in 2008) received a contract as an external staff care consultant on a global level. The organization's justice work focuses on violence against women and children; modern-day slavery, including sex trafficking, labor trafficking, and online sexual exploitation of children; and police abuse of power. The goal is to strengthen national justice systems by partnering with local law enforcement officers, members of the judicial system, and social service workers whose mission is to investigate crimes, rescue victims, convict perpetrators, and support survivors through the healing process.

My initial assignment as an external consultant was to complete a needs assessment of the existing staff care program and make recommendations toward the development of a comprehensive program for approximately 1,000 global workers. At that time, staff care was managed by the human resources department and was limited to traditional employee benefits. New employees were given a job description but did not receive orientation regarding the risks associated with specific jobs. Strategies and programs related to prevention, wellness, and resilience development were not part of the organization's human resource services. Instead, it functioned in a reactive manner when a traumatic event or crisis occurred. Tactical debriefings following rescue operations were often utilized. However, the concept of psychosocial individual or group debriefings was not included as part of a post-operational response.

Development of a Comprehensive Staff Care Program

Development of a comprehensive staff care program from prevention to intervention, embodying best practices, was the primary goal following the initial needs assessment. This section discusses my recommendations to the organization (in italics) followed by my comments on each item.

1. Staff Care Specialist in Every Field Office—Each Human Resource (HR) department across the organization will have a designated role that focuses on the development and administration of a comprehensive staff care program.

This individual will be responsible for completing and implementing a staff care plan for all staff members with assistance and accountability from a global staff care specialist.

2. Community Mental Health Referrals—Each field office's staff care specialist will identify and vet local pastors and mental health professionals as community referrals for staff members.

Feedback from staff members regarding the most critical factors in their meetings with pastors or mental health workers strongly emphasized that all conversations must be confidential. Other important factors were the availability of providers who spoke the same heart language, understood and were sensitive to the organization's mission, held similar religious beliefs, and were exposed to the potential providers by inviting them to lead workshops or inspirational times of sharing.

3. Crisis Response and Contingency Planning—*Each field office will develop a crisis response plan for large-scale events such as a death in the line of duty or a natural disaster.*

Often, a crisis can be handled utilizing local resources. If needed, the global staff care specialist is alerted and briefed about the event, and then a decision can be made about reaching out to a global staff care consultant for support. Some large-scale or severe crises might impact most or all staff members; for these situations, it is important to have a plan of action in place that includes a designated person or command center for communication, mobilization of staff members to come on site and assist with the crisis response, and consultation from key individuals who have expertise with how to lead and manage a large-scale crisis event. Advanced preparation is crucial to a successful response in such crisis events.

I was involved in several crises that involved all members of the field office. I learned from experience that the following structures are helpful to mitigate negative effects of the traumatic event: (1) a chain of command to ensure an effective decision-making process; (2) a clear communication system; (3) mobilization of external personnel to assist local staff members and provide staff care support; and (4) group events in the early phase of a crisis to ensure cohesion and connection among the staff. I found it important to have all available staff participate in a briefing and time of sharing each morning and, if possible, to attend a debriefing time at the end of each day.

4. Cross-Cultural Assignments for Specialized Positions—*Organizations that hire expatriate specialists for positions that cannot be filled by a local hire must provide specialized services to ensure a positive adjustment and transition to new assignments.*

For example, an Australian investigative specialist with experience in child trafficking might be hired to work in an office in the Philippines. A cross-cultural assignment involves unique challenges for new staff members. The global HR individual responsible for onboarding expatriate hires should work with field office HR workers to develop a transition plan.

5. Family-Accompanied Cross-Cultural Assignments—*The global human resources department hiring expatriate workers for a cross-cultural assignment with accompanied family members will coordinate with a local field office a specialized plan to provide* care *for the family members.*

Staff care for accompanied family members was not part of a new hire package when I began my role as consultant.

My professional belief is that family members' adjustment to a new assignment is just as important as the employee's adjustment. Therefore, it is important to assess the risk factors that might indicate difficulty with a cross cultural adjustment. For example, a child diagnosed on the autism spectrum might need specialized educational services. Performing a home visit before a family deploys for their first assignment with an organization is a positive way to learn about the family as well as to establish a relationship of trust. Family debriefings can be managed by sending a family to a program that specializes in this activity. Otherwise, a global staff care consultant with whom the family is already familiar can perform this function.

6. *Individual and Group Debriefing*—Organizations will develop debriefing practices for front-line justice workers.

The term "debriefing" can be used in a variety of professional contexts. One example of debriefing involves investigators who have daily exposure to the sex trafficking world. They might meet informally to process the challenges of their work and encourage each other through sharing ways to leave behind the visual images associated with their work. Another form of debriefing concerns individuals who experience exposure to a distressful or traumatic event that elicits strong emotional reactions. Critical Incident Stress Debriefing (CISD) is an evidence-based group practice that can be useful as part of an overall staff care response to critical incidents. Mitchell (2000) states:

> A Critical Incident Stress Debriefing can best be described as a psycho-educational small group process. In other words, it is a structured group storytelling process combined with practical information to normalize group member reactions to a critical incident and facilitate their recovery. A CISD is only used in the aftermath of a significant traumatic event that has generated strong reactions in the personnel from a particular homogeneous group. The selection of a CISD as a crisis intervention tool means that a traumatic event has occurred, and the group members' usual coping methods have been overwhelmed and the personnel are exhibiting signs of considerable distress, impairment, or dysfunction.

7. *Psycho-Educational Staff Training*—All staff members will be trauma-informed to create and ensure a culturally sensitive staff care program.

Trauma-informed training for staff members involves an overview of the following trauma-related topics:

- What is trauma in the context of work related to human trafficking?
- How does trauma affect us physically, psychologically, cognitively, and spiritually?
- How does the brain respond to traumatic events?
- Basic debriefing techniques following a stressful or traumatic work-related event
- Developing a self-care plan that includes work-related strategies and non-work-related strategies

Once staff members have become adept at integrating trauma-informed principles, the leadership can plan specific training seminars. One field office struggled with negotiating through conflicts and therefore requested a seminar specific to this issue. Training seminars on topics such as stress management, using Kelly McGonigal's research in *The Upside of Stress* (2016), has become a means of building community and getting to know how staff function as a collective system. Staff development also includes becoming trauma-informed with an understanding of terminology used in the field of traumatology including primary trauma versus secondary trauma, vicarious trauma, compassion fatigue, and burnout. *Primary trauma* refers to an individual having direct contact with a traumatic event whereas *secondary trauma* refers to the psychological impact from hearing or viewing traumatic events experienced by others. *Vicarious trauma* refers to a shift in a person's attitude and world view due to prolonged exposure to the suffering and painful experiences of others. *Compassion fatigue* is common among humanitarian workers and involves a person's decline in performing their assigned tasks in a timely and competent manner due to physical fatigue and an accumulation of the negative effects of exposure to stress and trauma.

Information Gathering to Evaluate Staff Care Needs and Trends

As a global staff care consultant, I visited all the field offices during my early years with the organization. I learned through experience what it was like to be a frontline justice worker who had direct engagement with the crimes perpetrated upon people living in poverty. On one occasion, I was embedded in a team of investigators and researchers who were measuring the incidence of sex trafficking in a country where the organization was considering the establishment of a new field office. My role included leading psycho-spiritual briefings each day to prepare the team that would be visiting establishments where victims of sex trafficking might be found. While investigators were scouting out establishments for possible sex trafficking victims, I rode around in the van so that I could be available for an informal debriefing or a critical incident debriefing. At the end of each night, we all met for a debriefing on any specific events the investigators had encountered. This opportunity to work closely with investigators gave me insight into their very difficult work.

Visiting each of the field offices helped me establish my role as a staff care consultant and become a known entity to staff members. Each time I visited a field office, I requested meetings with the field director, leadership team, heads of departments, investigative team, and any staff who wanted an individual session. Through these encounters, I assessed the team's general health and developed a plan of action with the field director and leadership.

After visiting all the field offices, I met with organizational leadership, such as regional vice presidents, to share general trends I was observing in the field. I protected confidentiality by sharing trends that were evident across several of the field offices. I withheld specific information that would identify a location or specific staff members. Informing leadership regarding staff care trends led to elevating staff care as a global initiative.

Staff Survey
After several years of consulting with global teams, we conducted a survey (unpublished) to better understand how field workers integrated staff care into their vocation as justice workers. The survey was structured to elicit feedback on trauma, debriefing, self-care, and resilience—all topics closely related to staff care. We held group and individual sessions and asked first how a person living in their community would respond when asked about the meaning of these concepts. Different cultures can have very different views and terms related to these and other "mental health" concepts and must be considered when working in a community. The second level was to ask staff members to define what these concepts mean within the context of working for a justice organization. Lastly, the questions related to how they personally integrated these concepts into their work life, along with cultural factors that might restrict integration into their professional and personal life.

A common response to the first question was that these concepts are not known within their communities. For example, mental health services were for those identified as "crazy." Regarding their knowledge within the work environment, most workers reported that they had received training related to the meaning of these concepts. Lastly, there was great variance as to whether individuals incorporated these concepts into their lives within and outside the workplace. One important outcome was a recognition that educational training needed to go beyond just the informational level to an experiential level that intentionally integrated these concepts into staff's daily routines. Another outcome was the development of a peer support model to assist in making these concepts more relevant. This involved training managers in basic coaching techniques, psychological first aid, and helping workers construct a self-care plan that included goals specific to their job descriptions and strategies to maintain a healthy work-life balance. This review provided a natural experience for workers to connect to their managers regarding these issues.

The Need for Self-Care
Many justice workers view themselves as deeply compassionate people who are highly dedicated to their work and tirelessly give their time and energy. Sometimes this dedication leads to an unhealthy work-life balance, which affects one's personal wellness and relational health. In some cases, a compassionate drivenness for helping others can be influenced by a mixture of virtuous and unresolved personal issues. In the short term, this lifestyle can be sustained, but over time it is not a viable way to function. Self-care is critical for humanitarian workers who encounter high levels of stress and secondary trauma each day.

The Green Cross Academy of Traumatology (2005, 1) established the following standard practices related to self-care: "First, do no harm to yourself in the line of duty while helping/treating others. Second, attend to your physical, social, emotional, and spiritual needs as a way of ensuring high quality services for those who look to you for support." Their ethical principles for humanitarian workers declare that it is unethical not to attend to your self-care as a humanitarian worker because sufficient self-care prevents harming those we serve:

1. Respect for the dignity and worth of self: A violation lowers your integrity and trust.
2. Responsibility of self-care: Ultimately it is your responsibility to take care of yourself and no situation or person can justify neglecting it.

3. Self-care and duty to perform: There must be a recognition that the duty to perform as a worker cannot be fulfilled if there is not, at the same time, a duty to self-care.

Development of a Safeguard Program: Specialized Interventions for Workers with Direct Engagement

Trafficking girls to become commercial sex workers (CSWs) was a common way to prey upon the vulnerable poor in the Philippines. International Justice Mission (IJM), as a large justice organization, studied the prevalence of CSWs in a region north of Manila, using time-space sampling and undercover data collection (IJM 2016). An outcome-based study was conducted after interventions that included the rescue of victims and prosecution of perpetrators. The results indicated a prevalence of child sex trafficking in the region at 1.21 percent. This meant that one out of 83 CSWs identified by the data collectors was a minor. When we compared the baseline prevalence study in 2012 in the same region to the 2016 prevalence study, we found an 86.23 percent reduction in minor CSWs (IJM 2016). The organization celebrated this significant reduction in the sexual exploitation of minor girls not only in the area researched, but also throughout the Philippines where IJM was working.

Online Sexual Exploitation of Children

However, despite these positive results, a new, darker, and widespread form of crime emerged in the Philippines and elsewhere, involving online sexual exploitation of children (OSEC). "Cybersex trafficking is a form of modern slavery that was unimaginable prior to the digital age. Cybersex trafficking is the live sexual abuse of children streamed via the internet, set up by adults who receive online payment from predators and pedophiles located anywhere in the world" (IJM 2020).

My first encounter with OSEC casework occurred in the Philippines while I was debriefing a group of social workers who described their horrific experience of rescuing victims of OSEC living in extreme poverty. Removing these children, as young as three years old, from their homes and placing them in a government facility was unimaginable to them. It triggered strong reactions that challenged their deepest moral beliefs regarding the significance of family. Another example involved justice workers prosecuting local perpetrators who represented the middle person for OSEC crimes. These perpetrators were often family members. Court judgments were often harsh toward Filipino perpetrators. Again, the high value of family relationships was challenged. In contrast, perpetrators from other countries who instigated and perpetuated this crime were often given a minimal sentence. It was hard for these workers to accept this discrepancy. Finally, just watching videos of children engaging in sexual acts is horrifying for the workers, also challenging their moral system.

Moral Injury

In a similar situation, soldiers who participate in acts of war, such as collateral deaths of civilians, often return from their wartime service highly affected by their actions. Their compliance with the rules of military engagement may run counter to their moral beliefs and values. The term "moral injury" was first used by Jonathan Shay in *Achilles in Vietnam* (1994) to describe the dissonance between wartime line-of-duty actions and an individual's moral conscience. Shay (2014, 183) defined moral injury as "a betrayal of what is right by someone who holds legitimate authority in a high stakes situation." Litz et al. (2009, 700) defined moral injury as "the lasting psychological, biological, spiritual, behavioral and social impact of perpetrating, failing to prevent, or bearing witness to acts that transgress deeply held moral beliefs and expectations." Litz et al. (2016, 21) added that "moral injury is a syndrome of shame, self-handicapping, anger, and demoralization that occurs when deeply held beliefs and expectations about moral and ethical conduct are transgressed. It is distinct from a life-threatening event, as it is also not inherently fear-based; it can arise from killing, perpetration of violence, betrayals of trust in leaders, witnessing depraved behavior, or failing to prevent serious unethical acts."

In response to the potential for moral injury and other trauma-related reactions, it is critical to develop safeguard training for workers who have direct engagement with OSEC casework. I was part of a team that developed a safeguard program for OSEC caseworkers which involved the following components:

1. Candidate Screening Practices

Mitchell (2011, 121), writing about the inevitable negative personal and professional effects of working in a traumatic situation, says that the "collateral behavioral health damage in first responders may owe to being unfit mentally or physically prior to a disaster to perform relief work, as well as inadequate training, and unrealistic expectations from leadership." It is critical to identify the risk factors associated with each job and apply appropriate interviewing and assessment techniques to determine if a candidate is mentally and emotionally fit. Not all candidates—or their family members—will fit. The organization must be willing to decline such candidates and their families.

2. Orientation for New Hires
The onboarding process includes the following activities: (1) orientation to the safeguard program; (2) introduction to the concept of self-care and a review of common reactions to stress and positive coping strategies; and (3) exposure to OSEC casework using Stress Inoculation Training (SIT), an evidence-based intervention developed to manage the impact of a stressful situation. New hires receiving SIT view videos related to less severe events they will encounter in their work and then receive input about developing preventative measures to counteract the exposure. The fourth and final activity is a debriefing to process the SIT and any other reactions to the topics discussed.

3. Psychological First Aid
All staff members who have direct engagement with victims of OSEC receive training in psychological first aid (PFA) so that they can support one another during and after an operation. PFA is an intervention with peers or teammates to defuse any lingering acute stress reactions, encourage engagement with emotional and social support networks, and develop an action plan of strategies to implement until a follow-up encounter. If symptoms continue, then it is important to recommend that the OSEC worker pursue a personal debriefing.

4. Peer Coaching
OSEC field workers expressed a need for more support beyond debriefings. Training in peer coaching was offered to a group of staff members chosen by their managers. Along with psychological first aid, informal conversations between peers are a positive way to offer support and defuse stressful situations. Becoming trained in basic coaching techniques helped to promote positive conversations between the coach and worker. Psychological first aid training gave peer coaches an understanding of helpful resources to recommend, as well as criteria regarding when to make a referral to an external counselor. Feedback from the peer coaches indicated that common issues involved interpersonal conflicts with a manager or teammate.

5. Leadership Development
Justice organizations must function as thoroughly trauma-informed. It is essential for primary and secondary leaders in a field office to model wellness

and resilience and to recognize the symptoms associated with compassion fatigue, secondary trauma, and burnout. Leaders must develop a culture that advocates for needed prevention and intervention. Training leaders to include psycho-social-spiritual questions during routine check-ins helped to build a trauma-informed culture. Field directors often found it hard to share with peers about their workplace challenges and concerns. Field directors themselves often need regular check-ins with a confidential person external to the staff. This can be a global staff care consultant or a local mental health professional.

6. Routine Debriefings
It is important to set standards for routine and critical incident debriefings of OSEC workers. Routine debriefings can include individual meetings and group discussions. I recommend that OSEC workers who have direct contact with OSEC victims should participate in a routine debriefing every quarter. This debriefing helps with recognizing the impact of stress, processing strong emotions, identifying healthy coping strategies, and development of a personal narrative that encourages awareness of personal growth. Group debriefings help to build a cohesive team and to process difficult experiences related to OSEC casework. There are times when a critical incident affects a team, and it is necessary for the entire team to receive a group debriefing.

7. Trauma-Informed Organization Targeting Wellness, Resilience, and Post-Traumatic Growth
A justice organization is responsible for the provision of staff care. However, individual staff members should also be caring for themselves. Workers who follow a wellness program for the body, mind, and soul tend to be motivated and resilient. According to Figley (2012, 10), "Resilience is the ability to physiologically and psychologically adapt to environmental changes." Resilience means that we can face adversity and have the adaptive skills not only to bounce back but to grow to greater levels of functioning. Such post-traumatic growth has positive outcomes such as greater emotional capacity, spiritual growth, improved relationships, and greater appreciation for life (Tedeschi and Calhoun 1996).

8. Spiritual Formation
Developing rhythms or regular practices of spiritual formation within a justice organization benefits the individual and the organization. Being mindful of one's spiritual health is a core part of holistic health and will improve our

capacity to care for ourselves and others. Important rhythms include daily times of prayer and reflection, scheduled times for retreats and solitude, and development of rituals that help daily with entering and leaving OSEC work. In addition, having wrestled with a theology of suffering, injustice, and God's goodness can contribute to spiritual and emotional resilience.

Potential Challenges to the Development of a Comprehensive Staff Care Program

Staff care for a large organization has its challenges. Often the greatest challenge is to convince top leadership that staff care needs to be a priority for their workers. Senior leadership should illustrate that they value staff care in their reporting to an organization's board of directors. Data can be gathered through employee satisfaction surveys. Staff care without an endorsement from senior leadership is likely to be ineffective. The quality of staff care can be limited by lack of budgeted funds and lack of information gathered from workers about their satisfaction with the organization. I believe that staff care must be woven into the ethos of an organization and the daily lives of its workers so that it becomes a normal way of functioning. I have observed organizations that value spiritual formation and integrate it into daily functioning, such as reserving a time for prayer and reflection each day.

Some individuals are strong advocates for self-growth and wellness within an organization and wholeheartedly support staff care efforts. Others may be more resistant to staff care initiatives based on their previous exposure to mental health services. For some who have a history of military or government careers, mental health problems may be viewed as a sign of weakness that can negatively affect an individual's security clearance or ability to function in their job. For these individuals, it can be difficult to comply with a culture that fully endorses staff care. I have known some individuals who verbally assent to the policies regarding staff care but find ways to be passively resistant. When this happens, it is important to continue to find ways to build trust and assure confidentiality.

Being People of Hope

It is an honor to serve as global staff care consultant for a justice organization and to take part in building a comprehensive staff care program. I am grateful for those who trust me, share their struggles and challenges with me, and trust me to work with their families. When meeting with an individual or group connected to the organization, I like to share words of hope that may perhaps remain with them and inspire them to continue in the fight against injustice.

"May your light cause us to shine so bright that we bring hope into the dark. Hope for the hopeless, your love is," says the song "Open Up" by The Brilliance (2010). Hope reflects the light and God's love that we can share with others. Hope coming from a place of love can permeate the darkness where the evil of human trafficking prevails. "We cannot continue to do the work we do or to survive as a people or a society without hope. Yet we cannot be repeatedly exposed to trauma without building up defenses against the pain and sorrow of our work….We cannot afford to ignore vicarious traumatization or to abandon hope at any level—personal, professional, or society" (Saakvitne and Pearlman 1996, 140). Being an agent of hope for others means that we have encountered pain and have grown through our personal adversity.

The apostle Paul wrote:

> And we rejoice in the hope of the glory of God. Not only so, but we also rejoice in our sufferings, because we know that suffering produces perseverance; perseverance, character; and character, hope. And hope does not disappoint us, because God has poured out his love into our hearts by the Holy Spirit, whom he has given us." (Rom 5:2–5)

The promise that hope will not disappoint us reassures me that love overcomes the darkness associated with the heinous crimes perpetrated against humanity in the form of violence and slavery.

Applications: Staff Care in the Fight Against Human Trafficking

Core Strategies

1. Work closely with organizational leadership in the development and implementation of a comprehensive staff care program. It is critical that leaders validate, endorse, and model staff care in the organization.

2. Maintain a posture of learning when functioning as a staff care expert for staff members who live in a different cultural context. Learn through being curious about the experiences of all staff members. Every staff member has a story to share about how their work has shaped their lives.

3. Process and debrief with other professionals who do similar work, to encourage each other to maintain proper self-care.

Core Resources

1. Diane Langberg. 2015. *Suffering and the Heart of God: How Trauma Destroys and Christ Restores.*
2. Brett Litz, et al. 2016. *Adaptive Disclosure: A New Treatment for Military Trauma, Loss, and Moral Injury.*
3. Bessel van der Kolk. 2014. *The Body Keeps the Score: Brain, Mind, and Body in the Healing of Trauma.*

Reflection and Discussion

1. Does your organization have a comprehensive staff care program from prevention to intervention? What components are like those shared in this chapter? What additional components do you have, or what components are missing?
2. What are the benefits and challenges of having staff care managed solely by the organization's human resources function, compared to having an external consultant providing services who is affiliated with the organization but is not an employee?
3. What possible encounters might workers from your organization have that would fall into the category of a moral injury? Does your organization have a safeguard program for those who have frontline exposure to trauma?

References

The Brilliance. 2010. "Open Up." https://www.youtube.com/watch?v=ayieu0zRnnM.

Figley, Charles. 2012. "Basics of Compassion Fatigue." Figley Institute. http://www.figleyinstitute.com/documents/Workbook_AMEDD_SanAntonio_2012July20_RevAugust2013.pdf.

Green Cross Academy of Traumatology. 2005. *Standards of Care.* https://greencross.org/about-gc/standards-of-care-guidelines/.

International Justice Mission. 2016. "Child Sex Trafficking in Angeles City." https://ijmstoragelive.blob.core.windows.net/ijmna/documents/studies/ijm-pampanga-final-web-pdf-v2_2021-02-05-064344.pdf.

International Justice Mission. 2020. "Philippines: Fighting Cybersex Trafficking." http://www.ijm.org/philippines.

International Labor Organization. 2022. "Global Estimates of Modern Day Slavery: Forced International Labor and Forced Marriage." https://www.ilo.org/global/topics/forced-labour/publications/WCMS_854733/lang—en/index.htm.

Langberg, Diane. 2015. *Suffering and the Heart of God: How Trauma Destroys and Christ Restores*. Greensboro, NC: New Growth Press.

Litz, Brett, Leslie Lebowitz, Matt Gray, and William Nash. 2016. *Adaptive Disclosure: A New Treatment for Military Trauma, Loss, and Moral Injury*. New York: Guilford Press.

Litz, Brett, Nathan Stein, Eileen Delaney, Leslie Lebowitz, William Nash, Caroline Silva, and Shira Maguen. 2009. "Moral Injury and Moral Repair in War Veterans: A Preliminary Model and Intervention Strategy." *Clinical Psychology Review* 29 (8): 695–706.

Livermore, David. 2011. *The Cultural Intelligence Difference*. New York: AMACOM.

McGonigal, Kelly. 2016. *The Upside of Stress: Why Stress Is Good for You*. New York: Avery.

Mitchell, Jeffrey. 2000. *Critical Incident Stress Debriefing*. International Critical Stress Foundation. Ellicott City, MD. Trauma. https://icisf.org/.

Mitchell, Jeffrey. 2011. "Collateral Damage in Disaster Workers." *International Journal of Emergency Mental Health and Human Resilience* 13 (2): 121–125.

Saakvitne, Karen, and Laurie Pearlman. 1996. *Transforming the Pain: A Workbook on Vicarious Traumatization*. New York: Norton.

Shay, Jonathan. 1994. *Achilles in Vietnam: Combat Trauma and the Undoing of Character*. New York: Scribner.

Shay, Jonathan, 2014. "Moral Injury." *Psychoanalytic Psychology* 31 (2). https://www.sheldonhub.org/usercontent/sitecontentuploads/3/92D00AA2F618149F979A1277D0033657/moral_injury-shay.pdf.

Tedeschi, Richard, and Lawrence Calhoun. 1996. "The Posttraumatic Growth Inventory: Measuring the Positive Legacy of Trauma." *Journal Trauma Stress* 9 (3): 455–471.

van der Kolk, Bessel. 2014. *The Body Keeps the Score: Brain, Mind, and Body in the Healing of Trauma*. New York: Viking.

Timothy Friesen, PsyD, is a graduate of the Rosemead School of Psychology at Biola University and a licensed clinical psychologist in Michigan, USA. While in Chiang Mai, Thailand, Tim helped to develop professional counseling and member care services for mission workers. He is the founding director of the Cornerstone Counseling Foundation. In 2010, he started a non-profit organization, Twelve12:Hope, which provides services to humanitarian and mission workers and their organizations and child trauma recovery training using the Jacaranda Communities of Hope program (www.twelve12hope.org and connect@twelve12hope.org).

PART 4
Staying the Course in Good Practice

Grace Shim & Tim Hibma, Consulting Editors

Introduction to Part 4

Grace: My journey in mental health care as mission began in Kyrgyzstan (2003) when I was a new mission worker with my husband (a physician) and our three young children. These were some of the most difficult years for us as a family. Yet they gave me firsthand experience of some of the challenges those who serve in mission face. In 2009, we transitioned our family to Chiang Mai, Thailand, where I joined Cornerstone Counseling Foundation's staff as a therapist and eventually as executive director. My years of ministering to many mission workers, couples, and families further deepened my compassion for them and for the intensity and impact of their struggles. I also gained respect for their courage and resilience as they took active steps to address the issues and pain that surfaced in the stress of cross-cultural ministry. These experiences greatly inform my current role as the executive minister for Serve Globally, the global mission arm of the Evangelical Covenant Church.

Whether from the Global North or South, we as Jesus's followers are invited to participate in the whole mission of God, actively engaging in many ways to see God's kingdom come on earth. This includes a commitment to being whole persons as we minister and serve. Member care's emphasis on holistic wellbeing is vital for the longevity and thriving of those who have said yes to God's invitation.

Tim: My professional work as a specialized member care provider has been highly rewarding and meaningful. My area of expertise is in social work-based mental health care. I had the privilege of working as a therapist at Cornerstone Counseling Foundation in Chiang Mai, Thailand for nine years (2005–201). I treated traumatized, burned-out, and bewildered mission workers. I also consulted with regional leaders regarding spiritual, emotional, and relational care for their field personnel. Currently, I am president of the Narramore Christian Foundation in California. My wife, Cindy, and I lead the annual Counseling and Member Care Seminar near Athens, Greece. The target audience for this seminar consists of people who have organizational responsibility to provide member care to their field personnel. The seminar builds awareness and skills needed in caring for oneself and for organization members.

My experiences with these precious ministers of the gospel taught me that member care is critically important in the efforts to bring the good news of Jesus Christ to hard places in the world. It also taught me the essential need for supporting good practice—the theme of Part Four—through training and mentoring member caregivers.

Overview and Perspectives

The five chapters in this part focus on providing and developing member care via mission organization staff, the local church, field-based mutual care, coaching, health care, and pastoral care. Linking the chapters together are many examples of good practice to support mission workers, their families, and leaders as they face the many challenges of ministry.

Chapter 16 by Doug Lucas, Jacquie Kubr, Mary Kranick, Jonathan Trotter, and Renee Witkowski, share Team Expansion's development of its member care strategy to address the growing needs of their workers. Through their experience, the writers reflect on what they discovered to be good practices for the challenging contexts in which their members serve. The section on trauma-informed care highlights that coming alongside and believing in others are powerful ways to offer support. Through these actions and attitudes by caregivers, workers can experience God as the Good Shepherd, knowing that they do not struggle alone. In addition, "spiritual bypassing," a negative coping mechanism by which people in religious settings and systems unconsciously avoid dealing with personal struggles, is discussed. The readers are challenged to consider how this form of avoidance may be an obstacle to healthy spiritual growth, relationships, and ministry. Through this chapter, we learn of one organization's willingness to observe, respond, and adapt to workers' needs over the course of time. May it stimulate ideas for sending groups in different stages of member care development and encourage patience and trust that God will unfold the way forward in their member care.

Chapter 17 by Jeremy and Anastasia Thomas, focuses on the variety of member care resources that should be organized and offered by those who send workers, those who lead workers, and those who meet face-to-face with field workers, particularly in an African context. The Thomases show that member care needs vary greatly from pre-field to post-field and retirement. Cultural norms and expectations highly impact how workers' needs are understood and are or are not met. Where mission leaders graciously use their power and authority to encourage their field workers both to reach out for assistance and to accept offers of help, workers feel cared for, valued, and loved. This is the body of Christ in action!

Chapter 18 by Mulugetta Demissie Dagne, Rich Hansen, and Keith Webb, focuses on the skills that coaches can bring and teach as part of good practice in member care. A special emphasis is on how coaching can improve the interactions between mission workers and leaders in their sending organizations. The authors draw on research and personal experiences with cross-cultural mission workers from the Global South—primarily in Africa and secondarily in Asia and Latin America—and share stories and principles regarding good practices in caring for mission workers through coaching. A core part of their coaching practice involves "non-directive interaction with empathic, active listening, as part of a Holy Spirit-driven process of reflection, discussion, and discernment." This chapter effectively demonstrates how good coaching is relevant for missions.

Chapter 19 by Ted Lankester and Brian Wainaina, addresses an aspect of care that is often neglected, namely physical health. Lankester shares honestly about how his own lack of attention to physical health, even as a medical doctor, negatively impacted him and his family. This experience helped stimulate his passion for the physical health of mission workers and for encouraging them to prioritize their physical health. Through evidence-based research, we learn of lifestyle diseases that can have significant impact, from mild to severe, and can even put an end to a mission career. The chapter includes practical advice and specific recommendations for individuals, teams, and organizations to consider—and hopefully follow! The authors also address some special health issues and questions pertinent to mission workers, given the unique challenges of travel and possible lack of local medical resources. Sometimes we can all fall prey to elevating spiritual and emotional health above physical care, routine medical visits, and basics such as diet, exercise, and sleep. The authors exhort us to obey the greatest commandment to love God with our whole selves, which includes our body!

Chapter 20 by Edward Bruce, Kendall Johns, Chloe Raphael, and Denise Lee, discusses the two primary practices in Frontiers' model for member care. The first is the training and utilizing of pastoral coaches for their workers. The second is the incorporation of these coaches in a member care team composed of other specialists who together provide care for those serving cross-culturally. The authors use personal testimonials to give a framework for how a pastoral coaching team strategically addresses a variety of issues among workers. Coaching has proved effective through periodic visits and calls or on home assignments to meet with workers for issues such as burnout, trauma, crisis management, debriefings, and development of healthy rhythms of rest and sabbath. One author specializes in working with women and singles, who make up a large percentage of mission workers yet can often be undervalued. From the first months to home assignments to reentry, coaches can be vital to the health of workers, walking beside them at every stage. Sending organizations wanting to improve their quality of member care can certainly learn from this team model of pastoral care.

Final Thoughts

The authors in Part Four remind us that field workers' main need is to be lovingly understood and to know that their experiences are valid and important. When coaches, counselors, and member care teams exhibit humility, empathy, and presence, these traits help to foster genuine relationships with leaders as well as field workers. One of the many applications is that spiritual bypassing by member care workers themselves can impair good practice. Viewing most workers' needs as spiritual and needing spiritual remedies can have the effect of misunderstanding and minimizing needs, and sometimes even shaming workers. Truth with grace sets people free. Member care workers must consider spiritual, relational, intrapsychic, and physical aspects of any concern and should provide or advocate for resources appropriate to meet those holistic needs.

We close with a quotation to encourage the core *relational* component of good member care practice: "Suffering is inevitable. Suffering alone is intolerable." Those individuals and organizations entrusted to care for these precious cross-cultural workers participate in the sacred work of God's Immanuel presence of "being with." Thanks to the authors who contributed these chapters to expand our understanding of how to do better incarnate Immanuel's presence.

Grace Shim is the executive minister of Serve Globally in the Evangelical Covenant Church. She is a licensed clinical professional counselor, ordained pastor, and former executive director of Cornerstone Counseling in Chiang Mai, Thailand. Grace and her family served in mission for nineteen years in Kyrgyzstan and Thailand in mental health and medical care. She and her husband Bob, a physician, have three adult children and enjoy exploring new cultures, relaxing in coffee shops, and spending time with their families.

Tim Hibma, MSW, is the president of Narramore Christian Foundation in California. His forty-six years of work as a clinician have included nine years as a therapist and executive director for Cornerstone Counseling Foundation in Chiang Mai, Thailand. Prior to that, he worked in a psychiatric inpatient unit and outpatient counseling centers. Tim and his wife, Cindy, have four adult children and sixteen grandchildren. He enjoys choral singing, bird watching, hiking, and engaging with his grandchildren.

16

Tough People for Tough Places

Member Care Reflections from Team Expansion

Doug Lucas, Jacquie Kubr, Mary Kranick, Jonathan Trotter, and Renee Witkowski

In this chapter, we describe the development and practice of member care in our organization, Team Expansion. We now have ten member care specialists on staff (four full-time and six part-time) who work closely with our leadership structure. The stakes can be very high for our workers and those whom they serve, so we want to do all we can to back them up with good member care.

We have organized this reflective chapter into five sections—one per author. We cover the development of member care during the forty-five-year journey of a mission CEO, managing chronic stress and trauma in the field, drawing near to the Good Shepherd, understanding how "spiritual bypassing" can hinder personal growth, and identifying what is working well in our member care approach.

Searching for Helpful Member Care Systems

Doug Lucas, President

The idea for Team Expansion began one night in a dorm room prayer meeting in 1978. Eight of us were kneeling around a world map on the floor, praying and pleading that "someone should do something about these unreached peoples." Suddenly, it seemed unfair to ask for "someone" to do something that we wouldn't first strike out to do ourselves. Several of us signed our names beside a particular country, as a commitment to see the unreached people groups (UPGs) in that nation reached. Little did I know that, some forty-six years later, I'd be serving as the president of the organization whose ministry was born that night.

We started as just a handful of families, with minimal understanding of how to care for our mission workers. But from the start, I could sense that member care would be a critical need. We did the best we could.

On an as-needed basis, we sought outside help from trainers at resource agencies such as Missionary Internship (later renamed Mission Training International or MTI).

By God's grace, we grew—little by little at first, and then more quickly, in waves. Almost suddenly, there were 100 full-time mission workers and I was still largely working solo in the "home office," such as it was. I knew we needed help. We began asking other agencies what they did, attended personnel conferences (e.g., "Pastor to Missionaries"), and read everything we could.

We continued to send everyone to pre-field orientation and language acquisition training at MTI. We also added new training elements before, during, and after mission service. We introduced a one-week training called Launch that would help workers understand our organizational culture, including our core values of grace, accountability, and coaching. We worked hard to ensure that everyone served as a part of a caring and close-knit team, modeling our approach closely after Jesus, who sent workers out two by two. We articulated a set of "great passions" that included effective communication, creative strategic perseverance until the results are achieved, and growth in every way." These passions fueled most of our workers, but there were still some who, in spite of our best efforts, needed more than passion-based stamina—they needed care. Some of the care they needed was beyond our scope.

I remember receiving a phone call early on from one of our team leaders. He explained that his wife and he were sitting on the floor of their hallway. He had caught his wife on the way to the bathroom, razor blade in hand. The stress was so heavy that she had lost all hope. She said she was headed to slit her wrist. I listened carefully, trying not to judge. But their words were difficult to hear. "She's saying you never told us it would be this hard." I bit my lip, trying not to become defensive. But I did venture so far as to remind the speaker, ever so gently, of the opening session of our Launch training, in which I tell our new workers, "This will be the hardest thing you've ever attempted. In fact, it's so hard, it's a wonder anyone should ever even have attempted it." They were quiet and then I heard the woman's voice through the phone: "Yes, but you didn't say it loudly enough." We sent them a counselor and thankfully, in this case, the couple stayed in the fight. Some 15 years later, they were two of our best leaders. They had embraced the words "creative, strategic perseverance." Unfortunately, not every story ended so favorably.

Shortly after *Doing Member Care Well* (O'Donnell 2002) was published, one of our workers became a member care champion for our organization. By this time, we had reached around 200 full-time workers. We knew that we had to take action. We empowered this worker to speak, placed her on our leadership team, connected her well with our board of directors, and sent her regularly to all our fields. For a while, it seemed as if momentum was with us. But as we grew, I feared she might have become overwhelmed. She finally had to take a step back. I went off for a personal prayer retreat, coming back with the proposal that we "infuse member care." Instead of relying on member care specialists, we would train *everybody* to do member care with one another. Looking back, I think that was a grand idea that worked—until it didn't.

When we became an organization of 300 or so full-time workers, it seemed more and more difficult to keep up with all the unique situations popping up in multiple fields. By this time, we were working in about forty countries. Looking back, I can perceive one of our key leaders in outreach underappreciated the value of emotional, social, and mental health. He believed that if we set people up with a good job description, challenged them to strong faith, and made sure that they had effective ministry training, then fruitfulness should follow. As a result, the member care specialist mentioned above probably always felt a bit on the outside. Don't get me wrong—her opinion was always heard. But in retrospect, there wasn't much integration between our mission leadership and member care. Still, somehow, the member care system worked for a while. To this day, I have great respect for the outreach leader mentioned above. But when he resigned, we redesigned and radically reworked the system.

We intentionally began to grow member care significantly by adding four full-time and six part-time specialists. All were highly trained and passionate about the Great Commission *and* member care. There was no longer any polarity or unclarity. By God's grace, the new outreach leader took up my challenge to stage a retreat for all our field coordinators (15 to 20 mentors who coach our team leaders) and member care specialists, to get all of them on the same page. So much energy came out of his first retreat that we have made it an annual event ever since. Now, whenever there's a problem with a particular team or family, our field coordinators meet with our member care specialists to sort out possible root causes. They pray hard and propose scenarios. Together with the team or family, they come up with a way forward—a treatment plan of sorts. Working in harmony like this is so invigorating for them, and the outcomes so far have been stellar.

More recently, we're welcoming on staff more workers from other countries. In fact, today, more than one-fourth of our 380 workers grew up outside the United States. We are committed to developing our cross-cultural competencies as a mission and learning from these mission workers about ways to support them with member care. Mutual support within all our teams—including our growing number of multi-national teams—and building relationships with locals in the host cultures are keys for adjustment and growth.

Interpersonal conflicts still occur, though seemingly less frequently than before. We suspect that some of our workers are still resigning due to conflict, although in their exit interviews they cite other reasons, perhaps to protect the parties involved. But we aren't giving up. We've fashioned protocols modeled after Christ's instructions on handling fault-finding (Matt 18). It's still early and we need to keep working on this, but we're encouraged by the results so far. We've combined these efforts more recently with the resources provided by Peace Pursuit (peacepursuit.org).

In all the above stories, one thing has continued to stand out: praying together is imperative. It's hard to argue with people when we're praying with them. But when conflict (personal or interpersonal) arises despite our best efforts to prevent it, we now have clearer paths, more help, and more optimism than ever before.

Managing Stress and Trauma in the Field
Jacquie Kubr, Third-Culture Kids (TCK) Care Associate

When mission workers are willing to sacrifice everything, it's apparent that the reason why they have chosen to live abroad is of the utmost importance to them. The stakes and stress are high. The new challenges can be physically and emotionally exhausting. The slow results over years of commitment and loneliness add to the difficulties. It is understandable why they'd feel depleted or burned out. Add to this high investment level the ongoing stress of living in dangerous or developing nations, seeing people die without hope in Jesus, chronic and complicated grief, or other stressful and traumatic experiences. No wonder that mission workers can experience seasons of serious physical, psychological, relational, and managerial struggles (Fawcett 2003).

Over the past several months, I have heard accounts from people of multiple agencies and denominational backgrounds where one spouse burned out and slipped into unhealthy and sometimes abusive behaviors as a result. When the non-offending spouse reached out to their sending entity for help, the results were not what either spouse would want. Often, the couple is pulled from the field with little to no notice or choice. Children are not allowed to finish school years or sports seasons, or to say goodbye to friends. Few return to the field. Even if healing occurs, there is still hurt and a wish that things had been handled differently. This is why we've come to believe that member care practice must include trauma-informed care, which should, in turn, not only shape our approach and policy but permeate our organizations and cultures.

The impact of chronic stress and trauma varies, based on factors such as the type and severity of the event, cumulative exposure, individual characteristics, and any intergenerational patterns of trauma. Cumulative exposure and poly-victimization (i.e., multiple types of violence) often lead to more severe symptoms and impairment, amplifying existing physical and mental health struggles and straining relationships. Trauma-informed care, which considers the social, psychological, and biological consequences of trauma with cultural sensitivity and humility, has gained attention as an approach to delivering member care services. It focuses on trust-building, safety, transparency, empowerment, and collaboration to promote resilience, coping, and social connectedness.

Six core principles for a trauma-informed approach include safety, trustworthiness, peer support, collaboration, empowerment, and consideration of cultural, historical, and gender issues (Menschner and Maul 2016). Here are some examples of what's involved which have helped to shape our trauma-informed approach to caring for Team Expansion staff.

Safety is established when people *perceive* themselves to be safe, not just when they have physical safety. Ask workers what will help them feel safe and if they're able to make and act on a safety plan (with your input as needed). Developing a plan will also help them feel more in control. If they're not capable, ask their permission to make one with them and implement it with their approval. No plans should be made and implemented without their knowledge, involvement, and consent. Well-meaning decisions that overlook workers' choice are harmful. If someone needs to leave the field for a period, involve them in the exit plan. If there is conflict in marriages or teams, mediate but refrain from making unilateral decisions about their family or team.

Trustworthiness is of the utmost importance. Workers who know that their member care providers maintain confidentiality are more likely to open up when struggling. They will reach out for help when experiencing discord, suicidal ideation, abuse, or other serious threats. When these disclosures happen, confidentiality may need to be broken for legal and ethical reasons. Of course, we make it a point to seek permission from people first. This will maintain the safety of the relationship. Conversely, when people disclose hurt and then feel betrayed because information is shared without permission, more harm is caused and restoration of trust becomes more difficult.

Creating intentional opportunities for *peer support* and community is a gift to mission workers. The Lord created us for community. We cannot go without it. Regular conferences, opportunities for team retreats or training, and accountability groups with other workers are all great options for authentic sharing and mutual support. Community care can assist with a variety of issues, including marital struggles, team conflict, depression, grief, and parenting issues. Peer support, when delivered well, provides safe spaces to struggle, grow, and heal.

Collaboration and *empowerment* go hand in hand. Collaborating with workers to create and implement goals, care plans, and strategies is a high priority. Empowering others supports a greater sense of autonomy and competence along with providing momentum to achieve their goals. Empowering care involves understanding the importance of working together to identify what is needed to make people healthier and more effective. If high-level decisions must be made that affect the person or team, then the reasoning behind those decisions should be explained and as much control as possible within those directives should be delegated to those whom the decision is impacting.

Consideration of cultural, historical, and gender issues can offer increased insight and sensitivity to the contributing factors in trauma. Mission workers can learn more about themselves and their backgrounds in the process, including their vulnerabilities to stress and trauma.

Adopting a trauma-informed approach requires ongoing attention, sensitivity, and possibly organizational culture change. It cannot be achieved through a single technique or checklist. Internal organizational assessment and engagement with board members, leadership teams, and member care professionals help to monitor and improve the quality of stress and trauma-related care.

Drawing Near to the Good Shepherd

Mary Kranick, Member Care Associate

I am privileged to come alongside the staff of Team Expansion as they live and work in difficult, unreached fields. I have found that it is important to evaluate their existing support systems and especially their time with the Good Shepherd. After assessment and providing possible needed resources, I help them connect more deeply with the Good Shepherd by praying holistically with and for the workers, their families, their teams, and their work. I take the time to listen well and take all of it to the Good Shepherd to discern how he is working in and through them each day.

Believing in Others

Member care plays a critical role in conveying that we believe in our workers and in encouraging them each step of the way. I would like to share the story of a woman who felt called to the field later in life. Meg (not her real name) was single, with grown children and one grandchild. Because she had asthma and was overweight, she had to take several medications. Nonetheless, she still felt called to Asia. She had already gone there several times and served alongside her sending church's ministry there.

We had some concerns about the situation, beyond Meg's health limitations. For example, our agency didn't have any workers in that part of Asia. She wouldn't have a team with her. Learning the local language at any age is hard. Meg and I started meeting on a regular basis over several months. She steadily lost weight and, under medical supervision, was able to discontinue some of her medications. Along the way, we became great prayer warriors for the people of Asia. She was approved for the field. She worked through every obstacle, and I was able to encourage her every step of the way. We took everything to the Good Shepherd, and I saw her blossom! What a great gift it is to have somebody believe in you! I also see the fruit of her love for others. She has connected with so many people while learning the language. Her zeal for Jesus is contagious.

In Meg's own words:

> I knew God had called me to go, but there were health challenges to overcome, and starting the journey to the mission field at an older age comes with disadvantages. Sometimes you may know what you need to do, but having a member care worker to walk beside you as a cheerleader and to encourage you when the challenges come is a game changer.

Their belief that you can do it and their encouragement along the way help you stay engaged in the journey to the field. Unexpected challenges once I was in the field were navigated with my member care worker. Knowing she was just a message or call away meant the world to me, especially as I grieved the loss of both parents and a child's life partner.

Good member care can be the difference between flourishing where God plants you and giving up and heading home. I am encouraged every time Meg and I talk, and new courage rises within me too.

Understanding and Addressing Spiritual Bypassing

Jonathan Trotter, Member Care Associate

Mission workers go to hard places and do hard things. Often, they've chosen to sacrifice because of life-altering spiritual convictions and a deep desire to spread the news of God's wonderful kindness, love, and salvation. Those are beautiful and inspirational qualities, to be sure, and they can anchor someone during horrible hardships and struggles in the field.

But what happens if our sincere desire to cultivate authentic and robust spirituality is blindsided by our denial of personal problems and an unhealthy spiritual zeal that blocks spiritual growth? For instance, what happens when our use of the Scriptures ceases to be a balm to the brokenhearted and instead becomes a tool for self-deprecation and hurting others? These things—and more—can happen!

Here's how people become blindsided. Mission workers beat themselves up with guilt and denial, believing that "spiritual people don't get depressed," even though they are definitely depressed. Someone lectures an anxious spouse (or child or teammate) for struggling with anxiety, using Scripture to harshly admonish a hurting and vulnerable soul. A husband whose marriage is struggling continues to believe that the couple is just under a spiritual attack, and that if they could just pray or worship more, or if she would submit more, their relationship would be miraculously reconnected and healed. Perhaps a teammate or team leader, failing to see that their own unresolved childhood struggles are causing serious team conflict and misunderstanding, instead condemns everyone around them for disrespect, arrogance, and rebelling against authority. Or fellow workers may have little patience for and may thus invalidate normal and appropriate grief.

All these cases are examples of *spiritual bypassing*, which blocks emotional, psychological, and spiritual health and growth. John Welwood

(2000) defined spiritual bypassing as using "spiritual ideas and practices to sidestep personal, emotional 'unfinished business,' to shore up a shaky sense of self, or to belittle basic needs, feelings, and developmental tasks" (pages 11–12). He noted that spiritual bypassing can be used as a tool of avoidance and emotional repression within many religious and spiritual systems.

As a Christian coming alongside Christian mission workers, I believe that spiritual bypassing is especially insidious yet seems attractive to many of us. It has the deceptive appearance of holiness but blocks the road to Christlikeness.

"Leave God Out of It"
Those who provide member care to mission workers have an amazing opportunity to gently guide people who are using or succumbing to spiritual bypassing into a better way. In our role as pastors or counselors, we can invite people to deal with roots of problems or with difficult unfinished business in a safe place and in a safe way, with a safe person. But sometimes, such an invitation to engage with their issues can be a real shock.

When I am counseling a mission worker and sense a dynamic of spiritual bypassing, I often suggest that they leave God out of it. This often causes quizzical looks; occasionally it leads the listener to question me and their decision to meet with me. However, it can be enough of a jolt to start a new way of thinking.

"Of course," I tell my clients, "I love God and I think the Scriptures are vitally important." I reassure them that I am *not* advocating for some type of non-biblical approach. Rather, I am inviting them to consider how some of their spirituality might be blinding them to their actual reality. If enough trust has been developed and enough rapport has been built, this approach often produces wonderful fruit. Clients lay down their clunky shells of spirituality and begin to look at their very real, heart-level pain. Sometimes, shedding the shell helps clients to see the underlying cognitive distortions, fears, and hurts that are actively sabotaging their emotional and relational health.

Curiosity has been shown to reactivate the prefrontal cortex, bringing the rational and cognitive parts of the brain back online after a crisis or traumatic experience. Spiritual bypassing, however, shuts down curiosity and problem solving. Thus, one of my main goals in asking this provocative question is to spur curiosity. I might ask, "If, for a minute, we left God out of it, what do you think you yourself might do? What issues, questions, or concerns might bubble up?"

I have seen these questions bring freedom to tired workers—including the tiredness that comes from avoiding important issues in one's life. And I have seen these questions eventually bring tired workers closer to God. For more on my approach to spiritual bypassing, see my "Shapes Diagram" listed in the references.

None of us—whether we are mission colleagues, leaders, or member care providers—want to heap spiritual burdens on mission workers or reinforce ones they already have. Nor do we want to join the loud chorus that already exists in many people's souls, telling them that their problems would go away if they would just be better, do better, or know better. Rather, we can be empathic people who help to open the door to a more pleasant road, one that leads toward healing and mercy. As counselors, we can risk some curiosity with our clients, knowing that our God is a gracious healer of his beloved people.

I encourage us to be willing to risk an odd question for the cause of healing. Let's be on the lookout for spiritual bypassing tendencies in ourselves, our clients, and our colleagues. Let's explore, with gentleness and compassion, helpful ways to guide people out of spiritual bypassing and into a healthier spirituality and healthier ways of relating to themselves and others.

Identifying What Is Working Well
Renee Witkowski, Member Care Coordinator

In the past few years, we have increased the number of member care providers in our organization to ten. Everyone, from the receptionist in the home office to the mission family more than 8,000 miles away, has a member care associate assigned to them. We also have specialized care for the children in our organization. Every infant, child, teen, or young adult has an assigned TCK specialist. This relatively large team of member care providers knows every individual in the organization by name. The team considers the most convenient ways to contact and stay connected to people in the organization and to other members of the member care team. These strong relationships between member care providers and mission workers and families have changed our organization's view of the member care department. From being primarily a place to call when workers are struggling with serious issues, it has now become a place with loving professionals available to support our staff's holistic health including healthy relationships and mutual support among team members.

Examples with Staff

One of our families lives in an isolated area with limited local support. The family's teenage girls and elementary-age son get up early once a month to join our organization's TCK calls for their age group. Here, they meet with our mission children from all over the world, to get to know each other and share things like the names of their pets, their favorite subject in school, or some of the anxieties they experience while living in different cultures. The mother meets monthly with her member care associate for prayer, encouragement, and support. Recently, one of the mother's parents was diagnosed with a terminal disease. The supportive and practical discussions that ensued covered how she can grieve over this diagnosis, how to support her extended family from a distance, and when she should return home to visit her parent.

One married young couple has taken advantage of our marriage enrichment services and personal and marriage counseling with our volunteer therapists. The mother stays home with her newborn and toddler and enjoys connecting monthly with our online support group for moms. This couple has said multiple times that they have grown in their emotional awareness, communication, and love for each other. They are grateful for the opportunities for personal growth offered to them and do not believe they would be in the field without our services.

Many single workers also enjoy connecting with their member care associate to process ministry challenges such as conflict with teammates, a spiritually dry season, or stress. We've heard more than once the gratitude they feel because someone knows them, cares for them, is praying for them, and is available whenever they run into a difficulty or want to celebrate a breakthrough or answer to prayer.

Our development of member care staff and our shift from crisis care to more proactive member care have had a huge impact on our organization. From the office worker who encounters health challenges, to the mission teen who struggles with anxiety and depression, to the single who wants to share the joys of starting a fitness class with her colleagues, everyone knows someone is there for them who will reach out to them monthly and who is just an email, text, or call away if they need extra support.

Conclusion

Team Expansion's involvement in member care has certainly been a journey! Starting as a small group with minimal understanding of how to care for mission workers, we sought external help and gradually developed a comprehensive member care system. More recently, we are utilizing trauma-informed approaches and emphasizing safety, trustworthiness, mutual support, collaboration, empowerment, and cultural sensitivity. Through it all, we are committed to maintaining good relationships with one another, prayer in all things, and diligently supporting our staff's relationship with the Good Shepherd.

One thing we will not do on this journey is to view ourselves as having "arrived." We are excited about moving from reactive and crisis care to more proactive and relational care. We will continue to evaluate and get feedback from staff about our member care program and approaches. We will keep nurturing close relationships between care providers and mission workers, including children. And with God's help and with healthy workers, we will increase our positive impact on the world with the good news of Jesus Christ.

Applications: Tough People for Tough Places

Core Strategies

1. Maintain the organization in "learner" mode at all times as you face new challenges, try new strategies, and monitor and reflect on your organization's ministry.

2. Focus deeply on relationships in all you do, organizationally and in ministry. Pray together regularly as you weather the ups and downs of mission life.

3. Develop cohesion among the team of member care practitioners and in their relationship with the leaders in the organization.

Core Resources

1. Doug Lucas. 2019. *More Disciples: A Guide to Becoming and Multiplying Followers of Jesus*; Doug Lucas and Tina McCormick, *Brigada: Missions Resources, Information, and Trends* (weekly news).

2. Jonathan Trotter. 2023. *Digging in the Dirt: Musings on Missions, Emotions, and Life in the Mud*; Jonathan Trotter and Elizabeth Trotter. 2019. *Serving Well: Help for the Wannabe, Newbie, or Weary Cross-Cultural Christian Worker*; Elizabeth Trotter, *A Life Overseas* (blog).

3. Member Care Associates. 2021. "Tough People and Teams for Tough Places and Times: Featuring the Work of Team Expansion."

Reflection and Discussion

1. Take some time to review the main highlights of your own organization's journey in member care.
2. What seems to be working well and what isn't working well in your different contexts? Are there approaches that worked well in some contexts but not others, or in the past but no longer?
3. What lessons have you been learning in your own ministry of member care?

References

Fawcett, John. 2003. *Stress and Trauma Handbook: Strategies for Flourishing.* Monrovia, CA: World Vision.

Lucas, Doug. 2019. *More Disciples: A Guide to Becoming and Multiplying Followers of Jesus.* Monument, CO: WIGTake Resources.

Lucas, Doug, and Tina McCormick. *Brigada: Missions Resources, Information, and Trends.* www.brigada.org.

Member Care Associates. 2021. "Tough People and Teams for Tough Places and Times: Featuring the Work of Team Expansion." Member Care Update, August 2021. https://mailchi.mp/59cc2dc209e4/resiliency-for-team-leaders-special-news-may-2018-member-care-updates-10361892.

Menschner, Christopher, and Alexandra Maul. 2016. "Key Ingredients for Successful Trauma-Informed Care Implementation." Center for Health Care Strategy. https://www.samhsa.gov/sites/default/files/programs_campaigns/childrens_mental_health/atc-whitepaper-040616.pdf.

Mission Training International. https://www.mti.org/.

O'Donnell, Kelly, ed. 2002. *Doing Member Care Well: Perspectives and Practices from Around the World.* Pasadena, CA: William Carey Library. https://passionexchange.files.wordpress.com/2008/10/doingmembercarewell.pdf.

Peace Pursuit. https://peacepursuit.org/.

Trotter, Elizabeth. *A Life Overseas* (blog). https://www.alifeoverseas.com/.

Trotter, Jonathan. 2023. *Digging in the Dirt: Musings on Missions, Emotions, and Life in the Mud.* Independently published.

Trotter, Jonathan. "The Shapes Diagram." https://trotters41.com/tag/shapes-diagram/.

Trotter, Jonathan, and Elizabeth Trotter. 2019. *Serving Well: Help for the Wannabe, Newbie, or Weary.* Resource Publications.

Welwood, John. 2000. *Toward a Psychology of Awakening: Buddhism, Psychotherapy, and the Path of Personal and Spiritual Transformation.* Boston: Shambhala Publications.

Doug Lucas has served as Team Expansion's president since its founding in 1978. His passion is multiplying disciples and groups (simple churches) among the unreached. He longs to learn more every day about caring for Team Expansion's more than 300 workers worldwide.

Mary Kranick is a member care specialist for Team Expansion workers. She provides pastoral care with a strength in drawing workers to the Good Shepherd. Her calling to care for mission workers has grown out of her own mission service dating back to the early 1990s. She works internationally from the United States.

Jacquie Kubr serves on Team Expansion's Third Culture Kids care team. She is a clinical mental health counselor specializing in trauma studies. Jacquie is dedicated to empowering families of third-culture kids, fostering resilience and growth, and creating a supportive space for healing and thriving.

Jonathan Trotter provides pastoral care and coaching through Team Expansion. He and his wife are the authors of *Serving Well: Help for the Wannabe, Newbie, or Weary Cross-Cultural Christian Worker*. From 2012 to 2020, they served as mission workers in Cambodia.

Renee Witkowski directs the member care team at Team Expansion and provides care to several teams and field workers. She and her husband served in East Asia from 2003 to 2009, and both now serve at Team Expansion's home office in Louisville, Kentucky.

17

Member Caring and Linking Ministries

The Strategic Role of the Local Church

Jeremy Thomas and Anastasia Thomas

In this chapter, we share how we have engaged in member care for mission workers in Africa and helped to link ministries together. From our home base in Mauritius, we have visited mission workers and pastors in various countries of Africa and beyond, hearing about their mental, emotional, and relational struggles. Some of these struggles have been augmented by cultures that tend to view asking for help as a sign of weakness or failure. They shared how glad they were to have an opportunity to talk about their lives with people like us, and that they often do not know to whom they can turn since there is no member care structure in their community. As a result of these experiences, we developed a model of member caring and wrote an e-manual called the *Inreach Manual for Member Caring, Encouraging, and Linking* (Thomas 2021) along with a first-year implementation program for community settings. During the COVID-19 pandemic, we facilitated several online trainings on this material to support churches and senders who recognize the need to develop member care for their mission workers, ministers, staff, and their families. Throughout this chapter, we discuss member care for mission workers within the broad context of holistic wellbeing for all members of the global church, with an emphasis on the local church.

The Church and a Culture of Care: Caring for One Another

All Christians are broken sinners who need a Savior, Jesus, to rescue and restore us. We all know Psalm 23, which explains how God takes care of our needs, makes us rest in green pastures, refreshes our soul, walks with us, and comforts us. But we often forget that God does much of this through his hands and feet on earth—that is, his disciples and servants. We yearn for the global body of Christ, blessed with so many human and material resources, to experience in a tangible way what the early church was experiencing in Acts 4:32–34:

All the believers were one in heart and mind. No one claimed that any of their possessions was their own, but they shared everything they had. With great power the apostles continued to testify to the resurrection of the Lord Jesus. And God's grace was so powerfully at work in them all that there were no needy persons among them.

Several years ago, our hearts were moved when we discovered that a lack of caring and strong links (i.e., communication and support networks) among members of the body of Christ are some of the main reasons why people leave the church, ministers leave the ministry, and mission workers leave the field. Many people who previously devoted their lives actively to God's Kingdom have stopped due to lack of caring support for them as workers. In fact, it is estimated that 3 percent of all mission workers will leave the field prematurely each year for reasons that are preventable (O'Donnell 2002, 6–7).

Since our human desires are often selfish, we need God's grace and help in caring for one another and ensuring that our fellow Christians, including ministers and mission workers, have their needs met. Having our needs met does not mean being financially well off, living in luxury, or having the latest model of everything. In the book of Acts, the early Christians did everything possible to ensure that no one in the church had unmet spiritual, physical, or emotional voids. God provides for our needs through the body of Christ, and not only through leaders and elders, but through all of us serving one another!

Paul received member care from his coworkers on different occasions (Ellis 1995). He stayed with Peter for two weeks in Jerusalem (Gal 1:18). Barnabas provided member care to Paul in the form of encouragement and support when the disciples did not trust him at first (Acts 9:27). During their mission trip, Barnabas did not preach much but mainly encouraged his coworker Paul (Acts 14:12). Epaphroditus risked his life to bring Paul what he needed (Phil 2:25–30). Stephanas and two members of his household visited Paul in Ephesus and refreshed his spirit (1 Cor 16:17–18). Tychicus and Onesimus kept Paul informed about the situation in the churches while he was not there (Eph 6:21–22; Col 4:7–9), making a communication link between Paul and the churches to encourage them. These coworkers of Paul were so important to him that he described them as faithful servants who should be valued (Eph 6:21; Col 4:7–9).

Care for Mission Workers

Having the caring support of a mission agency and the pastoral support of a local church is very important for a mission worker. And having a person or team appointed by a local sending church to provide care, encouragement, and links with a mission worker really makes a big difference in providing holistic care (Pirolo 2012). Some member care is best provided by a local church or by a person or a team not in church leadership. This helps a church ensure that their precious members involved in ministry have what they need, especially when serving overseas. Through our encounters with mission workers from several countries, we have seen the difference between mission workers whose local churches were just sending money and those who had a member care team from their local church doing regular check-ins and trying their best to help their mission workers feel well supported (Thomas, Thomas, and Tindall 2022).

As part of the Global Member Care Network, we facilitate a bimonthly member care newsletter focusing on Africa (Africa Member Care Network). We compile and advise readers of available resources in our region and beyond for those who are caring for mission workers and others involved in ministry. We receive and disseminate information from many member care providers in Africa who work to ensure that all types of mission workers can have proper rest, counseling, inner healing and reconciliation, debriefing, and other tools to equip them in the field.

We are also glad to see the growing amount of interest and training in the field of member care around the world. Many member care providers are not psychologists or doctors but have a sincere desire and commitment to care for and support, in a competent and skillful way, those involved in ministry within God's Kingdom worldwide.

Inreach Resource Servants

We commonly refer to those who are in member caring and linking ministry as *inreach resource servants*. These combined functions in different contexts can also be known as servant, caregiver, facilitator, administrator, coordinator, people helper, assistant, mediator, communication officer, ambassador, or champion. We define an inreach resource servant as *someone actively caring for, encouraging, and listening to the members while making links between the available resources and the individuals' needs.*

Usually, the term *member care* is associated with care provided to cross-cultural mission workers. We prefer using the term *inreach* to be more inclusive of the broader member care provided to all types of mission workers, ministers, and clergy.

The African Context

We regularly visit countries in Africa, helping Christian communities develop their member caring and linking ministries according to their context and culture. We have opportunities to share how useful it can be to have an inreach (member care) team, which does not need to be composed only of church elders and leaders. We've heard from several pastors that they have not really experienced member care themselves. Too often, church leaders are familiar only with the concept of a pastor caring for mission workers and other ministers in a community and have not considered that other servants (like Tychicus, Onesimus, or Stephanas) can play a vital role in caring for mission workers (like Paul). This is why we don't hear many teachings on member care per se, which is different from pastoral care.

Out of conversations and requests in Africa to set up an inreach ministry within local communities, we wrote an e-manual called *Inreach Manual for Member Caring, Encouraging and Linking* (Thomas 2021) and constructed a first-year implementation program to accompany the manual. Both resources are available online for free (Daybreak Academy). We have also facilitated several online and in-person trainings and workshops on this material as churches around the world become more aware of the need to develop member care for their mission workers, ministers, and clergy.

For example, in 2023, we were invited by the Ethiopian Council of Gospel Believers' Churches, which represents more than 40 million Christians from different denominations, to facilitate a workshop. We witnessed them making a stand as one body in Christ to intentionally develop their contextualized inreach support for more mission workers locally, nationally, and internationally. They shared with us that our workshop and resources helped them ensure that their active members have what they need to fulfill their God-given mission. Most cross-cultural mission workers started serving within their local churches. Accordingly, local churches should ensure that their members feel well listened to, valued, and invested in (cared for) when they start serving locally before they go to the ends of the earth.

In the African context, when leaders ask for help, it may be perceived as a sign of weakness. Often, mission workers or people in full-time ministry are placed on a pedestal, as supposedly more spiritual, more resilient, and stronger believers. They often feel lonely and do not know to whom to turn when they encounter challenges. Looking for a member care provider in such a context might be a courageous act of humility and vulnerability, and those to whom they turn need to understand the central biblical calling to support one another.

An evangelist from Liberia whom we met recently expressed gratitude for having an inreach resource servant assisting him in his outreach trips. But because his companion wasn't the one preaching and "bringing people to Christ," the evangelist also realized how little this precious coworker—his Barnabas—was valued by his community. Nevertheless, the coworker was extremely valuable in constantly offering encouragement in ministry, such as by helping the evangelist push a car through miles of mud on one occasion to reach their destination! Christian leaders appreciate knowing that they have people who are willing to support them through tough times without passing judgment.

Through our experience as inreach resource servants in our local churches, we have seen how local pastors and ministers, some of whom are mission workers, have felt blessed that they can turn to us when they face a challenge or need. They know that we are here to serve and care for them so that they can be more effective in their ministries.

A cross-cultural mission family lost a child some years ago. Their senders provided member care through a trauma debriefing, furlough for proper rest, and ample recovery time. Though the loss was tremendous, so was the senders' outpouring of care. Now, they are back in ministry, blessing those among whom they serve (Thomas and Thomas 2023).

A mission team serving in a remote Ugandan village learned that war had broken out in their home country. Concern for their families and limited internet access made it difficult to focus on ministry. Their mission agency sent a member care person to debrief and counsel them. This helped some of the mission workers to decide to return to their families who were enduring the war. Others chose to stay, knowing they had access to a counselor for help to process their personal trauma as they continued to serve in Uganda (Thomas and Thomas 2023).

Another example was a mission couple from Zimbabwe who had to come and serve for two to three months in our country, Mauritius, for a church plant. Based on their culture, for the wellbeing of their children, they discerned that it was better for the children to stay in Zimbabwe with another family who were trustworthy members of their local church. There were also inreach resource servants from their community who were ensuring that the kids were going to school and that their needs were met (such as food, outings, materials, internet connection to speak with their parents every day, etc.). These mission workers were able to do short-term ministry in Mauritius because their local church back home had a good inreach team caring for the needs of their children.

If a church community doesn't have an established member caring and linking ministry or an inreach team looking after its mission workers, ministers, and clergy, then you should look around and get to know the people God has already placed in this community. There might be a *resource person* to whom people feel comfortable coming with questions and challenges, and who can link them with needed resources inside or outside a community. Or a *welcoming and caring person* who is always ready to listen, encourage, and pray. Or a person with strong *administrative* skills who often volunteers for logistical aspects of the work. If you can identify at least two such people, then you may already have the beginnings of your inreach team!

Every Christian community or organization has its own particular history, context, and structure. This is why it is necessary to understand the difference between a pastor or community leader, a counselor or therapist, and an inreach resource servant. Here are some potential responsibilities for each role:

Pastors and Community Leaders

- Preaching and teaching
- Praying for others
- Providing guidance and direction for the development of members in the community
- Holding services, Bible studies, and community devotional programs
- Overseeing administrative functions and ministries within the community
- Providing pastoral counseling and listening
- Extending care and debriefing in crisis situations
- Mentoring people in ministry, marriage, and parenting

Therapists and Counselors (who may be from outside a community if no one is certified locally)

- Offering therapeutic intervention in emotional and psychological crises
- Providing professional counseling services for members on personal and family issues
- Providing conflict mediation, trauma care, and debriefing for members
- Consulting with leadership regarding members' issues and policymaking
- Offering training in interpersonal skills, debriefing, or stress management
- Developing and maintaining a referral network

Inreach Resource Servants

- Identifying member care needs within the community, coordinating and mobilizing resources to meet these needs, and working to establish a supportive community
- Networking with local, national, and international member care colleagues and other communities' inreach resource servants
- Offering training in member caring and linking ministry and in self-care skills
- Recommending programs or plans of action to respond to members' needs
- Attending to the specific concerns of families, singles, new members, transitioning members, and aging members; facilitating dialogue and conflict resolution
- Orienting new members regarding member care and personal development
- Consulting with leadership and members on needs, policies, and resources; helping leadership coordinate activities and programs within the community; and liaising between members and leadership.

The function of member caring and linking ministry within a community is to care for, encourage, and link the members. But individual inreach resource servants are not expected to do everything. Following are four typical types of inreach resource servants (inspired by Gardner 2018). They and their most suitable assignments can be identified through prayer, conversations with leadership, and practical involvement in caring for mission workers, ministers, and clergy. We encourage you to consider which types, or combined types, of servants you may already have within your community, which ones you need, and which set of roles you may gravitate toward.

Champion
- Influencer: promotes or recommends member caring and linking ministry through interaction with people or on social media
- Advocate: publicly supports or recommends member caring and linking ministry
- Writes articles to explain the importance of caring for and linking members
- Prepares Bible studies on the importance of supporting one another
- Speaks to leaders and elders on behalf of members or to deal with specific issues

Coordinator
- Contact person for member caring and linking requests from members, or for questions
- Coordinates links between needs and resources
- Networker: looks for resources and specialists

Facilitator
- Actively makes plans and programs about member caring and linking ministry
- Prepares necessary structures to support people from the start to the end of their community involvement
- Uses teaching and coaching skills to equip members accordingly
- Networker: looks for external resources according to the needs of the community

Provider
- Gives member caring and linking support for community members, either individually or in small groups
- Follows up to support the members' holistic wellbeing

God has given the global church so many resources to help us care for one another and to reach out into the whole world. We have seen churches grow because they were humble enough to realize that they needed help and tools from other churches, to become stronger not only in evangelism (outreach),

Member Caring and Linking Ministries

but also in caring for one another (inreach). We are disciples of Jesus and citizens of heaven (Phil 3:20) even before our national, organizational, or denominational allegiance, and the body of Christ is a holy nation (1 Pet 2:9). This mindset and culture can be imparted to others as we intentionally do our best, as inreach resource servants, to live out our values and actively care for, encourage, and link those who belong to the family of believers (Gal 6:10), Jesus's disciples.

Member Support Circle

Diagram used with permission of Jeremy Thomas.

Member Support Circle: A Model to Assess and Guide Care

We encourage every Christian community to appoint at least one inreach resource servant to develop a member caring and linking (inreach) team. We also recommend having the pastor or at least one of the church leaders/elders be involved in or oversee this ministry. The team members can meet with community members, especially those involved in missions locally and abroad, to assess their needs and areas of required support. You can use the Member Care Circle (inspired by Prins and Willemse 2009) with your members to assess what you already have and what can be developed.

Every member needs to recognize that they need support from other people in the different areas of life and ministry that make up the circle. The Member Support Circle is relevant for mission workers and their families, especially those serving in demanding and risky places. Thus, they should identify specific people to whom they can generally turn when they have questions or issues. They do not need a different person or group of people for each area, as one person or group can cater to several areas at the same time. All these people do not have to know each other; they can even be from different Christian communities, but they should all be people with whom mission workers have a personal relationship.

Leadership Support
Community leaders must be aware of, support, and value the mission workers whom the church appoints and sends on mission. If this is not the case, then those providing pastoral or caring and linking support can become the link between the mission workers and the leadership.

Pastoral Support
This person ensures that people and families develop and grow spiritually, receive the necessary fellowship with other believers, and have enough time and opportunities to study the word. Mission workers should feel comfortable turning to this person when they have spiritual questions or need guidance.

Caring and Linking Support
These people are inreach resource servants who do their best to ensure that people are well cared for, encouraged, and linked to the resources they need. This role can also include advocating for mission workers and their ministries and mobilizing and gathering volunteers, partners, and resources to help where needed.

Ministry Support
This person is a mentor or coach who can help people reach their ministry goals and objectives and get appropriate training for the ministry they are involved in.

Logistical Support
This person provides others with the necessary information and contacts they need. They must be trustworthy in fulfilling practical, everyday needs, both ministry-related (transport, Bibles, literature, projectors, materials, sound equipment, props, etc.) and family-related (medical contacts, legal contacts or other services, school materials, etc.).

Prayer Support
These people receive prayer requests from mission workers and pray for and with them, or they may communicate with other prayer warriors on their behalf (respecting confidentiality).

Communication Support
This person is readily reachable and helps by sharing mission workers' news with the right people, such as by distributing newsletters. He or she keeps mailing lists up to date and ensures that communication channels are kept open. This person can also ensure that communication is two-way and that important feedback is shared.

Financial Support
This person can help to plan budgets and manage financial matters (banking, insurance, loans, etc.) that mission workers might be struggling with, as well as organizing appropriate fundraising activities and possibly supporting them financially at times according to their ministry needs.

Work Support
These are people engaged in the same occupation as a mission worker who can provide assistance with the actual work they carry out. For example, an engineer working in a mission field may need very specific technical information on a project. A group of engineers in his or her home community could help find the needed information along with offering general support. A teacher might need information on a curriculum or recommendations of teaching materials.

Transition Support
Mission workers and mission families go through different types of transitions such as departure, reentry, cross-cultural experience, and

traumatic experiences. It is good to have someone ready to walk alongside them as they process and pass through these transitions. Someone who has gone through similar experiences and is skilled in empathic support is ideal.

Challenges and Strategies

Sometimes church leaders have difficulty in understanding the role and purpose of an inreach team as they have not received this type of care or training themselves. If you are facing such a situation, we encourage you to be patient and take these steps:

1. Spend time in prayer to seek God's guidance and wisdom.
2. Meet with your elders and pastor to clarify your objectives and your accountability toward them.
3. Present examples and share stories when member care and inreach support played a key part in positively impacting the well-being of mission workers and boosting their ministries.
4. When the ministry and partnership with the leadership is clear, seek support from other members of the community and build a team!

Another challenge of being involved in an inreach team can be the lack of interest and understanding from church members which might affect the quality of practical caring and linking support received by mission workers and ministers. There might be a false impression that such men and women of God "should be fine." If this is your situation, look for creative ways to communicate to your local church about the value of inreach teams, such as through posters, videos, sermons or simply speaking with those who have questions about this ministry and how it is beneficial to God's Kingdom.

One more challenge is that caregivers may become tired or even overwhelmed in caring for, encouraging, and linking others and may not receive sufficient care themselves. A complete care system must also meet the needs of an inreach team's own members, as well as networking with other inreach resource servants nationally and internationally. These relational networks can provide mutual support in this ministry, share up-to-date resources, and equip people to face ongoing and new challenges in caring for church members and mission workers.

Final Thoughts

We pray that Christian communities will develop inreach teams so that, as "ligaments" in the body of Christ, they can make the link between needs and resources. Such people can take pressure off pastors and elders, who can then focus more on time in the word and in prayer to nurture and lead their members. We envision seeing Christians—especially mission workers and their families—have their needs met by one another as in Acts 4, whatever challenges they may face.

Our vision is to see tangible love and unity within the global body of Christ, spurred by interdependent inreach ministries. Such ministries would have at least one inreach resource servant for every Christian community around the world, developed according to their own cultural contexts. We invite you to contact us at Daybreak Academy if you find this vision compelling. Let's care better for our mission workers and for one another locally, nationally, and internationally!

Applications: Member Caring and Linking Ministries

Core Strategies

1. Help to connect the caring support of a mission agency and the pastoral support of a local church for mission workers and their families. Having a person or team appointed by a local sending church to care, encourage, and link mission workers to resources makes a big difference in providing holistic care.

2. Be intentional in developing contextualized inreach ministries in local communities that can effectively send and support mission workers locally, nationally, and internationally. Caring and linking are essential so that mission workers can flourish in their ministries.

3. We encourage Christian communities to appoint at least one inreach resource servant who can help to develop an inreach team. The team can then work with others to meet community members (especially those involved in missions locally and abroad), assess their needs, and identify some resources to help. The Member Support Circle provides a model to assess what is already available and what can be developed.

Core Resources

1. Jeremy Thomas. 2021. *Inreach Manual for Member Caring, Encouraging, and Linking.*
2. Marina Prins and Braam Willemse. (2009). *Member Care for Missionaries: A Practical Guide for Senders.*
3. Laura Mae Gardner. 2018. *Healthy, Resilient, and Effective in Cross Cultural Ministry: A Comprehensive Member Care Plan.*

Reflection and Discussion

1. What are some of the main types of care that you receive and from whom? What other types of care would you like to receive, and how could you connect to them? Identify some of the types of care you provide to others.

2. How is the member caring and linking (inreach) ministry functioning within your local community? What can you and your community do to develop it further? Consider having at least one inreach resource servant actively developing it and discussing how to do this with others.

3. Review the Member Support Circle model to assess your own ministry and the types of support you need. Think about your local community too, considering what types of support are already available and what can be developed to support mission workers and other members involved in ministry.

References

Africa Member Care Network. Newsletter. https://memcare.us2.list-manage.com/subscribe?u=895d43ef69926eab7812e0395&id=72bb7e4778.

Daybreak Academy. https://daybreak-academy.org/.

Ellis, Jeffrey. 1995. "Stephanas: A New Testament Example of Frontier Member Care." *International Journal of Frontier Missions* 12 (4):1 71–175. https://www.ijfm.org/PDFs_IJFM/12_4_PDFs/02_Ellis.pdf.

Gardner, Laura Mae. 2018. *Healthy, Resilient, and Effective in Cross Cultural Ministry: A Comprehensive Member Care Plan.* Condeo Press.

O'Donnell, Kelly. 2002. "To the Ends of the Earth, To the Ends of the Age." In *Doing Member Care Well: Perspectives and Practices from Around the World*, edited by Kelly O'Donnell, 1–10. Pasadena, CA: William Carey Library. https://passionexchange.files.wordpress.com/2008/10/doingmembercarewell.pdf.

Pirolo, Neal. 2012. *Serving as Senders Today*. San Diego, CA: Emmaus Road International.

Prins, Marina, and Braam Willemse. 2009. *Member Care for Missionaries: A Practical Guide for Senders*. Member Care Southern Africa. https://www.memcare.co.za/index.php/resource.

Thomas, Jeremy. 2021. *Inreach Manual for Member Caring, Encouraging, and Linking*. Daybreak Academy. https://daybreak-academy.org/resources/.

Thomas, Jeremy, Anastasia Thomas, and Mary Tindall. 2022. "The Local Church Is the Foundation of Member Care." *Evangelical Missions Quarterly* 58 (2) (special issue on member care). https://missionexus.org/the-local-church-is-the-foundation-of-member-care-2/.

Thomas, Jeremy, and Anastasia Thomas. 2023. "Instruments of Care." *Afrigo* 8 (3): 5. https://afrigo.org/articles/instruments-of-care/.

Jeremy Thomas and Anastasia Thomas (originally from Mauritius and Ukraine, respectively) are certified in counseling and life coaching. Based in Mauritius, they are part of Daybreak Academy, a resource center encouraging love and unity within the global church. Jeremy and Anastasia provide member care to Christians in ministry and missions; offer training and tools to develop member caring and linking ministries (inreach) in Christian communities; lead inner healing and reconciliation workshops; and facilitate ministry collaboration between Christians, churches, and organizations. They are passionate about cultures, art, nature, and the global church. See: https://daybreak-academy.org/; Contact: daybreakacademy@live.com.

18

Caring for Mission Workers Through Coaching

Good Practices in the Global South

Mulugetta Demissie Dagne, Rich Hansen, and Keith Webb

For centuries, most nations in the Global South were mission-receiving cultures. Now they are increasingly mission-sending cultures (Love 2017, 17). This shift should be celebrated, but it comes with its own set of unique issues and needs, especially in effectively caring for Global South mission workers.

In this chapter, we explore how coaching can improve the interactions between mission workers and their sending organization's leadership. Challenges in these interactions—with implications for staff well-being and effectiveness—often emerge due to cultural norms and expectations of both the workers and leaders. We draw on research conducted on cross-cultural mission workers from the Global South and our personal experiences—primarily in Africa and secondarily in Asia and Latin America—and share stories and principles regarding good practices in caring for mission workers through coaching. Central to coaching well is the practice of non-directive interaction with empathic, active listening, as part of a Holy Spirit-driven process of reflection, discussion, and discernment. We encourage that coaching skills be further developed as a core part of member care programs and practices.

Challenges in Caring for Mission Workers

For the past twenty-five years, I (Mulugetta) have led church and parachurch organizations and participated on the boards of both church and multicultural mission organizations. For the past fifteen years, I have been involved in equipping both domestic and international mission workers. Through all these experiences, I have observed the challenges that Global South mission workers face before, during, and after their mission service.

One primary challenge is the communication gap between mission organization leaders and their workers. I did my doctoral research on this topic and spent many hours listening to numerous painful stories from both mission workers and leaders. Most of the challenges were related to lack of preparation and accompaniment and can be placed in three categories: spiritual, emotional, and lack of skill. They often arise because many leaders do not see the disruptive gaps between themselves and their workers. These gaps include lack of trust, disappointments, grudges, and anger (Dagne 2022, 183).

My research in Africa has revealed that the sense of urgency about sending African mission workers often has the darker underside of inadequate care for the very mission workers that organizations are so excited to send. I interviewed one mission worker who, with his wife and five-year-old boy, was sent to Central Africa for five years. He summed up the support he received from his sending agency with the words, "They don't listen to us. If they had only listened to us and prayed with us, I would have had a much easier time and borne better fruits." When he tried to explain some of the challenges his family and he were facing in a new culture, his mission leaders repeatedly responded that he was "complaining a lot." He added, "By those responses, my own leaders made me feel ignored, rejected, disregarded, and cornered. Sometimes, I felt I was invisible to people around me and forgotten by my own leaders. Then the pain became too much, and I lost hope."

Another mission worker sent to a Muslim country in West Africa reported being challenged by language and cultural barriers. He told me, "I know God called me to be a mission worker for him to that least-reached people group. But to be honest, I was not well prepared in terms of the knowledge, attitude, and skills I needed for my mission. Besides the linguistic and cultural challenges that I faced there, the most difficult thing for me was that I had no one to share my burdens. Most of the discussion topics with my mission leaders were reports of how many people were saved, baptized, or became followers of Jesus. All that was good, but it also made me feel no one wanted to hear about the difficulties I was facing. Any time I mentioned those challenges, they would either push them aside, preach to me, or offer irrelevant advice. That response drained my energy. I stopped telling them what they didn't want to hear and started telling them only what they wanted to hear. This, in fact, increased the damage to me. Finally, I decided not to return to that field after my vacation."

The wife in another mission couple who served in a Muslim country in the Middle East told a similar story. I asked her if she was willing to return to the mission field. She replied, "I don't even want to hear the word 'mission' anymore, let alone go there again." Unfortunately, such stories are far too common.

It is wonderful that churches have a genuine enthusiasm to share the gospel and eagerly send out mission workers. Unfortunately, they often pay little attention to preparing workers before they are deployed or following up with them after they are sent. This is a major obstacle to offering proper care to mission workers. The following responses from mission workers illustrate the results:

- "I wish I had known twenty years ago that all my reactions to leaving my home culture were normal! How much struggle and discouragement I could have avoided."
- "I thought something was wrong with me spiritually, that this was a demonic attack and that I was losing my faith. Now I see that I was undergoing culture shock."
- "Silence from the sending church and sending organization is painful. So is impatience. I have basic questions that I have a right to know the answers to but am told that I just have to endure. And then I am asked, 'After all, are you not a mission worker?'"
- "It's painful to be told how I have to feel and behave, when what I need is comfort and encouragement."
- "I really worry when I think of our future workers, knowing almost all of them will pass through the same crisis I and my family experienced. It is sad that most of these challenges are avoidable if we, mission workers and leaders, know how to communicate in a better way."

In fact, churches and mission-sending organizations in Ethiopia (where I live) are not totally negative in how they support their people. Many of them have been trained in theological seminaries and are good counselors. They also have honest commitment to the *missio Dei*. Unfortunately, their effectiveness is limited by cultural barriers, including traditional leadership styles, and lack of training in member care for people before, during, and after their mission service.

Why Mission Workers Are Often Disappointed by the Care They Receive

My (Mulugetta) extensive research interviewing cross-cultural mission workers has caused me to conclude that a traditional and hierarchical leadership style has prevented mission organization leaders from listening well to mission workers.

Listening from the heart, with empathy and without judgment, is one of the key principles of member care. Yet many African church and mission organization leaders—accustomed to hierarchical, traditional, and authoritative leadership mindsets and influenced by the general advice-giving culture of Africa—have a hard time listening. They assume they already have the answers when, in fact, many leaders have little (if any) firsthand experience of the many complex cross-cultural, social, spiritual, and logistical challenges their mission workers face.

During my interview sessions with church and mission organization leaders, I learned that most of these leaders had no mission field experience. Most of them are graduates of theological institutions where they learned to serve as local church pastors. The teaching methodology in their schools of theology is mostly the "banking approach." Students are "banks" where teachers "deposit" knowledge; students memorize and repeat what they are taught. "The teacher plays an active role while the student plays the passive role of absorbing the information" (Freire 1985). Leaders with such an education might be tempted to lecture mission workers rather than giving them opportunities to explore their challenges and possible solutions.

In addition to these limitations, mission leaders told me they do not have accessible cross-cultural materials for mission worker self-development. The available books are often written by and addressed to Western mission workers who are living in and adapting to Global South mission fields. Though these works are still helpful, other resources must be developed to support new Global South mission workers moving into other cultures.

A Biblical Shift in Helping Mission Workers

I (Keith) want to share how I transitioned from advice-giving to a more reflective and helpful approach.

When someone shares a struggle or challenge, my default response is to share my experience and what I know about that topic, or to give advice. My years in Indonesia changed my advice-giving habit.

Indonesia has the largest Muslim population in the world. There is also an active and substantial Christian population. I worked in leader training with young Indonesians who served in Muslim contexts. Then, as now, religious and ethnic tensions can lead to violence.

Indonesia, a nation with a strong social hierarchy, places great importance on heeding the counsel of those in higher positions. Despite my teaching and encouragement that they should find their own way, my Indonesian friends would faithfully follow any advice I gave them to the letter. To them, being a good follower meant obeying their teacher without question; doing otherwise would be considered disrespectful.

I must admit that I enjoyed seeing that they wanted my advice and followed it. It made me feel important and needed.

One day, as I thought about this dynamic, I realized that my advice could get one of these young Indonesians killed, beaten, arrested, or thrown out of the villages they served in. Suddenly, I came face-to-face with the consequences of my advice-giving.

I wasn't their supervisor. It wasn't my place to make decisions for them. Each person and team needed to seek guidance from the Holy Spirit regarding their next steps. If the Holy Spirit directed them toward actions that resulted in persecution, then it was God's will, and he would provide the strength to endure it. The crucial thing was for them to seek God's guidance, not rely on my advice.

Jesus explained the Holy Spirit's role: "But the Counselor, the Holy Spirit, whom the Father will send in my name, he will teach you all things and will remind you of everything I have said to you" (John 14:26). The Holy Spirit will teach and remind. I am not a substitute for the Holy Spirit. Sometimes I forget that. Often, I jump into teaching or advice-giving before giving the person a chance to reflect and hear from God.

I needed to change my conversations from giving advice and teaching to drawing out what the Holy Spirit put in the person. As I asked questions and listened, the young Indonesians I worked with began to hear from God and develop strategies to move forward. Some of their ideas were similar to mine, but some of their ideas would never have occurred to me. They reflected and answered through their own cultural lens. Their reflections and ideas were formed by their age, gender, culture, experience, and personalities—not mine.

A Coaching Approach in Latin America

Félix Ortiz (a close colleague of ours) has had a long trajectory of more than thirty years in Christian leadership positions. He took it for granted that he was responsible for the changes in people's lives—which implied that his sense of dignity, value, and even identity depended on his success in changing the lives of people under his responsibility. At the same time, as a leader, he felt obliged to have answers to any potential question or need his followers could have. That was overwhelming, but he did not know a different paradigm of how to lead.

Becoming trained as a coach revolutionized Félix's way of leading and his way of living. His leadership changed as he started empowering people and helping them take responsibility for their lives and ministries. His way of living was transformed as he became free of the personal burden of being responsible for all the needs of the world.

When Félix started using coaching in his leadership, he realized that it wasn't true that Latin Americans generally preferred to be told what to do. Like most people, they prefer to be empowered and grow in responsibility, because that is the only way to grow as human beings and followers of Christ. It is true that some cultural preferences may exist, but those may change when people understand other ways of being led and leading.

Ramón (not his real name) is a prominent pastor and leader in one of the most important denominations in Latin America. This denomination is characterized by a top-down approach to leadership. Ramón came to one of Félix's trainings on how to integrate coaching skills into his leadership style. Throughout the training program, he remained quite skeptical regarding its utility for practical ministry and leadership. After the training, he established a coaching relationship with Félix. Through this personal experience, Ramón realized how useful coaching skills were for empowering people and helping them to think, reflect, and find their own solutions. Ramón now applies this learning to his leadership at the local and denominational levels.

Coaching Offers a Much-Needed Alternative

We recommend a coaching approach that will provide a nurturing and safe environment for both mission workers and their leaders in the Global South. Coaching skills such as active listening, goal setting, building genuine relationships, and giving and receiving feedback can contribute to narrowing the gaps between mission leaders and mission workers. Non-directive coaching empowered by the Holy Spirit results in a process of reflection and discernment. This process helps mission workers grow in self-discovery and become motivated and energized to solve their problems by themselves, as we will see later in this chapter.

Mulugetta observes that coaching for mission workers and mission organization leaders is indispensable in the African context. It can create a safe place for mission workers to "breathe their pain" freely. It also helps mission leaders to cultivate their potential to listen well, be less judgmental, and understand others. Through a coaching approach, leaders can help mission workers discover their own weaknesses and limitations, as well as their own strengths and creativity.

One day, an African mission worker called a mission leader whom Rich knows. This worker urgently needed to make some difficult choices. "I need your advice!" was her plea. When they met over a cup of coffee, rather than giving her advice, the mission leader instead asked her what she would like to see as a result of her choices. What would good results look like? What was keeping her from getting the results she desired? Her eyes lit up, and she started listing what she wanted to see and do. The leader just continued to listen, with occasional clarifying questions.

After a while, the mission worker stopped speaking and, with a big smile on her face, said "Thank you, this was really helpful!" But the mission leader had not given her any advice! Indeed, the leader reported that she had not said much at all. Yet she offered exactly what her mission worker most needed—not advice but an open, supportive space where she could explore her feelings, clarify her options, and choose her own solution. Summing up the whole experience, the mission leader concluded, "Helping people find their own solutions is just so much more effective."

Basic Coaching Skills

Listening

Genuine, deeper listening is often not culturally valued. Talkers are presumed to be smarter, wiser, and of higher status than listeners. Thus, giving advice is often the cultural default. During Rich's training of over 300 Ethiopian leaders in coaching skills, he asked each cohort of 25 to 30 students, "Are Ethiopians generally good listeners?" Ninety percent or more immediately answered in the negative. They recognized that Ethiopia, like other African nations, is a "telling" culture, not a listening culture.

A coaching approach turns this cultural predisposition upside down. In our coaching training, we help leaders make a mental shift and focus their energy on genuinely hearing and honoring the heart, mind, and spirit of another human being. The Bible greatly values listening: "My dear brothers and sisters, take note of this: everyone should be quick to listen, slow to speak and slow to become angry" (Jas 1:19).

This kind of listening may require a difficult and sometimes painful change in the leader's mindset. Leaders must no longer bring their own content or answers to a conversation; instead, they use coaching skills to facilitate a self-discovery process within the person being coached ("coachee"), who then discovers his or her own answers.

The Humility to Listen

Inherent in a coaching mindset is a quality we have seen many mission workers deeply desire but often fail to find in their leaders: humility rather than judgment.

In traditional hierarchical cultures, people at the top develop a know-it-all mentality. Because they are rarely questioned, they assume that they even know all about areas where they have little experience or direct knowledge. Thus, they may perceive any question or objection from mission workers trying to explain the deep challenges they face as "complaining." Rich recalls one meeting of mission executives at which one leader of a major denomination's mission program brushed aside any talk of cross-cultural challenges with the comment that "If they were really called as mission workers, they wouldn't have any problems."

A humble coaching mindset trusts the mission worker to be the "expert" about his or her own life situation, which is often thousands of miles away geographically (and even farther away culturally) from the mission director's office. This mindset allows the coachee/mission worker to be in the driver's seat, navigating his or her own cross-cultural context, with the mission leader offering helpful listening and emotional support rather than judgment.

An example of how dramatic these shifts can be was offered by a pastoral leader whom Rich is currently training in Zimbabwe:

> I have learned the importance of using coaching skills within my pastoral work. Before I attended the coaching training sessions, I met with our student pastors to evaluate their performance and give them advice.
>
> After going through four sessions of coaching training, I met again with a student pastor using my new coaching skills. I noticed that the student pastor was engaged and excited about our discussion. Between our previous four meetings, he never sent me a message. But after the

fifth meeting, he sent me this message: "I appreciate your meeting with me. Thank you for your help and your ear to listen. Naturally I will be more open when we speak next time."

This was a great learning experience for me. I realized that I could achieve more and be more effective by using coaching skills.

Asking Questions
A second way that a coaching mindset helps leaders care for Global South mission workers is by changing the way they ask questions. After undergoing coaching training, the director of the mission-sending agency of one of the largest denominations in Ethiopia reported a breakthrough to his cohort group:

> When I used to talk with my mission workers, in the former days I used to ask very definite questions. Not open-ended questions. But after my coaching training, I tried not to push them into a corner for an answer. As a result, their answers became far more descriptive, and I was able to grasp much more information. … They were now telling me things they never told me before. Previously, they just answered the question that I asked. But now they tell me more things that I never expected. I found that very important. Especially in communicating with my mission workers, I found it indispensable.

In hierarchical leadership structures, asking closed questions—those that are answered yes or no—allow the leader to keep control of the conversation. It's easy to guide people toward your answer using a closed question, or a leading question (which is usually structured to try to get someone to respond or act in a certain way). "Have you prayed about this? Are you still committed? You don't want to give up on God's calling, do you?"

Asking closed and leading questions can feel more like finding fault than finding a solution. In Lebanon, a group that was learning coaching skills with Keith initially had a negative reaction to being asked questions. This was because the only people who typically asked them questions were authority figures trying to find fault so that they could then extort a bribe.

If we want to hear someone's story, understand their perspective, and explore their situation, we need to ask different kinds of questions. Begin questions with the word "what" to generate more expansive thinking and explanation. "What are you experiencing in your ministry?" "What impact is this having on you and your family?" "What does this mean to you?" "What would need to change for that to happen?"

We ask reflective questions based on the assumption that God is already at work in the life of the mission worker. "Jesus said to them, 'My Father is always at his work to this very day, and I, too, am working'" (John 5:17). Asking open, exploratory questions is an effective way to help people reflect on their situation, go deeper in their understanding, generate options, and commit to a path forward.

These examples of coaching skills all flow from a coaching mindset that believes mission workers are guided by the Holy Spirit and have within themselves the creativity, skills, and resources they need to solve their problems by themselves for the most part or at times with the help of skilled others (e.g., counselors and consultants). When this mindset is in place, leaders no longer need to be know-it-all experts imparting advice. As coaches, they can relax and focus all their energy on listening deeply and well. Out of that deep listening come powerful questions as keys to unlock the self-reflection process that empowers mission workers to determine their own direction.

Clear Goals for Conversations

In our experience, conversations between mission leaders and mission workers are often not clearly focused. Since traditional, hierarchical leaders often dominate discussions, it is important to put the mission worker in the driver's seat and choose a clear focus for conversations. This helps both the leader and worker to interact using a purpose-driven approach. This coaching skill gives direction for both parties to clarify the mission worker's challenges and pursue achievable solutions. Best of all, setting clear outcomes will help mission workers in their everyday conversations and ministries.

Action Steps

Almost all traditional discussions between African mission leaders and their mission workers end with unilateral commands from the mission leader, often without clear action steps. However, part of coaching is helping the mission worker determine clear action steps that will empower helpful change. When coaches help workers choose their own action steps, the workers will be far more motivated to complete them. Action steps chosen by workers can be followed up in subsequent meetings to ensure accountability. In this way, mission leaders will begin to see tangible outcomes of their discussions with their workers.

Build a Genuine Relationship

Most countries of the Global South, including Africa, are relational cultures. Sadly, many mission leaders and mission workers, due to the previously discussed issues and gaps, do not have genuine interpersonal relationships.

In Africa, it is easier to share personal problems with a peer group friend than with a supervisor or leader. As a result, many mission workers suffer from hidden personal, family, and social challenges. A coaching style of conversation can bridge this gap; mission workers are far more likely to trust leaders who listen empathically without judgment. Mission workers will feel safe in sharing their challenges with their leaders, and at the same time, they will learn ways to develop more genuine relationships with the people and disciples in their host culture(s).

Mission workers in the Global South have often received inadequate care and support for two main reasons. First, mission agency leaders have been the only people offering care. Second, for a variety of reasons, these mission agency leaders are not well-equipped to offer care and are often so overburdened with other tasks that care is neglected once their mission workers are deployed. We propose that a coaching style of interaction with mission workers is an essential and necessary first step to close the gap between agency leaders and mission workers. However, it is *only* a first step.

A second step is to build a larger support system for mission workers that does not depend solely on the mission agency leader. Mission agency leaders can begin building such a system by facilitating one-to-one relationships between mission workers. This arrangement enables them to become peer coaching partners with each other, thereby fulfilling the many "one another" commands of Scripture. We find that many mission workers would welcome—or are even desperate for—such partnerships. But they need their mission agency's help in creating them. Another important aspect of a larger support system is trained volunteer mentor coaches who will walk alongside mission workers outside the mission organization's chain of command. Mentors become recognized as "safe" people who will listen confidentially to the challenges mission workers face, even within their organization.

A Way Forward

The way forward begins with re-equipping leaders of churches and mission-sending agencies for their critical role of preparing, sending, and caring for Global South mission workers. Leaders may rise to church and mission organization leadership positions either as a reward for their long years of service in a local church or through nepotism, which is common in Africa. Such mission agency leaders often bring great passion to share the gospel and send out home-grown mission workers but are handicapped by traditional and cultural mindsets that create major gaps between them and their mission workers.

Once church and mission organization leaders have realized that such gaps exist, they can take intentional steps to close them. We believe that adopting a coaching mindset and building conversational coaching skills are crucial ways to close the gaps. We acknowledge, of course, that not all mission and church leaders will want to do this and may instead engage in resistance. It is hard to give up power, privilege, and control. As mission leaders experience a coaching mindset, however, their self-driven transformational change will likely have ripple effects that can improve the member care their organizations offer.

In this chapter, we have tried to be realistic and honest in describing both the challenges that Global South mission workers face in receiving care and those that mission agency leaders face in offering effective care. It has been a steep learning curve for everyone involved. Fortunately, many of the mission agency leaders we know already have significant personal spiritual, social, and cross-cultural experience; most have grown up in a multilingual and multicultural society. As they realize the distance that often exists between them and their mission workers, they are well-positioned and ready to adopt a coaching mindset. Creating intentional and well-designed opportunities for these leaders to experience coaching themselves and learn basic coaching skills will be a major step forward toward creating a better member care system (Koteskey 2013). In addition, taking advantage of the various member care training opportunities can further develop leaders' skills for self-care, management, and staff support.

Going forward, we hope that some of the first-generation Global South mission workers whose stories and challenges we have shared above will themselves become leaders of mission agencies, committed to training the next generation of mission workers. Their own cross-cultural experience in mission will be essential to inform their development of leadership and member care structures and of good practices, since they will have walked in the shoes of the mission workers they seek to lead and will have faced similar challenges in the mission context.

Equally importantly, we hope mission agency leaders can learn to share the burden of leadership more widely. Because many African churches are traditionally hierarchical, mission leaders often wear every hat in the recruiting, training, and sending process, including caring for their mission workers after they enter the field. This is an impossible task for leaders! By the time mission workers are on the field, their leaders have little time or energy left for proper member care. Mulugetta is currently bringing together several church and mission agencies in Ethiopia to raise awareness of cross-cultural training and member care needs and start discussions on how to minister jointly. Simply gathering several agencies to share training for their workers (rather than saddling each one with the burden of doing all their training in-house) will free up more time and energy that leaders can devote to member care.

As mentioned above, new experiments in creating teams of trained mentor coaches who can offer confidential, proper member care are underway. This requires trust on the part of the sending agencies, as well as good support for the mentor coaches who are on the front lines of member care. Ideally, training for these mentor coaches will be offered by indigenous leaders who already have cross-cultural mission worker experience. Rich is part of such an experimental program and is currently training Ethiopian lay church leaders in building one-to-one coaching relationships with Ethiopian mission workers. Training mentor coaches who could be assigned to regularly walk alongside just one mission worker family on the field is one creative step with great potential for replication in many organizations and settings.

Applications: Caring for Mission Workers Through Coaching

Core Strategies

1. Show empathy to mission workers, recognizing that the many struggles they face and the questions they ask are not signs of a lack of faith, but are parts of living out their difficult calling.
2. Listen to others actively, with a humble spirit.
3. Ask open questions that enable mission workers to share their stories and struggles, as well as their victories.

Core Resources

1. Certified coaching training is available through Rich Hansen's Leadership Coaching Network in Africa and Keith Webb's Creative Results Management.
2. Keith Webb's book, *The COACH Model for Christian Leaders* (2019), provides an overview of the principles and practices of coaching conversations. It is available in several languages.
3. Mulugetta Demissie serves at the Summer Institute of Linguistics Languaculture Center (SIL-LC), focusing on cross-cultural ministry training in Addis Ababa, Ethiopia. You can follow the SIL-LC's work at https://www.facebook.com/languacultureethiopia/.

Reflection and Discussion

1. Consider a recent conversation with a mission worker. How much did you ask questions and listen as opposed to speaking or giving advice?
2. What do you believe about the abilities of mission workers to reflect and find their own way forward if we provide empathy, a listening ear, and some non-judgmental questions?
3. How might you incorporate coaching skills and contextualize some of these approaches into your member care practices?

References

Creative Results Management. https://creativeresultsmanagement.com.

Dagne, Mulugetta. 2022. "Equipping Ethiopian Intercultural Workers for Mission." PhD diss., Fuller Theological Seminary. https://www.proquest.com/openview/299cd6fe33ba8ad96ec21fed18355905/1?pq-origsite=gscholar&cbl=18750&diss=y.

Freire, Paulo. 1985. *Pedagogy of the Oppressed*. Harmondsworth, Middlesex, UK: Penguin.

Koteskey, Ronald. 2013. "Missionary Member Care: An Introduction." https://www.missionarycare.com/ebooks/Member_Care_Introduction_ percent20Book.pdf.

Leadership Coaching Network. https://www.leadercoachingnet.com/.

Love, Rick. 2017. *Glocal: Following Jesus in the 21st Century*. Eugene, Oregon: Cascade Books.

Narramore Christian Foundation. Counseling and Member Care Seminar. https://ncfliving.org/what_we_do/counseling-member-care-seminar.html.

Webb, Keith. 2019. *The COACH Model for Christian Leaders*. New York: Morgan James. https://store.keithwebb.com.

Mulugetta Demissie Dagne, DIS, is a leader in the mission worker training department at SIL Ethiopia. Mulugetta's doctoral research in intercultural studies at Fuller Theological Seminary focused on developing effective models for training African mission workers. He has fifteen years of experience in equipping mission workers for cross-cultural mission.

Rich Hansen, DMin, has pastored local congregations for over forty years and served for several years as Lecturer in Theology and Academic Dean at the Ethiopian Graduate School of Theology in Addis Ababa. He founded the Leadership Coaching Network in 2020 to offer leadership coaching training to African leaders and organizations.

Keith Webb, DMin, is the author of *The COACH Model for Christian Leaders* and the founder of Creative Results Management, a global training organization focused on equipping ministry leaders. For twenty years, Keith lived in Japan, Indonesia, and Singapore.

19

Physical Health for Mission and Humanitarian Workers

Ted Lankester and Brian Wainaina

In this chapter we address physical health problems faced in mission and humanitarian work by those who live and work locally and those who travel and work internationally. Unfortunately, many organizations can neglect their duty of care regarding staff members' health issues. Through medical screening and advice regarding self-care and prevention, health problems affecting specific assignments can be recognized. In addition, mid- to long-term issues can be identified and addressed so as to prolong the lives and productivity of workers. This chapter is based on the best available evidence regarding the type and standard of care that should be provided, though we realize that in some countries, accessing such care may be difficult and quite expensive (Lankester 2005). We conclude the chapter with an imaginary but realistic case study that indicates actions to take when people realize that their health is less optimal than they thought.

Ted's Story and Medical Work

Every week, I see mission and humanitarian workers at my clinic in London. I've been doing this for more than twenty-five years, first with InterHealth Worldwide and now with Thrive Worldwide.

I co-founded these organizations because I was passionate about preserving the physical health of people who were traveling internationally due to their desire to serve and care for our world. This concern arose out of my own life experience as a humanitarian. My family and I were not always as healthy as we should have been. Nor was I reliable in getting appropriate immunizations and antimalarials.

During our years working in a remote part of the Himalayas in the 1980s and subsequently, my family and I suffered from the following illnesses: dengue, glandular fever, tooth abscess, deep vein thrombosis, pulmonary embolism, Henoch Schoenlein Purpura (swelling of small blood vessels), a scratched and bitten face from a potentially rabid cat, chronic coughs, giardiasis, and acute bilateral sciatica. My wife had two miscarriages, one involving severe blood loss. On one of my medical expeditions, I caught malaria. I share more of my story in a podcast by the Arukah Network (Lankester 2017).

When I returned to the UK in the late 1980s, I knew exactly what I wanted to do with my career: to make sure that others carrying out similar service globally could take better care of themselves through advice, better understanding of care and self-care, and preventing avoidable illness.

I distinctly remember one comment from an aid worker: "Do you realize, doctor, that most of us spend more time looking after our car's insurance, body work, and annual safety checks than we do on ourselves?"

What Are the Key Physical Health Needs?
Physical health should be viewed as part of overall holistic health care, including behavioral and psychosocial support. There are a very wide range of physical needs, but we can group the most frequent (and often the most important) ones into a few categories.

At the top of the list are non-communicable diseases (NCDs), which kill more people worldwide than any other single cause, even in low-income countries (NCD Alliance; WHO 2023). These include cancers, cardiovascular diseases, chronic respiratory diseases, and diabetes. Nearly half of the deaths attributed to these causes occur before age 70 (Lankester and Grills 2019, 388–403). We rightly worry and grieve about the deaths of premature babies, but many of us think a lot less about premature and preventable deaths among our fellow adults.

NCDs can be referred to as *lifestyle* diseases when they result from such factors as inactivity, poor nutrition, stress, and harmful use of tobacco and alcohol. They also include common mental health conditions such as depression and anxiety.

In the past twelve months, I have seen numerous diabetic patients, many of them previously undiagnosed, including two apparently healthy men in their early thirties who had no symptoms and were about to be deployed to field locations. Both, unknown to themselves, had Type 1 diabetes (insulin-dependent).

Nearly one-third of all adults I see (most of whom are not traveling but are busy managers and caregivers) have elevated blood pressure, often untreated or inadequately treated. More than half have an elevated cholesterol level, and most are overweight (Lankester 2018).

Cancers may have early "red flag" signs such as blood in the urine or from the bowel, chronic coughing, certain types of breast lumps, or persistent pain with no obvious cause. However, in most cases these symptoms do not indicate cancer.

Another group of conditions falls in the category of chronic obstructive pulmonary disease (COPD). This term refers to issues with breathing, including severe asthma and various other lung conditions. Some, but not all, cases of COPD are caused by heavy past or current cigarette smoking, or by chronic exposure to air pollution.

During a medical examination, anything relevant that may have an impact on fitness and safety during travel and deployment should be explored, with appropriate advice and follow-up. Key areas include specific health advice for the proposed mission location, including immunizations and antimalarials, and mutually agreed-upon follow-up of any important existing conditions, such as hypertension or abnormal blood tests.

It's Never Too Late to Turn Your Health Around

At age 51, I went to three different intensive care units with heart problems, including a cardiac arrest. Before and since then, I've had elevated blood pressure (now treated), my cholesterol has been brought down by statins, I've prioritized healthy eating, and more recently I have achieved a fully normal Body Mass Index (BMI). Now, twenty years later, I can run nonstop for an hour and forty minutes on a rough, muddy country trail.

So Why Are We Not Looking After Ourselves Better?

Here are some common "reasons" that I have heard for poor health care practices:

"I feel fine, so why see a doctor?"

"I'm just too busy to fit in any more appointments."

"Other people need to see their doctor more than I do."

"My family all lived to a good old age, so I probably will."

"My general practitioner is too busy to see people unless they are really ill."

"I may be overweight, but I always have been, and I seem to manage fine."

"I used to play rugby and became very fit, so I assume I'm still good to go."

"If I become sick, I pray that God will heal me."

"I don't like seeing doctors!"

Lack of access to good healthcare is an important reason too, especially in some low- and middle-income countries where overall facilities and health systems are often weak, though good care is often available for those able to afford it.

What Can We Do about This Problem?
First, look after yourself. Take steps to stay as healthy as possible. Exercise regularly, eat healthily, get enough sleep and rest, and stay connected with others. And crucially, stay informed about your health. Not being aware of your health needs can obviously have serious consequences.

I recommend the following suggestions to my family, friends, and patients and make an effort to follow them myself:

1. Find out your Body Mass Index (BMI). Type "BMI calculator" into a search engine and put in your weight and height, and the algorithm will calculate your BMI. If it's over 25, prioritize losing weight. If it's over 30, make this a top priority. BMI is a screening tool, not a diagnostic tool, but is very helpful in identifying a specific health risk.

2. Know your blood pressure. Either see a health professional or, if possible, buy a machine to measure your own blood pressure. If the reading exceeds 140/90 on three or more occasions, you will probably need to start medication, but reduce your salt intake first as this may help. If your blood pressure remains too high, consult your healthcare professional. An ideal blood pressure is 130/80 or below.

3. Check if you have diabetes. Know your blood sugar by testing your hemoglobin A1c (HbA1c). A healthcare professional and some pharmacies can arrange this. You can also buy a glucose monitor, which uses a finger prick test to measure this indicator yourself. A normal result taken when you wake up and before eating is 4 to 7mmol/L. If your level is too high, see your healthcare professional and take action.

4. Comprehensive medical check. If you are deploying outside your own country, you should get a comprehensive medical check before leaving, unless it's a short trip to a relatively healthy and low-risk location. Identifying any potentially problematic but not-yet-diagnosed condition, such as diabetes or HIV, is one crucial reason.

5. Mental health. There is a connection between mind and body—the wellbeing of one directly influences the other. Chronic stress is a silent killer and a precursor and amplifier of many illnesses. Making healthy choices such as eating well, staying active, getting enough sleep, maintaining strong social connections, can improve your mental health and contribute to the prevention of NCDs, cardiovascular diseases, and diabetes. On the other hand, ignoring these healthy habits can increase the risk for these health issues. Prioritizing your mental health is a huge part of staying healthy overall. Thrive Worldwide has a variety of mental health resources on its website (www.thrive-worldwide.org).

Second, look after your team.

1. Medical checks. As described above, ensure that each member who travels has had a thorough medical check within the past year, ideally in the last six months. This check includes blood tests, advice about immunizations and antimalarials when necessary, and arranging travel health insurance.

2. Prioritize team resilience and organizational health. Mutual care and maintaining friendships are foundational to good health, as is peer support in the field. The websites for Thrive and Member Care Associates website have multiple resources on these subjects.

Third, look after your organization.

1. Duty of care. Organizations have a moral and legal obligation to ensure the safety and wellbeing of employees and volunteer staff. An organization's duty of care covers both the medical and psychological health. Ensure that the necessary steps to fulfill this duty are reliably organized and consistently carried out. Missions and other agencies need to ensure that these actions are taken by an organization or medical center with specialized experience in assisting people who are traveling and working internationally and cross-culturally. Prioritizing staff members' physical and mental health saves an organization time and money, reinforces its positive reputation, and helps to retain staff (CHS-Alliance 2014).

Many organizations are good at delivering pre-travel care, but post-travel care is just as important and often neglected. During one of our periods of service, while working with people with substance addictions in a remote part of the world, my wife and I (Ted) noticed that we had less energy and were losing weight. But since the symptoms seemed mild, we resolved to wait until we returned home before seeking some medical advice. By the time we got an examination, it revealed that we had severe tropical malabsorption. We received an accurate diagnosis and good treatment, even agreed to be placed in a research project, and were fortunately cured! I frequently see people returning from abroad with undiagnosed conditions that need to be diagnosed and treated.

Any organization that routinely sends staff to different parts of the world should have a duty-of-care policy that clearly spells out the need for health screening and appropriate advice before leaving, and for medical care on return. Duty of care should never stop at passport control.

Specific Health Issues in Your Future Location

Hopefully, you are already aware of the likely illnesses and risks that may be present in your new location, such as malaria, dengue fever, or Japanese encephalitis. One frequently neglected condition is bilharzia, commonly picked up unknowingly when one is swimming in some alluring lake or river (or even carrying out a baptism in such an area). Lake Malawi is well known for posing this threat.

In addition to finding a reliable and recommended doctor or allied health worker when traveling, you need to avoid two extremes. The first extreme is to be insufficiently treated and rely too much on guesswork without sufficient medical investigation; the other extreme is to be investigated too much. If in doubt, don't hesitate to ask why a particular investigation is being done and whether it's relevant to the health problem you have described. In this way, you can avoid the small but significant danger of being over-investigated and over-treated, with unnecessary expense. As one aid worker stated, "If you have an itchy bum, you don't need a whole-body scan." If you are in doubt about advice or investigations that have been recommended to you, ask a trustworthy colleague, ideally a healthcare professional. Sometimes it's useful to follow up with your healthcare provider at home to ensure that the advice and proposed investigations are appropriate.

One common health danger worldwide is road traffic accidents. In many countries, this is the likeliest cause of death or serious injury affecting mission and aid workers. Take all precautions possible as a pedestrian, driver, or passenger (InterHealth and People-in-Aid 2002).

How Do I Obtain Reliable Medicines When I'm Away from Home?

First, determine whether the medicines you need are available and of good quality. In some countries, many medications are of poor quality, contain irrelevant ingredients, or are past their expiration date. Check with a well-respected pharmacy rather than going to other outlets that offer medicines for sale over the counter or ordering online.

It's important to always have a two- to three-month supply of your regular medications when you leave home, since it may take time to arrange their availability in your new location. If the medicine you need to take long-term is not reliably available, you may need to have a safer supply brought from home by someone who comes to visit you, after getting a prescription from your own healthcare provider. Be aware of regulations regarding this practice, as sometimes it is technically illegal to bring certain medications with you or have visitors bring them into the country on your behalf.

It is often helpful to have a healthcare professional write a note to this effect: "These medications are solely for the personal medical use of [your name] and are not being sold or made available to others." Having this note written in the main language of the country you are going to is an additional benefit.

One important concern is whether it is necessary to take all the medications prescribed for you if you fall ill while abroad. You may have more prescriptions than you actually need. One classic situation is as follows. Suppose that you fall ill with a fever in a remote part of sub-Saharan Africa. You go to a doctor who does some basic tests and informs you that you have both malaria and typhoid. Consequently, you are prescribed treatments for both conditions, along with various additional medications to alleviate symptoms, control your temperature, and settle your stomach. You may wonder, "Do I really need five to ten different medicines?" Of course, any possibility of malaria calls for immediate treatment. But seeking guidance from an informed colleague or reaching out to your home doctor can often be a big help as you navigate a variety of situations.

What Action Should I Take If I Become Ill Abroad?
If you are being deployed for a long period of time, you should find out the most widely respected doctors, clinics, and health facilities where you will be living. It's better to know these in advance so that you don't struggle to find the best treatment should you become ill.

Your in-country colleagues will often have the best advice. In many, but not all, good quality private care is increasingly available. You can supplement this information using search engines or review apps which are commonly used in your location.

If you or your children need special or important care, check if your home-based healthcare professional or specialist has connections with medical facilities in your new area. If you're seriously worried about yourself or a family member, especially a child, consider visiting the health facility. It's ideal to meet with the relevant healthcare professional beforehand, especially if the health situation is complex or crucial.

If you become seriously ill, either you or a colleague should contact the emergency help line of your medical insurance company. It's their responsibility to suggest and ideally to arrange the best options for treatment, which may include being flown to another country with better facilities or to your home country. Always have this number on hand, written down and easily accessible for you and others. Sometimes the decision may require either you (if you are feeling well enough) or a colleague accompanying you to engage in discussion with the insurance company. Most organizations have policies and protocols as well. Be sure to inform your organization so that its staff can help monitor and manage the medical situation or emergency.

One action I take when seeing someone who has returned early from an assignment for any medical reason is to ask directly yet empathically ask, Do you think you could have done something to prevent this illness from happening?" If the response isn't clear, I reframe my question and ask, "Was there something that you didn't do which, upon consideration, you think caused this illness to bring you home early?" One important example is failing to continue with antimalarials. Usually, when someone becomes ill while abroad, some underlying issue is involved. Often the cause could have been recognized earlier and the problem prevented. When I ask these questions, I do not intend to stir up guilt, but rather to facilitate an important learning experience to safeguard the person's health in the future.

What Steps Should I Take When I Return Home?
Each organization and each individual will need to consider how to proceed or what advice to give according to their different circumstances. The following suggestions, however, represent a minimum pattern that should be observed.

How you handle being back home depends on how long you have been away, as well as whether you have any health concerns upon return. For any trip of six months or longer, or for a shorter but difficult assignment such as working in unhealthy situations, it is good practice to get a full medical examination and appropriate blood tests from a medical practitioner experienced in travel medicine, ideally the same person or organization who carried out your pre-assignment medical exam.

It is surprising how frequently health concerns gradually accumulate. It can be helpful and sensible to discuss these once you are back in your home country. If you received good medical care and your health issues have been satisfactorily addressed while abroad, your regular family doctor or general practitioner can ensure that you are now fit and well based on an examination. For shorter missions, provided that you don't have any complex or specialized health problems, you can also simply consult with your regular family doctor or general practitioner.

Face-to-face medical exams are generally more valuable than virtual consultations in the context of travel medicine, due to the more complex medical history and psychosocial concerns that are commonly experienced. In addition, blood tests are often needed. If you have any significant abnormalities on any test prior to leaving for your assignment, these tests should be repeated upon returning home.

Finally, if you are experiencing any stress-related symptoms, emotional disturbance, poor sleep, or symptoms of anxiety or depression, discuss these in more detail, ideally with a counselor or clinical psychologist. You may just be experiencing normal reactions arising from abnormal life situations, but they can still be troubling.

How About Those Who Live in Their Home Country but Make Frequent Trips Abroad? An Imaginary but Realistic Case Study

Short-term travelers are an important and often neglected group of people (Chomorro-Premuzic 2015; Lankester 2011). Let's consider one such hypothetical person who frequently travels globally to support humanitarian staff in his organization. Much of what he says can also apply to other travelers and mission and humanitarian workers.

> My name is Charlie Sponks. I am on the Senior Leadership Team of a humanitarian aid agency called Support the Whole World. I'm proud of the care we give our staff. For me, it's a no-brainer that mission workers, aid workers, and other worthy long-term travelers should have careful health checks before they venture abroad—and when they come back. In contrast, I assumed that since I worked at our headquarters, my own health risks were rather insignificant. But were they?
>
> Last week by our coffee machine, a colleague claimed that people who normally work at headquarters or virtually at home but who also make frequent trips abroad often have poorer health and greater long-term risks than the aid workers we send out. Apparently, a few years back there was a program about this on the BBC World Service. So I thought, "Help, is that me?"

I'm preparing for another overseas trip in just five days. My line manager asked me this morning if I could follow that trip with another one a week later—not long before Christmas. "It's just your cup of tea," she said. Before going, I still have all my day-to-day work to do and (don't tell my colleagues) I'm still writing up a proposal following my last trip, which ended a full three weeks ago. This means my spouse and our three teenage kids will get even less attention from me—and less help with their homework than usual. But as my wife sighed, "Yes, we're getting used to this."

I have to admit that on my travels I don't follow the best advice about self-care, healthy eating, and maintaining exercise. In fact, eating nice, tasty meals somehow compensates for the trip—accompanied by a little more alcohol than usual. And I'm usually too busy to exercise.

It's not okay, though. I've made a decision. It was triggered by seeing my larger paunch in the shower and getting out of breath more quickly when I run up the stairs to my office.

I told my human resources manager that I wanted one of these medical exams we are entitled to every two years but which I and most of my colleagues never schedule. I think more colleagues would probably have medical exams if we were sent reminders by the human resources department. ...

I arrived in time for the medical exam. I actually filled in most of the online form the night before. The facilities were nice, the doctor was on time, and thank God, she was friendly and welcoming. They even had a good coffee machine.

The consultation went well. The doctor was actually interested in what I'm doing because she worked for a few years in East Africa. She asked me surprisingly relevant questions and examined me carefully after explaining what she was about to do and why.

"Just jump on the scales and we'll do your weight." Whoops, my Body Mass Index was 32—far too high based on my height and weight!

"I'll now take your blood pressure," she said. A moment later, a frown on the doctor's face accompanied her advice that I'd better buy myself a blood pressure cuff and take my pressure regularly at home, as it was a bit on the high side.

Next was the blood test. The results came back as promised three days later. I was alarmed to discover that the blood sugar test indicated I probably had developed type 2 diabetes. Another red flag was my cholesterol levels, and in particular one called "low-density lipoprotein," which seemed to be the "bad" type of cholesterol.

This story has a good ending. I set up an action plan. The kind doctor helped me to do this. We've actually worked on and agreed on it together. And I've been following it the last few months. As a result, I feel better! I have more energy! I'm more comfortable with my body. Mandy even finds me more attractive and romantic! My colleagues have also noticed the difference. They say, "You look different—a really good kind of different." I reply, "Have you thought of getting one of those health checks yourself? You might be surprised at what you find. Don't leave it as late as I did."

Applications: Physical Health for Mission and Humanitarian Workers

Core Strategies

1. Be aware of your own health status and health risks including high or low blood pressure, elevated cholesterol, obesity, lack of exercise, and diabetes. Monitor your stress levels.

2. Take action to deal with these issues through self-care based on good evidence, advised as necessary by your regular healthcare professional. Support groups and accountability partners can be very helpful.

3. Be sure to get a medical examination before and after any significant overseas deployment, or if traveling abroad regularly. The need for regular medical exams also applies to local and national staff.

Core Resources

1. Thrive Worldwide. This is a global travel and organizational health company that provides a wide range of medical care, psychosocial support, information, and other resources. The procedures and advice in this chapter largely follow those used by Thrive Worldwide.

2. Travel Health Pro's "Country Information," National Travel Health Network and Centre. See also the resources from the NCD Alliance.

3. Journals, including the *Journal of Travel Medicine*, *Christian Journal for Global Health*, and *Travel Medicine and Infectious Disease*.

Reflection and Discussion

1. As health workers, we often receive our greatest satisfaction by providing cure and care. We know that prevention and advice are important, but we usually default into what we were mainly trained to do—treat people who are ill. But could good prevention enable us to have a few less ambulances at the foot of the cliff and a few more fences at the top? How can we think creatively about ways to prevent people from falling over the cliff in the first place?

2. Relief and development agencies, faith-based entities, and other civil society organizations have amazing resources, skills, and passion to bring comfort and healing to ailing people and our troubled planet. But what is their greatest resource? It's obvious—people! List a few ways in which your organization demonstrates that it values its staff.

3. How can working together as agencies, care providers and thought leaders help mission and humanitarian workers to have not just quality care available at the bottom of the cliff but also, critically, effective prevention measures at the top? How is such cooperation part of our duty of care as well as good financial stewardship that benefits everyone?

References

Arukah Network. https://www.arukahnetwork.org.

Chomorro-Premuzic, Thomas. 2015. "The Health Risks of Business Travel 2015." *Harvard Business Review.* https://hbr.org/2015/11/the-health-risks-of-business-travel.

Christian Journal for Global Health. https://journal.cjgh.org/index.php/cjgh.

CHS Alliance. 2014. "Core Humanitarian Standard." https://corehumanitarianstandard.org/language-versions.

Grills, Nathan. 2019. "Non-Communicable and Chronic Diseases." In *Setting up Community Health and Development Programmes in Low and Middle Income Settings*, 4th ed., edited by Ted Lankester and Nathan Grills, 388–403. Oxford: Oxford University Press. https://doi.org/10.1093/med/9780198806653.003.0022.

InterHealth and People in Aid. 2002. "Health and Safety Guidelines for Preventing Accidents." In *Doing Member Care Well: Perspectives and Practices from Around the World*, edited by Kelly O'Donnell, 377–390. Pasadena, CA: William Carey Library. https://passionexchange.files.wordpress.com/2008/10/doingmembercarewell.pdf.

Journal of Travel Medicine. https://academic.oup.com/jtm.

Lankester, Ted. 2005. "Health Care of the Long-Term Traveller." *Travel Medicine and Infectious Disease* 3 (3): 143–155. http:// DOI: 10.1016/j.tmaid.2004.09.002.

Lankester, T. 2011. "Frequent Travellers Have High Obesity Risk." InterHealth. https://www.interhealth.org.uk/news_frequent_travellers_high_obesity.html.

Lankester, Ted. 2017. "How to Build Community: Podcast with Arukah Network's Co-Leader in Conversation." https://share.transistor.fm/s/244c32bb.

Lankester, Ted. 2018. "Non-Communicable Diseases: Why Are They So Important to Know About? https://thrive-worldwide.org/blog/why-are-non-communicable-diseases-so-important-to-know-about/.

Member Care Associates. "Team Resiliency." https://membercareassociates.org/getting-equipped/team-development/.

NCD Alliance. "NCDs." https://ncdalliance.org/why-ncds/NCDs.

Thrive Worldwide. https://thrive-worldwide.org.

Travel Health Pro. "Country Information." National Travel Health Network and Centre. https://travelhealthpro.org.uk/countries.

Travel Medicine and Infectious Disease (open-access journal). https://www.sciencedirect.com/journal/travel-medicine-and-infectious-disease.

WHO. 2023. "Noncommunicable Diseases." https://www.who.int/news-room/fact-sheets/detail/noncommunicable-diseases.

Ted Lankester, MD, is interested in global health, particularly community healthcare in developing countries and those involved in faith-based and humanitarian programs. For over forty years, he has worked in different nations, written books on travel medicine and community health, and founded three organizations dedicated to these causes.

Brian Wainaina is a communications specialist who uses his gifts in writing and training to help people and organizations share their stories. He is currently the communications lead for Arukah Network which connects and supports local community leaders to improve the health and wellbeing of their communities.

20

Pastoral Coaching

A Team Model for Member Care

Edward Bruce, Kendall Johns, Chloe Raphael, and Denise Lee

Jesus is walking dusty streets in the Middle East and North Africa. He is present on crowded, noisy streets in Asian cities. He is loving and revealing himself to Muslim men, women, and children as he builds his Kingdom among them. Beside him walk many disciples who have given up lives of comfort and safety in their home country to join him in this work. As they do so, he helps them adapt to a new culture and learn new languages. He teaches them to draw on his word for wisdom, strength, and truth. He heals past wounds and holds believers in his arms through trauma and loss. He mends marriages. He sits with children and helps them process all the changes. He waits with them for the release of a loved one from prison. He travels with them back to their sending country when their host government forces them to leave behind their homes, friends, and ministry, comforting them in their grief.

Jesus ministers to these apostolic believers sent out by Frontiers, the mission organization to which we belong, through a group of pastoral coaches called the Barnabas Team. In this chapter, we share some of our experiences and approaches as members of the Frontiers pastoral coaching team. All names have been changed to protect the identity of the workers. First, co-founder Edward Bruce shares how this team began.

> It all began in the 1990s due to a dysfunctional relationship with our team leader. Four years earlier, my wife and I had joined Frontiers, an agency committed to church planting among unreached Muslim people groups. God had called us to a people in Central Asia, where we served as members of a large team in a city beneath a majestic range of mountains. We were excited to have roles with a team and organization we respected and to see our calling become reality.
>
> I remember the feeling in the pit of my stomach. After months of failed negotiations between leader and team, our entire team resigned. We could no longer follow our leader's controlling and

manipulative leadership. Too many were being wounded in this young national church. Hoping that things would change, I had held out too long, nearing a nervous breakdown from the burnout and stress.

What were we going to do now? We felt alone in the decision. At first, it seemed that no one from our organization was really paying attention.

Months later, after we were back in the US, two pastors from partnering churches, who provided pastoral care for cross-cultural workers, reached out to us. Don said, "Come, let's meet for a debrief." John added, "We need to hear your story and learn from your situation."

This began our journey of restoration. Their compassionate listening and encouragement were crucial in our healing. A few of us gathered with them for a group debriefing. It felt so good to be with others and share stories.

During this time, I noticed other hurting workers in need of someone who would listen to their stories and provide support. During our Frontiers US Sending Base (USSB) meeting, one international leader presented a call for couples who could provide "pastoral coaching" to field teams. Then it hit me: this was what we had needed!

After I had been off the field for just over a year, when I had recovered from burnout and depression, Bart, a Frontiers leader, invited Don, John, and me to the USSB to discuss forming a member care department. God had birthed in both Bart and me a vision for better serving our workers, who were toiling faithfully in difficult lands among unreached, often unengaged Muslim peoples. After their invitation for me to join this endeavor was confirmed by God in prayer and the counsel of others, we made plans to move our family to Phoenix.

The Barnabas Team, named for the "son of encouragement" (Acts 4:36), began in March 2000 with two pastors (Don and John), a psychologist (Randy), and a field worker (me). We divided the approximately 300 American field workers serving with Frontiers between Don, John, and me. We began by contacting those who were struggling, on home assignment, or in transition between teams. We sought to build trusting relationships with workers who needed support, approaching them as their new pastoral coaches. Randy, an experienced member care psychologist, joined us as a consultant and guided us in handling crises.

Member care at the USSB had a small but intentional beginning, as was the case for Frontiers in general (Livingstone 1995). But the Barnabas Team was beginning to offer much more than had been available to me and my team in Central Asia.

Introduction

Since 1999, Frontiers USA has been developing a model for member care that focuses on two central practices:

1. The recruitment and training of mature pastoral coaches, preferably with field experience, who develop and maintain trusting relationships with the individuals, couples, and families to whom they are assigned. Coaches are not meant to be therapists. They provide a listening ear and neutral voice to field workers from their launch to the mission field to their return, utilizing resources for growth and resilience as well as responding to crises and transitions.

2. The establishment and development of a team composed of pastoral coaches and other specialized member care providers who meet regularly, working and praying for the ongoing care and ministry delivered to field members. Pastoral coaches come from a variety of ministry backgrounds. Most have several years of field experience and pastoral gifting. Training is provided for coaching, debriefing, communication, and conflict resolution. Coaches also meet weekly to pray for field workers and monthly for ongoing training on a variety of topics related to pastoral coaching.

These two modalities have created a vibrant community that has developed and effectively applied valuable tools and resources to the task of member care. In this chapter, we illustrate the value of the pastoral coach model and its synergy with the larger team community, as well as highlighting some of the tools and opportunities that have enhanced the care provided to field members.

Burnout, Trauma, and the Value of a Field Visit

Edward: I first met Brad and Carolyn at candidate school, Frontiers' two-week training event for potential field workers. I came to know them more deeply later when the international office requested a field visit to them. Brad met me at the airport in one of the largest cities in Southwest Asia. With his long brown beard and local dress, he blended in well with the Muslim men around us. His smile and engaging manner concealed the serious burnout with which he was struggling. Here, Brad tells their story.

> Almost five years into life on the field, multiple stressors and crises had left us burned out and ready to return to the US. At the very beginning, the leader of the team we hoped to join died unexpectedly, causing me to be appointed team leader. In the early years, one team member

needed confrontation and eventually had to be sent home. This was a stressful time that our coach, Edward, walked us through. We had also been coordinating many short-term teams, which escalated into more relief teams than we could handle after a major earthquake occurred. We were responsible for difficult negotiations for a coworker's release from jail. When one of our national leaders was kidnapped, we were in the midst of the crisis, helping believers and teammates cope with the danger as well as the presumption that he had been killed.

Carolyn became overwhelmed with all the hospitality and transporting visitors, which continued into her pregnancy and the birth of our first child, just months before the earthquake. When everything culminated in a panic attack for me, we knew we needed help. That was when Edward made a field visit to our home, five years into our stressful life on the field.

The days he spent with us were a lifesaver. He helped us recognize the incredible number of stressors and traumas that were contributing to our exhaustion and our difficulty in communicating with each other in our marriage. He asked good questions to help us see more clearly the effects of multiple stressors on our lives. He helped us slow down and listen to each other, where we hadn't been able to do that before. He joined in our daily life as a family in our neighborhood. He met our friend and national leader, Henry. He played with our daughter and watched in surprise as I jumped up from the dinner table one night to kill a rat.

Just surviving day to day with recent crises and all the demands on us, we were unable to process everything on our own. We were in burnout, exhausted on all levels from the last several years, and felt confused about where to turn. Family members in the US often reacted to our stress in unhelpful ways, as they had no idea of our life and what we had lived through. We needed someone who did understand, and who would listen to help us make sense of it all and hear God speaking into our situation. We needed someone sitting down across from us to help us map the events of those messy years, bringing perspective to our critical situations.

Edward brought his own experience with stress and trauma on the field, but with a calm demeanor that our anxious hearts needed. He led us through the passage in 1 Peter on suffering, helping us apply it to our lives. It felt like uncovering the turmoil inside, then letting the Scriptures do the healing work. He prayed with us, using inner healing prayer to begin to address the effects of trauma.

At that time, if we had gone back to the US for this intervention, I doubt that we would have returned. Having coaching in our home on the field led to lasting, healing changes within our host culture. It felt like cold water in a desert to us! If Edward hadn't come in 2008, we are certain that we would not have reached our 23rd year serving with Frontiers.

Inner healing prayer, sometimes called Immanuel prayer, is used widely in Frontiers. It has become a valuable tool for facilitating intimacy with God as well as for resolution of painful memories and past trauma (Immanuel Prayer).

Frontiers has an international Risk and Crisis Management Team that now monitors crisis situations like the ones Brad mentioned. The death of nationals, natural disasters, imprisonments, kidnappings, and other critical events are part of the fabric of life for mission workers serving among frontier peoples, particularly Muslims. The Barnabas Team's partnership with these risk and crisis experts helps us immensely and provides the kind of backup field workers need.

Coaching Women and Singles

As the number of workers we served grew, the need for more coaches for women, couples, and singles grew as well. During the early days of the Barnabas Team, some workers did not get the care they needed, mainly because our relatively few coaches were all married males. Married women and singles, particularly women, needed female pastoral coaches with whom they could talk openly about their challenges and be understood. God provided several married and single women gifted in coaching who had served on the field. One of us, Chloe, is a veteran single worker. She picks up the story here.

Chloe: A single male colleague was recently asked, "What do you wish your leadership understood about the single field experience?" He responded, "When a married person on the field has an issue, the issue is viewed by others as the issue. When a single person on the field has an issue, it is not always viewed as the issue itself, but as a result of their singleness."

Singles have an extensive legacy of service in overseas missions. Twenty percent of our 1,200 Frontiers field workers worldwide are single, and 85 percent of these singles are women. Our singles are taking their place in our leadership structure as well, with 30 single team leaders. Among these single team leaders, 87 percent are women, and some of them are leading men, couples, and families. With such a strong presence in the field, our member care team has learned that it's vital to offer member care in a way that best suits the needs of those receiving care. For singles, this begins with valuing them as whole people.

Our international director team recently posed this question: "How can we bless our singles at our upcoming international conference?" I shared with them how one female field worker with many years of experience confided that the largest felt need of singles is affirmation, especially by top leadership. This was echoed in a conversation I had with an Asian-background field worker, who described the desire "to be seen as a whole person, not as incomplete or 'in a phase,' especially by leadership."

On the opening night of our recent international conference, our international director team welcomed various groups to the conference. The speaker began with singles, inviting them to stand. I was delighted that spontaneous applause broke out. Then he said, "We want you to know that we see you. We honor you for serving in a world in which you are often invisible."

Many singles told me later that when they were asked to stand, they were embarrassed, a common occurrence for singles in a world dominated by married people. "To hear those words of affirmation," said one single man, "brought tears to my eyes."

As pastoral coaches, we must relate to single field workers as men and women first, not as unmarried persons. One of our single pastoral coaches offers a workshop at our candidate school that encourages both marrieds and singles to remember that "teams where singles thrive are teams where everyone thrives." That includes married women, single men, and third culture kids (TCKs). In a healthy community, everyone is seen, valued, and cared for.

Pastoral Coaching in the Early Months

Harold and Tanya served in North and East African nations with unstable societies plagued by the threat of civil war, tribal factions, and other conflicts. The stressful challenges of cross-cultural life brought out brokenness and unhealthy patterns in their marriage and family.

> *Tanya:* These pressures threatened to derail us. Working with our first pastoral coach was a huge help. Don always seemed available! He talked us through situation after situation, helping us think through our options and stay connected to Jesus and each other. Everything was new for us—not just culture and language but marriage, parenting, and team leading. He helped a lot with our marriage!

Harold: Don was available over Skype and at Frontiers regional gatherings to help normalize what we were going through. He helped us process culture shock, team conflict, and gender role challenges. Don prayed for us and with us, and he taught us more effective prayer. He used inner healing prayer ministry, which became key to our individual and marital health. Don was the one available in those early years to troubleshoot problems, establish healthy life rhythms, and spiritual growth.

The first years on the field are typically when the highest attrition occurs. People often don't make it beyond two or three years. Pastoral coaching seeks to connect proactively with field workers as they land and establish themselves in a new and sometimes hostile environment. Tools such as the CernySmith Assessment (CSA) and the Cerny Resilience Inventory (CRI) can be helpful in identifying specific pressure points that have been weighing on field workers' hearts and minds (CernySmith Assessments). A variety of different team building exercises have helped workers bond with their teams, grow in their understanding of gifts and roles, and connect more deeply with one another (Jones and Jones 2003). And having a neutral, thoughtful, skilled, and compassionate pastoral coach can be a key determinant of emotional wellbeing in the first terms of service, increasing the likelihood of long-term viability on the field and greater fruitfulness in ministry.

Proactive pastoral coaches create their own unique rhythms of connection with each field worker according to their strengths, availability, and vision. These include monthly or quarterly check-ins by Zoom, virtual cards or greetings for each family member's birthday and anniversary, and prayerful replies to newsletters and prayer requests. We believe that such personal connections can help reduce early attrition.

Debriefing and Dealing with Crises

After some time on the field, Harold and Tanya were confronted with the crisis of tribal warfare and the imprisonment of expatriate workers. Pastoral coaches Don and Kendall were sent to East Africa, where they met for several days with the team, providing critical incident stress debriefing.

Tanya: I remember these two not-so-young coaches coming all the way across the world, withstanding all the inconveniences of life here to accompany us in our crisis. We felt so loved by that. It made a big difference in our processing and healing journey.

Harold: When we were forced out of our second field home, Don was unavailable. But Kendall debriefed us in person. He typed up our whole story, word for word. We felt that our story was important, worth remembering and processing. Amid our shock and loss, he welcomed and gently cared for us, as a father loves his kids.

Debriefing is critically important, especially after potentially traumatic events such as sudden deportation, accidents, and threats (Holloway and Holloway 2002). Since extended debriefing for everyone on the team, including the children, is essential, other staff engage in debriefing if one's own coach is unavailable. Debriefing, coaching and counseling are provided with clear confidentiality guidelines to protect the worker from inappropriate use of their information (see Core Resources at the end of this chapter).

Early on, we began hosting retreats called "Oasis" for deeper debriefing in a supportive group setting, where Scripture study and inner healing prayer enable healing and restoration. We also saw the value of developing a special team focused on the specific needs of families and their TCKs. As Tanya notes, "Oasis retreats were really important for us, especially for our kids. We've always appreciated how the TCK team has helped them process their overseas experiences. Plus, it's fun! They feel seen and loved for who they are."

As time passed, our member care team developed partnering relationships with several mental health professionals who provided consultation and counseling services. Their participation contributed to the breadth of the team's care. Our vision became helping workers not only to survive but to thrive in some of the most difficult places to live on earth.

Tanya: After a serious accident in which we rolled our car on a dirt road out in the bush, Kendall debriefed us and connected us with Tammy, the TCK coach, who debriefed the kids. As a family, we all had the chance to tell our stories and were able to reframe the whole experience in the light of God's presence. I don't think anyone involved has residual trauma! We wouldn't have made it through that season in East Africa without our coaches' support.

When God calls us to a risky life, it's a bit like rock climbing. If you have a climbing harness, you can do crazy things like attempting a tall, sheer, mountain cliff—things you would never do without a harness. Kendall and Don have been like harnesses for us, and we feel that we can take bigger risks because of their support.

Guided Sabbaticals Enable Workers to Recover, Reflect, and Refocus

Chloe: An intentional, guided sabbatical can enable field workers to recover from cumulative stress and even burnout, reflect on their unique design, and realign their contribution.

As a nurse, Jennifer jumped at the opportunity to work with national believers at a clinic in the Middle East. What seemed a great fit initially became a dissatisfying experience, leaving Jennifer discouraged and worn out. As I coached her through the sabbatical process, she was able to refine her passion to empower people in holistic care. She now works with national believers to develop curriculum and training so that they can care for others.

Sometimes a worker discovers that how they've been working relative to their gifting needs to change so that they can avoid unnecessary stress or even burnout. When field workers discover that they've been doing things that lie outside their personal design and passion, chronic discouragement, a tendency to question their call, or even burnout and possible resignation can be more effectively addressed. Sabbatical coaching helps field workers understand themselves better and refine their ministry contribution, discovering the role and opportunities for which God designed them. It also helps them make better contributions to their teams.

Helping Workers Reengage after Deportation

Kendall: My first Frontiers field experience involved leading a team in an unreached part of Central Asia in the mid-1990s. For our teammates Lloyd and Donna and their young children, it was their first long-term overseas experience. Language learning and team bonding had gone well, and we were already seeing some fruit. Rhythms of Sabbath, monthly half-day retreats, accountability partnerships, rich team worship, and deep sharing from the heart created solid relationships. However, local politicians plotted to expel the whole team. After months of tension, a court trial, and a very difficult exit, everyone on our team was traumatized.

Finding ourselves suddenly back in the USA, we (as a team) received a four-day debriefing by Randy, a psychologist colleague of the Barnabas Team. This was followed by the six-day Oasis retreat. These debriefing events plus continued coaching paved the way for processing our expulsion and considering future options. Our only regret was that our teenage daughter did not participate. Future Oasis retreats would include age-appropriate debriefing for children and youth.

Most of the team returned to Central Asia with Lloyd as the new team leader. As the former team leader, I stayed actively involved from a distance in the ongoing life of the team, overseeing, coaching, and pastoring them as they re-established themselves not only in this second country, but also later in two different locations in a third country. Instead of ending the first four years of ministry due to a traumatic deportation, they (three families and some singles) went on to thrive in long-term fruitful service.

During one season, I helped a field worker process difficult team memories and achieve reconciliation with Lloyd. Inner healing prayer and conflict resolution sessions guided by the Peace Pursuit approach helped restore their relationship (Peace Pursuit). When marriage or character issues threatened to sideline whole families, our pastoral coaching team, along with other specialists and agencies, helped to create space for healing, transformation, and relational growth. These opportunities were crucial in enabling a healthy return to the field.

One team member spoke for the whole team: "Kendall's support was crucial. All the vehicles for support offered by Frontiers helped us stay the course and remain healthy. I don't think every team takes advantage of what is available."

Another team member suffered a bout of depression for three years. She explained:

> I was on the verge of burnout and ready to give up. I had to confront false beliefs about God, myself, and the work. God worked through Frontiers staff and pastoral coaches to bring growth in awareness and healthy trust, and I became more emotionally and spiritually healthy. And that helped our family remain on the field.

This grace-oriented team, with mature leadership, let Darcy take the necessary time to work through her questions and depression and to utilize the available member care resources, even while still on the field.

Collaborating to Support Reentry

Kendall: Each time field workers return to their sending countries, they return changed. They have become accustomed to life in their host culture and see the world with new eyes. Upon returning, however—as is well-known—they can face unexpected difficulties in adapting back to their culture of origin. This can be especially true for their children, for whom the field culture may be the "home" culture in their hearts. Pastoral coaches can help to prepare field workers for this challenging time of reentry.

Kyle and Janet had to leave the field twice for a substantial period before returning. The first time was after armed militia violently carjacked them and deserted them on the side of the road, resulting in PTSD. On the second occasion, Janet suffered a health condition. Kyle explained, "Leaving the field the first time brought about an identity crisis. If I'm not the guy who goes to hard places, then who am I? I was confusing calling with identity."

A team approach was used to help this couple through reentry to their home culture, deploying the necessary resources and strategies to deal with the emotional and physical effects of their experiences. Referrals to therapists, member care counseling centers such as Link Care in California, retreat and residential renewal ministries including Restoration Farm in Virginia, and medical professionals were central to the recovery process. Ongoing coaching and support also provided encouragement and continuity throughout the process.

When I visited them at Kyle's parents' home in Oregon (USA), I was thankful for the significant progress they had made. Working together with family, leaders, pastoral coaches, counselors, counseling organizations, and sending church supporters facilitated their healing and return to the field.

Edward: In another family, twelve-year-old Ryan had become very frustrated with his life. He had grown up as a TCK in Southeast Asia with his parents and three older siblings. Struggling to communicate and having trouble with school and peers, he began acting out. One day, his parents discovered that he was missing. After four hours of searching, Ryan was found to have run away to a local carnival. The family soon returned to the US in search of answers, and their home stay ended up lasting several years. They found medical and psychological help, through which Ryan was diagnosed with high-functioning autism. Therapies and a six-month stay in a residential treatment center for adolescents made a difference. Their coach and TCK team staff were available to support Ryan and his family throughout their extended leave.

Transition Coaching and Renew and Retool are two helpful programs that we offer during extended leaves between terms overseas. This family eventually returned to the field and joined a different team in their host country, near an international school where Ryan would receive the ongoing help he needed in order to thrive.

Summary: A Pastoral Coaching Team as a Strategic Model

We have illustrated the pastoral coaching and team approaches to member care within Frontiers USA. Each worker or family has at least one pastoral coach who seeks to establish a long-term relationship of trust, participating in occasional face-to-face meetings and offering availability in moments of crisis and trouble. Early in field life, active coaching helps field workers survive and thrive through culture shock, team storming (learning to work together), and various bumps in the road. As needs arise, the coach can utilize a variety of tools (such as those listed below under Core Resources) to enhance their coaching effectiveness. Sometimes, using these tools requires a field visit, but often it involves simply staying in contact and using online tools to enhance and maintain the connection.

A team approach offers opportunities for collaboration with multiple resources for the benefit of field workers as well as the pastoral coaches themselves. As the Barnabas Team develops meaningful community and mutual support, we discover each other's strengths and capabilities in meeting the needs of field workers. They encourage and pray for each other as well as for the field workers we serve. This strengthens our group identity and sense of calling. Knowing that the team also includes and consults with professionals in various fields such as psychology, medicine, and nutrition extends the reach of the pastoral coaches and keeps them from needing to have all the answers or tools that a given person needs.

We know that we in the West have been blessed with a wide variety of resources and that younger sending agencies and countries might find it overwhelming to try to generate a similar set of tools. But the future belongs to a new generation of senders, and we are committed to supporting their innovation and empowerment going forward. We have found that the model of pastoral coaching as a team, including collaboration with other talented people and thoughtfully developed programs, has given our field people a better chance at both fruitfulness and healthy longevity. Praise God for his leading of this ministry!

Applications: Pastoral Coaching–a Team Model

Core Strategies

Some of the Barnabas Team's key strategies are:
1. Assignment of pastoral coaches to all field workers.
2. A team approach to collaboration and community.
3. Standard and extended debriefings that help workers process their cross-cultural experiences, including structured transition coaching, "Renew and Retool" programs, and TCK/family coaching and debriefing.

Core Resources

1. Various debriefing tools and confidentiality guidelines (Pastoral Coaching Resources).
2. Special programs and services such as the Renew and Retool Program, Healthy Life Plan, Sabbatical Coaching, and Oasis Retreats.
3. Personal and relationship healing and growth tools including Immanuel Prayer, CernySmith Assessments, Relational Skills (THRIVE Today), and Peace Pursuit.

Reflection and Discussion

1. What factors did you observe that helped the field workers highlighted in this chapter not only to survive but to thrive in fruitful cross-cultural service?
2. In what ways could you encourage team leadership to support member care among your field workers? Which methods might you pursue to develop your agency's member care ministry?
3. What are the essential values embodied in the Frontiers pastoral coaching team model? How might these values contribute to the quality of life and longevity of cross-cultural workers?

References

CernySmith Assessments. https://https://cernysmith.com/assessments/.

Holloway, Steve, and Kitty Holloway. 2002. "The Perils of Pioneering: Responsible Logistics for Hostile Places." In *Doing Member Care Well: Perspectives and Practices from Around the World*, edited by Kelly O'Donnell, 445–446. Pasadena, CA: William Carey Library. https://passionexchange.files.wordpress.com/2008/10/doingmembercarewell.pdf.

Immanuel Prayer. https://mercytransformation.com/.

Jones, Gordon, and Rosemary Jones. 2003. *Teamwork: How to Build Relationships*. Bletchley, United Kingdom: Scripture Union Publishing.

Livingstone, Greg. 1995. "Reflections on Pastoral Care in Frontiers." *International Journal of Frontier Missions* 12 (4): 209–210. https://www.ijfm.org/PDFs_IJFM/12_4_PDFs/10_Livingstone.pdf.

Pastoral Coaching Resources. bit.ly/PastoralCoachingResources.

Peace Pursuit. https://peacepursuit.org/https://peacepursuit.org/.

Relational Skills. https://thrivetoday.org/the-19-skills/.

Edward Bruce is the director and co-founder of the Barnabas Team, Frontiers' US Sending Base member care department. Collaborating with team members, he has served their field workers and sought to develop a pastoral coaching model in member care for over twenty-four years.

Kendall Johns has been active in cross-cultural ministry since 1978, serving as chaplain, church planter, pastor, team leader, overseer, trainer, and pastoral coach on the Frontiers member care team. He has worked in North and South America and in Central Asia.

Chloe Raphael served on Frontiers teams for over a decade in Central Asia. She is a pastoral coach with the Barnabas Team and serves as singles coordinator for the agency. She also ministers to field workers as a spiritual director.

Denise Lee enjoys working with her husband, Edward Bruce, as a writer and editor. As a survivor of long-term chronic illness, she is thankful for walks, bike rides, and visiting friends once again. Her call to mission came at age 16 while she was studying as an exchange student in South Africa.

Afterword

What lies ahead for the member care field, and for our world at large? What are the future challenges and opportunities for member care in mission as we resolutely stay the course in sharing the good news and good works among all peoples?

Our developing field needs good learner-practitioners who are growing in character (virtues), competency (skills), and compassion (love). We need to be willing to cross boundaries, work cooperatively across sectors, and cross "deserts" (i.e., our internal journeys of faith and external places of difficulty). We must grow together through the hard times, listening to and learning from our colleagues around the world, inspired by the vision to see member care develop globally—for all peoples and from all peoples.

As a diverse, resilient, international community of member care workers, we need clear ethical commitments to providing and developing quality services to mission workers in many settings, often in unstable locations permeated by poverty, conflict, calamity, and corruption. And as earthen vessels, we must develop the personal resiliency and mature faith that can sustain us as we take risks to do good and to resolutely confront evil in its many forms.

The material in this book and the historical flow of our field are intentionally leading us toward an ultimate destination. That destination is also the foundation and motivation for our field: resilient, sacrificial, celebratory love that flows from duty, desire, and delight. We seek to live God's *agape* as we actively await the blessed hope and coming of our Lord Jesus Christ.

Amo neniam pereas.
Love never fails.

# Index

A

advocacy 60
Africa Member Care Network, newsletter 281
African mission leaders 282
after-actions review (AAR) 68
air pollution 225
attrition 140, 161, 329

B

Back to Jerusalem (BTJ) 93
Barnabas Team, Frontiers' pastoral coaching model 323
Barnabas Team—Indonesia 139
Barnabas Training courses—Indonesia 146
bereavement 156, 162
building community 133
burnout 108, 161, 325, 326
business and ministry model 132

C

Cape Town Commitment 220
career development 102
caring communities 161
Chad and environment issues 228
Changing the Climate 230
children's education 98, 124
Chinese member care 91, 93
Chinese mission history 92
Chinese mission workers 91
  issues and struggles 94
  stress 99
church community 129, 130
church member care 138
climate and environment
  member care and mission 225, 233
climate-aware therapy 231
Climate Change/An Evangelical Call to Action 232
climate change concerns 227
climate change surveys 228, 230
coaching and peer partnerships 305
coaching, non-directive
  listening and self-discovery 301
  skills, mindset, process 300
coaching, role of the Holy Spirit 304
cognitive dissonance 196
collective cultures 108, 115
compassion fatigue 247
confidentiality 330
contextualization 107, 116
contextually informed 59
Convention on the Rights of Persons with Disabilities (CRPD) 209, 215
Cornwall Alliance 230
corruption 202
corruption, defined 194
counseling 115, 148, 166

creation care, biblical reeasons   231
creation stewardship   225, 230
   Lausanne Movement   232
   local and plant-based food   237
   plastics   237
   policies   233, 237
   travel   234, 236
crisis care   156, 163
Critical Incident Stress Debriefing (CISD)   246
cultural relevance   59
cultural sensitivity   59, 188, 269, 270

D

debriefing   111, 130, 146, 246, 253, 329
depression   209, 213, 219, 232, 270, 332
diaspora   121
disabilities and access   217, 219
disabilities and accommodations for mission workers   215
disability, defined   209
disability, models   211
disabled community, meeting needs   218
discipleship   125
displaced people   121
displacement by weather-related events   227
duty of care, defined   313
dysfunction and deviance (DD)   195
   organizational tactics   195

E

ecclesiastical crime   202
eco-anxiety   231
environmental missions   232
ethics in work   63

F

Faith and Public Integrity Network   203
financial planning   103
frequent international travel, health concerns   317
frontier mission task   111
Frontiers US Sending Base (USSB)   324
fruit of the Spirit   157

G

global citizens   203
global integrity   194, 203
Global Integrity/Anti-Corruption Network   203
Global Integrity Day (GID)   203
Global Member Care series   73
global mental health   179
Global Mental Health (GMH), defined   177
Global South   179, 295
   member care context   295
   member care challenges
   leadership style   298, 300
grief and loss   63, 123, 139, 270

H

health care   156, 163
homesickness   130
Hong Kong   129
honor/shame cultures   97, 141
hope   237, 254
host cultures   100, 114
human rights and member care   73
human rights and missions   73, 79
human rights instruments   80
human-trafficking and member care comprehensive staff care program   244
human trafficking, statistics   243
humility and coaching   302

I

identity struggles   98
Immanuel Approach   182, 185
Immanuel prayer   327
India Missions Association (IMA)   155
Indian member care   155
   challenges and unmet needs   156
Indonesian member care   137
Indonesian Peoples Network   137
Integrity, defined   194
internally displaced persons (IDPs)   181
International Organization for Migration   121
international psychology (IP)   57

J

Jesus Christ   183, 185, 218, 299, 337

K

Korean Member Care Network   110
Korean missions   107
Korean mission workers psychological traits and expectations   113

L

leaders   149
Least-Reached Peoples and Places (LPPs)   137

M

marriage and family life   131, 155, 157, 246, 328
medical investigation, pros and cons   314
member care and love   35
member care and the apostle Paul   280
member care and the local church   279
Member Care Circle. *See* member caring and linking ministry; *See* member caring and linking ministry
member care consultations   138
member care definitions   142, 156
Member Care Formula—Indonesia   143
Member Care Indonesia   137
Member Care in India   161
member care, online, proactive, preventive TCKs, mothers,

couples, singles, all staff 274
Member Care Training Course (MCTC) 142
member care workers training 110, 139
member caring and linking ministry
   inreach resource servants, defined, types 285
   inreach resource servants, defined, types, team 289
   inreach resource servants, defined, types, teams 281
   manual 282
mental health as mission 178, 188
mental health resources 313
mentor coaches 307
Middle East 123
migrant workers 124
Missionary Upholders Trust (MUT) 155, 162
mission children (MKs) MUT study 159
mission kids (MKs) 110, 114, 158, 163
mission motivations 103
mission trainers and mentors 97
moral injury 251
multiplication of trainers 148

N

non-communicable diseases (NCDs) 310

O

Oasis Retreats 330, 331
online sexual exploitation of children (OSEC) 250
organizational culture 161
OSEC and member care, safeguard program components 251
Overseas Filipino Workers (OFWs) 121

P

participatory action 62
partnering 133
pastoral coaching
   deportation 331
   described 325
   guided sabbaticals 331
   rhythms of connection 329
   team 325, 333
peace 6, 13, 23, 36, 41, 45, 63, 72, 176, 187, 262, 326
peer support 249, 313
PETRA People Network 203
Philipine member care 123
Philippine Christians 121
physical health, part of holistic health 310
post-traumatic growth 253
post-traumatic stress disorder (PTSD) 179, 182, 184, 187, 215, 247, 333
prayer, place of 271
psychological first aid (PFA) 252

R

reentry medical exam 316
refugees xxv, 49, 55, 117, 223
relationship and task orientations 109
reliable medicines 314
residential member care 333

resilience   143, 149, 231, 253
rest and recuperation   162
retirement   155, 157, 163
retreats   149
risk and crisis management team   327
road traffic accidents   314

S

sabbath   141
sacrifice, suffering, and risk   166
self-care and mutual care   103, 111, 115, 249, 312
sending churches   99, 109, 165
short-term mission   109
specialist care   112
spiritual bypassing   272
spiritual disciplines   130
spiritual formation   253, 254
spiritual warfare   36, 156, 165
staff care, challenges   254
stress assessments   329
Sustainable Development Goals (SDGs)   59, 178, 202

T

TCKs   226, 330
team-building tools   329
Team Expansion, history and member care   265
temperature rise target 1.5°C   226
temptations   157
tentmaking   96, 128
training   102, 129, 133, 166

trauma   112, 177, 178, 180, 181, 182, 184, 187, 247, 270
trauma-informed care   269
  core principles   269
trauma-informed training   247
trauma training   179
Tree of Life (ToL) workshop metaphor explained   181
Tree of Life (TOL) workshop research outcomes   184

U

Universal Declaration of Human Rights   73
Unreached People Groups (UPGs)   155

V

vicarious trauma   247

W

We'll Never Let Go of That Rope   152
wellbeing and effectiveness   xv, xviii, xxvi, 32, 55, 87, 109, 152
World Development Report   121
World Health Organization (WHO)—mental health resources   178

visit us at missionbooks.org

Global Member Care (Vol. 1):
The Pearls and Perils of Good Practice
Kelly O'Donnell

If you are interested in growing as a person and developing your member care skills, then this book is for you. Part One reviews member care history and includes future directions in light of global realities. Part Two examines the crucial area of health/dysfunction with specific suggestions for good relationships, management, and governance. Part Three explores core ethics and human rights principles that are essential for good practice. This book is a contemporary text for training in universities, seminaries, and mission/aid settings. Its principles and resources also make it a great handbook for sending groups and all those with member care responsibilities.

Global Member Care (Vol. 2):
Crossing Sectors for Serving Humanity
Kelly & Michèle O'Donnell, editors

Global Member Care: Crossing Sectors for Serving Humanity, the latest book from the O'Donnells, is part of an ongoing effort to help a diversity of colleagues keep current with a globalizing world and the global field of member care. This second volume in the Global Member Care series encourages readers to connect and contribute to various international sectors on behalf of mission/aid workers and humanity. The book's thirty-five chapters include a wealth of practical resources: guidelines, codes, resolutions, perspectives, principles, case examples, videos links, human rights instruments, and more. Get ready to venture into the heart of global issues and opportunities—from the trenches to the towers and everything in between!

www.ingramcontent.com/pod-product-compliance
Lightning Source LLC
Chambersburg PA
CBHW052130070526
4458SCB000178/1776